Tourism Research Meth

Integrating Theory with Practice

_____

Tourism Research Methods

Integrating Theory with Practice

_____

Edited by

Brent W. Ritchie

University of Canberra, Australia

Peter Burns

University of Brighton, UK

Catherine Palmer

University of Brighton, UK

CABI Publishing

CABI Publishing is a division of CAB International

CABI Publishing
CAB International
Wallingford
Oxfordshire OX10 8DE
UK

Tel: +44 (0)1491 832111
Fax: +44 (0)1491 833508
E-mail: cabi@cabi.org
Website: www.cabi-publishing.org

CABI Publishing
875 Massachusetts Avenue
7th Floor
Cambridge, MA 02139
USA

Tel: +1 617 395 4056
Fax: +1 617 354 6875
E-mail: cabi-nao@cabi.org

A catalogue record for this book is available from the British Library,
London, UK.

Library of Congress Cataloging-in-Publication Data
Tourism research methods : integrating theory with practice / Brent W. Ritchie,
Peter Burns, Catherine Palmer (eds.).
    p. cm.
  Includes bibliographical references and index.
  ISBN 0-85199-996-4 (alk. paper)
  1. Tourism--Research. 2. Tourism. I. Ritchie, Brent W. II. Burns, Peter (Peter M.)
III. Palmer, Catherine (Catherine A.) IV. Title.

  G155.A1T59246 2004
  910′.72--dc22
                    2004014901

ISBN 0 85199 996 4

Typeset by MRM Graphics Ltd, Winslow, Bucks
Printed and bound in the UK by Biddles Ltd, King's Lynn

Contents

Contributors

Cara Aitchison, Professor of Human Geography, School of Geography and Environmental Management, Faculty of the Built Environment, Bristol, University of the West of England, Frenchay Campus, Coldharbour Lane, Bristol BS16 1QY, UK. E-mail: Cara.Aitchison@uwe.ac.uk

Sue Beeton, Senior Lecturer, School of Tourism and Hospitality, La Trobe University, Victoria 3086, Australia. E-mail: s.beeton@latrobe.edu.au

Peter Burns, Professor of International Tourism Planning and Development, Centre for Tourism Policy Studies, University of Brighton, Darley Road, Eastbourne BN20 7UR, UK. E-mail:pmb18@brighton.ac.uk

Stroma Cole, Senior Lecturer, Buckinghamshire Chilterns University College, High Wycombe HP13 5BB, UK. E-mail: scole01@bcuc.ac.uk

David Crouch, Professor of Cultural Geography, Tourism and Leisure, School of Tourism and Hospitality Management, University of Derby, Kedleston Road, Derby DE22 1GB, UK. E-mail: d.c.crouch@derby.ac.uk

Alan Fyall, Senior Lecturer, International Centre for Tourism and Hospitality Research, Bournemouth University, Poole BH12 5YT, UK. E-mail: afyall@bournemouth.ac.uk

Brian Garrod, Institute of Rural Studies, University of Wales Aberystwyth, Llanbadarn Campus, Aberystwyth, Ceredigion SY23 3AL, UK. E-mail: bgg@aber.ac.uk

C. Michael Hall, Professor, Department of Tourism, University of Otago, PO Box 56, Dunedin, New Zealand. E-mail: cmhall@business.otago.ac.nz

Simon Hudson, Associate Professor, University of Calgary, 2500 University Drive NW, Alberta T2N 1N4, Canada. E-mail: shudson@mgmt.ucalgary.ca

Gayle Jennings, Associate Director, School of Marketing and Tourism, Faculty of Business and Law, Central Queensland University, Rockhampton, Queensland 4702, Australia. E-mail: g.jennings@cqu.edu.au

Laura Lawton, Assistant Professor, Department of Health, Fitness & Recreation Resources, George Mason University, 10900 University Boulevard MS 4E5, Manassas, VA 20110, USA. Present address: Assistant Professor, School of Hotel, Restaurant and Tourism Management, University of South Carolina, Columbia, SC 29208, USA.

Jo-Anne Lester, Senior Lecturer, Centre for Tourism Policy Studies, University of Brighton, Darley Road, Eastbourne BN20 7UR, UK. E-mail: jl1@brighton.ac.uk

Graham Miller, Lecturer in Management, School of Management, University of Surrey, Guildford, Surrey GU2 7XH, UK. E-mail: G.Miller@surrey.ac.uk

Catherine Palmer, Principal Lecturer, Centre for Tourism Policy Studies, University of Brighton, Darley Road, Eastbourne BN20 7UR, UK. E-mail:cap@brighton.ac.uk

Brent W. Ritchie, Head of Tourism Research, Centre for Tourism Research, University of Canberra, ACT 2601, Australia *and* Faculty Fellow, Centre for Tourism Policy Studies, University of Brighton, Darley Road, Eastbourne, BN20 7UR, UK. E-mail: Brent.Ritchie@canberra.edu.au

J.R. Brent Ritchie, Chair, World Tourism Education & Research Centre, Scurfield Hall, Room 499a, University of Calgary, 2500 University Drive NW, T2N 1N4 Calgary, Alberta, Canada. E-mail: brent.Ritchie@haskayne.ucalgary.ca

Chris Ryan, Professor in Tourism, Department of Tourism Management, University of Waikato Management School, Private Bag 3105, Gate 7, Hillcrest Road, Hamilton, New Zealand. E-mail: caryan@mngt.waikato.ac.nz

Carla Almeida Santos, Assistant Professor of Tourism, Department of Recreation, Sport and Tourism, University of Illinois at Urbana-Champaign, 104 Huff Hall, 1206 South Fourth Street, Champaign, IL 61820, USA. E-mail: csantos@uiuc.edu

Pascal Tremblay, Chair of Tourism, School of Tourism and Hospitality, Charles Darwin University, Darwin, Northern Territory, Australia. E-mail: pascal.tremblay@cdu.edu.au

Rochelle Turner, Market Research Manager, TUI-UK, Greater London House, Hampstead Road, London NW1 7SD, UK. Email: Rochelle_Turner@Tui-uk.co.uk

Andrea Valentin, Postgraduate student, Department of Tourism, University of Otago, PO Box 56, Dunedin, New Zealand. E-mail: avalentin@business.otago.ac.nz

David Weaver, Department of Health, Fitness & Recreation Resources, George Mason University, 10900 University Boulevard MS 4E5, Manassas, VA 20110, USA. Present address: Assistant Professor, School of Hotel, Restaurant and Tourism Management, University of South Carolina, Columbia, SC 29208, USA.

Clare Weeden, Senior Lecturer, Centre for Tourism Policy Studies, University of Brighton, Darley Road, Eastbourne BN20 7UR, UK. E-mail: chw3@brighton.ac.uk

Preface

The idea for this book developed from a discussion between the editors suggesting that few research books in the tourism field integrate theory with practice and bridge the divide between business research methods and the growing social science perspective. Many tourism courses do not use one sole textbook for tourism research subjects. This is partly because the tourism industry can be viewed in a multi-disciplinary way, with an interest in tourism as a business and/or as a social phenomenon from a multitude of perspectives (geography, anthropology, psychology, etc.). Although many institutions elect to consider, and indeed place, tourism in business faculties or schools, some are located in social science divisions or schools and there is growing interest in researching tourism from a social science perspective.

Teaching staff and students may find themselves in a position in which they either adopt business or social science research textbooks, which lack specific tourism examples and case studies, or use tourism research texts, which frequently do not discuss different research approaches or methodologies located in some social science books. To date, research textbooks are often focused on tourism as a business and either ignore alternative social science approaches to tourism research or provide them with little attention. Students also complain that texts do not provide relevant examples or case studies on how these research approaches may be undertaken and operationalized or indeed how to go about analysing and interpreting research findings. Furthermore, students are not exposed to different research approaches and are often constrained in undertaking positivistic or business/social science types of research depending on the faculty or school that they find themselves attached to and the research books used by staff.

Therefore, we saw a need for a specific tourism research textbook that:

- went beyond the business/social phenomenon divide of tourism research;
- provides a discussion of theory but integrates this theory with specific tourism research examples and case studies to assist student learning and application, of research approaches and techniques;
- outlines alternative research approaches and techniques that may be adopted by tourism researchers from different disciplines and research positions; and,
- sourced experts (and new researchers) who have had relevant experience related to tourism related research issues, approaches and techniques.

The result is what we hope is a tourism research book that provides a fresh perspective by integrating theory with practice while considering a wide range of research issues, approaches and techniques. The chapter topics vary but all authors have attempted to integrate theory with practice and reflect on their own research practice, which is an important component of the research process for all researchers (including students).

Acknowledgements

We would like to thank several people and organizations for their support in the production of this book. First, thank you to the School of Service Management at the University of Brighton for providing the right intellectual environment for ensuring that this book was developed and completed. Thanks also go to the Tourism Programme at the University of Canberra for providing time for Brent to complete the final stages of the book with Peter and Catherine in Eastbourne, UK.

A big thank you also goes out to all of the individual contributors who have written chapters from all parts of the globe. Thank you for your excitement over the project and your excellent contributions! We also acknowledge the support of the publishing team at CAB International for their assistance throughout this process, in particular Rebecca Stubbs. Finally, thanks to all our families and partners for their love and support in all of our endeavours.

Brent W. Ritchie
Peter Burns
Catherine Palmer

Eastbourne, UK
June 2004

1 Introduction: Reflections on the Practice of Research

BRENT W. RITCHIE,[1,2] PETER BURNS[2] AND CATHERINE PALMER[2]
[1]Centre for Tourism Research, University of Canberra, ACT 2601, Australia;
[2]Centre for Tourism Policy Studies, University of Brighton, Darley Road, Eastbourne
BN20 7UR, UK

Just as research generally takes place in a moment of time, so does writing. At the time of preparing the present book, two things occurred as part of the social, political and economic milieu within which everyday life occurs. Neither of them has anything to do with tourism. The first incident concerns the traumatic war in Iraq (2003) led by the USA and the UK. The foundation for this war against Saddam Hussein's regime was based on data gathered by scientists, journalists and intelligence agencies from a complex and frequently opaque range of sources. These data were used as evidence to confirm the existence in Iraq of a sustained and deliberate campaign to both accumulate and deploy weapons of mass destruction (WMD). As one might imagine, huge controversy surrounded the means by which the data were gathered, how they were to be interpreted and the uses to which they were put (for a particular controversy about how a student's PhD thesis, published some 12 years earlier, was plagiarized from the Internet by officials in the UK Prime Minister's office and included as evidence, see Norton-Taylor and White, 2003).

Evidence was presented to global publics that was designed to assure us that, for example, the UK was in immediate, clear and present danger from these WMD. Yet, despite the bewildering array of 'evidence' presented, no such weapons have been found. As a result, the justification for the war and the control of its aftermath continue to be mired in controversy and dissent. Seemingly, noone can conclusively prove that these weapons did or did not exist (for researchers interested in semantics and linguistics, the phrase has been subtly changed in official discourse from 'Weapons of Mass Destruction' to 'Programmes for Weapons of Mass Destruction'). The point of retelling this episode is to highlight the fact that research findings can have explosive, dramatic and permanent consequences, and that the way in which research results are written and forwarded to various audiences is just as important as the methods, tools or instruments employed.

The second incident is much more of a domestic UK issue and involves a controversial immunization programme given to all infants in the UK as part of the national campaign to prevent the childhood diseases measles, mumps and rubella (the 'triple jab' MMR scheme) (http://news.bbc.co.uk/1/hi/health/3530551.stm). Whether or not the MMR immunization programme is 'safe' has become a hostage to vested interests' (political, pressure group, medical) claim and counter claim, so much so that parents are often confused and concerned about whether to have their children immunized using the free triple jab scheme or to pay to have three single jabs. The scientific research of Dr Andrew Wakefield and his team, which first suggested a possible link between the MMR vaccine and autism in children, has been the subject of fierce criticism from a variety of quarters, most notably politicians and the medical profession. However, Dr Wakefield's research and his hypothesis are not without support. Both of these incidents highlight the contested nature of research and the problems involved when supposedly more objective 'scientific' research delivers results that are highly controversial.

Moving on to tourism, it could be argued that tourism research, whilst not devoid of controversy, is unlikely to cause such major trauma. However, thinking at a very local level, if a tourism researcher were invited to investigate the likely social impacts of tourism on a given population and got it wrong, through the careless application of specific methodologies, by talking to the wrong people, or as a result of being influenced by government or client pressure, then the future lives of the local population could be adversely affected. This would, to say the least, be a most unfortunate, but highly contained problem. So, let us move up a notch.

Fuel emissions from aircraft are directly injected into the air at high altitudes. There is existing evidence to suggest that these polluting carbon emissions are causing damage to the ozone layer. An article in *New Scientist* cites a UK Commission on Environmental Pollution as 'predicting that air travel could account for nearly 75 per cent of the UK's greenhouse gas emissions by 2050' (Ananthaswamy, 2004). Even so, policy makers (politicians and governments) seem unwilling to act at even a basic level, such as with the introduction of taxes on aviation fuel with the specific aim of bringing about reductions in fossil fuel emissions. This is a case where the science is known, but pressure from the aviation industry shifts governments away from sensible, negotiated positions that help to alleviate the problem (see Aviation Environment Federation, 2004; Jarman, 2004).

The examples shown above illustrate a number of things. First, they emphasize the need to ensure that the end users of research results can have an assurance either that the results are value-free (i.e. a scientific reporting of facts that have arisen from a regulated programme of research that has been thoroughly tested and reviewed) or that the results are coming from a particular perspective (i.e. the 'values' are known). For example, if the World Wide Fund for Nature were to undertake research into the impacts of tourism on species in a certain location, you would not expect a particularly balanced report, but this would not take away the idea that they could produce good scientific evidence to promote or support their particular viewpoint. In both cases, the science is good; one is considered neutral, the other biased. However, the real danger comes when either science purports to be neutral and is not or when the science is sloppy (incidentally, place the phrase 'sloppy science' into an Internet search engine for some fascinating discussions on controversial scientific results).

Where does this leave tourism research? While we do not claim to present an exhaustive list, the following general components can be said to frame or determine tourism research agendas. Most of these agendas can be seen reflected in the chapters contained in this book, all of which serve to illustrate the rich and varied nature of tourism research. These agendas are:

- Variability: recognizing that tourism is a form of consumption and as such varies according to economic, social and cultural dynamics.
- Performance: whereby tourism is seen as an embodied act performed by tourists at and through the spaces of tourism.
- Ritual: here myth and metaphor help us to understand tourism as a ritual activity for many, although not all, societies.
- Mediate: where tourism enables people to make sense of the world in all its myriad, contested and contingent forms.
- Agency: the idea that at the level of society and culture, human-induced change can be planned and controlled to provide beneficial outcomes.

- Response: which in a sense provides the linking theme emphasizing the interdisciplinary necessity of tourism research.
- Consequences: including studies of what happens at destinations, to communities and society at large. The focus here is likely to be applied research.
- Prediction: asking the question 'can innovative use of research data be used to predict changes in tourism, hospitality and retail patterns and consumption?'.
- Ambiguity: the knowledge that tourism remains an ambiguous and somewhat unpredictable subject for research.

In recent years there has been a general upsurge in the number of publications devoted to aspects of tourism research and, in particular, the wider philosophical debates underpinning specific methodologies (Phillmore and Goodson, 2004). This is important because it points to the increasing maturity and sophistication of the field of tourism, whether viewed as a business/industry to be predicted, managed and controlled (Cooper, 2002), or as a social/cultural phenomenon capable of illuminating aspects of the modern condition (Franklin, 2003). These two sides of tourism have increasingly become polarized within the nomenclature of *Tourism Management* or *Tourism Studies*. Such aspects of tourism have often followed the predictable route whereby tourism management research is seen to be dominated by positivism and the laws of natural science, whilst tourism studies research tries to counter what it sees as a somewhat mechanistic approach, by highlighting the advantages of phenomenological methodologies (Franklin and Crang, 2001).

This bipolar position is driven by the different demands on those that undertake tourism research. On the one hand, some tourism academics may consider their task as being to help bring 'respectability' to tourism as a worthwhile subject for study and a serious university topic. In this search for peer recognition they focus on theory building and the search for deeper meanings in tourism. For them (Selwyn, 1996; Edensor, 1998; Hollinshead, 1998) the pur-

pose of tourism research is to try to understand what tourism means in various societies in what is sometimes called the postmodern world. Such work is published in journals such as *Annals of Tourism Research* and, more recently, *Tourist Studies*. Others, such as Fletcher (1989), see the role of tourism research more as reporting its value to particular economies and how visitor experiences can be improved through better understanding their behaviour and better business practice, leading to a generally more profitable industry. Such work tends to be found in *Tourism Management* and the *Journal of Travel and Tourism Marketing*.

The situation has been described as the 'tourism as industry vs. tourism as problem' paradox (Burns, 1999) or 'the constant tension between academic and industry-based researchers' (Cooper, 2002: 375). Nowhere is this better observed than in two contrasting articles. The first, by Franklin and Crang (2001) acts as a sort of position paper in the first edition of a new tourism academic journal. Their central argument is that tourism research has grown in such a way as to have become muddled and bogged down. They express three specific concerns:

1. While tourism, both as business and social phenomenon, has grown immensely over the past decades, the research community has struggled to keep up with this growth, leading to a situation whereby 'tourist studies has simply tried to track and record this staggering expansion, producing an enormous record of instances, case studies and variations' (p. 5).
2. Much of the research into tourism that lies outside the economic functionalist domains of 'counting' tourism for policy and planning purposes has been dominated by 'a relatively small core of "theorists" whose work has tended to become petrified in standard explanations, accepted analyses and foundational ideas' (p. 6).
3. The approach to tourism research has been as fragmented as the industry itself. This fragmented character affects the study of both supply and demand where tourism is

seen 'as series of discrete, localized events, where destinations ... are subject to external forces producing impacts ...' and those impacts are themselves 'simply' 'a series of discrete, enumerated occurrences of travel, arrival, activity, purchase, [and] departure ...' with the tourist being viewed as a 'grim' reality (p. 6).

Franklin and Crang go on to criticize the preoccupation with 'typologies' and the 'obsession with taxonomies', citing Lofgren (1999), who clearly states that such approaches to complex ideas 'represent a tradition of flatfooted sociology and psychology ... [representing] an unhappy marriage between marketing research and positivist ambitions of scientific labelling' (p. 6).

The second article, by Cooper (2002: 375), starts with the proposition from the Australian Institute for Commercialisation (AIC) that 'Research may be the world's best, but it is of limited value unless it successfully enters the commercial market and the resulting commercial opportunities are maximized'. Cooper goes on to claim that 'Knowledge Management delivers both a complementary and contemporary approach to tourism research which is not evident in the academic tourism literature'. This is a big claim to make, but what does it mean? Using a research tool known as critical discourse analysis (CDA) we can assume that Cooper was making a point, indeed staking out a position, by using the somewhat alarmist quote from the AIC. Moreover, by referring to the tensions between different approaches to tourism research he purports to make a case for more applied research that can help businesses to be more effective. While he is right elsewhere in the article to remind us that tourism is generally fragmented and comprises mainly small businesses that are, in general, 'research averse', he seems not to mention another underlying tension, which is the industry's failure to properly fund research.

In the experience of many tourism researchers, the industry is mean with its money and will not fund research aimed

at improving our understanding of its complexities but only that for mechanistic, commercial purposes such as market or product research. To be fair to Cooper, in another paper he makes the point that in arguing for a knowledge management (KM) approach 'all' he is asking for is 'that research is undertaken to understand processes and practices for the generation, identification, assimilation and distribution of knowledge' (Ruhanen and Cooper, 2003: 13).

In general terms, approaches whereby data are generated from a so-called 'real world' of statistics, visitor satisfaction surveys and the like may be termed 'positivist' in approach and those dealing with abstract matters such as social impacts and the role of tourism in postmodern societies as 'hermaneutic'. The claim for the latter is that such a discursive, reflective and reflexive approach will provide 'new dimensions to the body of knowledge in their respective fields' (Riley and Love, 2000).

The articles by Franklin and Crang and Cooper are illustrative of most debates in the tourism literature, which tend to coalesce around the merits of qualitative versus quantitative research methods – the 'hard' science versus the 'soft' science dichotomy (Burns and Lester, 2003). The arguments within the quantitative 'good', qualitative 'bad' scenario have tended to mirror those which have taken place over many years in the more established disciplinary areas such as geography, psychology and the social sciences. However, as with all such debates, the pragmatic position is more often than not one where sometimes quantitative methods are best, sometimes qualitative methods and sometimes a mixture of both. It all depends on what you want to find out.

Such a view provides the underlying rationale for this book, which has two key aims: first, it seeks to move beyond the business/social phenomenon divide by highlighting the diversity and richness of tourism research across both the quantitative and qualitative approaches. In this respect we asked the contributing authors to widen the usual case study discussion by linking the research projects examined more closely to their philosophical foundations. Hence, all the authors represented here were asked not to report or dwell on the specific findings of their research but to discuss how their methodological approach influenced the design, planning and implementation of their particular project.

Secondly, the book seeks to highlight what happens when the philosophy and theory of a particular method meets the practice of research out in the field. Too often, research texts give the impression that once a researcher (whether student or academic) has mastered the theory behind a certain method – the advantages and disadvantages, issues of validity, bias, etc. – then putting this into practice is actually quite straightforward. But as anyone who has ever tried to master a complex dish by following the recipe to the letter will know, theory and practice do not always coincide. The perfectly planned piece of primary research may not go according to plan since fieldwork is more often than not a messy business. As the sociologist Norman Denzin (1970: 315) once remarked, theory and research is far from an idealized process immaculately conceived in design and elegantly executed in practice. In reality, concepts do not automatically generate operational definitions and theories do not fall into place once all the data have been gathered. This is not the way research gets done.

This is not to say, however, that fieldwork should not be rigorously and thoughtfully designed, carefully and cautiously executed. As previously noted, we would not wish to advocate 'sloppy' or unreliable research practices, but, rather, suggest that dry theoretical discussions are not always the most helpful in terms of the practical challenges almost every researcher is faced with at one time or another. For example, students and many academics are frequently unclear as to how to construct a focus group. Just from where and how do you contact suitable participants? How long is a longitudinal study? What is it like to question participants about their personal experiences and lives? These are the sorts of issues and questions we asked our contributors to consider when preparing their chapters.

Structure of the Book

Following this chapter, which sets the contextual scene for the book, Chris Ryan and Cara Aitchison examine two of the most important perspectives in tourism research: those of ethics and gender. Ryan argues that complex issues such as ethics and 'truth' lie at the heart of the research process. By way of illustration he examines these issues through the prism of his own personal experiences as a member of an academic community and as a researcher. These experiences cause him to reflect that there is no given right for others to respond to the questions asked of them, and, as a consequence, care and nurturance might be the ethical stance appropriate to the research complexities of contemporary tourism experiences.

Ryan's chapter on ethics in tourism research offers no certainties, except for the certainty that research is a complex business, which does not line up with the idea that 'objective truth' is subject to social and interpretive vagaries. The chapter is inevitably presented as a personal narrative, drawing on the author's own experience of dealing with university ethics committees which may not understand the nature of reflexive research and the realities of the dilemmas arising during the course of fieldwork. Note that towards the end of his chapter, as the narrative gets more personal, the use of the first person singular, 'I', becomes the most appropriate way of addressing the issues. This should not present any sort of problem for researchers with a background in anthropology, but may well cause positivists some sleepless nights! (See Riley and Love, 2000, for an interesting discussion of the importance of the first person to reflexive narratives in tourism research.)

Cara Aitchison discusses the relationship between epistemology, methodology and method in relation to gender perspectives in leisure and tourism studies. She argues that our view of the world, and thus leisure and tourism's place within the world, shapes the way in which our leisure and tourism relations, and our knowledge of these relations, is produced and understood.

Sue Beeton presents a thoughtful examination of the usefulness and applicability of the case study as a research method in tourism. She maintains that this research method can provide insightful data over a long period of time because it enables theoretical concepts to be tested against localized experiences.

Peter Burns and Jo-Anne Lester argue that qualitative methods in tourism research should make greater use of visual evidence as a way of understanding tourism as a social construct. This form of data has, they maintain, considerable potential to add value to more normative data collection methods, yet to date it has been either under-utilized or ignored. They offer a useful framework for analysing/reading films as data/text, which can be used to make connections with the theoretical context in which a particular film is discussed.

Stroma Cole discusses the concept of action ethnography, a subdivision of applied anthropology concerned with producing data that are useful to the participants in the research process. Focusing upon a research project in Eastern Indonesia, she presents a useful insight into the practicalities of ethnographic research and of the dilemmas frequently faced by a researcher who is at the same time an outsider and an insider.

David Crouch presents an interesting discussion of tourism as *encounter*, and of the embodied nature of the performative act in tourism. Drawing upon conceptual developments in cultural geography he argues that, in order to understand the increasingly complex character of being a tourist, it is necessary to empirically investigate the tourist–space encounter, the construction and constitution of space. In his examination of caravanning he seeks to understand the processes involved in visiting tourist locations and in so doing constructs a kaleidoscope of the components that comprise the *encounter* a tourist makes in relation to material and metaphorical geography.

Brian Garrod and Alan Fyall present a very detailed account of how the Delphi technique can be used 'to dig beneath the surface of issues' that 'would otherwise be unavailable to the researcher'. They start by giving an historic context to the Delphi technique, fully explaining and acknowledging its limitations. However, they then go on to revisit the method, so to speak, and provide very clear and precise detail as to how these problems can be avoided. The case study they use to illustrate the method ('defining marine ecotourism') provided them with some very novel results that may well not have arisen without the use of this particular method.

Gayle Jennings examines the qualitative interview and the particular skills required of the researcher utilizing this method. She considers definitional aspects of such interviews, the philosophical debates underpinning this method and practical guidelines for conducting this type of interview. She argues that this method enables the researcher to access the multiple voices and views inherent in the complex world of tourism.

Graham Miller, Simon Hudson and Rochelle Turner consider the value and applicability of mystery shopping to the tourism industry through an analysis of a research programme designed and implemented by Lunn Poly, the retail arm of Thomson, the largest tour operator brand in the UK. They examine some of the issues involved in the recruitment and training of the mystery shoppers and of the impact of such a research instrument on those employees being observed.

J.R. Brent Ritchie examines the fundamentals of longitudinal research and the special challenges it presents to researchers. For Ritchie this method is particularly valuable and rewarding since it can provide the kind of in-depth understanding that simple cross-sectional studies are unable to supply.

Carla Almeida Santos examines how framing theory can assist tourism research by shaping textual analysis of mass mediated tourism narratives. Framing analysis permits researchers to advance conceptual and theoretical discussions by revealing the embedded socio-cultural components of tourism marketing. She argues that tourism narratives are framed by the social, cultural and political world view of those people who construct them.

Pascal Tremblay focuses upon geographic information systems (GIS), the computerized system for storing, analysing and displaying data of a geographical nature. He argues that this method is particularly useful for evaluating the appeal to tourists of a place or region, for predicting the number of potential visitors to a recreational area or for assessing the impact of tourists on wildlife. Such information can help to identify ecological and tourism hotspots and in so doing make a valuable contribution to conservation and public policy concerns.

Clare Weeden provides us with specific detail about how she used focus group discussions to elicit and construct meaning about varying attitudes towards and perceptions of 'ethics' in tourism. In her frank account of the advantages and disadvantages of the method, a narrative unfolds that allows real insight into the researcher's approach. As well as providing an account of how to conduct a focus group meeting, Weeden also takes us through the findings to give an illustration of one approach to writing up results.

C. Michael Hall and Andrea Valentin place their focus on the use of content analysis in tourism research. From an initial discussion of the ways in which this method has been employed they go on to illustrate the utility of the method through an examination of media coverage of the terrorist attacks of 11 September 2001. They argue that the judgement and analytical skill of the researcher is a significant factor in the successful application of this method.

David Weaver and Laura Lawton's chapter also has as its subject ecotourism. But for them, the approach used was 'cluster analysis'. They wanted to find out if ecotourists could somehow be categorized along a 'hard–soft' continuum. This would help ecotourist lodging businesses to ensure some match between their products and potential clients. What is particularly interesting about their chapter is the way in which they describe how cluster analysis of existing survey data can move approaches to marketing to ecotourists to new levels of sophistication. Weaver and Lawton, just like Ryan and other contributors to this book, acknowledge the existence of bias and doubts about objectivity, but the clarity of their explanations about how such issues are taken into account will help overcome doubts about this and other methods.

C. Michael Hall's comments on the future of tourism research are set within the environment which produces and funds research and make the point that, in future, those of us concerned with tourism's social consequences should be thinking more about the intellectual baggage that comes with mobilities (in its various forms) than what we now term 'tourism'.

References

Ananthaswamy, A. (2004) Soya powered planes promise greener air travel. *New Scientist*. Available at: http://www.newscientist.com/news/news.jsp?id=ns99994813

Aviation Environment Federation (2004) *Aviation and Global Climate Change*. Available at: http://www.aef.org.uk/PDFs/GlobalChangeLeaflet.pdf

Burns, P. (1999) *An Introduction to Tourism and Anthropology*. Routledge, London

Burns, P. and Lester, J. (2003) Using visual evidence in tourism research. *Tourism, Recreation, Research* 28(2), 77–83.

Cooper, C. (2002) Knowledge management and research commercialisation agendas. *Current Issues in Tourism* 5(5), 375–377.

Denzin, N. (1970) *The Research Art in Sociology: a Theoretical Introduction to Sociological Methods*. Butterworth, London.

Edensor, T. (1998) *Tourists at the Taj: Performance and Meaning at a Symbolic Site*. Routledge, London.

Fletcher, J. (1989) Input–output analysis and tourism impact studies. *Annals of Tourism Research* 19(4), 541–556.

Franklin, A. (2003) *Tourism. An Introduction.* Sage, London.

Franklin, A. and Crang, S. (2001) The trouble with tourism and travel theory? *Tourist Studies* 1(1), 5–22.

Hollinshead, K. (1998) Tourism and the restless peoples: a dialectical inspection of Bhabha's Halfway Populations. *Tourism, Culture and Communication* 1(1), 49–77.

Jarman, M. (2004) *Temperature Gauge.* Available at: http://www.redpepper.org.uk/June2004/x-June2004-Temp.html

Norton-Taylor, R. and White, M. (2003) Blunkett admits weapons error: dossier on Iraqi threat 'should not have been published'. *The Guardian.* Available at: http://www.guardian.co.uk/uk_news/story/0,3604,973450,00.html

Phillmore, J. and Goodson, L. (eds) (2004) *Qualitative Research in Tourism. Ontologies, Epistemologies and Methodologies.* Routledge, London.

Riley, R. and Love, L. (2000) The state of qualitative tourism research. *Annals of Tourism Research* 27(1), 164–187.

Ruhanen, L. and Cooper, C. (2003) Developing a knowledge management approach to tourism research. *Tedqual* 1/2003, 9–13.

Selwyn, T. (ed.) (1996) *The Tourist Image: Myths and Myth Making in Tourism.* John Wiley & Sons, Chichester, UK.

2   Ethics in Tourism Research: Objectivities and Personal Perspectives

CHRIS RYAN

Department of Tourism Management, University of Waikato Management School, Private Bag 3105, Gate 7, Hillcrest Road, Hamilton, New Zealand

Essentially, the structure of this chapter comprises two sections. These sections are premised on the notion that tourism research is primarily about the behaviour of tourists; that is, it is a study of people as sociable entities within the context of travel away from home, which travel is primarily motivated by holidaying. The first segment is a discussion about the nature of ethics within social science research in general, while the second considers more specifically various issues pertaining to some aspects of tourism research drawn from the author's own experience. It should also be added that as the author has conducted research from within a university setting, this locates the perspective and background of the author's experience. Equally, as will be evident from the discussion of research ontologies, any consideration of the ethics of research requires conceptualizations of 'truth' that become increasingly complex the more closely they are examined. As participants, shapers and beneficiaries of research, academic researchers adopt varying roles in relationship to the subject of their research, and hence may speak with different voices. In recognition of this 'truth' the author adopts different voices – initially using the third person, but then being forced to use the first as the discourse requires, particularly in the latter part of this chapter where the examples are specific and peculiar to a

time, place and stage in the author's own research career.

In any process of research, three processes of learning occur. First, something is learnt about the subject of the research. Second, something is learnt about the process of research. Finally, albeit in not every case, something may be learnt about oneself, particularly in those processes of research that engage the researcher with a group of people over a fairly lengthy period of time. The issue of ethical behaviour is woven through all of these learning processes, and thus the very core of research itself. The researcher is faced with a series of self-accepted domains of responsibility – to be responsible: in the modes of research selected, to those who participate in the research as respondents, to the readers of the research findings, and, that most difficult of issues, to the 'truths' of the research circumstance. The act of asking a question is not a neutral act – to ask a question bestows legitimacy upon the question as the question forms an agenda to be considered by the respondent. It causes a response requiring thought from a respondent – a response, however, that may or may not be to the forefront of the normal consciousness of the respondent, or of a limited 'truthfulness' given that respondents may not wish to divulge all of their thoughts about a situation or subject. The answer to the question is a construct of subject, interviewer–interviewee relationship, other relationships, context and place. Hence on the one hand it is possible to discuss the power of the researcher as an originator of agenda, and actor in agenda setting, yet on the other hand the researcher possesses power only insofar as a respondent permits. It is often stated that a 'good' research project is one that possesses a 'rich' dataset – that is, samples are large and/or respondents have been articulate and thoughtful – but that in itself implies absence of inarticulacy – while such an attribute of inarticulacy on the part of respondents may itself be a 'truth' of the research. To further compound the difficulties facing the researcher, today researchers are very aware that the silences are important aspects of the research. Whose voice is not heard reflects power structures; what view is not expressed indicates the hidden possibilities of the marginal.

Complexities in research abound, many of which imply questions of ethics. Additionally, in universities and other institutions today, researchers are asked to meet the requirements of 'ethics committees', whose very existence and adherence to statutory rules is a recognition and codification of issues pertaining to ethical concerns. Practice, however, differs from faculty to faculty, determined in part by the culture of the scientific discipline, the institution, the location of the university and concerns of grant-providing organizations. The polyvocal nature of such issues is perhaps best observed in New Zealand, by the clashes of perceived priorities where those researching in the natural sciences are asked to consider the implications of their research upon Maori culture (NZPA, 2003a), and whether there is specific 'Maori science' that can attract separate funding from the Foundation of Research, Science and Technology (NZPA, 2003b). Equally, in the regime of social sciences, following partially the issues that pertain within the medical sciences, social science researchers, within which tourism is located, are increasingly being asked to indicate means by which the privacy of respondents is being respected.

This is partially a response to the legal considerations generated by various privacy acts found around the western world. Given the one-shot questionnaire-based research that is characteristic of much reported tourism research, especially when based upon postal surveys, and where names and addresses of respondents are not required, such a concern seems, to this author, misplaced and one-sided. Misplaced because, again in the experience of this researcher, potential respondents are more than capable of failing to respond to a postal questionnaire, however carefully crafted the covering letter might be, or, in face to face circumstances, indicating that the researcher should 'get lost' with varying degrees of politeness; one-sided, because in many instances the other responsibilities of the researcher as listed above are not enquired into, often, it has to be said, for good reason. Such reasons include a lack of expertise on the part of panel members in a given subject area or technique, and a belief that the probities of the research project are subsequently assessed through procedures such as double blind refereeing or the examination of colleagues at public presentations at conferences. The degree to which this faith is, in turn, potentially misplaced is discussed below.

A third aspect of the ruminations of ethics committees in university tourism departments or faculties is the degree to which permissions are granted on the basis of rule adherence. While the rules may be motivated by a desire to enforce ethical research, is such adherence to rules by both committee and researcher moral? If it is ethical in the sense that parties are adhering to what may be assumed to be ethical rules pertaining to respondent rights, are the behaviours or outcomes necessarily moral? From a utilitarian or Benthamite perspective, does the potential good of the research outweigh the concern over the rights of the respondent? It could be argued that respondents possess not only a right to privacy, but also a responsibility to a wider community. For example, research associated with the impacts of tourism (and the associated research project itself) may benefit or inhibit social wellbeing. The researcher, by obtaining answers, is the conduit through which the individual respondent discharges the responsibility to the community. Consequently the adherence of a rules-bound university department's ethics committee based on the primacy of one stakeholder's interest may mitigate the very ethical outcomes apparently sought by such a committee.

This concept of ethics as adherence to a set of rules was considered, among others, by Foucault (1985), who noted that morality consists of codes of behaviour as well as the ways in which individuals choose to adhere, or not, to those rules. His consideration of ethics and morality are expressed in his work, *The Use of Pleasure: the History of Sexuality, Volume Two* (Foucault, 1985: see particularly pages 26–28). This is particularly notable perhaps to the present author because of his own work on sex tourism, which is discussed below. Foucault draws a distinction between morals and ethics based on the ways in which individuals work out their own relationships to the codes and ways in which they adhere to them. Foucault suggests four ways by which these relationships can be developed, and these are applicable to the ways in which tourism researchers work. First, what part of one's behaviour is concerned with moral conduct – is one faithful to the rules because of a resolve to follow the rules, feelings for significant others or the mastery and control of ego? Second, is the source of moral behaviour external or internal? Third, how does the researcher change in order to become an ethical subject? Finally, what type of person does one aspire to be when acting ethically?

For Christians (2000), the existence of ethics committees indicated two distinct parameters. First, the concern expressed by such codes of conduct with the need for informed consent by respondents, the avoidance of deceit, the maintenance of privacy and confidentiality and accuracy. Second, however, he argues that the primacy of such concerns represents the ethics of value-neutral paradigms of research associated with a Weberian analysis of a need

for the scientific exclusion of values associated with evaluation. Christians (2000) interprets Weberian analysis as being driven by a pragmatic analysis of relevance contextualized in a period when German managerial classes required training in the 'how' while remaining silent about the 'ends'. Christians (2000: 142) concluded that 'This constricted environment no longer addresses adequately the complicated issues we face in studying the social world'. By the same token, the pragmatic concerns of a code-bound ethics committee that adopt rules for the Weberian needs of even-handedness in coming to decisions are also likely to engage the ire of social scientists sponsoring research agendas that are value driven and post-stucturalist. Hence the leading question that invades privacy may be essential to their research.

It can be argued that for the tourism researcher who seeks to investigate a range of topics not considered specific to the tourist experience and formation of self (e.g. about levels of satisfaction with theme parks or price sensitivities) by means of a questionnaire comprising Likert type items that avoid personal questions (e.g. of the nature 'How many times did you visit a massage parlour while on holiday?' or 'What is your sexual orientation?'), then to be acting ethically in adherence to the codes required by an ethics committee poses no problem, particularly if no names and addresses are required. The researcher acts ethically, but no moral challenge is involved. On the other hand the researcher who examines a subject such as sex and gender issues in tourism enters a minefield of moral conundrums.

This issue of ethical behaviour and subject matter raises issues about the nature of tourism research and the desire of the researcher. Is the curiosity of the researcher sufficient justification to obtain the cooperation of the respondent and the discharge of the respondent's wider social responsibility by provision of information that might have some wider public good? It cannot be pretended that all tourism research engages fundamental social questions. For example, destination exit surveys at airports about expenditure patterns or levels of satisfaction about specific attractions possess value, but the value may be of limited social use. On the other hand, research about the ability of a community in a developing nation to absorb visitor numbers and the impacts of such numbers on a way of life may be said to possess more significant value. Does this imply that subject matter of the research determines whether it is more or less ethical, or more or less moral? The issue of the morality and importance of an issue has a long history. At what point does the pragmatic person draw the line in the sand to distinguish between that which is not approved of, but which is condoned by lack of action, and that which is not approved of, and is condemned and acted against?

So, what is meant by the expression 'to be ethical in research'? To be acting ethically might be said to act with integrity, with honesty, but also to act in a manner sensitive to the concerns of others. Yet, in a sense, such definitions of ethical behaviour are tautological. To act with integrity is ethical, to be ethical is to act with integrity – but what does this mean in a practical sense? Aristotle, in *Ethics* seeks to answer the question by making further sub-divisions. For him the soul comprises both the rational and the irrational, and virtue is equally so divided.

> Some virtues are called intellectual and others moral; Wisdom and Understanding and Prudence are intellectual, Liberality and Temperance are moral virtues. When speaking of a man's character we do not describe him as wise or understanding, but as patient or temperate. We do, however, praise a wise man on the ground of the state of his mind; and those states that are praiseworthy, we call virtues.
> (Aristotle, c. 370 BC/1986: 90)

Under this schema, it might argued that the researcher operates within spheres of wisdom, understanding and prudence, and that indeed may be an effective approach to the nature of ethical research given that the different ontologies of research recognize different constructions of truth. There exist different classifications but Guba (1990) suggests four main categories: positivistic, post-

positivistic, constructionist and critical theory. Other writers suggest additional paradigms. Jennings (2001), for example, argues that feminism is not simply an example of critical theory, but has evolved into its specific form so as to establish itself clearly as another form of enquiry. This author is not wholly in agreement, in that for agreement to be so constituted implies homogeneity of thought within feminism, which is now not present. Faulkner and Russell (2000) suggested a further categorization associated with chaos theory, a point accepted by Jennings (2001), but one amended by McKercher (1999), who draws a distinction between chaos and complexity theories. Each of these paradigms, these frameworks of thought, constructs a relationship between the researcher and the 'truth'. The implications of such relationships were discussed by Bogdan and Taylor (1975) over a quarter of a century ago and it is worth quoting them at length on this issue:

> Two major theoretical perspectives have dominated the social science scene. One, *positivism*, traces its origins to the great social theorists of the nineteenth and early twentieth centuries and especially to August Comte and Emile Durkheim. The positivist seeks the facts or causes of social phenomena with little regard for the subjective states of individuals. Durkheim advises the social scientist to consider 'social facts', or social phenomena, as 'things' that exercise an external and coercive force on human behaviour. The second theoretical perspective, which, following the lead of Irwin Deutscher, we will describe as *phenomenological*, stems most prominently from Max Weber. The phenomenologist is concerned with *understanding* human behaviour from the actor's own frame of reference ... The phenomenologist examines how the world is experienced. For him or her the important reality is what people imagine it to be.
> *Since the positivists and the phenomenologists approach different problems and seek different answers, their research will typically demand different methodologies.*
> (Bogdan and Taylor, 1975: 2; italics in the original)

Inherent in these differences lie varying understandings of the role of the researcher. Those concerned with the 'facts' of the situation, whether positivist, post-positivist or (to an extent) constructionist, recognize that 'facts' exist independently of the researcher. The researcher's role is to discover those 'facts', and there is little that the researcher can do to change the nature of those 'facts'. The researcher is thus concerned with the nature of the tools used to discover those facts, and hence a concern emerges about the reliability of datasets and an ability to generalize from what is learnt about the specific. The researcher seeks therefore to prove that samples are representative and the results derived are replicable by others.

However, while there are 'social facts' and 'things' about tourism, such as the fact that a hotel exists, and that a given number of flights occur between two locations, arguably 'truths' that are the concern of 'ethical research' are concerned with more than the 'facts'. Tourism researchers, like other social science researchers, are concerned with the implications of the 'facts' for people, communities, business organizations and natural environments, to list but some stakeholders. It is possible to locate an analysis of implications within a positivistic reference. Arguably, Butler's (1980) destination life cycle model is one such example. From a positivistic perspective, destinations rise in popularity, change their nature and spatial patterns, are used differently over time by different groups of tourists, and subsequently enter periods of stagnation and then decline unless certain forms of corrective action are engaged upon. On the other hand, tourism researchers have argued that the inherent purpose and rationale of tourism is the search for experience. Conventionally tourism researchers have argued that this is a search for difference (Dann, 2000; Ryan, 2002) – a difference of place, activity and experience. Accordingly researchers have argued that the tourist is a displaced person, spatially and temporally, and used the conceptualizations of commentators like Derrida (1976) and Bourdieu (1978) to analyse the tourist as a person apart from both the host- and tourist-gener-

ating communities (e.g. Wearing and Wearing, 1996). Other writers have attributed different social connections to tourist behaviour, including, notably, Urry's (1990, 2002) conceptualization of the ludic post-tourist. On the other hand, Prentice and Andersen (2003), in an analysis of visitors to Edinburgh, have argued that tourists do not actually seek difference, but familiarity. Trauer and Ryan (2005) amended Prentice and Andersen's view with reference to adventure tourism, attributing an importance to the media as generating a familiarity of 'sign'. The proposition is made that tourists are able to locate themselves within expectations as to place, activity and experience through the media – they are actors about to fulfil a role seen many times previously on their television sets. Experiences are evaluated against images derived from the 'Discovery Channel'.

To elicit research findings from such constructions of experience requires methods not easily derived from the quantitative, empiricist traditions of tourism research. Patton (1980: 159) discusses the importance of field notes in participant–observer research and emphasizes that '*the documentation would not have made sense without the interviews and the focus of the interviews came from the field observations. Taken together, these diverse sources of information and data gave me a complete picture of staff relationships*' (italics in the original). He then proceeds to note that 'fieldwork is a creative process' (Patton, 1980: 159). Fieldwork does not begin with a comprehensive checklist of what is to happen, and the researcher is continually making judgements about what is noteworthy, if only because selection of material is required for to do otherwise is to be overwhelmed by detail.

Taking these themes of creativity in fieldwork and the importance of experience within tourism research, the tourist researcher is often faced with a quandary of discourse. The debate of difference–familiarity is in itself a discourse about tourism and its relationship with the mainstream of social organization. The researcher seeks to locate the tourist experience both within and outside of the parameters of conventional social organization – the special nature of the tourist experience as the memorable experience has sense as being memorable only by comparison. But to adopt the language of conventional social interaction is to not fully capture the nature of the exceptional. Hence in the case of adventure tourism Trauer and Ryan (2005) have recourse to theories of flow, involvement and risk to assess the nature of the experience even while the research is contextualized within a consumerist society of demand, supply and image formation by the media. How much more do these remain problems when controversial issues like sex tourism are approached?

Derrida (1976: 158) famously wrote that 'there is nothing outside the text' (*il n'y a pas de hors-texte*). That is to say there is nothing outside of human relationships and social organization that is not conditioned and structured by language. The text of social relationships is language that both reflects and shapes the process of social discourse. The text is predominant. Consequently, the researcher into sex tourism enters a domain whereby, arguably, the sex worker and the client (the tourist) have not been given access to the text – they have been silenced in the processes of social legitimization – they are illegitimate. The text of the researcher derived from the field notes and the creativeness of which Patton writes become therefore significant utterances by giving voice through publication. For some feminist tourism researchers this poses a problem: the language of the text itself is determined by a patriarchal society. Feury and Mansfield (1997: 129) express this by stating,

> If morality is a social convention, which is defined, articulated, and sustained within the cultural world order, then, according to feminist theories, this morality must reflect a patriarchal bias. It will also operate largely within the symbolic realm, through laws, taboos, and regulations.
> Transgressions against this moral structure can take place in the *sémiotique* – which leads to the difficult question of whether this order is potentially immoral or moral, or of a different type of morality altogether.

Accordingly, following their argument, what one finds is that the hitherto silent capture the language of the power elite to transform it by different usage. Black rappers use the term 'nigger', lesbian feminists speak of the 'power of the cunt' (Murray, 1998) and, perhaps more blandly, tourism researchers give voice to and legitimize the sweat of the massage parlour and strip joint (Donlon, 1998; Suren and Stiefvater, 1998).

Thus far, much of what has been written may seem theoretical and far removed from the experience of the academic researcher asking their questions of managers, tourists and politicians. It might also be objected that discussion of the subject of sex tourism represents an extremity not representative of much of that which is written in the literature. To which one response is that like all extremes, or margins, it illustrates wider problems. Consequently, the remainder of this text will draw upon three examples derived from my own experience wherein ethical considerations have a role to play. Of the three examples, two represented decisions with which I was at ease, the third was one where, even now, I still possess a sense of hesitation.

The first example relates to an issue of code adherence; namely that the tourism researcher should utilize carefully and professionally the research techniques that they profess to be expert in. As an editor of a journal I am only too aware of just how much depends on trust in the author's expertise. I receive many papers that are quantitative in nature, particularly of a market research nature. Within such papers the authors report results, and in the better cases, are able to demonstrate why such results have significance beyond the particular time and place within which they were derived. Yet how is a referee, or an editor, to fully assess the ability of the researcher and the accuracy of the statistics without access to the original raw data set and the questionnaire? I have reached the stage where I do request copies of the questionnaire used in the research as this potentially is of value to future researchers who may wish to replicate or otherwise confirm findings inasmuch as they relate to underlying factors. Arguably the progress made in the confirmation–disconfirmation debate surrounding the SERVQUAL model of Parasuraman, Zeithmal and Berry (1994) resulted precisely because researchers had access to the items that comprised the SERVQUAL scale. However, what is notable is that many researchers do not consider the issue of non-response and the implications it may possess for their work. Two aspects of non-response exist. First, there is the issue of whether those who do not respond display the same socio-demographic and other characteristics as those who do reply to questionnaires, particularly postal questionnaires. At least two methods of checking exist. First, to check that the characteristics of the sample match those of the target population. Second, that some follow up of non-respondents is undertaken. One such method used by this author is to phone a sample of non-respondents and use a shortened version of a questionnaire and then match responses between those who initially reply and the 'telephone sample of non-respondents'.

The second example of non-response is the issue of those who do not or may not wish to reply to certain items within a questionnaire. For this author (as discussed in Ryan and Garland (1999) and Ryan and Cessford (2004)), there is a need to provide an option of non-response to Likert type items in a questionnaire. The reason for this is predicated on an argument that a genuine difference exists between the respondent who is indifferent to an item and may therefore select the mid-point of any scale, and a respondent who feels they have insufficient information from which to make a judgement.

Such issues are those of the exercise of technical expertise and thus lie within the Weberian ethical principles as indicated above. The proper exercise of skill is, however, more than simply a technical matter. It is an issue of respecting the informants and their information and adhering to the principle of accuracy. Poor and shoddy acts of statistical analysis or interpretation are therefore unethical. Additionally, it represents a lack of respect not only for inform-

ants, but also for fellow researchers (and, arguably, particularly for editors and referees if work is being submitted for publication).

My second and third examples come from areas of research that are more contentious in many respects. In 1997 I had published an article relating to the rites of Maori and the implications for representations of Maori within the New Zealand tourism industry. That article was informed by various conversations with several informants, including Maori. The full manuscript (before being sent to the publishers) was seen by a small number of these informants, not only to check that their views had been correctly represented, but also to assess the overall tone of the piece. I was somewhat taken aback when one of these informants, with whom I had a good relationship and had worked with before on issues pertaining to Maori tourism, wrote back a long letter taking me to task for some of the statements about Maori ethical principles. The comments were of a nature that while what I had written was accurate, it was not for me as a *Pakeha* to reveal or discuss Maori ethics. Therefore I was asked not to proceed with publication. It is evident that finally I did decide to place the article with a journal, but that was not until I had discussed the issue with Maori colleagues, including those at different Ministries in New Zealand. The consensus was that the paper could be published. The academic researcher, working within a Western tradition whereby knowledge is to be freely disseminated to all that may benefit from it, at times will work within cultures where knowledge is exclusive. In such societies some types of knowledge may be disseminated only among the initiated, and in some instances, the initiated may only come from certain families or groups. The ethical dilemmas quickly become apparent. How does a researcher access the knowledge, how do they know they fully understand that which they are told, and to what extent may they reveal that knowledge?

To my mind the ethical conundrum is partly solved by the researcher's recognizing that a mutual set of responsibilities exists.

This is fully consistent with, at least in my experience, the culture of gift giving within the cultures wherein I have worked. Maori are fully aware that there are academics who have 'made a reputation' by publishing pieces about Maori culture and cosmology in different journals, and thereby enhanced their own careers. But what benefit have Maori received in return? These feelings are, perhaps, particularly strong when the academic does not sustain a long-term relationship with the group concerned. Feelings of trust need to be sustained, and these can only develop over long periods of time. In short, the researcher must return some value to the group from which the information has been obtained. I have to admit that this is something about which I have strong feelings, and such an admission cannot be explained by the scientific objectivity of a positivistic stance. For example, I have misgivings about articles that adopt a deconstructionist approach to the text of tourism brochures and other promotional literature that effectively isolate the voice of the people about which the representations are made. The attempt to further justify the interpretations obtained with a few quotes from some informants representing the culture being portrayed is little more, in my view, than tokenism. Yet, and there is a 'yet', the interpretations may not be, and, indeed, often are not, wholly 'wrong'. In short, the published pieces may meet the ethical principles of accuracy and be true to the data, but are they true to the ethics of mutuality desired by the peoples about whom the author has written? To my mind the answer has to be 'no'!

Yet such a discourse implies that research can be about more than simply the revealing of 'truths' or the deconstruction of the text. It is about relationships and the nature of those relationships. In a metaphor that I used in Ryan and Hall (2001), it seemed to me that the truth was like an onion. The context of this metaphor was discussing research into sex tourism and the relationships that one establishes with informants. It is first argued that there is a necessity for a long-term relationship to be established, and that trust is an important component within these relationships. It is argued that the women involved as sex workers have excellent social skills, and they construct roles and truths for given situations for many different reasons. Consequently, the one-off meeting is capable of discerning some 'truths' – but the emphasis is upon the word 'some' and the plurality of the 'truth'. Therefore, the metaphor argues that the various layers of the onion represent truths as they are slowly peeled away, and eventually a core is reached. But is there a 'core truth'? The answer has to be 'no' because the truth is the whole onion, with not only the hidden core, but all the hidden layers that lay between it and the surface. And, to press home the metaphor, just as one cuts the onion, so one cries. It is but a metaphor, but the nature of the long-term relationship is that the researcher becomes a friend to the informant, and repetition of the fact that one is doing research and the showing of the papers one produces does not wholly hide or change any friendship or familiarity with the subject that is created. The researcher can only experience a tension, between being the participant in a process and also seeking to be reflective. Note that I say here 'reflective' whereas some researchers might speak of trying to establish a distance to be objective. I am not sure that is possible, because in many circumstances I would suggest that among the data present are the researcher's own emotions and reactions. This was an issue that I faced in Ryan and Martin (2001), and the article specifically makes explicit the relationship between the authors as observer and observed. Whilst the ambience of a strip club seems extreme, the same issues occur elsewhere. For example, Jennings (1998) has to explicitly address the nature of her relationship as a researcher who had 'been there, done that', and being perceived by her informants as having that experience, when discussing the female experience of sailing yachts for long cruises (both spatially and temporally) in the South Pacific while undertaking her doctoral studies. As part of the ethical responsibility to the reader, the role of the researcher, and the way the researcher is used by informants, has to be stated because it is a process that has informed the research.

At times, ethical dilemmas can be many and unexpected. Ethics committees may require full disclosure of information to the informants, and hence notes of any conversation may have to be made available to the informant. But to my mind this is not axiomatic, and the principle is based upon a scientific conceptualization of the nature of the 'truths' to be discerned. In long-term relationships between respondent and researcher, the process of discovery is exactly that: a process of maturation of understanding. Indeed the relationship may require maturation because the respondent may not want to face the 'truths' about their own attitudes or the implications of those attitudes. The researcher assumes, perhaps, degrees of self-knowledge (or a degree of willingness for self-revelation) on the part of the respondent which may or may not be present. The post-positivistic researcher using a questionnaire with Likert type items does not ask what lay behind the choice of a number on a scale – the qualitative researcher may find the understanding of that choice to be detailed or limited. To repeat, the act of asking a question is not a neutral act. In one of my research projects, that of Ryan and Martin (2001), which is about strippers, I was asked by one of the informants if she could see my notes; a request echoed by the other women concerned. For me, this was an ethical issue – because what my field notes clearly showed was a series of contradictions and inconsistencies in stories. I had accepted these as being reflections of time and stage in understanding, but I came to the decision that for the respondents to be faced with these would not be appropriate. This, I admit, may have been a wrong decision – I would claim no infallibility in such situations. I therefore decided to write a poem that used the words of these women. It consisted of a number of verses, and included:

We are the women of Sinsations Bar,
We twist, gyrate and strip,
Pout and smile, we want your money

Not a dollar or two,
but ten or twenty will do.

We are professional,
Our bodies glisten with our sweat,
We dance and hussle
To the wimps, lonely and neanderthal,
Drink, stare, fantasize at our shopping mall!

But can you see beyond our tits
Our bums and cunts with fingers hid,
Slyly, shyly enticing your stupid leers,
Can you see who we are
What we think, our histories and our fears?

I had resolved not to show the poem unless I was asked for my notes. As it happened, I was asked, showed the poem, which was read by the women involved, and in consequence of their reaction began to acquire new insights and knowledge that had not been previously revealed.

In one way, therefore, perhaps this example illustrates the observation made by Patton (1980) that qualitative research is a creative act. But the act of creation and the elicitation of data through such acts means that the researcher may well be a participant and not simply an observer, an actor and not simply a provider of critique. Within some schools of research thinking, this is perfectly acceptable – notably, perhaps within feminist studies (if it is possible to discern a homogeneity within feminism, something that I doubt). However, there does remain a test for such qualitative research, and that is the test of credibility. Do the findings seem credible to the actors and to the readers? It is, possibly, a dangerous test, for self-delusion is not unknown, but it is not possible in multi-layered, polyvocal circumstances to determine an objectivity that is consistent with the approach adopted by the mathematical modelling of the positivist. Indeed, it is possible to go further and argue that critical theorists and post-structuralists cannot construct models or meta-theories – at best frameworks might be established specific to given contexts bounded by space and time.

In conclusion, therefore, research processes are complex, and not only is the asking of a question not a neutral act, but the very shape and mode of asking the question possesses importance in determining the nature of the answer. Given this, the value-neutral processes of the social scientific method themselves exhibit values about the nature of truths and the relationship of the researcher to the discovered. One can only reiterate that the ethical researcher is a reflective researcher, continuously mindful of sets of competing and complementary responsibilities to respondents, other researchers, those who commission the research, to readers and to those who may wish to follow by building upon the findings and research methods. In some ways to be a researcher is to adopt an arrogant role – there is no God-given right for others to respond to our questions; and in remembering that, perhaps care and nurturance might be the ethical stance appropriate to the research complexities of contemporary tourism experiences.

References

Aristotle (c. 370 BC/1986) *Ethics*. Translated by Thomson, J.A.K., revised by Tredennick, H. Penguin Books, Harmondsworth, UK.

Bogdan, R. and Taylor, S.J. (1975) *Introduction to Qualitative Methods*. John Wiley, New York.

Bordieu, P. (1978) Sport, status and style. *Sport History Review* 30(1), 1–26.

Butler, R. (1980) The concept of a tourism area cycle of evolution. *Canadian Geographer* 24(1), 5–12.

Christians, C. (2000) Ethics and politics in qualitative research. In: Denzin, N.K. and Lincoln, Y.S. (eds) *Handbook of Qualitative Research*, 2nd edn. Sage Publications, Thousand Oaks, California, pp. 133–155.

Dann, G. (2000) Differentiating destinations in the language of tourism: harmless hype or promotional irresponsibility? *Tourism Recreation Research* 25(2), 63–75.

Derrida, J. (1976) *Of Grammatolog*. Translated by Spivak, G.C. Johns Hopkins University Press, Baltimore, Maryland.

Donlon, J.G. (1998) A travel model in the runway setting: strip-tease as exotic destination. In: Oppermann, M. (ed.) *Sex Tourism and Prostitution: Aspects of Leisure, Recreation, and Work*. Cognizant Communication Corporation, New York, pp. 116–122.

Faulkner, B. and Russell, R. (2000) Turbulence, chaos and complexity in tourism systems: a research direction for the new millennium. In: Faulkner, B., Moscardo, G. and Laws, E. (eds) *Tourism in the 21 Century*. Continuum, London, pp. 328–349.

Feury, P. and Mansfield, N. (1997) *Cultural Studies and Critical Theory*. Oxford University Press, Melbourne.

Foucault, M. (1985) *The Use of Pleasure: the History of Sexuality*, Volume Two, Translated by Hurley, R. Vintage Books, New York.

Guba, E.G. (1990) *The Paradigm Dialog*. Sage Publications, Newbury Park, California.

Jennings, G.R. (1998) *Towards an Understanding of Travel Motivations: Cruising Yachtspersons' Motivations and the Overall Travel Experience: a Critique of Theory and Practice*. 1998 International Society of Travel and Tourism Educators Annual Conference Proceedings, Cleveland, Ohio, pp. 15–18.

Jennings, G.R. (2001) *Tourism Research*. John Wiley and Sons, Milton, Australia.

McKercher, B. (1999) A chaos approach to tourism. *Tourism Management* 20(4), 425–434.

Murray, A. (1998) Femme on the streets, butch in the sheets (a play on whores). In: Bell, D. and Valentine, G. (eds) *Mapping Desire*. Routledge, London, pp. 66–74.

NZPA (2003a) Claims Maori have too much say on GE research are 'absurd'. *New Zealand Herald*, 4 January. Available at: http://www.nzherald.co.nz/storydisplay.cfm?thesection=news&thesubsection=&storyID=3049854

NZPA (2003b) Millions go to Maori Science. *New Zealand Herald*, 16 January. Available at: http://www.nzherald.co.nz/storydisplay.cfm?thesection=news&thesubsection=&storyID=3051602

Parasuraman, A., Zeithmal, V.A. and Berry, L.L. (1994) Alternative scales for measuring service quality: a comparative assessment based on psychometric and diagnostic criteria. *Journal of Retailing* 70(3), 201–230.

Patton, M.Q. (1980) *Qualitative Evaluation Methods*. Sage Publications, Beverley Hills, California.

Prentice, R. and Andersen, V. (2003) Festival as creative destination. *Annals of Tourism Research* 30(1), 7–30.

Ryan, C. (2002) *The Tourism Experience*. Continuum Books, London.

Ryan, C. and Cessford, G. (2004) Developing a visitor satisfaction monitoring methodology. *Current Issues in Tourism* 6(6), 457–507.

Ryan, C. and Garland, R. (1999) The use of a specific non-response option on Likert type scales. *Tourism Management* 20(1), 107–114.

Ryan, C. and Hall, C.M. (2001) *Sex Tourism: Marginal People and Liminalities*. Routledge, London.

Ryan, C. and Martin, A. (2001) Tourists and strippers: liminal theater. *Annals of Tourism Research* 28(1), 140–163.

Ryan, C. and Trauer, B. (2005) Adventure tourism and sport – introduction. In: Ryan, C., Page, S.J. and Aieken, M. (eds) *Taking Tourism to the Limits: Issues, Concepts and Managerial Perspectives*. Elsevier Pergamon, Oxford, UK.

Suren, A. and Stiefvater, R. (1998) Topless dancing: a case for recreational identity. In: Oppermann, M. (ed.) *Sex Tourism and Prostitution: Aspects of Leisure, Recreation, and Work*. Cognizant Communication Corporation, New York, pp. 107–115.

Urry, J. (1990) *The Tourist Gaze*. Sage Publications, London.

Urry, J. (2002) *The Tourist Gaze*. Routledge, London.

Wearing, B. and Wearing, S. (1996) Refocusing the tourist experience: the flâneur and the choraster. *Leisure Studies* 15, 229–243.

3 Feminist and Gender Perspectives in Leisure and Tourism Research

CARA AITCHISON

School of Geography and Environmental Management, Faculty of the Built Environment, Bristol, University of the West of England, Frenchay Campus, Coldharbour Lane, Bristol BS16 1QY, UK

Introduction

In the last two decades of the 20th century a number of social science disciplines experienced what has come to be known as 'the cultural turn'. In leisure and tourism studies this turn to culture coincided with the turn of the new century and was evident in the publication of a range of research that embraced new theoretical perspectives, methodological approaches and research techniques (Aitchison, 2000a; Fullagar, 2002; Jordan, 2004). Unlike leisure and tourism studies, which have become established areas of research and scholarship within the social sciences over only the last three decades, feminist and gender studies have a longer history that straddles both the social sciences and the humanities. Thus, well known writers such as Virginia Woolf, Simone de Beauvoir and Germaine Greer, who came from literary backgrounds, have authored classic texts now seen to underpin the course of social scientific research in feminist and gender studies.

The cultural turn represented a narrowing in the gap between social science disciplines such as sociology and geography in relation to humanities subjects such as literary criticism and cultural theory. This closer relationship between the social and the cultural was informed by the increasing engagement with poststructural theory within the academy. Originating in literary criticism within the humanities, poststructural theory contested the 'grand theories' of both positivism and structuralism. Instead of claiming to know the totality of relationships between social and cultural phenomena, poststructuralism introduced uncertainty into our ways of knowing about the social and cultural world. This uncertainty, or 'crisis in representation' as Denzin and Lincoln (2002) have defined it, contested the post-Enlightenment view that knowledge could be produced in a rational, scientific manner to discover 'the truth' and that such truths could be represented in social models that could be replicated across time and space. In contrast, by placing stress on difference and diversity, poststructuralism emphasized the relative nature of knowledge and the existence of multiple truths that are not necessarily fixed in time and space. Moreover, poststructuralism, like earlier feminist writings, drew attention to the ways in which knowledge of the social and cultural world is produced, legitimated and reproduced by dominant groups. By revealing the power relationship inherent in the production of knowledge, poststructuralism opened the way to the possibility of contesting and reworking these privileged epistemologies or ways of knowing and seeing.

This chapter first seeks to outline the relationship between epistemology, methodology and method in relation to gender perspectives in leisure and tourism studies. In doing so, the chapter reveals how particular leisure and tourism policies and practices are the outcome of equally particular perspectives and philosophies. In other words, our view of the world, and leisure and tourism's place within the world, shapes the way in which our leisure and tourism relations, and our knowledge of these relations, is produced and understood (Aitchison, 2001a, 2003). In the second section of the chapter three different perspectives from feminist and gender theory are introduced and evaluated: feminist empiricism, standpoint feminism and post-structural feminism. Each of these broad perspectives has served to shape our multiple understandings of the relationships between gender, leisure and tourism. What the chapter addresses here is the complex and competing nature of knowledge and understanding, the multiple ways of knowing about social and cultural relations including gender relations, and our different understandings of social and cultural phenomena including leisure and tourism. This section introduces examples from a range of studies of feminist and gender research in leisure and tourism that exemplify these different ways of knowing about leisure and tourism.

The final section of the chapter, whilst acknowledging the positive influence of the cultural turn within feminist and gender studies of leisure and tourism, offers a note of caution in the wholesale adoption of post-structural approaches to the neglect of structural and material analyses. Here, the concept of the social–cultural nexus is introduced as a framework within which to explore the mutually informing nature of social and cultural relations in shaping gender relations within leisure and tourism. The chapter concludes by arguing that whilst women and girls still suffer structural oppression within almost all social and cultural arenas it is inappropriate to discontinue a research tradition that has served feminism well in highlighting the material constraints that women and girls face as part of everyday life, including within leisure

and tourism. The chapter therefore stresses the importance of developing theoretical critiques that integrate material and cultural analyses of gender and leisure and tourism relations.

Feminist and Gender Research: Understanding Epistemology, Methodology and Methods

Epistemology, or research philosophy, is concerned with the examination of the nature of knowledge and the links between theory and data in the construction of knowledge (Mannheim, 1952). In relation to gender, leisure and tourism, this means asking ourselves what we know, how we come to know, how our beliefs and values shape what we know and what evidence there is to support or refute our claims to knowledge (Stanley, 1997; Oakley, 2000). Feminist critiques of what counts as knowledge and who creates knowledge are therefore fundamental to feminism as an academic field of enquiry; to feminist ideology and the academic discussions that seek to increase knowledge, understanding and appreciation of gender–power relationships. Feminism is also an applied field of study and instrumental in political activism, decision making, policy making, planning and management. In both of these endeavours, a reappraisal of traditional epistemologies has been a necessary prerequisite for change.

The debates concerning the existence and nature of a feminist epistemology have been documented clearly elsewhere (Stanley and Wise, 1983, 1993; Stanley, 1990; Weedon, 1997; Jackson and Jones, 1998; Evans, 2003; Letherby, 2003). Within these and other writings extensive debate has taken place concerning the nature of feminist epistemology or epistemologies; the relationships between epistemology, methodology and methods; and the existence of feminist research methods (Roberts, 1981; Stanley and Wise, 1983, 1993; Harding, 1987; Dyck, 1993; Katz, 1994; Gray, 1997; Madge et al., 1997; Jackson and Jones, 1998; Oakley, 1998; Jackson and Scott, 2002). In recent years, feminist academics have attempted to retrace the footsteps of these debates in an attempt to uncover where a crucial and damaging misunderstanding about the relationship between feminist theory and method occurred (Stanley and Wise, 1993; Oakley, 1998).

Stanley and Wise (1993) contend that this criticism of feminist research was founded largely on a semantic misconception whereby many academics assumed that feminist researchers had been calling for a radical change to *research methods* when, in reality, they were seeking changes to *research epistemologies*. To emphasize this point, Stanley (1990: 26), in *Feminist Praxis*, notes that many reviewers of *Breaking Out: Feminist Ontology and Epistemology* (1983) interpreted the book 'as a discourse on either method or methodology, while it was produced as a discussion of epistemology', which, together with Wise, she defined as:

> ... a framework or theory for specifying the constitution and generation of knowledge about the social world; that is, it concerns how to understand the nature of 'reality'. A given epistemological framework specifies not only what 'knowledge' is and how to recognize it, but who are the 'knowers' and by what means someone becomes one, and also the means by which competing knowledge-claims are adjudicated and some rejected in favour of another/others.
> (Stanley and Wise, 1993: 188–189)

The misunderstanding relates to what is now recognized as an inappropriate conflation of feminist epistemology with qualitative research methods. The perceived narrowness of methodological approach employed in feminist research resulted in criticism and marginalization from the male-dominated academy where a plurality of approaches, albeit informed by what Spender (1981) defined as the 'patriarchal paradigm', were in operation. The patriarchal paradigm refers to the ways in which researchers have 'extrapolated results from research into male behaviour across the entire population' (Pillimore and Goodson, 2004). Thus, research has been constructed

to explain social phenomena pertaining to both men and women, but where only men's experiences have been investigated and where these male experiences then come to be seen as 'the norm' and where women's experiences are viewed as secondary, as deviant from the norm, or as Other. Feminists have therefore rejected these interpretations of their lives because they have been made by undertaking research within a patriarchal framework that neglects or negates women's experiences, both as the 'subject' of the research and as the researcher.

Feminist research acknowledges the significance of the researcher or writer in shaping the research process and written outcomes. Moreover, the relationship between the researcher and the research 'subject(s)', or 'participants' as feminist researchers prefer to define them, has received scrutiny from a number of feminist researchers (Code, 1981; Oakley, 1981; Gilligan, 1982; Stanley and Wise, 1983, 1993; Farran, 1990; Seller, 1994). From here on, this chapter will therefore refer not to 'research subjects' but to 'research participants'. This attempt to create a less hierarchical relationship within the research process is in line with what Morris *et al.* (1998: 221) see as the 'third tenet of feminist methodology, which is the rejection of hierarchical relationships within the research process by making those being researched into partners or collaborators'. The other tenets of feminist methodology, outlined by Morris *et al.* (1998: 220–222) include: a 'commitment to feminist principles' in the purpose, conduct and reporting of the research; a commitment 'to doing feminist research *for* women, and not just *on* them'; and a 'commitment to reflexivity, based on notions of openness and intellectual honesty'. In contrast to conventional notions of objectivity in research, Letherby (2003: 45) has stressed that for 'the supporters of feminist standpoint epistemology, reflexivity within research is not a problem but a scientific resource, and the use of reflexivity leads to "strong" objectivity'.

This relationship between the researcher and the researched is also highlighted by Oakley (1981, 1998) and Farran (1990), who both give detailed accounts of their own experience of interviewing for research purposes. Both researchers have written of the constraints that the traditionally defined research interview places on both feminist analysis and feminist practice as a result of the predetermined relationship between researcher and researched. In her study of women travelling solo, Jordan (2004) interviewed 39 women about the ways in which they experienced both constraints and feelings of empowerment during the course of their journeys. She explores the issues at stake in trying to interpret the data and in 'giving voice' to the women who participated in the research project. With over 200,000 words of interview transcript Jordan (2004: 78) recognizes that, 'Whilst I have endeavoured to ensure that I represent as many views as possible I acknowledge that I, as the interpreter of women's solo travel stories, am the one who has either given voice or silenced them':

> ... having a 'researcher' interpret the stories of the 'researched' implies a power relationship that can create the researcher as more powerful through their selection and interpretation of the data. On the other hand, as Jackson and Jones (1998) point out, even in everyday life we constantly interpret and endeavour to make sense of our own experiences and those of people around us. Our responsibility as researchers then is to make this process visible in the way we write up our research.
> (Jordan, 2004: 77)

In other recent studies of women as solo travellers and tourists, Simmons (2003) stresses the role that the researcher plays in the telling of travellers' tales, and Small (1999, 2002) emphasizes the role of 'memory work' as a set of research techniques that seek to uncover shared meanings in women's travel experiences. This emphasis on the form of the narrative has been informed as much by research perspectives adopted and adapted from the humanities as the social sciences. Here, the tourism-related work of Botterill (2003), developing sport and leisure-related 'auto-ethnographic'

research undertaken by Sparkes (1996), has also been important in acknowledging further the role that the researcher plays in the research process and the ways in which the researcher simultaneously constructs and is constructed by the telling of the narrative. What all of these approaches have in common is their acknowledgement that social and cultural research, including research exploring gender and tourism relations, cannot be undertaken without acknowledging the impact of the research process and its impact upon both the researcher and research participants.

Different Perspectives in Feminist and Gender Theory

It is appropriate, within the context of this chapter, to distinguish between feminist research and gender research. The former has an explicitly political purpose in seeking to highlight, and subsequently improve, conditions for women within society. Whilst all feminist research and researchers place gender relations at the centre of their investigations, not all gender research embraces a feminist perspective or is undertaken by feminist researchers. For example, much of the human geography research undertaken in the late 1990s, and which contributed to the cultural turn in geography, had a focus on gender and/or sexuality but was not explicitly feminist in orientation (Bell and Valentine, 1994; Bell et al., 1994). Feminist research began to emerge in leisure studies from the late 1970s and grew significantly during the 1980s (Talbot, 1979; Deem, 1986; Green et al., 1987; Woodward et al., 1988; Henderson et al., 1989). However, it was not until the early 1990s that tourism studies really embraced feminist epistemology as a legitimate research perspective (Kinnaird and Hall, 1994). Swain (1995) chronicles the rise of what she terms 'gender in tourism' and there has subsequently been what appears to be an exponential increase in the breadth and depth of feminist and gender research in tourism. This research has been informed by a variety of feminist perspectives and has been published both in tourism studies and in the 'parent' disciplines of anthropology, geography, politics, psychology and sociology.

Feminist research has an explicit political purpose and distinct schools of thought within feminism have placed political significance on different power relations that are seen to subordinate women. This has resulted in differences within feminism and between different feminisms. For example, whereas liberal feminism sees the lack of equality of opportunity within organizations and institutions such as education and work as being a major cause of inequality, socialist and Marxist feminism view the very structure of such institutions as inherently patriarchal. Radical feminism, in a further contrast, directs attention towards the institution of the family, sexuality and the oppression of women through unpaid domestic labour and reproduction. Marking a further difference, poststructural feminism would view such a perspective as essentialist and to be over homogenizing women, and postcolonial and black feminism would emphasize further the cultural diversity of women and the legacy of colonial power in shaping gender relations.

It could be argued that the formation of typologies representing different schools of thought, constructed according to the perceived locus of gender–power relationships within society, has come to form a preoccupation of feminist and gender studies. Thus we have many different labels for different kinds of feminism: liberal feminism, radical feminism, cultural feminism, socialist feminism, Marxist feminism, poststructural feminism, postmodern feminism, eco-feminism and so the list goes on. The difficulty with assigning such labels is that they tend to invoke fixed categories and are usually apportioned by readers of feminist research rather than by the writers themselves. The result, as Letherby (2003: 58) points out, is that 'many writers and thinkers are labelled in ways that they themselves challenge' and I can identify with this myself having been 'accused' of being both a radical feminist and a postmodern feminist within the space of only a few years even though none of my writings purports to advocate either 'position'.

An alternative, and less restrictive, means of providing clarity regarding different perspectives in feminist and gender theory has been to group related perspectives under one of three categories. By examining the different groupings proposed by a selection of feminist scholars it is then possible to explore the relationship of each broad grouping to feminist and gender research in leisure and tourism. Harding (1986) defined three kinds of feminist approach to research as *feminist empiricism, standpoint feminism* and *postmodern feminism*.

First, *feminist empiricism* encompasses research approaches that seek to work within the dominant scientific paradigm that was developed as a result of Enlightenment thinking and that seek to uncover 'the truth' by establishing 'the facts', using accepted scientific methods of 'objective research'.

Second, *standpoint feminism* embraces those approaches that question the authority of the dominant social science paradigms and starts from the premise that the 'personal is political' (Letherby, 2003: 44). Like feminist empiricism, standpoint feminism seeks to provide a greater focus on women within the research process. However, standpoint feminism goes beyond calling for changes in research methods by also seeking epistemological change. In contrast to feminist empiricism, standpoint feminism asserts that 'the truth', uncovered by research, can neither be revealed nor known independently of the researcher or knower. In other words, reflexivity or the importance of acknowledging the ways in which the researcher's experience both shapes and is shaped by the research process is of central importance in uncovering 'the truth'. Standpoint feminism therefore acknowledges the significance of the researcher or writer in shaping both the research process and the outcome of the research. Thus the relationship between researcher and research participant(s) is of central importance and has been discussed at length by many feminist writers (Code, 1981; Oakley, 1981; Gilligan, 1982; Stanley and Wise, 1983, 1993; Farran, 1990; Seller, 1994).

Third, *postmodern feminism* seeks not so much to establish but to deconstruct established truths. Thus, as Flax (1990: 41) has emphasized, 'Postmodern discourses are all deconstructive in that they seek to distance us from and make us sceptical about beliefs concerning truth, knowledge, power, the self, and language that are often taken for granted within and serve as legitimation for contemporary Western culture'. One of the main concerns of poststructuralism is therefore to refute the notion of one single theory or 'grand narrative' capable of explaining social, cultural and power relations throughout time and across space. In particular, poststructuralism denies the existence of one single truth or logical reason; logocentric constructs that have been so important in Western philosophy since the Enlightenment. As Bryson (1992) states:

> ... the search for a single all-encompassing theory is therefore rejected in principle, as is the very possibility of objectivity. Western philosophy's quest for truth and certainty (described as logocentrism) is therefore abandoned and is seen as the product of a particular historical era that is becoming inappropriate in a postmodern society that is increasingly characterized by fragmentation, diversity and diffuseness in all spheres of life. Existing theories,

particularly Marxism, which claim to embody certainty and objectivity are rejected as totalitarian; here it is not simply the conclusions that are rejected, but the quest for truth itself.
> (Bryson, 1992: 225–226)

Harding's three categories of feminist empiricism, standpoint feminism and postmodern feminism have been reworked and represented by a number of different feminist writers. Alvesson and Billing (1997), in their research of gender and management, referred to three categories as 'gender as variable', 'feminist standpoint' and 'poststructural feminism'. Hearn et al. (1989), in their research of gender and organizations, equated these previous categories with 'social roles', 'political categories' and 'discourses of power'. Di Stefano (1990) then defined three categories of feminist research as 'feminist rationalism', 'feminist anti-rationalism' and 'feminist post-rationalism'. Letherby (2003) most recently wrote of 'feminist empiricism', 'feminist standpoint epistemology' and 'postmodernism or poststructuralism'. Adapted from an earlier publication, Table 3.1 illustrates the ways in which each of these categories has adopted and adapted different research philosophies, methodologies, methods and research foci in their pursuit of knowledge.

Table 3.1. Feminist and gender theory: different research approaches.

Feminist researchers	Feminist research	Feminist research	Feminist and gender research
Harding (1986)	Feminist empiricism	Standpoint feminism	Postmodern feminism
Alvesson and Billing (1997)	Gender as variable	Feminist standpoint	Poststructural feminism
Hearn et al. (1989)	Social roles	Political categories	Discourses of power
Di Stefano (1990)	Feminist rationalism	Feminist anti-rationalism	Feminist post-rationalism
Letherby (2003)	Feminist empiricism	Feminist standpoint epistemology	Postmodernism or poststructuralism
Research philosophy or epistemology	Liberal feminism	Socialist feminism Marxist feminism Radical feminism	Poststructural feminism
Research methodology	Distributive research	Distributive and relational research	Relational research
Research methods	Quantitative research emphasis	Mixed method research	Qualitative research
Research focus	Structural power systems	Structural power systems	Cultural power relations

Feminist empiricism

Feminist empiricism, like liberal feminism, is concerned with reform rather than wholesale change. It seeks to make such reforms within existing scientific structures and systems rather than by challenging the foundations upon which these systems and structures are based. This approach therefore advocates changes to the ways in which research is designed and research methods employed so that women are fully included in the research process, both as researchers and research subjects. By operating wholly within existing structures and systems, feminist empiricism cannot provide a complete feminist research perspective as it does not address the underpinning epistemological issues of knowledge construction, legitimation and reproduction. For example, feminist empiricism might inform research into employment patterns within tourism or on leisure participation statistics between the sexes. Such a focus on descriptive statistics that answer questions of 'what' and 'where', whilst important in illuminating and enumerating women's position in leisure and tourism, tells us little about 'how' and 'why' such patterns exist or the gender–power relationships inherent in the construction of such patterns. This concentration on quantifiable and measurable assessment can be seen as positioning feminist empiricism rather too close to positivism to be an appropriately challenging perspective for research into the complexities of the interrelationships between gender and power.

One emphasis of feminist empiricism has been on *Catching Up The Men* (Dyer, 1982) and on identifying and overcoming visible barriers to women's leisure and tourism participation. Barriers or constraints to women's participation have been described under the headings of biological, social, physical, legal and financial, but these all tend to concentrate on the symptoms of gender–power relationships within society rather than the underlying structures and cultures which might be challenged by standpoint feminism and poststructural feminism, respectively. This concentration on effect rather than cause has been particu- larly prevalent within leisure and tourism policy and management research dominated by a liberal feminist perspective. Such research could be accused of providing rather partial and superficial explanations resulting in equally partial and superficial measures advocated to address inequality. For example, in spite of Sports Council efforts to attract more women into sport and active leisure during the 1980s, the numbers participating in outdoor sport actually fell between 1983 and 1988, thus suggesting that there may be wider structural and cultural barriers to women's sport and leisure participation (Sports Council, 1993). Similarly, research conducted within commercial tourism organizations recommended that women's experiences of travel and tourism would be enhanced by the provision of safety measures such as providing male escorts to and from their cars rather than actually tackling the underpinning issues of fear of male violence. Notwithstanding these shortcomings, feminist empiricism has made a major contribution to gathering and disseminating data that has served to inform later feminist analyses of sex segregation and sex role stereotyping in tourism. For example, research into employment patterns and management structures has revealed the gendered structure of work and related pay differences between men and women (Bagguley, 1990; Hicks, 1990; Adkins, 1994; Kinnaird and Hall, 1994; Jordan, 1997; Aitchison *et al.*, 1999).

Standpoint feminism

'Standpoint feminism' is an umbrella term that embodies a number of different 'standpoints', including Marxist feminism, socialist feminism and radical feminism, with each position derived from a different emphasis on the locus of power within society. Marxist feminism locates gender relations within an explanation of economic and class relations. A central tenet of Marxist feminism is that any improvement in women's situation requires economic change as a precondition. The family is seen as propping up capitalist society by providing unpaid domestic work and a reserve army of labour to service the economy as the need arises. As such, Marxist feminist theory is concerned with examining the material base of women's subordination in both employment and family relations. Although Marxism has been criticized for failing to address issues of gendered power, Marxist feminists emphasize that Marx referred to both *production* and *reproduction* in his theory of the creation of a surplus value of labour:

> The private sphere, so dear to the liberal feminist's heart, is a veritable prison to the Marxist feminist. It subordinates woman by permanently excluding her from the public, productive world and leaving her with a life comprising little more than the emotional support of man who engages in 'real' human activity.
>
> (Tong, 1989: 67)

Whilst Marxist and socialist feminism have a number of features in common, they are separated by the different relationships they identify between class and gender relations. Whereas Marxist feminism emphasizes economic relations over patriarchal relations as the cause of women's oppression, socialist feminism sees both patriarchy and capitalism operating together as a 'dual system' of oppression with neither being dominant. Evans (1995), for example, states that 'following the perception that the relationship between feminism and Marxism was fraught, marred by the primacy of capitalism and class, the distinctive socialist feminist project became the analysis of capitalism and patriarchy, and the relationship between the two' (Evans, 1995: 108). Socialist feminism thus emphasizes the 'dual system' of oppression brought about by both capitalism and patriarchy operating in unison without one system necessarily having primacy over the other. It can be argued that socialist feminism has been the acceptable face of feminism within academia as it provides a more clearly articulated theoretical and hence academic base than liberal feminism, but is not as unpalatable to a

male-dominated establishment as radical feminism. A socialist feminist perspective argues that many of the barriers that prevent women from participating in leisure are the result of capitalism's private–public patriarchal dichotomy, women's unpaid domestic and child-rearing role and their status as a reserve army of labour. Socialist and Marxist feminists assert that it is these underpinning structural constraints that must be challenged if social policy interventions are to have any significant impact on women's position in relation to leisure and tourism, as both participants and providers.

The influence of socialist feminism is evident throughout the major case studies of women's leisure undertaken in the UK in the 1980s and referred to in the section above. There seems little doubt that the majority of previous feminist leisure studies have viewed class relations as a major determinant of leisure relations. For example, Woodward *et al.* (1988: 99) list six determinants of women's leisure with the first three emphasizing the influence of social class: '... the most significant influences on women's leisure were their social class, level of household and personal income, employment status, age group, marital status and stage in the family life cycle'. Thus, whilst the major feminist studies of leisure conducted in the 1980s undoubtedly disrupted the discourse of leisure studies, they can also be viewed as part of leisure studies' own structuralist sociological tradition where '... from the very beginning, leisure research in Europe was a topic oriented field of research dominated by sociological perspectives but strongly leaning toward public policy interest' (Mommaas, 1997: 241). This statement again highlights the rather different trajectories of leisure research and tourism research. Although both have been informed by sociology, recognized in the UK through the Research Assessment Exercise as the major single discipline within which women's studies is situated, it is only relatively recently that feminist sociology has been developed within and in relation to tourism studies.

As an influential writer of radical feminist critiques, MacKinnon (1983: 227) has asserted that 'sexuality is to feminism what work is to Marxism: that which is most one's own yet most taken away'. Because feminism takes sexuality as its starting point, and Marxism takes the economic relations of work and employment as its starting point, MacKinnon (1983) has argued that the two philosophies are mutually incompatible. Moreover, she has stressed that attempts by socialist feminists to integrate the two theories 'have not recognized the depth of the antagonism or the separate integrity of each theory' (MacKinnon, 1983: 236).

The radical feminist perspective states that neither a traditional liberal feminist approach nor a Marxist or socialist feminist approach provides an adequate analysis of the complex structures that interact to subordinate women. Unlike the liberal feminist perspective, which views the state as essentially neutral, radical feminism sees the state as but one of many manifestations of patriarchal power. This perspective is equally critical of Marxist feminism, which is seen to ignore the non-economic bases of male power and female subordination.

Radical feminism therefore views patriarchy, rather than class or a combination of patriarchy and class, as the cause of women's subordination and oppression. Patriarchy is seen as being present in all structures and processes within society, in both the public and private spheres, and is seen to precede all other forms of oppression related to class and 'race'. Male sexual power is seen as the root of patriarchal power. Radical feminism has paid particular attention to patriarchal constructions of society through sex role stereotyping, heterosexism and compulsory heterosexuality, the institution of marriage, and practices of pornography, prostitution, rape, sexual abuse of women and children, and other forms of abuse of power including 'domestic' violence (Millet, 1970; Daly, 1973, 1978; Rich, 1977; Firestone, 1979; Dworkin, 1981, 1982; Griffin, 1981; MacKinnon, 1995; Jeffreys, 1997, 1999).

However, radical feminist critiques of patriarchy tend to view power relations as a 'zero-sum game' in which power is gained by one side at the expense of the other. This

dualistic view of power can also be seen in the writings of major social theorists such as Marx and in C. Wright Mills' *The Power Elite* (1957), criticized by Parsons shortly after its publication:

> To Mills, power is not a facility for the performance of function in, and on behalf of, the society as a system, but is interpreted exclusively as a facility for getting what one group, the holders of power, wants by preventing another group, the 'outs', from getting what it wants.
> (Parsons, 1960: 221)

Walby (1990: 177) emphasizes the all-pervasive power of patriarchal capitalism and suggests that a fuller explanation of women's subordination must take account of the interaction of patriarchal relations in both the public and private spheres by examining the mode of production, relations in paid work, in sexuality and in cultural institutions, and must also consider male violence. It could be argued that leisure and tourism, in both the public and private spheres, as an area of academic study, policy making, management and practice, has the potential to provide an arena where all of the above patriarchal relations are manifested in some form or another. However, radical feminist analysis has been relatively absent within tourism and leisure-related studies. There appears to be no radical feminist research in tourism studies *per se* although Enloe (1989) and Jeffreys (1999, 2003) do provide analyses that draw on both radical and socialist feminist theory to critique the political economy of international sex tourism. There are, however, a number of radical feminist critiques of sport, such as Brackenridge (2001), Lenskyj (1986, 1990) and Theberge (2000), who provide useful accounts of patriarchal constructions of sexuality in sport and child sexual abuse in sport. In relation to education and research, Stanley (1980) appears to provide the only radical feminist critique of leisure studies as an academic field of enquiry.

Critiques of the patriarchal construction of language have also played an important role within radical feminist analysis, with the work of Spender (1980), referred to earlier, being particularly influential. But it is within poststructural feminism that the role of language in creating, maintaining and reproducing power has formed a central theme in feminist critiques.

Poststructural feminism

Poststructuralism and postmodernism are frequently used interchangeably and it is important to acknowledge that, although they are overlapping and mutually informing, they are also differentiated by their objects of study. Postmodernism is concerned with the critical study of modernity whereas poststructuralism is concerned with the critical study of the power relations inherent in, and resulting from, the structures and structured order of modernity. Thus postmodernism seeks to deconstruct the meta-narratives and grand theories of modernist society whereas poststructuralism seeks to reveal the power relations upon which the construction, legitimation and reproduction of modernist society depends. This difference in object and method of study has resulted in postmodern accounts remaining largely within the realms of the humanities whilst poststructural critiques have crossed into the social sciences where critical engagement with theories of social, economic and cultural power is already established. Poststructural analyses of gender, leisure and tourism have become increasingly visible over the last decade, and although there are some studies that could be identified as 'postmodern', these have largely been undertaken in tourism and have involved critiques of the visual and semantic representation of tourism imagery, a research technique developed in the humanities subject fields of cultural studies and media studies (Crouch et al., 2004).

The previous sections have demonstrated that each feminist perspective focuses on what it deems to be the major cause of women's oppression. Liberal feminists are largely concerned with male domination of public institutional structures; radical feminists are primarily concerned

with male domination of private familial and sexual relations; Marxist feminists are concerned with male domination of economic relations; and socialist feminists point to the duality of the social relations of the family and the economic relations of the market as being the cause of women's oppression by and for the benefit of men.

In contrast, poststructural feminism draws our attention to the way in which ideology and cultural relations serve to shape gender relations. Instead of focusing on the political, social and economic manifestations of the gender order, poststructural feminism seeks to uncover the very cultural codes by which such an order is constructed, legitimated and reproduced (Weedon, 1997). This means that a 'poststructuralist feminist challenge for women [is] to subvert male colonization of knowledge and theory' (Wearing, 1998: 143) that informs the way we think about, represent and normalize political, social and economic relations in both the public and private spheres. Indeed, poststructural feminism calls into question the post-Enlightenment grand narratives that have served to construct the world into dualistic categories of public/private, male/female, work/leisure, nature/culture and self/other. Wearing, writing in relation to leisure studies, questions these dualistic categories, boundaries and hierarchies when she states:

> While some male writers on leisure have begun to apply poststructuralist theory to leisure in a questioning of the work/leisure and production/consumption dichotomies where the former are prioritized and latter inferiorized...it has been left to post-structural feminists to suggest ways in which the deconstruction of these dichotomies may be specifically applied to women's experiences of leisure.
>
> (Wearing, 1998: 148–149)

Wearing's work has been instrumental in introducing poststructural analyses of gender to the subject field of leisure studies. In earlier writings (1996: 186), and drawing on poststructural feminist theory, she offered a critique of the 1980s feminist leisure research identified earlier in this chapter when she stated that, 'Feminist theorists have challenged the male bias in such [leisure] theories, but still have concentrated on the labour aspects of the family as explanation'. In contrast to the frequently levelled criticism that poststructuralism and postmodernism are theoretical projects devoid of real-life application or meaning for women outside academia, Wearing points to the lives of ordinary women as giving sense to poststructural critique:

> ... one of the dangers of the socialist feminist position in the late 1980s was that such thorough documentation of women's oppression, theoretically linked to structural causes, implied that nothing that individual women could do would make any significant change in their lives. A pessimistic position, to say the least. And one which breeds a victim mentality. There was a shift from the 'victim blaming', 'bootstraps' approach of liberalism to the 'poor victim' approach of socialism. Yet in the everyday lives of the women I knew, and those I came to know through my research, women were continually constructing survival strategies, struggling, negotiating, contesting and sometimes transforming power relationships at an individual and group level.
>
> (Wearing, 1998: 37)

Within tourism studies poststructural perspectives have offered insight into the unhelpful rigidity of previously established and taken-for-granted dualistic concepts such as the binary construct of hosts and guests. Edensor (2000: 334–335), for example, refers to ways in which the performances of tourists are similarly constructed by hosts to form 'disciplined rituals', 'improvised performances' and 'unbounded performances'. The sights that tourists consume may be staged but the tourist is both audience and cast member in a performance that is not entirely directed by them. Eschewing such a poststructuralist reading, Roy (1997), in her novel *The God of Small Things*, is critical of the impact of guests upon hosts when she points to the way in which the performance of Kathakali dancing in Kerala in India has forced local people to engage in 'corrupting stories' handed down

by their ancestors and participate in 'encashing identities' to benefit financially from tourism. These two examples, whilst both embracing postcolonial critiques, are differentiated by the ways in which they align themselves with poststructuralism in the case of the first example and a more radical form of anti-capitalism or anti-globalization in the case of the second example. Although complex, the formation of critiques that integrate both poststructuralism and postcolonialism whilst also acknowledging the influence of wider structural power relations is possible:

> Tourist destinations and tourism hosts are represented as pure and authentic rather than being viewed as constantly evolving places and people with changing characteristics resulting from the mutually informing process of productive consumption derived from that in-betweenness of global and local, tourist and host. Feminized, sexualized and racialized imagery can be seen to inform a symbiotic relationship between colonialism and sexism that constantly reinvents itself within the globalized tourism industry. Whilst there are tensions between poststructural and postcolonial feminisms, the contribution of both to a feminist analysis of tourism is acknowledged here.
>
> (Aitchison, 2001b)

Building Bridges between Standpoint and Poststructural Feminism

Whilst the introduction of poststructural critiques to leisure and tourism research has clearly added sophistication, nuance and diversity to the knowledge creation and dissemination process, it is important to caution against the wholesale adoption of a poststructuralist perspective. A significant part of the feminist project is highlighting and challenging systemic power relations that oppress or undermine less powerful groups within society, most notably women. Poststructuralist perspectives are contextually specific and run the risk of negating theories of power as systemic phenomena. With no systemic power relations, there can be no overall system of domination and oppression, only specific contexts of subordination, resistance and transformation. A key question for feminist research in leisure and tourism is therefore to enquire as to the extent to which systemic male power – that is, patriarchy – exists in relation to the production and consumption of leisure and tourism and/or the extent to which localized, contextualized and pluralized power relations exert their influence on gender relations within leisure and tourism. This questioning and cautionary note has been signalled recently by a number of feminist theorists and was flagged up over a decade ago by the social and cultural geographer Liz Bondi (Bondi, 1992: 166) who urged against prioritizing the cultural over the social or the 'unharnessing of the symbolic and the sociological'. It is therefore important to maintain the dual influences of the humanities and the social sciences, the cultural and the structural, the symbolic and the material in feminist analyses of leisure and tourism, which are themselves both social and cultural phenomena.

Conclusions

This chapter has drawn on materialist, structuralist, poststructuralist and postmodern accounts of gender, leisure and tourism in recognition of the interconnections between material, social, cultural and symbolic relations. The chapter concludes by calling for the development of theoretical critiques that further integrate social *and* cultural perspectives by accommodating elements from both standpoint and poststructural feminism. This accommodation of the social and the cultural can be articulated through the conceptualization of the social–cultural nexus, where the social–cultural nexus is explained as both a site and process of construction, legitimation, reproduction and reworking of

gender relations (Aitchison, 2003). In this way, feminist research is able to engage with poststructural theories to explore the contested workings and reworkings of gender–power relationships in localized leisure and tourism. Simultaneously, however, the concept of the social–cultural nexus values materialist analyses of patriarchy and capitalism or patriarchal capitalism in shaping the power relations that construct, legitimate and reproduce gender relations in leisure and tourism, often on a global scale. Moreover, and in addition to linking social and cultural analyses, the concept of the social–cultural nexus recognizes the mutually informing nature of social and cultural power. Thus, it is often at the nexus of social and cultural relations that one type of power relation supports or contests another.

By engaging with the plurality of feminist perspectives developed with feminist and gender studies, and more recently applied within leisure and tourism studies, it is possible to develop a sophisticated area of research that has a central place within the developing subject fields of leisure and tourism studies in addition to studies of leisure and tourism within single disciplinary contexts. Such research, I have argued, should seek to go beyond the earlier empiricist accounts but pull back from the extremes of the cultural turn and its denial of systems of oppression. As long as women experience inequality and oppression on a global scale, but differently across space and time, we need more than simply the polemic of radical feminism or the rhetoric of academic poststructuralism to bring about meaningful change. Both standpoint feminism and poststructural feminism have useful critical insights to offer and these insights are at their most powerful when developed in combination rather than in isolation, as has previously been the case.

References

Adkins, L. (1994) *Gendered Work: Sexuality, Family and the Labour Market.* Open University Press, Milton Keynes, UK.
Aitchison, C. (2000a) Poststructural feminist theories of representing Others: a response to the 'crisis' in leisure studies' discourse. *Leisure Studies* 19, 127–144.

Aitchison, C. (2000b) Women in leisure services: managing the social–cultural nexus of gender equity. *Managing Leisure* 5, 81–91.

Aitchison, C. (2001a) Gender and leisure research: the 'codification of knowledge'. *Leisure Sciences* 23, 1–19.

Aitchison, C. (2001b) Theorising Other discourses of tourism, gender and culture: can the subaltern speak (in tourism)? *Tourist Studies* 1, 133–147.

Aitchison, C. (2003) *Gender and Leisure: Social and Cultural Perspectives.* Routledge, London.

Aitchison, C., Jordan, F. and Brackenridge, C. (1999) Women in leisure management: a survey of gender equity. *Women in Management Review,* 14, 121–127.

Alvesson, M. and Billing, Y.D. (1997) *Understanding Gender and Organizations.* Sage, London.

Bagguley, P. (1990) Gender and labour flexibility in hotel and catering. *The Service Industries Journal* 10, 737–747.

Bell, D. and Valentine, G. (eds) (1994) *Mapping Desire: Geographies of Sexualities.* Routledge, London.

Bell, D., Binnie, J., Cream, J. and Valentine, G. (1994) All hyped up and no place to go. *Gender, Place and Culture* 1, 31–47.

Bondi, L. (1992) Gender and dichotomy. *Progress in Human Geography* 16, 98–104.

Botterill, D. (2003) An autoethnographic narrative on tourism research and epistemology. *Leisure and Society* 26, 97–110.

Brackenridge, C. (2001) *Spoilsports: Understanding and Preventing Sexual Exploitation in Sport.* Routledge, London.

Bryson, V. (1992) *Feminist Political Theory.* Macmillan, Basingstoke, UK.

Code, L. (1981) Experiences, knowledge and responsibility. In: Garry, A. and Pearsall, M. (eds) *Women, Knowledge and Reality.* Allen and Unwin, London, pp. 245–264.

Crouch, D., Jackson, R. and Thompson, F. (2004) *The Media and the Tourist Imagination.* Routledge, London.

Daly, M. (1973) *Beyond God the Father: Towards a Philosophy of Women's Liberation.* Beacon Press, Boston, Massachusetts.

Daly, M. (1978) *Gyn/Ecology: the Metaethics of Radical Feminism.* Beacon Press, Boston, Massachusetts.

Deem, R. (1986) *All Work and No Play: the Sociology of Women and Leisure.* Open University Press, Milton Keynes, UK.

Denzin, N. and Lincoln, Y. (2002) *The Qualitative Inquiry Reader.* Sage, London.

Di Stefano, C. (1990) Dilemmas of difference: feminism, modernity and postmodernism. In: Nicholson, L. (ed.) *Feminism/Postmodernism.* Routledge, London.

Dworkin, A. (1981) *Pornography: Men Possessing Women.* Perigee, New York.

Dworkin, A. (1982) *Our Blood: Prophesies and Discourses on Sexual Politics.* Women's Press, London.

Dyck, I. (1993) Ethnography: a feminist method. *The Canadian Geographer* 20, 410–413.

Dyer, K. (1982) *Catching Up The Men: Women in Sport.* Junction Books, London.

Edensor, T. (2000) Staging tourism: tourists as performers. *Annals of Tourism Research* 27, 322–344.

Enloe, C. (1989) *Bananas, Beaches and Bases: Making Feminist Sense of International Politics.* Pandora, London.

Evans, J. (1995) *Feminist Theory Today: an Introduction to Second-wave Feminism.* Sage, London.

Evans, M. (2003) *Gender and Social Theory.* Open University Press, Buckingham, UK.

Farran, D. (1990) 'Seeking Susan': producing statistical information on young people's leisure. In: Stanley, L. (ed.) *Feminist Praxis: Research, Theory and Epistemology in Feminist Sociology.* Routledge, London.

Firestone, S. (1979) *The Dialectic of Sex.* Women's Press, London.

Flax, J. (1990) *Thinking Fragments: Psychoanalysis, Feminism, and Postmodernism in the Contemporary West.* University of California Press, Berkeley, California.

Fullagar, S. (2002) Narratives of travel: desire and the movement of subjectivity. *Leisure Studies* 21, 57–74

Gilligan, C. (1982) *In A Different Voice.* Harvard University Press, Cambridge, Massachusetts.

Gray, A. (1997) Learning from experience: cultural studies and feminism. In: McGuigan, J. (ed.) *Cultural Methodologies.* Sage, London.

Green, E., Hebron, S. and Woodward, D. (1987) *Leisure and Gender: a Study of Sheffield Women's Leisure Experiences.* The Sports Council/Economic and Social Research Council, Sheffield, UK.

Griffin, S. (1981) *Pornography and Silence: Culture's Revenge Against Nature.* Women's Press, London.

Harding, S. (1986) *The Science Question in Feminism.* Open University Press, Milton Keynes, UK.

Harding, S. (ed.) (1987) *Feminism and Methodology.* Open University Press, Milton Keynes, UK.

Hearn, J., Sheppard, D.L., Tancred-Sherrif, P. and Burrell, G. (1989) *The Sexuality of Organisation.* Sage, London.

Henderson, K.A., Bialeschki, D., Shaw, S.M. and Freysinger, V.J. (1989) *A Leisure of One's Own: a Feminist Perspective on Women's Leisure*. Venture Publishing, College Park, Pennsylvania.

Hicks, L. (1990) Excluded women: how can this happen in the hotel world? *The Service Industries Journal* 10, 348–363.

Jackson, S. and Jones, J. (1998) Thinking for ourselves: an introduction to feminist theorising. In: Jackson, S. and Jones, J. (eds) *Contemporary Feminist Theories*. Edinburgh University Press, Edinburgh, UK.

Jackson, S. and Scott, S. (2002) *Gender: a Sociological Reader*. Routledge, London.

Jeffreys, S. (1997) *The Idea of Prostitution*. Spinifex, Melbourne, Australia.

Jeffreys, S. (1999) Globalising sexual exploitation: sex tourism and the traffic in women. *Leisure Studies* 18, 179–196.

Jeffreys, S. (2003) Sex tourism: do women do it too? *Leisure Studies* 22, 223–238.

Jordan, F. (1997) An occupational hazard? Sex segregation in tourism employment. *Tourism Management* 18, 525–534.

Jordan, F. (2004) Gendered discourses of tourism: the experiences of mid-life women travelling solo. PhD Thesis, The University of Gloucestershire, UK.

Katz, C. (1994) Playing the field: questions of fieldwork in geography. *The Professional Geographer* 46, 67–72.

Kinnaird, V. and Hall, D. (1994) *Tourism: a Gender Analysis*. Wiley, London.

Lenskyj, H. (1986) *Out of Bounds: Women, Sport and Sexuality*. Women's Press, Toronto, Canada.

Lenskyj, H. (1990) Power and play: gender and sexuality issues in sport and physical activity. *International Review for the Sociology of Sport* 25, 235–241.

Letherby, G. (2003) *Feminist Research in Theory and Practice*. Open University Press, Buckingham, UK.

MacKinnon, K. (1983) Feminism, Marxism, method and the state: an agenda for theory. In: Abel, E. and Abel, E. (eds) *The Signs Reader*. Chicago University Press, Chicago, Illinois.

MacKinnon, K. (1995) Speech, equality, and harm: the case against pornography. In: Lederer, L. and Delgado, R. (eds) *The Price We Pay: the Case Against Racist Speech, Hate Propaganda, and Pornography*. Hill and Wang, New York.

Madge, C., Raghuram, P., Skelton, T., Willis, K. and Williams, J. (1997) Method and methodologies in feminist geographies: politics, practice and power. In: Women and Geography Study Group (eds) *Feminist Geographies: Explorations in Diversity and Difference*. Addison Wesley Longman, London.

Mannheim, K. (1952) *Essays on the Sociology of Knowledge*. Routledge, London.

Millet, K. (1970) *Sexual Politics*. Abacus, London.

Mommaas, H. (1997) European leisure studies at the crossroads? A history of leisure research in Europe. *Leisure Sciences* 19, 241–254.

Morris, K., Woodward, D. and Peters, E. (1998) 'Whose side are you on?' Dilemmas in conducting feminist ethnographic research with young women. *Social Research Methodology* 1, 217–230.

Oakley, A. (1981) Interviewing women: a contradiction in terms. In: Roberts, H. (ed.) *Doing Feminist Research*. Routledge, London.

Oakley, A. (1998) Gender, methodology and people's ways of knowing: some problems with feminism and the paradigm debate in social science. *Sociology* 32, 707–732.

Oakley, A. (2000) *Experiments in Knowing: Gender and Method in the Social Sciences*. Polity, Cambridge, UK.

Parsons, T. (1960) *Essays in Sociological Theory*. Free Press, New York.

Phillimore, J. and Goodson, L. (2004) *Qualitative Research in Tourism*. Routledge, London.

Rich, A. (1977) *Of Woman Born: Motherhood as Experience and Institution*. Virago, London.

Roberts, H. (ed.) (1981) *Doing Feminist Research*. Routledge, London.

Roy, A. (1997) *The God of Small Things*. Flamingo, London.

Seller, A. (1994) Should the feminist philosopher stay at home? In: Lennon, K. and Whitford, M. (eds) *Knowing The Difference: Feminist Perspectives in Epistemology*. Routledge, London.

Simmons, B. (2003) Travel overseas by Australian women in midlife. PhD thesis, University of Newcastle, Australia.

Small, J. (1999) Memory-work: a method for researching women's tourist experiences. *Tourism Management* 20, 25–35.

Small, J. (2002) Good and bad holiday experiences: women's and girls' perspective. In: Swain, M. and Momsen, H. (eds) *Gender/Tourism/Fun(?)*. Cognizant Communiction Corporation, New York.

Sparkes, A. (1996) Writing the social in qualitative enquiry. In: Radnor, H.A. (ed.) *Educational Research Monograph Series*, Vol. 8. School of Education, University of Exeter, Exeter, UK.

Spender, D. (1980) *Man Made Language.* Routledge and Kegan Paul, London.

Spender, D. (ed.) (1981) *Men's Studies Modified: the Impact of Feminism on the Academic Disciplines.* Pergamon Press, Oxford, UK.

Sports Council (1993) *Sport in the Nineties: New Horizons.* Sports Council, London.

Stanley, L. (1980) *The Problem of Women and Leisure: an Ideological Construct and a Radical Feminist Alternative.* Sports Council/Social Science Research Council, London.

Stanley, L. (1990) *Feminist Praxis: Research, Theory and Epistemology in Feminist Sociology.* Routledge, London.

Stanley, L. (ed.) (1997) *Knowing Feminisms.* Sage, London.

Stanley, L. and Wise, S. (1983) *Breaking Out: Feminist Ontology and Epistemology.* Routledge, London.

Stanley, L. and Wise, S. (1993) *Breaking Out Again: Feminist Ontology and Epistemology.* Routledge, London.

Swain, M.B. (1995) Gender in Tourism. *Annals of Tourism Research* 22, 247–266.

Talbot, M. (1979) *Women and Leisure.* Sports Council/Social Science Research Council, London.

Theberge, N. (2000) *Higher Goals: Women's Ice Hockey and the Politics of Gender.* State University of New York Press, Albany, New York.

Tong, R. (1989) *Feminist Thought.* Routledge, London.

Walby, S. (1990) *Theorising Patriarchy.* Blackwell, Oxford, UK.

Wearing, B. (1996) *Gender: the Pleasure and Pain of Difference.* Longman, Melbourne, Australia.

Wearing, B. (1998) *Feminism and Leisure Theory.* Sage, London.

Weedon, C. (1997) *Feminist Practice and Poststructural Theory,* 2nd edn. Blackwell, Oxford, UK.

Woodward, D., Green, E. and Hebron, S. (1988) Research note: the Sheffield study of gender and leisure: its methodological approach. *Leisure Studies* 7, 95–101.

4   The Case Study in Tourism Research: a Multi-method Case Study Approach

SUE BEETON

School of Tourism and Hospitality, La Trobe University, Victoria 3086, Australia

Introduction

Case studies are used extensively in tourism research and teaching. This publication alone applies case studies to each chapter. It is such a pervasive methodology in tourism research and study that it appears that its justification is no longer deemed necessary, if it ever was. Leading scholars in world tourism take for granted the application of case study methodology, yet when queried decry it as an over-simplistic option (see Pizam, 1994). Accepted (and often celebrated) 'case studies' include work by Rapoport and Rapoport (1975), Craik (1991), Murphy (1991), Harris and Leiper (1995) and Singh and Singh (1999), yet they have not discussed the pros and cons of the methodology within the reporting of their cases. Is it that they take the case study as such a well established method that it does not need to be justified, or are they concerned that tourism research will be dismissed by scholars from other areas because it is so extraordinarily dependent on the case study, avoiding any real discussion of the method for fear of being labelled 'unscientific'?

For a broad-ranging, psychologically complex field such as tourism, there is no singular pertinent research modality. In order to achieve the desired outcomes of tourism research, alternative methods must be considered and used conjointly, from experiments and surveys through to participant observation, histories and ethnographies as well as the case study. Case studies have the advantage of being suitable for both the more quantitative hypothetico-deductive and the holistic-inductive paradigms of tourism research, demonstrating a flexibility not evident in many alternative research modes (Jennings, 2001). Consequently, they are used extensively in tourism research.

One research discipline that can provide some guidance in this examination of the case study as a multiple methodology is the social sciences. Researchers in allied social science disciplines such as psychology, anthropology and sociology utilize a range of research methods that can be applied to tourism, providing a variety of modes that can be selected, depending on the type of research question and control the researcher has (or requires) over events and behaviour. The information-rich, interrelated nature of the case study is one such methodology.

There are a number of aspects of the case study that support its use as a valid methodological tool in tourism research. Table 4.1 summarizes the main features of the case study.

These features illustrate the power of the case study as a research method, begging the question why does it receive such bad press from the scientific community?

Table 4.1. Features of the case study. (Adapted from Hoaglin *et al.*, 1982.)

1. Can explain why an innovation worked or failed to work
2. Has the advantage of hindsight, yet can be relevant in the present and to the future
3. Can illustrate the complexities of a situation by recognizing more that one contributing factor
4. Shows the influence of personalities and politics on an issue
5. Can show the influence of the passage of time through longitudinal studies
6. The reader may be able to apply it to his/her situation
7. Can evaluate alternatives not chosen
8. Can utilize information from a wide variety of sources
9. Can present information in a wide variety of ways
10. Can illuminate a general problem through examination of a specific instance

While there are limitations (as discussed below), this does not adequately explain such attitudes.

The purpose of this chapter is to demonstrate the validity of taking a case study approach to research, particularly when using multiple methods in order to understand complex relationships and interactions. After outlining the philosophical context of the case study with a brief discussion on its place in the social sciences and the range of purposes of case studies, an explanation for the dismissive attitude towards the case study taken by some tourism researchers is postulated. The chapter ends with a description of a case where the multi-method case study approach was taken.

Philosophical Context of the Case Study Approach

Case studies have been broadly criticized as speculative, unreliable and too specific to be replicated or applied generally. However, this was not always the situation. In the pre-war years of the 1930s, case studies were considered a valid methodology and social science researchers such as Angell and Burgess (cited in Platt, 1992) began to address criticisms similar to those above within their own research. However, their recommendations were only applied specifically to their own work as opposed to case studies in general. Unfortunately, much of the work on developing, defining and justifying the use of case studies from that time was neglected after the Second World War,

when methodologies such as content analysis and schedules to measure attitudes replaced the case study as the main research mode, diminishing its recognition and distinctiveness. Platt notes that it was considered that a new paradigm had arisen that addressed the criticisms of the case study, ending the discussion along with any need to scientifically consider the case study as a research method. However, he argues that while the term 'case study' may have disappeared from methodological discussion in the social science literature of the 1940s and 1950s, the approach continued to be popular (Platt, 1992). In spite of this decline in overt recognition, there is growing evidence in the social sciences supporting its use today, particularly in situations where other research methods are not possible, due to pragmatic, physical or psychological constraints (Hall and Jenkins, 1995).

For much of the 20th century, research methods were viewed in a hierarchical manner with the case study being considered as appropriate only for the exploratory phase of an investigation. Surveys and histories were then utilized for the descriptive phase, and experiments provided data for explanatory or causal studies. Social scientists Dixon and Bouma (1984) stress that a case study is singular and as such can only establish whether there is a relationship between variables, not whether they are causally related. Such a view limits the use of the case study by relegating it to the early phases of an investigation, which tends to devalue its importance as a research methodology (Platt, 1992). However, in his 1994 publication on case study research, Yin argues compellingly that each strategy (case studies, surveys and histories, and experiments) can be used for all hierarchical phases (exploratory, descriptive and explanatory), challenging the common hierarchical view of research modalities as well as maintaining that there are large areas of overlap among each method (Yin, 1994).

Case studies need not be so specific as to preclude being applied to other situations, as they have the capability to take into consideration the effect of numerous study foci by encompassing several groups of individuals within the boundaries of the case, such as in a town or other social grouping (Stake, 1983). These case studies often have sub-cases embedded in them, providing a further richness and complexity of data and analysis (Miles and Huberman, 1994). For example, a town dependent on tourism will have groupings of sub-cases that could be identified as new residents, old residents, regular visitors, day-trippers and entrepreneurs, all of whom may contribute their own cases to the overall study and analysis, providing a range of results which may be applied on a broader scale.

The case study certainly has a significant place in the exploratory stage of an investigation, but it can also be extrapolated beyond that stage. The application of rigorous interpretation, combined with reason and logic, enables the researcher to obtain place-specific conceptual insights that may then be tested for wider applicability through further case studies or the use of additional methodologies, creating a multi-method case study. Conversely, theoretical concepts can be tested against local experiences using a case study (Yin, 1994). For example, Pearce et al. (1996) utilize case studies to illustrate the aptness of applying social representation theory to different types of tourist settings, using empirical and descriptive appraisals within the case studies themselves.

However, the criticisms of case studies are valid and cannot be simply passed off as mere historical or etymological aberrations. According to Yin (1994: xiii): 'Investigators who do case studies are regarded as having deviated from their academic disciplines, their investigations as having insufficient precision (that is, quantification), objectivity and rigour... [Yet] case studies continue to be used extensively ...'.

One explanation for this continued use of case studies may be that learning from what is observed is intrinsic to the development of the human psyche. From the moment of birth we learn from analysing and processing our observations of the world around us, from both direct and vicarious experience. Consequently, the case study is a process that provides instant recognition and understanding. This stance is supported by Stake (1983: 73) who claims that case studies may be 'epistemologically in harmony with the reader's experience ...'. However, such simple explanations belie the power and contribution to knowledge of the case study when it is rigorously planned, applied, reported and analysed.

Criticisms and Limitations of the Case Study

It has also been argued that case studies tend to reflect the bias of the researcher, who is the primary instrument of data collection and analysis. Hoaglin et al. (1982) maintain that the value system of the author tends to influence the presentation of the facts as well as analysis, and the usefulness of a case study can be influenced by the value system of the reader, who tends to remember results that support his/her values, rejecting the others that do not fit as neatly. However, bias can also enter into the conduct of other research modalities, such as the design of questionnaires and experiments, so while the possibility of bias in any case study must be recognized and dealt with, this issue is not restricted to this research method (Yin, 1994). One method proposed in the social science literature that may overcome some of the criticisms of researcher bias is 'triangulation'. By combining (or triangulating) a range of methodologies (including qualitative and quantitative), it is postulated that inherent bias would be neutralized and a convergence of results achieved (Creswell, 1994). Triangulating these within a case study should ameliorate criticism of researcher bias.

Stake sees limitations such as bias as positive, emphasizing that the case study is personal, situational and intricate, maintaining that recognition of researcher bias can be a positive trait. By making the reader aware of the personal experiences of gathering data and the previous experience of those involved in the work provides access to knowledge that the reader may not otherwise obtain (Stake, 1995). Another practical example of limiting bias would be to utilize at least two independent evaluators to review and analyse the data. Such independently made judgements and interpretations of the material, when combined with triangulation, will serve to reduce research bias to an absolute minimum (Patton, 1990).

While many of the criticisms of case studies can be eliminated or at least ameliorated (as illustrated in the earlier discussion on researcher bias), there are some limitations that need to be recognized. One of the major constraints is that of the length of the case study report. Due to the richness of data and complexity of analysis, case studies can be extremely long, deterring the intended audience, especially if they are in areas that already deal with intense information supply such as policy making – a significant field that case studies can inform (Hoaglin et al., 1982). While this can be reduced by designing the case study report in such a way that the main analysis is provided in the body of the work (with appendices providing the supporting data), or by producing a series of smaller, related subcases, it remains a core methodological limitation. Attempting to reduce the size of the report can be problematic, as the researcher may fail to include all of the material required for the reader to evaluate the outcomes of the study.

Setting boundaries for the case study enables the researcher to focus not only the research, but also the reporting process. Boundaries may be imposed either by physical research resources (such as time or funding) or by the nature of the research itself. The case study is the focus or 'heart' of the research as the unit of analysis, while the boundary defines the edge of the case, identifying what will not be studied. They may comprise a group of people with a common link, such as living in a town, being related or working in the same field, which is often used as the defining element of a case study (Merriam, 1998).

In a brief discussion of case study methodology in the tourism field, Pizam (1994) notes the importance of recognizing the need to be cautious when utilizing it as he considers many case studies to be singular instances that may provide misleading evidence when generalized, even with multiple cases. These limitations must be recognized, acknowledged or refuted, and dealt with by the researcher in the methodological discourse.

Notwithstanding the methodological limitations, the social/anthropological nature of tourism leads to widespread use of case studies. To date, they have been met with varying degrees of success, depending on the academic rigour applied and their original intention (as entertainment, instructional or research cases outlined in the following section).

In order to deal adequately with the complexity of many research aims, an ontological view that recognizes multiple realities needs to be taken. A combination of theoretical approaches is often required, which may range from descriptive observation through to the use of media reports and survey work, all of which can be incorporated into the case study. Researchers such as Hall and Jenkins (1995) and Jennings (2001) support this triangulated, multimethod approach, acknowledging the need to provide a richness of detail and explanatory power in tourism research that is not possible with singular methods.

One particular strength of taking a case study approach lies in its holistic-inductive nature and grounding in actuality with an emic (insider's) perspective, which is pertinent to applied disciplines such as tourism as well as to areas of policy development and examination. Such an approach is able to operate on a level of complexity and subtlety that is difficult to identify using purely experimental research methods (Adelman *et al.*, 1983). When deciding on methodology, it should be the type of questions that need to be asked in order to meet the research aims that inform the process. The types of many research questions considered by a researcher are often broken down into the basic 'who', 'what', 'when', 'where', 'how' and 'why' categories. A case study may be used to respond to various aspects of all the questions; however, the 'how' and 'why' questions are especially pertinent to this method as they deal with complex operational links that cannot be adequately examined using other research paradigms such as experiment and survey (Yin, 1994). Case studies are able to satisfy research aims that include the extension of experience and an increase in understanding (Stake, 1983).

During the 1980s, economists and quantitative social scientists, whose evaluation and assessment was undertaken using large-scale quantitative surveys and probabilistic sampling techniques, dominated international development agencies such as the World Bank. However, it was found that the data could not be trusted due to its scale and was so expensive to collect that there was little time or money left to analyse it, reducing its reliability and utility. Consequently, the World Bank (along with other international agencies) now advocates using case studies, as they are more manageable and readily accept multi-methods, which is particularly pertinent to the Third World countries that such agencies operate in (Patton, 1990).

Uses of the Case Study – to Entertain, Teach or Discover?

Journalists regularly utilize real-life examples (or 'cases') to explain the more complex aspects of their articles, especially if they are in the medical, scientific, business or political fields. At times, the simplification of concepts through the use of a case is utilized as an effective lead-in to a discussion of more elaborate concepts. Other times, the simplified version is all that is presented to the reader. However, journalists tend to adopt the anecdote with the most memorable features and extreme storyline available as the 'case', which can distort or even manipulate public understanding of an issue (Hoaglin *et al.*, 1982). While this usually renders an article easier to comprehend, helping to sell media publications and popularize broadcasts, such sweeping and ill-conceived use of case studies, or even just anecdotal evidence, has tended to devalue the scholarly standing of the case study.

In tourism academe (as in other social science areas) there has been some confusion between instructional case studies that have more in common with the journalistic versions of a case, and the more rigorous, independent research case studies. Many of the case studies that are used to instruct students have been manipulated and/or simplified to illustrate a particular point, or focus on just one aspect of a complex social system, whereas research-based case studies that are used to add to knowledge tend to be more complex, analytical and descriptive. This is an important distinction that has been missed by many tourism researchers who have equated instructional case studies with research case studies in their own work, resulting in under-developed research cases producing overtly biased and inaccurate results. Such instances support the rampant criticism of case studies as a valid research methodology.

In order to identify these differences, a definition must be established that specifically differentiates research case studies from the other illustrative and educational forms. According to Yin (1994: 13):

> A [research] case study is an empirical inquiry that
> • investigates a contemporary phenomenon within its real-life context, especially when
> • the boundaries between phenomenon and context are not clearly evident...
> [and]
> • relies on multiple sources of evidence, with data needing to converge in a triangulating fashion ...

Such a definition enables some differentiation between the teaching case study and research case study, particularly when the third aspect concerning multiple sources of evidence is applied. Merriam (1998) further identifies the use of the case study approach as a holistic method used to gain an in-depth understanding where the emphasis is on process rather than outcomes. Supporting Yin's multiple sources of evidence, Miles and Huberman (1994) define the case study by scoping it in terms of the nature and size of the social unit as well as temporally. They point out that a case, as well as being a unit such as an individual or community, can be an event, episode, encounter or sustained process. Combining the main contentions of these interpretations results in a more defined description of a research case study as being:

> a holistic empirical inquiry used to gain an in-depth understanding of a contemporary phenomenon in its real-life context, using multiple sources of evidence.

It needs to be re-emphasized that the purpose of the research case study, as outlined in the above discussion and resulting definition, renders it significantly different from a teaching case study, which tends to focus on specific parts of the case in order to illustrate or reinforce a certain aspect. Such a situation tends to occur in disciplines that may be more vocationally orientated, including tourism, where students are required to apply aspects of their education directly to specific circumstances. In order to assist in this application of theory (with which many students struggle) and develop their cognitive processes, specifically designed case studies and 'real-life' examples are presented. Even though they may be based on some research, they are rarely, however, research case studies.

The Need for Exemplary Case Studies

Due to the limited understanding and recognition of research case studies in tourism, it is important that a range of exemplary studies be identified, recognized and promoted. While not all case studies (including those that can be considered 'true' research case

studies, as opposed to instructional studies) will be exemplary, what constitutes an exemplary case study must be considered within this methodology discussion. An exemplary case study must do more than merely document a case. It must go beyond the technical aspects of methodology, producing insightful work that can be used to demonstrate not only appropriate use of the mode but also the insights obtained from the results of the case study. It must illuminate.

Yin identified five general characteristics that constitute an exemplary study, namely that it must be significant, complete, consider alternative perspectives, display sufficient evidence and be composed in an engaging manner. A case study is significant if it is atypical and of general public interest and/or has national importance in policy or practical terms, combining the concepts of discovery and theory development. In order for a study to be complete, the boundaries must be clearly defined at the outset, whilst considering alternative perspectives is crucial for any balanced, realistic discussion and discovery to occur. Sufficient evidence to support the propositions or conclusions is central to any research; however, there are numerous incidences where it has not been provided, making this somewhat obvious criterion one that must be enunciated. Finally, as noted previously, case study reports can be extensive; therefore they must be written and presented in a manner that engages the intended audience (Yin, 1994).

Such characteristics should be at the heart of all research, not just case studies, and as such the above discussion provides a valuable checklist at all stages of the tourism research process. It becomes crucial in this discussion due to the continued relegation of the case study methodology to the lower ranks of the tourism research hierarchy.

The Case Study: 'Film-induced Tourism'

This section reports on the design and conduct of a case study that was undertaken to understand better the impacts of a television programme on the community amongst which it was filmed. The highly popular Australian series *Sea Change* was selected as it became the nation's most popular series and was filmed primarily in the small seaside village of Barwon Heads. The study was undertaken over a 3-year period, taking a mixed-method approach, which included participant observation, photographic recording, self-completion surveys of visitors and residents, intercept face-to-face surveys and in-depth interviews as well as desk research of media stories and the series itself. The decision to take a multi-method approach came about due to the long-term and inclusive nature of the study. The final results were presented in a case study framework that allowed descriptive as well as quantitative and qualitative material to be introduced where and when relevant.

It is not possible within the confines of this chapter to discuss the results of the case study itself (see Beeton, 2001a, 2001b, 2002, 2005); however, the process applied is outlined in detail below.

The process

Participant observation, quantitative and qualitative surveys, in-depth interviews, informal discussions and secondary data such as media and government reports have all been utilized. Participant observation has been undertaken at all stages of the project, with photographic, anecdotal and personal data collected over a 3-year period. The use of these various methods enabled triangulation of the results. The concept map in Fig. 4.1 summarizes the methodological approach of the *Sea Change* study.

A major limiting factor for this research was the lack of visitor statistics. Barwon Heads is a small fishing, holiday and surfing town in Victoria, Australia, and whilst there are some broader regional tourism data, statistics for the village are not available. It was this lack of data that drove much of the research methodology. Keeping this in mind, it was crucial that some basic demographic data be collected as soon as possible. As the town had limited commercial accommodation, with two caravan parks, one motel, one hotel and two bed and

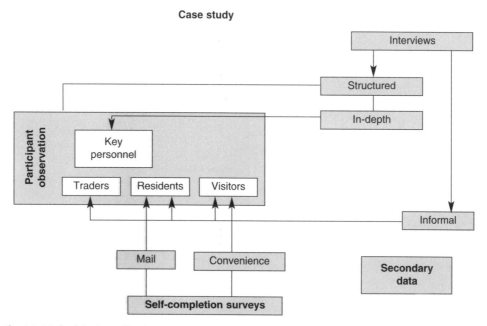

Fig. 4.1. Methodologies utilized.

breakfast establishments, the peak summer period from Christmas to February is virtually booked out with regular visitors. Surveying these visitors provides some base demographic data with which to compare new visitors, hypothesized as attracted by *Sea Change*, to visit the town.

A basic questionnaire was developed to obtain data on the overall visitor demographics to Barwon Heads, from day visitors as well as overnight visitors. The self-completion questionnaire was distributed through the commercial outlets in the town, such as restaurants and take-away food premises as well as accommodation outlets, including the caravan park and motel. Members of the Barwon Heads Traders and Tourism Association agreed to assist, providing a distribution base of more than 30 commercial operations.

The selection of questions for the survey was based on the prime need to obtain basic tourism data for the town, so they covered the usual demographic and length of stay questions included in such surveys. The TV series *Sea Change* had recently started airing on TV, so three basic questions related to *Sea Change* ('have you heard of the series?', 'did you know that some of the series was filmed at Barwon Heads?' and 'are you planning to visit any of the sites featured?') were placed on the reverse side of the survey. They were towards the end so as not to bias those respondents who were not aware of the television series. In an effort not to lead responses, as well as to ascertain the level of accurate knowledge respondents had regarding the filming of the series, the filming sites were not nominated.

Film-induced visitor motivation

Two waves of survey-based, formally structured intercept interviews of visitors to Barwon Heads were conducted at the film sites in the Barwon Heads Caravan Park in April 2000 and September 2001. As the interviews were conducted by a group of interviewers simultaneously, the questions were written out in full on the interviewer's form in order to maintain consistency of

reporting. However, there was a section for the interviewer to add their own comments as well as one for the interviewee, allowing for any aspects that were not covered, yet deemed important by either party to be included. Interviewers were instructed as to the appropriate protocols of approaching potential participants and given a script to work from as well as a covering letter of introduction and explanation for the participants, which included contact details of the main researcher and the university's ethics committee. Permission to conduct the interviews was obtained from the Barwon Coast Committee of Management, and the office at the park was also notified.

Informal, unstructured interviews (or conversations) and participant observation were used to aid in triangulation by supporting (or not) the survey-based data. In order to retain the natural flow of such a naturalistic mode, details of the informal conversations were not noted during the conversation, rather immediately afterwards in the field (away from the participants) and correlated the following evening. In order to maintain continuity, these were undertaken only by the main researcher. The manager of the Barwon Heads Park was also interviewed regarding her impressions of the importance of the series to the town and the park.

Community impacts and marketing

A self-completion questionnaire was mailed to each household in the town of Barwon Heads in March 2000. In an effort to reduce the bias of suggestion, the open-ended social representation questions were placed before structural questions such as those ranking lists of impacts. In order to verify the results, participant observation was undertaken, utilizing field notes, photographs and maps as well as informal conversations and in-depth interviews.

Due to the confidential nature and commercial concerns relating to individual economic analysis among the traders, avenues of secondary data were utilized, such as the Australian Bureau of Statistics and Real

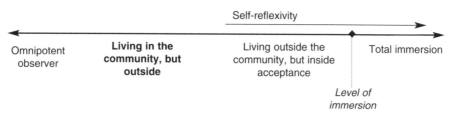

Fig. 4.2. Level of investigator immersion in Barwon Heads and *Sea Change.*

Estate Institute of Victoria figures. Data on regional development was also obtained from the City of Greater Geelong and the Department of Infrastructure. In order to ascertain the degree of use of *Sea Change* as an imaging tool for marketing the town and region, promotional material was gathered on each site visit, along with the data obtained from the visitor surveys, these being the primary destination marketing resources. The material has been used for textual analysis of the influence of film-induced tourism on destination marketing.

Depth of investigator immersion

Riley and Love describe the level of immersion of the investigator in the project as a continuum from 'omnipotent observer' at one end to the author's self-reflexivity of the personal lived experience at the other. Other points along the continuum could include living in the setting but outside the phenomenon, especially as temporary observers or foreigners (Riley and Love, 2000).

In relation to the television series *Sea Change* and the township of Barwon Heads, there was a high degree of immersion. As a fan of the series myself, there was a desire and interest to meet the characters and gaze on the sites 'for real'. On the three occasions that I stayed at Laura's Cottage, I felt part of the series and shared the gentle ambience of *Sea Change*. Also, Barwon Heads is a town that featured predominantly in my early years. Between the ages of 15 and 21, I spent many weekends and holidays there as well as working at the local hotel, becoming accepted as a 'part time local'.

Consequently, my return to Barwon Heads some 20 years later was not only emotional and nostalgic, but my earlier connections with the town gave me entrée to the current residents and traders, who saw me as having a personal investment in the town. This facilitated an openness from those I met that would not otherwise have been possible, yet I was still able to retain a certain amount of detachment due to not having been there for some time. This immersion is illustrated on the continuum in Fig. 4.2.

Due to the high level of immersion, a decision was made to record and report many of the personal experiences and observations at Barwon Heads in the first person (as in the discussion above).

Lessons learned from the case study case

The case study framework proved to be useful and valid, enabling multiple methodologies to be applied to the case of Barwon Heads and *Sea Change*. It was a good vehicle for using and presenting observation techniques, enabling them to be incorporated in other elements of the study. For example, when visitors were being surveyed on-site, observations such as the weather conditions, where they were, how they responded to the questions and who they were with could be included with other observational data as well as their actual responses to the questions.

Personal relationships had to be continually monitored, particularly given the level of investigator immersion in the study. Ethical issues such as whether something included in the description of the case would possibly offend one person or group had to be considered. I addressed these issues early on in the study by keeping a certain distance from the various factions in the town and not playing them off against each other. I also chose not to include some information that was personally sensitive and which would not affect the outcomes of the study. Being open with all actors and reminding them why I was there reduced these ethical issues. I do not support deception when undertaking such a long-term, in-depth study. These decisions require a level of maturity and life experience as well as skill from the researcher.

A benefit of this immersion and relationship development is that the actors are able to express any concerns they have regarding the research process. There were times where the method was slightly modified and improved after participants expressed or inferred some concerns or provided unexpected additional information.

Taking this approach allowed the depth and complexity of the relationships to be teased out and discussed; however, it threatened to become unwieldy due to this richness. The study was over a 3-year timeframe, which resulted in an enormous amount of information, so the writing up of the case threatened to be extensive. As this was about one small town, it is questionable how many people would read the case if it were presented in its entirety.

It became clear that merely relating the case as a descriptive 'story' would be far too unwieldy, so themes that could be linked into a logical progression needed to be teased out. In order to address this issue, the case was thematically divided into three elements: the effect of Sea Change on existing tourism, the effect of Sea Change on the residents, and how to incorporate these elements into community tourism planning. The importance of establishing boundaries is central to the case study process, and was reinforced by this study.

Taking a multi-method case study approach requires clear thinking and good record-keeping, especially when coming to tease out those themes and link them all together, as the themes may not have been evident from the beginning. It also requires the researcher to remain open to all possi-

ble outcomes of the study and not to become too attached to any particular elements (including people) of the study.

The decision to take a multi-method case study approach enabled a greater richness and depth to be brought to this study than any singular methodology would have produced. It provided levels of understanding that are still being uncovered. This was an appropriate approach to take for such a study, and, whilst some of the results may be specific to that town, possibilities were raised that others can explore. In terms of film-induced tourism, the main research questions were answered, and the study raised a number of issues that can be further examined in different cultures and situations.

Conclusions

Tourism, in the form of recreational travel and experience, has existed for hundreds, if not thousands, of years, arguably dating back to ancient Egyptian and Roman times, yet as an academic discipline it is among the most recent. Consequently, the majority of those currently studying tourism lack any grand academic heritage, other than the disciplinary training in one or more of the humanities or social sciences. Such scholastic 'youth' has circumscribed the pool of tourism knowledge, which academics have attempted to ameliorate through concerted research efforts. However, the need for recognition from the wider academic community is an imperative that has driven much of the research agenda and has continued to restrict the work of many researchers. It appears that, in order to achieve such recognition, tourism research has focused on a research modality within a hypothetico-deductive hegemony. This has resulted in undue focus and reliance on quantitative research methodologies, with qualitative work generally being relegated to a non-scientific/academic status, and case studies virtually ignored within the methodological debate. Nevertheless, case studies are central to most research in the humanities and social sciences, and have certainly found their way into tourism research.

For a number of reasons, the reputation of the case study has suffered since it was first introduced. Unfortunately, the case study has too often been viewed as a method that is too descriptive, specific and even 'unscientific'. This had led to teaching or illustrative case studies being applied in contexts where they were never intended to be applied, that is, as research cases.

According to Stake (1995: 133), '[there] is something that we do not sufficiently understand and want to – therefore, we do a case study'. By organizing the data gathering and reporting around an issue or theme, the research case study possesses focus and relevance to specific areas, being more than a general descriptive piece of work as in cases used for teaching purposes. Stake also stresses that the quality and significance of case study research is based on whether the meanings generated are valued, not its replicability or even impartiality.

A quote from the State Statistical Bureau of the People's Republic of China provides a pertinent metaphorical defence of the case study as a research methodology: 'In China there is a proverb: "The sparrow may be small but it has all the vital organs". After having "dissected" a few sparrows, one may have an idea about sparrows in general' (Hoaglin *et al.*, 1982: 188).

Case studies themselves are not the problem – the intent, use, application, development and understanding of their potential are the main issues that in turn reflect not only on the reputation of the case study as a valid research method, but also on those disciplines and individuals utilizing it. In the field of tourism research we must now face the imperative to 'get our own house into order' by establishing and applying rigour, recognition and understanding to tourism research case studies before we criticize the attitudes of others towards our field of study. Further discussion, debate and development in the area of this methodology is urgently required. Tourism academics need to constructively consider their research methodologies as well as their ontological and pedagogical stances.

In the majority of tourism research case studies published in academic journals and presented at tourism research conferences, this methodology is rarely discussed, debated or defended, indicating a lack of confidence in its use, even by those who employ this approach. Yet, most journals usually require appropriate literature reviews and discussion of the methodology for other forms of research undertaken. Such a contradictory position does little to further the development of tourism as a discerning and deserving academic discipline.

References

Adelman, C., Jenkins, D. and Kemmis, S. (1983) Rethinking case study: notes from the second Cambridge conference. In: *Case Study Methods I*, 2nd edn. Deakin University, Waurn Ponds, Australia, pp. 1–10.

Beeton, S. (2001a) Smiling for the Camera: the influence of film audiences on a budget tourism destination. *Tourism, Culture and Communication* 3(1), 15–26.

Beeton, S. (2001b) Lights, camera, re-action. How does film-induced tourism affect a country town? In: Rogers, M.F. and Collins, Y.M.J. (eds) *The Future of Australia's Country Towns*. Centre for Sustainable Regional Communities, La Trobe University, Bendigo, Australia, pp. 172–183.

Beeton, S. (2002) A (de-)marketing approach to enhancing capabilities for film-induced tourism. ANZAM 2002 *Conference Proceedings*, Melbourne, Australia.

Beeton, S. (2005) *Film-induced Tourism*. Channel View Publications, Clevedon, Australia.

Craik, J. (1991) *Resorting to Tourism: Cultural Policies for Tourist Development in Australia*. Allen and Unwin, North Sydney.

Creswell, J.W. (1994) *Research Design: Qualitative and Quantitative Approaches*. Sage Publications, Thousand Oaks, California.

Denzin, N.K. and Lincoln, Y.S. (1994) Introduction: entering the field of qualitative research. In: Denzin, N.K. and Lincoln, Y.S. (eds) *Handbook of Qualitative Research*. Sage Publications, Thousand Oaks, California, pp. 1–7.

Dixon, B. and Bouma, G. (1984) *The Research Process*. Oxford University Press, Melbourne, Australia.

Goeldner, C.R., Ritchie, J.R.B. and McIntosh, R.W. (2000) *Tourism. Principles, Practices, Philosophies*, 8th edn. John Wiley and Sons, New York.

Hall, C.M. and Jenkins, J. (1995) *Tourism and Public Policy*. Routledge, London.

Harris, R. and Leiper, N. (1995) *Sustainable Tourism, an Australian Perspective*. Butterworth-Heinemann, Australia.

Hoaglin, D.C., Light, R.L., McPeek, B., Mosteller, F. and Stoto, M.A. (1982) *Data for Decisions: Information Strategies for Policymakers*. Abt Books, Cambridge, Massachusetts.

Hollinshead, K. (1996) The tourism researcher as bricoleur: the new wealth and diversity in qualitative inquiry. *Tourism Analysis* 1, 67–74.

Jafari, J. (2002) Retracing and mapping tourism's landscape of knowledge. *ReVista – Tourism in the Americas, Harvard Review of Latin America*, Winter 2002. Available at: www.fas.Harvard.edu/~drclas/publications/revista/Tourism

Jennings, G. (2001) *Tourism Research*. Wiley and Sons Australia Ltd, Milton, Australia.

Merriam, S.B. (1998) *Qualitative Research and Case Study Applications in Education*. Jossey-Bass Publishers, San Francisco, California.

Miles, M.B. and Huberman, A.M. (1994) *Qualitative Data Analysis: an Expanded Sourcebook*, 2nd edn. Sage Publications, Thousand Oaks, California.

Murphy, P.E. (1991) Data gathering for community-oriented tourism planning: a case study of Vancouver Island, British Columbia. *Leisure Studies* 10(1), 68–80.

Patton, M.Q. (1990) *Qualitative Evaluation and Research Methods*, 2nd edn. Sage Publications, Newbury Park, California.

Pearce, P.L., Moscardo, G. and Ross, G.F. (1996) *Tourism Community Relationships*. Elsevier Science, Oxford, UK.

Pizam, A. (1994) Planning a tourism research investigation. In: Ritchie, J.R.B. and Goeldner, C.R. (eds) *Travel, Tourism and Hospitality Research: a Handbook for Managers and Researchers*, 2nd edn. John Wiley and Sons Inc., New York, pp. 91–104.

Platt, J. (1992) Case study in American methodological thought. *Current Sociology* 40, 21–35.

Rapoport, R. and Rapoport, R.N. (1975) *Leisure and the Family Life Cycle*. Routledge, London.

Riley, R.W. (1996) Using grounded theory analysis to reveal the underlying dimensions of prestige in leisure travel. *Journal of Travel and Tourism Marketing* 5(1–2), 21–40.

Riley, R.W. and Love, L.L. (2000) The state of qualitative tourism research. *Annals of Tourism Research* 27(1), 164–187.

Ritchie, J.R.B. and Goeldner, C.R. (1994) *Travel, Tourism, and Hospitality Research: a Handbook for Managers and Researchers*, 2nd edn. John Wiley and Sons Inc., New York.

Singh, T.V. and Singh, S. (1999) Coastal tourism, conservation and the community: case of Goa. In: Singh, T.V and Singh, S. (eds) *Tourism Development in Critical Environments*. Cognizant Communication Corporation, New York, pp. 65–76.

Stake, R.E. (1983) The case study method in social inquiry. *Case Study Methods I*, 2nd edn. Deakin University, Waurn Ponds, Australia, pp. 73–76.

Stake, R.E. (1995) *The Art of Case Study Research*. Sage Publications, Thousand Oaks, California.

Veal, A.J. (1997) *Research Methods for Leisure and Tourism: a Practical Guide*, 2nd edn. Financial Times, Pitman Publishing, London.

Walle, A.H. (1997) Quantitative versus qualitative tourism research. *Annals of Tourism Research* 24(3), 524–536.

Yin, R.K. (1994) *Case Study Research. Design and Methods*, 2nd edn. Sage Publications, Thousands Oaks, California.

5 Using Visual Evidence: the Case of *Cannibal Tours*

PETER BURNS AND JO-ANNE LESTER
Centre for Tourism Policy Studies, University of Brighton, Darley Road, Eastbourne
BN20 7UR, UK

Introduction

Tourism is an image-rich, political, cultural and commercial undertaking. Visual images in the form of brochures, advertising hoarding boards, TV advertisements and full colour spreads in Sunday newspaper travel supplements are used to promote products, cityscapes, landscapes, nation-as-destination and, uniquely in the case of tourism, material culture and social structures in the form of people's lifestyles and daily routines. On the consumer side, postcards, photographs and videos form an essential part of remembering and evocation that enriches the touristic experience and, in some cases, gives it purpose. These more intensive ways of using images have created change in the way in which tourism is communicated to potential tourists. A movement has taken place from passive consumption/reception of photographs, brochures, TV documentaries and postcards to activities and interactions such as home-made videos, flexible digital images and interactive websites (Naughton, 2004). It is, therefore, nothing short of astounding that visual images are not used more as both research data and as teaching material within tourism.

In deliberately provocative mood, Franklin and Crang (2001: 7) assert that tourism 'can no longer be bounded off as a discrete activity, contained tidily at specific locations and occurring during set aside periods.' They go on to point out tourism's scale, emphasizing its embeddedness in 'global social life …', attempting to shift the debates away from 'self styled tourist sites and encounters involving tourists away from home', making the point that 'tourism studies have become stale, tired, repetitive and lifeless … it seems almost impossible not to see tourist studies as one of the most exciting and relevant topics in these transnational times … and yet it is not'.

They are right. Part of the problem for those interested in pushing the boundaries of tourism research is captured by the lingering question: is tourism 'scientific' or simply soft science? In part answer to this question, respectability is sought through the seemingly scientific application of quantitative measure to what is essentially a social phenomenon. On the other hand, cultural analysts (Waldren, 1996) seem to draw far-fetched and even fanciful conclusions about what some observers see as people simply taking a vacation. These thoughts are framed by arguments about the relative values of qualitative (i.e. discursive, reflexive and open to nuance) versus quantitative (i.e. repeatability, numerical validity and a 'denial' that at the very centre of tourism lies a complex set of human motivations).

The argument put forward in the

© CAB International 2005. *Tourism Research Methods* (eds B. Ritchie, P. Burns and C. Palmer)   49 present chapter is that the use of visual evidence in its various forms has been held back because of lack of courage and imagination on the part of researchers who may be wary of entering what is for them relatively new territory. Established lecturers supervising students' work may feel more at home with questionnaires and other positivist approaches; perhaps journal editors prefer playing safe. As a consequence, a potentially rich seam of evidence that can inform our understanding of tourism as a social construct and set of phenomena has been under-utilized, not to say undermined. For example, tourism publications involving film have not really addressed issues of image or the film itself as visual evidence but, rather, ways in which the film has had impact in one way or another on tourism (for example, the movie *The Lord of the Rings* in New Zealand).

In an attempt to address these general problems the present chapter provides a practical example of how a film can be treated as data for the purpose of tourism and tourist studies. The four sections provide first an introduction and context setting about the nature, shape and style of visual data and the frameworks used to analyse them (with a note on visual literacy). Second, a review of how visual evidence has been used in the analysis of tourism and its multiple meanings. The third section moves from literature about images as data to more specific ground on how films can be analysed for purposes of critical review and as data, while the final part (the case study) uses Dennis O'Rourke's documentary film *Cannibal Tours* to demonstrate how such material can be analysed and what we can learn from such investigations.

Visual Data and Analysis

Just as a chapter on statistical methods might start with a word about numeracy, so this chapter on using visual evidence commences with a note on visual literacy. Neglect of visual evidence as scientific data may be a reflection of a wider societal problem of what is termed 'visual literacy', which

has been defined in various ways. In an article proposing the importance of visualization in computing skills, Stokes (2002) reviewed various definitions of visual literacy starting with Wileman (1993: 114), who defined it as 'the ability to "read", interpret, and understand information presented in pictorial or graphic images'. Stokes also discussed 'visual thinking', again drawing on Wileman (1993), who defines it as 'the ability to turn information of all types into pictures, graphics, or forms that help communicate the information'. In Stokes' own words, 'If visual literacy is regarded as a language, then there is a need to know how to communicate using this language, which includes being alert to visual messages and critically reading or viewing images as the language of the messages'.

Continuing this broader context, far-sighted educationalists were expressing concern about the neglect of visual literacy in school education almost two decades ago (Broudy, 1987). The role of visual literacy in stimulating 'interest, understanding, and achievement' has been cited as central in 'facilitating emotional success through improved self-concept and academic achievement' (Anderson, 2000). In his paper, Anderson captures the mood of the present paper in emphasizing the role of art in conveying meaning:

> The potency of the arts for learning has gone largely untapped despite years of evidence pointing to the important contribution the arts have to education and human development. This may be attributable to the false dichotomy in education between science and art …There is … a body of literature which shows the value of the arts to students' development in the cognitive, academic and social emotional domains.
>
> (Anderson, 2000)

So, here is a statement about the value not of art for art's sake (i.e. the pleasure of the aesthetic) but of the value of art and its cognitive framework (visual literacy) in helping to make sense of the world around us – which of course is one of the defining characteristics or purposes of scientific research.

Having made a start on establishing the legitimacy of visual data/evidence and the importance of visual literacy, the chapter now moves on to examine some literature on how tourism has thus far been analysed through a range of visual evidence.

Visual Evidence and the Analysis of Tourism and its Meanings

The use of visual evidence in the form of still images (photographs, postcards, brochure images) in tourism analysis was pioneered *inter alia* by Chalfen (1979), Uzzell (1984), Albers and James (1988) and Dann (1988, 1996), followed by some more recent work including that of Edwards (1996), Markwell (1997), Johns and Clarke (2001), Pritchard (2001), Markwick (2001) and Garlick (2002).

Chalfen's early work (1979) acknowledged that photography could be viewed not only as a common tourist behaviour but also as a source of images made available to tourists and mediated by members of the photographed community. His paper described significant relationships between tourist types and patterns of photographic behaviour and the content of photographs. While the work may now be viewed with a little scepticism on account of its naivety and assumptions made about the relationships between hosts and guests, it provided the first serious foray into the visual aspect of tourism. Uzzell (1984) conducted an analysis of visual images in six holiday brochures targeted to the 18–35-year-old holiday market. Uzzell's work focused on the symbolic structure of the holiday brochures in determining the myths and meanings that package holiday companies seek to convey through holiday brochures. Particular attention was given to the visual evidence and Uzzell commented on the power of photographs to convey multiple meanings.

Albers and James's (1988) study investigated the relationship between tourism, ethnicity and photography. Analysis of ethnographic postcards selected from a sample of around 40,000, collected over a period of 35 years from different parts of the world, was undertaken. As a medium of research the strength of the postcard is said to lie 'in the medium itself: its ubiquity, diversity, and narrative text'. Albers and James distinguished between the research methodologies of content analysis and semiotic analysis employed to analyse the postcards.

The use of brochure images employing the research technique of content analysis has been used in many studies, including Dann's (1988) content analysis of holiday advertising of Cyprus, in which he carried out a comparative analysis of images in nine tour operator brochures. In a later study Dann (1996) further developed this mix of content analysis and semiotics in his analysis of how people are represented in brochures; a study that suggested five categories around the theme of 'paradise'. In a far more sophisticated and detailed study, Edwards (1996) undertook an analysis of some 1500 postcards that form part of the collection at the Pitt Rivers Museum in Oxford, UK. Drawing on the work of Thurot and Thurot (1983) Edwards suggested 'one of the keys to understanding tourist phenomena is the analysis of tourist representations and their consumption' (1996: 197). The centre of Edwards's thesis was not so much the obvious stereotyping but rather that, first, photographic images of specific cultures tend to be made and controlled from the outside and, second, that such images in their form as objects of consumption (i.e. postcards), are 'appropriate[d] into the touristic discourses of ethnographic reality' (1996: 198). Edwards went on to link the making and consuming of 'authentic' portrayals of cultural identities with Selwyn's notion of tourism as a framework for modern myths claiming, quite reasonably that 'photography does indeed seem the natural conduit and the natural icon for tourist experience' (Selwyn, 1996).

Pritchard (2001) employed content analysis as a research technique to analyse visual representations of gender in a range of UK tour operators' brochures. Pritchard adapted existing work to develop a continuum scale for measuring 'sexism in tourism representations'. The analysis of 12,832 images in 14 UK tour operator brochures demonstrated that women in tourism advertising were still portrayed in stereotypical roles. Markwick (2001: 417) studied the symbolic meanings conveyed through an exploration of some 500 modern postcards representing Malta aiming to 'examine the role of postcards as symbols that sustain notions of exoticism and authenticity of destinations.' Like Edwards (1996), Markwick examined the extent to which (in the relatively economically advanced state of Malta) control of making and producing commercial images was influenced by the demands and expectations of tourists. Unlike Edwards's cases of African tribal peoples and Australian aboriginals, the majority of Maltese postcard imagery was produced within Malta, enabling Markwick to bring an added dimension: that of self-representation for the tourist market.

The semiotic framework for postcard imagery is linked to a number of interrelated theories surrounding motivation structures in the touristic process. The use of visual evidence in tourism research is extending beyond the steady growth in the use of content and semiotic analysis to examine visual imagery in tourism marketing literature. Markwell (1997) employed a mixture of quantitative and qualitative methods including ethnography, post-tour interviews and a content analysis of 2680 photographs taken by students on a 3-week nature-based tour in East Malaysia to examine the phenomenon of touristic photography. Markwell's empirical research sought to investigate what types of photographs were taken and when during the trip, the meaning and significance of the images within the content of the photographs, and the role of photography in the social interaction amongst the members of the tour group and between the guest and host. Tourist behaviour, motivations and experiences of travel and the use of photographic evidence have also been utilized by Johns and Clarke (2001) in their study of myths in tourism. They used photography to identify tourists' experiences on a boating holiday in the English river and lake complex, the Norfolk Broads. In their study, groups of tourists were given dispos-

able cameras and were requested to take pictures that they felt best expressed their holiday experiences. A semiotic analysis of the photographs was then used to explore the mythological elements of the tourists' experience.

Garlick (2002), in his conceptual paper, takes us full circle to Chalfen's study of 1979 in once again examining the relationship between tourism and tourists' photographic behaviour. He argued 'that by investigating the photographic practices of tourists we can learn more about the activity of "tourism" itself and about the importance both within Western cultures, and for the interaction between Western and non-Western cultures' (2002: 290). The literature discussed above is by no means comprehensive. The present authors have identified at least 40 journal articles and book chapters that directly deal with visual aspects of tourism.

With regards to moving images, the limited number of publications on the subject of films and tourism can be placed along a continuum. At one end are the cultural analysts who make links between tourism, the destination as a complex milieu, and the cultural impact on audiences, residents and tourists. Examples of this type include Tzanelli's (2003) analysis of how the Hollywood film *Captain Corelli's Mandolin* continues the sort of neo-orientalism and stereotyping seen in much earlier work. Winter's (2003: 323) article reflects on the paradox of official Cambodian policies that claim to 'treasure' Angkor as a serious site of cultural heritage and yet allowed its use as the backdrop to the Hollywood blockbuster *Tomb Raider – The Movie*. In particular, Winter remarks on how '"Tomb Raiders" creates new narratives for tourists; ones that undermine the efforts of conservation agencies looking to formalize serious, cultural tourism across the site'.

At the other end of the continuum lie articles on so-called 'movie-induced tourism' (which includes TV series and films following the pattern set by 'literary tourism'). In these articles the focus is on discussing visitor arrivals and how economic activity has increased as a result of a place being associated with a particular filmic event. This genre includes Gundle's (2002: 95) paper on how Hollywood's culture of glamour influenced the making of Fellini's 1960 film *La Dolce Vita*, which in turn created a favourable image of Rome as a cosmopolitan, fashionable city that 'boosted exports and tourism'. Beeton's (2001) case on how an Australian TV series, *Sea Change*, changed the nature of the traditional working class visitors to the town featured in the programme in favour of a more intrusive and higher spending middle class visitor whose tastes and demands altered the nature of the place. Busby and Klug (2001) drew links between movie-induced tourism and cultural/literary tourism through the example of the British film *Notting Hill*, which played an important role in creating pre-visit perceptions on the part of the tourist to that fashionable part of west London. Busby and Klug's paper used a quantitative measure in the form of a survey to try to understand links between the film and visitor motivations and expectations (see also Tooke and Baker, 1996).

None of the examples cited above sees the films themselves as a text, so to speak, with a view to uncovering the layers of meaning placed into and on to the film by players, directors and viewers (though, exceptionally, there is a body of literature on *Cannibal Tours* that will be introduced later in the present paper as the case study).

The literature cited above on still and moving images provides a potent mix of reflexivity and empiricism that leads to new insights that can only enrich our theoretical and practical understanding of tourism as both an act of consumption and a social construct. This section having provided an overview of the literature on how still and moving images have been used in the analysis of tourism, the next provides some observations on how moving images can be 'read' or treated as 'text'.

Frameworks for Analysing/Reading Films as Data/Text

'Reading' a film requires us to go beyond the plot, location, characters and other surface-level components and into how the elements of a film are presented to the audience. Brown (n.d.) reminds us that every single element of each shot is a conscious choice made by the director (even though a director may be influenced at a subconscious level by environmental conditioning and psychological make-up) and each shot is significant to the meaning of the film. This includes the music, the background, camera angles, costumes, positioning of actors in the frame and so on. Table 5.1 provides a structured basis or framework for undertaking a critical film analysis.

The framework suggested in Table 5.1 and also Table 5.2 can be used for both fiction and non-fiction films such as *Cannibal Tours*. Monaco (2000) developed a way of interpreting moving images and Rose (2001), in discussing the narrative (story telling) structures of films, provided a useful summary of the compositional aspects such as the spatial and temporal organization of a film, the former labelled 'mise-en-scene' and the latter 'montage'.

It is important to understand that while Tables 5.1 and 5.2 can help structure an analysis, they cannot be a substitute for intellectual reflection, deep thought and thick description (Geertz, 1973). In a discussion about the role of audience response to ethnographic films (especially 'scientific' audiences such as students, academics and researchers) Marcus Banks (2001: 140) suggests that:

> audiences, particularly student audiences, do not transparently and naturally read ethnographic films, but bring to them previously formed social and cultural understandings ... the 'meaning' of an ethnographic film was not inherent within either the film itself or in the intentions of its author(s), but was a negotiable property that lies within a conceptual triangle formed by the (film) subject, the filmmaker and the audience.

So, the problem expressed here – the assumption that a film carries only the meaning assigned to it by the director/filmmaker – is one that can be resolved by an understanding of the conceptual triangle

Table 5.1. Basic structure for critical film analysis. (Sources: adapted from Brown (n.d.) and Boraas (2000).)

Parameter	Description
Bibliographic information	Title: Director/filmmaker: Date of film: Length (in minutes): Distributor:
Type of film	Fiction (drama, character study, comedy, action, adventure, mystery, suspense, etc.). Historical fiction (ethnohistoric, historic). Documentary (ethnographic, historic, topical, etc.).
Literary analysis	What message does the film carry or what is the point being made? (This is different from the storyline.) Plot or storyline (going beyond simple description by identifying the 'conflict' (creative tension) and turning points in the film and how the conflict is resolved). What do the various characters personify or represent; what is their role in the central conflict of the film?
Aesthetic analysis	The film-maker sets the mood or feeling of a film by composing the scenes in particular ways including the shot itself (see Table 5.2). What are the perspectives from various actors' points of view? What is their positional relationship to each other? What is in the background? What role do light, colour and shadow play?
Editing	The extent to which scenes are long or short, their speed and rhythm. How are images and scenes juxtaposed (cut together) and what sort of meaning does this impose (clear, ambiguous)? Is the continuity editing (the cuts that narrate the story) clear? The beginnings of films (including the opening credits) are crucial in setting tone and mood and providing a key to important themes and motifs.
Soundtrack	Film sound can be categorized into three components (environmental, speech and music). What emotions do the sounds suggest? Is silence used? What is the effect of voice over narration and what might motivate its use?

(MacDougall, 1975) mentioned by Banks (2001: 140). What MacDougall's model shows us is that, while anthropologists have tended to use film as illustration (Offler, 1999) and 'subjects' as a mode of self-identity, not much thought has been given to emotional and 'scientific' responses by the audiences: in effect, the film is 'a product of the encounter between the film-maker, subject and audience' (Offler, 1999: 1, italics added).

This section has provided the framework for using films (fiction or non-fiction) as data or evidence. Though it should be noted that the rather prescriptive approaches of Brown (n.d.), Boraas (2000), Monaco (2000) and Rose (2001) as shown here (not the totality of their work) do tend to ignore the artistic merit of the film and seem to 'aim to distance, objectify and generalize, and therefore detract from the very qualities and potentials that the ambiguity and expressivity of visual images offers to ethnography' (Pink, 2001: 3). With this caveat in mind, the next section provides a narrative on how the film *Cannibal Tours* was analysed to make meaning of tourism in modern society.

Case Study: Dennis O'Rourke's Documentary Film *Cannibal Tours* (1987)

The background literature on *Cannibal Tours*

Note: The film is best described by a mini-literature review that will illustrate both the film's power and its controversial nature.

For example, Ball (1998: 5) considers the film to 'explore the notion of the Other' and that it 'raises fascinating questions concerning authority within accounts of encounters between cultures', whereas O'Rourke himself describes the film as a 'meditation on tourism' (in Lutkehaus, 1989: 423). The advertisement for *Cannibal Tours* states, 'This gently ironic film neither condones nor condemns the tourists or the Papua New Guineans' (in Bruner, 1989: 443). However, Bruner (1989: 443–444) is quite clear in his interpretation of the director's intentions, noting that 'O'Rourke's view is that tourism is neo-colonialism and that the New Guineans are exploited'.

As Bruner (1989) has argued, the title of the film derives from the tourists' fascination with cannibalism that used to be a tradition amongst the Iatmul people. The tourists want to see and feel and touch the places where cannibalism was once practised; however, they would prefer to do it from a safe point of view, from a point of luxury tourism. Bruner situates *Cannibal Tours* very firmly in the works of Baudrillard (1983) and of Eco (1986), who stated that 'tourism prefers the reconstructed

object, and indeed, this preference for the simulacrum is the essence of post-modern tourism, where the copy is more than the original' (cited in Bruner, 1989: 438).

MacCannell (1992) describes *Cannibal Tours* as a film that has two journeys. One is the physical journey of the rich Western tourists on a luxury cruise ship along the Sepik River in Papua New Guinea, the other journey is the metaphysical one – an attempt to discover the 'Other'. He goes on to review the evidence that the Other for whom the tourists are searching no longer exists due to the ravages and influences of colonialism, industrialization, modernization, tourism and globalization – themes that are present throughout the film. Instead the tourists find the 'ex-primitives', the people who have been experiencing 'civilization' for the past century or more, people (to the great disappointment and wonder of most tourists in the group) who are no longer cannibals but have, paradoxically, had their authenticity tainted by the civilizing work of the missionaries. In dealing with the brief encounters between the Westerners and the natives, the film focuses on the interaction between them and the perceptions that both

Table 5.2. Summary of Monaco's compositional interpretation of moving images. (Source: adapted from Rose (2001: 51–52).)

The mise-en-scene can be understood in terms of:

Frame	• Screen ratio
	• Screen frame: open or closed
	• Screen planes: frame plane, geographical plane and depth of planes
	• Multiple images
	• Superimpositions
Shots	• Shot distance: extreme long shot, long shot, full, three-quarters, medium, head and shoulders, close-up shot
	• Shot focus: deep or shallow, sharp or soft
	• Shot angle: angle of approach, angle of elevation, angle of roll
	• Point of view: character, third person, establishing, reverse angle
	• Pans, tilts, zooms and rolls, when the camera remains in one position
	• Tracking and crane shots, when the camera itself moves

The montage/assembly of a moving image can be described with reference to:

Cuts	• Type of cut: unmarked, fade dissolve, iris, jump
	• Rhythm/speed/logic

The sounds of moving images can be described by considering:

Type	• Music, environmental sound speech
	• Relation to the image: source, parallel with, contrapuntal

sides develop of Other and Self (Ball, 1998). Lutkehaus (1989: 423), in somewhat sarcastic mood, states that 'Cannibal Tours is about rich Western tourists on a cruise along the Sepik river in Papua New Guinea and their interaction, or lack of it, with the local villagers', while O'Rourke takes (somewhat disingenuously?) the position that 'Cannibal Tours [simply] ... looks at the incongruity of two cultures meeting, or not meeting in this particular context' (O'Rourke in Lutkehaus, 1989: 427). Many have criticized the film for not being politically correct, for not actually stating what it is that is wrong with tourism, but O'Rourke says of himself and the film, 'I'm trying to deal with the ineffable, with the metaphysical. I don't make any evaluation of whether tourism is bad or if it is good. Tourism exists. Why does it exist? The film is a meditation on the process, on this "shifting terminus"' (in Lutkehaus, 1989: 428).

O'Rourke also mentions that when tourists come home they have souvenirs, photographs, home videos and memories; however, what the filmmaker is more interested in is the tourists' state of mind. The concept of *loss* ventures throughout the film. The loss of identity, the loss of Christianity, the loss of a particular way of life – the sense of failure is being developed. Have the tourists found what they were looking for? Have they found the remedy for loss along the Sepik River and amongst the Iatmul people? (Lutkehaus, 1989). The answer to that lies with the climax of the film when the tourists have their faces painted into masks of death by the villagers and now the audience can see them dancing slowly onboard the luxury cruise ship. O'Rourke calls the scene 'The Dance of Death' and states that the scene represents 'a moment of ecstatic release' (O'Rourke in Lutkehaus, 1989: 428). Even though tourism and colonialism occur at different historical periods Bruner (1989) makes a connection between them, and they still share comparable social structures. To the natives, both the tourist and the colonialist are the 'Other' who have the same wealth and power as the colonialists and missionaries and who come to Papua New Guinea in order to show the natives 'the Other way of life' (Bruner, 1989). As MacCannell (1992: 46) reminds us, 'One does not find among the tourist any similar lightness of sensibility'.

It can be deduced from the foregoing that Cannibal Tours is likely to offer a rich seam of evidence about tourism, tourists, conflicts of motivation, and the multi-layered complexities of tourism – especially where there is stark contrast between the visitors and the visited.

How the film was analysed: practical aspects

In the first instance it is important to know that the present authors have used the film at least twice a year for several years as a teaching aid with undergraduate and postgraduate students studying tourism impacts and cultures. In this sense, the film was already familiar to the researchers. What changed that position was an undergraduate student (Yana Figurova) deciding to use Cannibal Tours as the basis of her dissertation, which provided the inspiration for the present chapter. A fuller account of the film can be seen in Burns and Figurova (2004). The stages of analysis are described in Table 5.3.

In terms of data validity, the mindset or working assumptions for this type of research and analysis are different from the more traditional approaches used in tourism (such as questionnaires). In essence, the researcher's communication with and response to the field (or in this case the object under review) is an explicit part of knowledge production. The subjectiveness of the researcher and of informants (or in this case the informants as seen through the eyes of Dennis O'Rourke) become data in their own right forming part of the interpretation – initially through the field notes. Pink (2001: 19) goes much further:

> Indeed, the assumption that a reflexive approach will aid ethnographers to produce objective data represents only a token engagement with reflexivity that wrongly supposes subjectivity could (or should) be avoided or eradicated. Instead, subjectivity

Table 5.3. Stages and approaches to analysing *Cannibal Tours*.

Stage	Approaches
1st viewing	The film was first seen in its entirety without making notes, just absorbing the film and contemplating it as an un-deconstructed whole; in a sense, seeing it as the director intended on a large screen. Writing down at the end of the viewing some impressions, memories and key issues.
2nd viewing	A short while after (no more than a week or two at most) we watched the film again, this time making notes as we went along. This provides multiple pages of hand-written notes. At the end, we reviewed the notes and wrote them up electronically to form the basis of 'field notes'. At this stage we started to pull out the conflicts, themes and meanings of the film as our personal response to it.
Literature review	We undertook a literature review of the film (the abridged results can be seen above in the preceding section). We categorized the writings into a formal literature review, which became the first completed section of the written output (in our case two book chapters). This process took about 2 months on and off, snatching time to do it alongside our other, regular, activities. Our knowledge of the film was by now enriched and we started to compare our own interpretation/responses with what we found in the literature.
3rd viewing	With the knowledge gained from the literature, we watched the film again, this time pausing the frames so as to make detailed notes about specific scenes, enabling us to identify particular themes we were interested in. Again, the notes were typed up and this description eventually informed our analysis.
Deciding a theme	At this point our writing theme emerged from the data (notes and observations). It could have been a general commentary about the film in its entirety, or a particular element such as economics, culture shock, tourist behaviour, the role of tour operators, etc. In our case, we chose to concentrate on the spoken word of two of the villagers and of two particular tourists.
Structuring the writing	At this point the essay or other academic output should be planned. For this, the basic pattern of an academic piece should be followed, for example: introduction and context setting, why the essay is important and what research questions it seeks to address, a review of relevant literature, the analysis or findings, a commentary on those findings, a concluding section that demonstrates how you have succeeded in answering the research question.
Detailed viewing	Using an edit suite (though a video recorder with remote control could have been used with reasonable effect) to aid detailed viewing of the film, we went to the scenes that we wanted to focus on and transcribed the words and detailed the scenes. We ended up with very detailed notes on the aspects we wanted to review.
Writing up	The intended audience defines the type of output. For example, academics will want to choose a journal and that journal will have its own defining styles. A student may be preparing a short (3000 words) or long (6000 words) essay or a dissertation (anything up to 25,000 words). The style and format of writing will therefore be defined externally but will always be based on the original 'field' notes.

Example of writing up film scenes

1: 'The experienced bargainer'
The scene is set somewhere in the middle of the village at medium long shot. There are about six to eight people wandering in and out of the frame, milling about; some of them are villagers trying to sell their wares, others are tourists thinking of buying. The background sound comprises burbling voices, raucous birds and the heavy sound of insects. The tourists seem hot and are swiping at flies around their heads. The camera zooms in on a medium close up to our German tourist. He is looking at a delicate carving about 8 inches high, 'How much?' The vendor, who is sitting down, looks away and says, 'Four kina.' [Four kina was about 3 dollars.] The tourist purses his lips, 'Four, that's the first price, four.' The vendor doesn't look up but looks disgusted, blowing away flies, doesn't respond. The German offers 3 kina. No response. He shrugs and places the carving back on the ground. The camera pans out and dissolves.

2: 'Bargaining tutorial'
Scene set in the same place as above but slightly further along the market. An old female tourist picks up an exquisitely carved story-stick. She looks nervous and uncomfortable, out of her depth. The scene shows about six people, again moving in and out of the static medium field shot. She says, 'Who is the spokesman? ... Is that right, twenty kina?' A male voice off camera (possibly the tour guide?) says, 'Look at it awhile, admire it.' The woman replies softly, seemingly embarrassed, 'Well that's so cheap, I can't say anything ... ten?' The male tourist, obviously her self-appointed tutor in this affair, urges her to, 'Ask for a second price.' She goes for it, holding the stick out as the camera gets in a little closer, 'Is there a second price for this?' An indistinct response from the woman selling the item, 'Huh?' The villager says more clearly, 'Thirteen.' To which the tourist says, 'OK, [then *sotto voce*] what a negotiation', as she struggles with her purse to take out the money. Her fellow tourists look proud of her. The villagers look as though they could cheerfully murder her.

3: 'First price, second price'
The shot is a close-up of a middle-aged villager with a white stubbly beard. His teeth and gums are stained with years of chewing betel nut. He is sitting against a hut of some sort and seems to be alone. Perhaps this is the place he does his carvings and makes his handicrafts for selling to the tourists. The conversation to camera is intimate, one-to-one. He does not seem angry, but is clearly unhappy. This is what he says in Pijin language, the words are taken from the translated subtitles on screen: 'The price I ask for my carvings is what I should be paid ... People should pay me the money that I ask. I don't agree with "second price" and "third price". I want them to pay without any fuss ... My own small amount of money but they ask for "second price" and "third price", it's wrong because when I go to those big shops – the town, I can't buy things for "second price" or "third price", I must pay the first price, for a shirt, trousers or whatever.'

Comment
What is interesting here is how O'Rourke has chosen to juxtapose these three scenes in sequence, which is not so obvious on the first, second, or even third viewing. It only becomes familiar as a sub-narrative when the film becomes so embedded as a piece of evidence to the viewer that sub-texts begin to reveal themselves. The translation of the villagers' words is done with great care, so that the subtitles appear in 'normal' flowing English, making the locals appear not ignorant but, rather, somewhat lucid in their opinions. The three scenes put together make a very powerful dynamic and this happens time and time again throughout the film, once again emphasizing the point that it is useless to try to pretend there is any sort of neutrality in film-making.

should be engaged with as a central aspect of ethnographic knowledge, interpretation and representation.

In our interpretation of *Cannibal Tours*, we recognized that we were already viewing the participants through the distorting lens of the director's thoughts. However, we were quite clear in our research intention: we wanted to know what this film told *us* about tourists, tourism and the interaction of hosts and guests, i.e. not attempting a 'scientific-realism', but rather a reflexive interpretation that acknowledged that the director's way of editing and the sequence he gave to the film is not the only interpretation: audiences (in our case, researchers) can place their own interpretive narrative on the visual evidence presented. There are no 'ethnographic truths' (Clifford, 1986) although the frameworks we used provided a consistent procedural validity in the same way that, say, a biography is 'valid' (Flick, 1998), or an 'ironic validity' that recognizes the validity of postmodern rhetorical reflections (Lather, 1993) such as films. We were not attempting 'generalizability' but were confident that our methods and findings had a high degree of 'transferability' (i.e. we could apply the same format to another context/film and develop another data set of comparative value for that new situation). As noted above, in qualitative research the notion of 'validity' is always at the forefront and is often framed by questions of reliability. In the case of qualitative research based on fieldwork (or film viewing in the case of visual evidence), Flick (1998) points us towards Wolcott's (1990: 127–128) elements of ethnographic validity (paraphrased): researchers should refrain from talking in the field but rather should listen as much as possible; they should produce fieldnotes that are as exact as possible; the writing should begin early; published writing should provide enough data for readers to make their own inferences and follow those

of the researcher; written outcomes from the fieldwork should be as complete and as candid as possible; researchers should seek feedback on the findings in the field or from colleagues; presentations should be characterized by balance and accuracy in writing.

Conclusion

As the social understanding of tourism broadens and progresses, we need to know the scope and scale of tourism not only through careful and sustained quantitative studies based on both testable empiricism but also by the use of qualitative (including visual) evidence and subsequential, careful, insightful reflection. This chapter suggests that questions and issues arising from the arguments raised above require more innovative research strategies than are often apparent from the published tourism literature or found in tourism curricula. Greater use of visual images as data and teaching material can tell us more about the multiplicity of meanings, messages and motivations inherent in the phenomenon than more traditional, normative data collection methods.

Tourism students and academics need to look beyond repetitive case studies or empirical studies that simply reassert the social and economic *importance* of tourism, to research approaches that focus much more on the *why* and *what for* of tourism, thereby avoiding what Franklin and Crang (2001: 6) have referred to as the 'petrification' of tourism research.

Acknowledgement

We would like to acknowledge the contribution of Yana Figurova, who undertook the literature review on *Cannibal Tours* as part of her dissertation studies at the University of Brighton.

References

Albers, P. and James, W. (1988) Travel photography: a methodological approach. *Annals of Tourism Research* 15, 134–158.

Anderson, D. (2000) Using the arts as a vehicle for educational and emotional success. Paper presented to the International Special Education Congress *Including the Excluded*. Manchester, UK, 24–28 July 2000. Available at: http://www.isec2000.org.uk/abstracts/papers_a/anderson_1.htm

Ball, M. (1998) Critical Design. *Subject, Author and Audience Revisited: Ethnographic Film Study, Winter Term '98*. Available at: http://www.criticaldesign.com/anthropo/ethno/ethno.htm

Banks, M. (2001) *Visual Methods in Social Research*. Sage, London.

Beeton, S. (2001) Smiling for the camera: the influence of film audiences on a budget tourism destination *Tourism, Culture and Communication* 3(1), 15–25(11).

Boraas, A. (2000) *Guide to Writing an Analytic Film Review*. Available at: http://chinook.kpc. alaska.edu/~anthro/anthropology/analyzingfilm.htm

Broudy, H. (1987) *The Role of Imagery in Learning*. The Getty Center for Education in the Arts, Los Angeles, California.

Brown, D. (n.d.) *Some Cursory Notes on 'Reading' a Film*. Available at: http://www.english. upenn.edu/Grad/Teachweb/dbfilm.html

Bruner, E.M. (1989) Of cannibals, tourists and ethnographers. *Cultural Anthropology* 4(4), 438–445.

Burns, P. and Figurova, Y. (2004) Tribal tourism in hidden places: the case of *Cannibal Tours*. In: Novelli, M. (ed.) *Niche Tourism: Contemporary Issues, Trends and Cases*. Butterworth Heinemann, Oxford, UK.

Busby, G. and Klug, J. (2001) Movie-induced tourism: the challenge of measurement and other issues. *Journal of Vacation Marketing* 7(4), 316–332(17).

Chalfen, R.M. (1979) Photography's role in tourism: some unexplored relationships. *Annals of Tourism Research* 6(4), 435–447.

Clifford, J. (1986) Introduction: partial truths. In: Clifford, J. and Marcus, G. (eds) *Writing Culture: the Poetics and Politics of Ethnography*. University of California Press, Berkeley, California.

Dann, G.M.S. (1988) Images of Cyprus projected by tour operators. *Problems of Tourism* 3(41), 43–70.

Dann, G. (1996) The people of tourist brochures. In: Selwyn, T. (ed.) *The Tourist Image, Myths and Myth Making in Tourism*. Wiley, Chichester, UK, pp. 61–82.

Edwards, E. (1996) Postcards – greetings from another world. In: Selwyn, T. (ed.) *The Tourist Image, Myths and Myth Making in Tourism*. Wiley, Chichester, UK, pp. 197–221.

Flick, U. (1998) *An Introduction to Qualitative Research*. Sage, London.

Franklin, A. and Crang, M. (2001) The trouble with tourism and travel theory? *Tourist Studies* 1(1), 5–22.

Garlick, S. (2002) Revealing the unseen: tourism, art and photography. *Cultural Studies* 16(2), 289–305.

Geertz, C. (1973) *The Interpretation of Cultures*. Basic Books, New York.

Gundle, S. (2002) Hollywood glamour and mass consumption in postwar Italy. *Journal of Cold War Studies* 4(3), 95–118(24).

Johns, N. and Clarke, V. (2001) Mythological analysis of boating tourism. *Annals of Tourism Research* 28(2), 334–359.

Lather, P. (1993) Fertile obsession: validity and post-structuralism. *Sociological Quarterly* 35, 673–693.

Lutkehaus, N.C. (1989) 'Excuse me, everything is not all right': on ethnography, film and representation. *Cultural Anthropology* 4(4), 422–437.

MacCannell, D. (1992) *Empty Meeting Grounds: the Tourist Papers*. Routledge, London.

MacDougall, D. (1975) Beyond observational cinema. In: Hockings, P. (ed.) *Principles of Visual Anthropology*. Mouton Publishers, Paris, pp. 109–124.

Markwell, K.W. (1997) Dimensions of photography in a nature-based tour. *Annals of Tourism Research* 24(1), 131–155.

Markwick, M. (2001) Postcards from Malta: image, consumption, context. *Annals of Tourism Research* 28(2), 417–438.

Monaco, J. (2000) *How to Read a Film: Movies, Media, Multimedia*, 3rd edn. Oxford University Press, London.

Naughton, J. (2004) We happy few, we band of brothers. *The Observer*, 11 January 2004.

Offler, N. (1999) Shock, judgement, and the stereotype: exploring the role of emotional response in ethnographic film reception. Available at: http://cc.joensuu.fi/naomi.htm

O'Rourke, D. (1987) *Cannibal Tours* [Videotape], 70 minutes, 35mm and 16 mm, Colour. Produced, directed and photographed by Dennis O'Rourke. Film editor: Tim Lichtenfield, O'Rourke and Associates, Canberra, Australia.

Pink, S. (2001) *Doing Visual Ethnograph*. Sage, London.

Pritchard, A. (2001) Tourism and representation: a scale for measuring gendered portrayals. *Leisure Studies* 20, 79–94.

Rose, G. (2001) *Visual Methodologies*. Sage, London.

Selwyn, T. (ed.) (1996) *The Tourist Image: Myths and Myth Making in Tourism*. Wiley, Chichester, UK.

Stokes, S. (2002) Visual literacy in teaching and learning: a literature perspective. *Electronic Journal for the Integration of Technology in Education* 1(1), 10–19.

Tooke, N. and Baker, M. (1996) Seeing is believing: the effect of film on visitor numbers to screened locations. *Tourism Management* 17(2), 87–94(8).

Tzanelli, R. (2003) Casting the neohellenic 'Other': tourism, the culture industry, and contemporary orientalism in 'Captain Corelli's Mandolin'. *Journal of Consumer Culture* 3(2), 217–244(28).

Uzzell, D. (1984) An alternative structuralist approach to the psychology of tourism marketing. *Annals of Tourism Research* 11(1), 79–99.

Waldren, J. (1996) *Insiders and Outsiders: Paradise and Reality in Mallorca*. Berghahn Books, Oxford, UK.

Wileman, R.E. (1993) *Visual Communicating*. Educational Technology Publications, Englewood Cliffs, New Jersey.

Winter, T. (2003) Angkor meets Tomb Raider: setting the scene. *International Journal of Heritage Studies* 8(4), 323–336(14).

Wolcott, H. (1990) On seeking – and rejecting – validity in qualitative research. In: Eisner, W. and Pershkin, A. (eds) *Qualitative Enquiry in Education: the Continuing Debate*. Teachers College Press, New York, pp. 121–152.

6 Action Ethnography: Using Participant Observation

STROMA COLE

Buckinghamshire Chilterns University College, High Wycombe HP13 5BB, UK

Introduction

Although anthropologists were slow to accept tourism as part of their studies (Din, 1988; Nash, 1996), following a number of conceptual shifts, the anthropology of tourism is now a well-established field. Following Smith's seminal collection of papers – *Hosts and Guests* – a number of monographs have been produced aimed at academics (e.g. Nash, 1996) and students (e.g. Burns, 1999). While critical debate continues on the content of the field and ethnographies are produced (e.g. Waldren, 1996; Kottak, 1999), little has been written on the methodologies used in this increasing, large sub-discipline.

This chapter examines the methods used by an anthropologist to produce an action ethnography of tourism. Following a brief introduction to action ethnography and participant observation this chapter examines how a trusted tour operator returned to carry out fieldwork in Eastern Indonesia. It examines how she dealt with selecting key informants, her various roles and the phases of her research. It discusses how interviews were adapted to the local ways of articulating and transmitting knowledge and how participation and data collection occurred concurrently. The chapter ends on the mutual benefits of action research.

Action Ethnography

Action anthropology is a subdivision of applied anthropology and is associated with Sol Tax, whose goals were 'to help people and to learn something in the process' (in Van Willigen, 1986). Anthropological commitment to the insiders' perspective and citizen advocacy (Preister, 1987) make it an appropriate discipline with which to work with those affected by, and learning to deal with, tourism. Tourism-induced change can be fast and far-reaching for participants in less developed countries who need to be able to derive benefits from anthropological research.

The term 'action ethnography' is employed to refer to my study as I addressed two objectives: to produce an ethnography of tourism, and to make it useful to the researchees, in the belief that 'the subject population have the right to the social power that comes from knowledge' (May, 1980: 365). Although MacClancy (2002) claims that much contemporary anthropology helps to empower the alienated and give voice to the otherwise unvoiced, there is a lack of data on how this can be done in the tourism literature (Berno, 1996). While anthropologists advocate steering a path between problem solving and interpretative anthropology by providing a means for a community to 'represent themselves and identify the nature and solutions to their problems' (Gardener and Lewis 1996: 41), there is little literature on how this can be done in practice.

Since Malinowski's work in the Trobriand Islands, extensive fieldwork has become central to anthropology (Kuper, 1983). Participant observation is the central methodology of ethnographic fieldwork. However, as Bernard (1988) argues, participant observation is not really a single method but a strategy that facilitates data collection. While direct observation is essential, participant observation includes casual conversations, in-depth informal unstructured interviews, structured interviews, and questionnaires (Jorgensen, 1999); and, in my case, focus groups. As I have written elsewhere (Cole, 2004) on this latter method I will concentrate in this chapter on the epistemological issues of some of the other methods that together make up participant observation.

Participant Observation

Participant observation involves attempting to understand and interpret the meanings and experiences of a group, a task which anthropologists argue is only possible through participation with the individuals involved (Burgess, 1984; Silverman, 1993; Selanniemi, unpublished). It is the most appropriate method when the research is concerned with human meanings and interactions from the insiders' perspective, especially where there are important differences between the views of insiders as opposed to outsiders. Participant observation seeks to uncover, make accessible and reveal the meanings people use to make sense of their everyday lives (Jorgensen, 1999).

In order to understand 'the natives'' point of view 'the twin ideals of empathy and objectivity' (Nash, 1996) are required. In order to achieve objectivity anthropologists adopt a self-reflective position. By taking themselves and their procedures into account 'a clear eye (is kept) on the potential bias that might come from one's own institutional, class and historical position'

(MacCannell, 1989: 3). Placing the researcher as central to the research process (Humberstone, 1997) is emphasized by the use of the first person singular in anthropological accounts. The use of the first person singular is an attempt to avoid disguising the researcher as neutral.

While participating with insiders it is clear that the researcher is part of the context being observed and therefore to some extent modifies and influences the data. Rather than seeing this as a negative form of bias triangulation, contextualization and reflexivity are used to remind the reader of the influence of the researcher on the research process. A further strategy to prevent biases and ensure validity and rigour is the use of 'respondent validation'. Once accounts from the field are written up the interpretation can be checked back with the participants. This is greatly aided by the use of e-mail.

The researcher relations in the field will heavily influence the accuracy and truthfulness of the data collected. 'Impression management' is necessary for the fieldworker to fit into his/her research setting. Appearance can be important in shaping relations and attention to dress can be particularly important in the initial phases of gaining trust (Hammersly and Atkinson, 1995). Rapport and trust need to be established before data collection proper can begin. Fieldwork roles are seen as developmental, moving through a series of phases as the research progresses. Bernard (1988) notes seven stages while Burgess (1984) quotes Janes (1961) as recognizing five phases and Olesen and Whittaker (1967) as identifying four.

Not only does participant observation involve a number of research methods, it covers a range of roles. The various roles that those carrying out participant observation adopt have been analysed and a distinction has been made between 'complete participant', 'participant as observer', 'observer as participant' and 'complete observer' (Gold, 1958 in Hammersley and Atkinson, 1983; Junker, 1960 in May, 1997). As a complete participant the researcher's role is concealed, e.g. when the researcher is already, or becomes, a member, or is 'totally immersed' in the group studied. In contrast a 'complete observer' has no contact with those she is observing. Most participant observation falls somewhere in between. The researcher may adopt different roles with different informants at different stages of the research, as I describe below.

The essential base of participant observation is the participation in, and observations of, everyday life. The method involves a flexible, open-ended opportunistic process (Jorgensen, 1999). It inspires concepts, generalizations and interpretations. The research question or questions are defined and redefined as the research process continues. The method is closely akin to in-depth case studies stressing a holistic examination in a particular setting.

Information gathered by a variety of techniques is recorded. A diary or logbook is nearly always used to keep records of observations and conversations. This may be supplemented with questionnaire surveys, recordings on tapes, photographs and film. The material so gathered has then to be sorted, organized and written up. Participant observation involves two activities concurrently: participation and data collection. Sometimes it is possible to write down, or otherwise record, activities as you go along; at other times, observations and conversations must be committed to memory and written down as the opportunity arises. The analysis of the data involves a multiple array of tasks: memorizing, note taking and interpretation. Frequently, once the research process is well under way, gathering and analysing data occurs concurrently.

Writing up the data produced by participant observation is done through a process of 'thick description' (Geertz, 1973). The researcher writes down only a small part of what is accessed. What is most important and meaningful is selected. This is a discriminatory process (Wickens, unpublished). Thick description implies layers, many and varied layers, which represent voices. One of the voices is the researcher's, who interpreted the voices of the participants. As I have suggested, being transparent about one's presence and the effect this has on the data is an essential part of writing up data produced by participant observation.

Participant observation in Ngadha Flores

The setting

The research took place in two villages in Ngadha, an area that approximates to the south-west third of the Ngada regency of Flores, Nusa Tenggara Timor, Indonesia. The area lies between East Indonesia's two renowned tourist attractions. To the east is Keli Mutu, a volcano with three different coloured lakes at its peak. To the west lies Komodo National Park, famed for its 'dragons' (*Varanus komodoensis*). The area is one of the poorest in Indonesia and tourism is considered the area's best option for economic development (Umbu Peku Djawang, 1991). The villages began to be visited by 'drifters' in the 1980s and have seen increasing numbers of tourists ever since. The most popular village received 9000 tourists in 1997 (Regency Department of Education and Culture, 1998, unpublished).

The villages lie in a rugged mountainous region with steep slopes and poor soils. The villagers are largely peasants eking out a hand-to-mouth existence. This is supplemented by craft production, which is subject to village and gender specialization. In one village a small proportion of men are blacksmiths while women in the other produce ikat[1] cloth. The spiritual heart of Ngadha villages, *nua*, lies around 30 wooden houses with high thatched roofs, arranged in two parallel lines or around the sides of a rectangle. In the centre are a number of *ngadhu* and *bhaga* (variously translated as totems, shrines and sacrificial posts) and a number of megaliths. The complex of attractions provides tourists with 'a feeling of being enclosed in antiquity' (Cole, 1997a). Four of the *nua*, including those where the research took place, have been

---

[1]Ikat, from the Indonesian *mengikat*, is a dye-resistant process that has entered the international textile vocabulary (Hitchcock, 1991).

designated prime tourist attraction status[2] by the government.

Access and initial contact

The research was conducted over a period of more than 10 years (1989–2000), in a number of roles. Between 1989 and 1994 I operated tours that included a 2-night stay in one of the villages. The success of the tours taken to the village influenced not only the selection of the research site but also the collection and analysis of the data. Many of the villagers had positive experiences of tourism as a direct result of my actions, bringing tourists, significant income, piped water and pride in their musical talents (Cole, 1997a). This gave me credibility and influenced the research process. After several visits the villagers had the opportunity to take part in an international bamboo music festival in Bali. When we met again they asked me, 'How can we have tourism and not end up like Bali?' They had noticed the volumes of scantily clad tourists, the wealth disparities, the traffic jams and no peace and quiet. The desire to answer the villagers' question became central to my research. I wanted to conduct research about how they should best develop their tourism.

In 1996 I carried out a Participatory Rural Appraisal to generate data for an academic paper (Cole, 1997b). The background, rapport, trust and language established during the previous visits was used to hold 30 questionnaire-based interviews with members of the village, to explore their ideas and views about tourism. I wanted to conduct research in a short space of time (10 days) to obtain some 'hard data'. Most of the villagers wanted to 'catch up'. The villagers wanted to know about me, what I had been doing, where my daughter was, why she wasn't with me, and so on. I struggled to steer conversations on to tourism and collect the data I wanted. However, the trip proved invaluable in reconnecting with the villagers.

[2]*obyek wisata unggulan* (*objek* = object, *wisata* = tourist, *unggulan* = superior).

Carrying out structured questionnaires was difficult for a number of reasons: a lack of familiarity with social science research among the respondents meant that many were anxious and worried about giving the 'wrong' answers. It was difficult to get a single opinion, as the villagers would gather around to see what was going on. When an elder gave a response, this was taken as the 'right' answer and then repeated by others.

In July 1998, I returned to carry out 8 months' fieldwork. During my early visits I had established an excellent rapport with the villagers. As I have suggested, the relationship between the fieldworker and the respondents is considered crucial to the research process. If 'the process of building a local acceptable persona is a trial and error affair' (Angrosino, 1986: 66) then by the time I came to live in the village I had found a persona that was both comfortable to me and non-threatening to my hosts. I had become *au fait* with the cultural norms, dress, behaviour and patterns of communication in the village during my earlier visits. I did not suffer from culture shock – I knew about the toilet facilities, the monotonous diet and the lack of privacy. I had worked out my coping strategies: going to town once a week or so for a relatively private night in a guesthouse, to get a bath and have a different meal.

My age and gender were also important aspects of my role and the nature of the data that I obtained. In Ngadha, men deal with outsiders. As a female outsider, I was in a superior research position to any male undertaking the same study, because as a woman I could also gain the female perspective and, as an outsider, I dealt with men. This ambiguous yet advantageous position has been identified by other female anthropologists (Hammersley and Atkinson, 1995). As a married woman, I was not a threat (cf. Angrosino, 1986, on the threat an unattached male anthropologist poses). I was married and therefore not competition. Golde (1986: 79–80) aptly describes the problems of being an older, unmarried, virginal anthropologist. My gender role changed over the course of the research process. When I had visited before my daughter was born, I had felt pushed out of some women's matters – although I only realized this afterwards. Later I became a 'real' woman. However, as I had only one child, I was considered poor. Considerable sympathy was extended to me for my impoverished status as a mother of only one child.

As other anthropologists have noted (e.g. Hendry, 1999), there are advantages in children accompanying anthropological field trips. My daughter's friendships gave me fruitful new openings that would not have otherwise existed. Further, a child's mind and line of questioning, often more direct and honest, frequently had significant benefits during the research process.

Participants and key informants

Following an initial introduction through the Department of Education and Culture and my long contact with the villagers, the minimum of formalities was required to access any information. Nobody attempted to block my access to anyone else, nobody declined to speak with me (although some were obviously less forthcoming than others). The voices of villagers in the ethnography included formal and informal village leaders, neighbours and other villagers. While I had conversations with very many villagers over the months of my research some voices proved more data-rich than others. These were my *key* informants.

According to Wolcott (1990: 195) a key informant is 'an individual in whom one invests a disproportionate amount of time because the individual appears particularly well informed, articulate, approachable or available'. Which informants should fall into the category of *key* informant is not defined. In my case all my hosts became key informants as I spent a disproportionate amount of time talking to them relative to other members of the villages. One non-host villager and a member of the Department of Education and Culture also became *key* informants because their voices were frequent in my notes and many of our conversations were directly relevant to my research.

According to Bernard (1988) key informants are selected for their competence. Hammersley and Atkinson (1995) note the importance of 'gatekeepers' and their impact on the choice of key informants. Here I would like to stress 'the click factor', i.e. bonding with participants. I use this to underline the importance of how well you get on with someone, how at ease one feels and the importance of this for the selection of key informants. The ease with which one can chat spontaneously without it being an effort, forging an intuitive bond that develops easily and can be maintained over time, is an aspect of 'the click factor'. With some of my key informants I could sit and chat for hours, like having a good gossip with a friend. Such chats could reveal interesting and important data.

In order to understand the development of tourism in Ngadha and to be able to make recommendations about it, it was necessary to contrast the experiences, attitudes and values of the villagers with other stakeholders. To this end I also collected data from guides, tourists and civil servants in relevant government departments.

The research process

As I have suggested, frequent visits over a number of years meant that my influence on the data was perhaps stronger than a once-in-the-field anthropologist. My essentially action-oriented approach, combined with a high level of trust and confidence, sharing of knowledge and experience and personal involvement, framed the study. Conversations were often more discussions than interviews because I was asked my opinion or frequently asked to give advice about what should be done. Many people were keen to use the influence they believed I would have on tourism policy.

My role, like other ethnographers, moved through a series of phases as the research progressed. During the 8 months, three phases could be discerned: first, 'getting to know you (again)', characterized as being treated like a guest, for example being served first at meal times. The second phase, 'acceptance', was characterized by being treated as one of the family, as a labour source to be tapped, and as someone who could be used to achieve political ends. During this phase, it is likely that the head of household would be served first, but in the family setting, order was unimportant. I ate from a shared gourd with female members of the family. The third and final phase, 'imminent departure', was characterized by special treatment and an effort to help me out. This phase was somewhat interrupted by Christmas, New Year, the villagers' annual festival (*Reba*) and my family visiting from England, at which point I reverted back to guest status.

According to Bernard (1988: 148), a participant observer is successful when 'informants laugh at what you say, it will be because you *meant* it to be a joke'. I felt rapport was established when my informants felt happy to ask me to do for them what they usually did for me. When I was requested to undertake domestic duties for the family such as lighting the fire and getting the rice and beans under way or I was left in charge of the dark inner kitchen I knew I was accepted. I had become a marginal family member and true rapport had been established. However, I always maintained special status. For example, I would be invited to events that my family position would not have allowed for and entered the inner house rituals for clans I was unconnected with.

While establishing true rapport is an essential aspect of participant observation it has drawbacks. While I was happy that I was accepted as a family member, demands on my time and emotional energies detracted from the research process. Furthermore, I had a problem of feeling too at home, which, as Hammersley and Atkinson (1995) suggest, leads to over-rapport. When life became too routine, I found that I was participating fully but not observing new things. My researcher role became eclipsed and I found the days passed without any new data.

In the 8 months I had three residences. Moving to new hosts allowed a balance between familiarity and rapport and the chores that went with it on the one hand, and the need to do my work but having to establish rapport on the other. By moving around I also got to experience the differences of living in traditional houses and in the 'modern, healthy' homes. I experienced living in the centre of a 'touristy' village with onlookers on my terrace on a daily basis. I also experienced living just outside a traditional village and seeing how little anything to do with tourism was part of some villagers' lives.

Data collection

I had different roles with different informants at different stages of my research. For the vast majority of my research I could not be a true 'complete participant' because the villagers were aware of my research. However, at times with tourists, in order to avoid reactivity, I was a 'complete participant', joining tours as a tourist and keeping my research concealed (until the tour was over). Also, some of my research on tourists was as a 'complete observer', just jotting down their behaviour and clothing for example. In the villages, my dress and conversation with villagers aroused suspicion among tourists that I was not a tourist. I found that tourists were attracted to me for conversation and to gather knowledge. Unable to converse with villagers, talking to me either filled the awkward vacuum of time or allowed them to feel they were blending in. However, the interest that tourists showed in me detracted from my ability to observe them and to carry out research with the villagers. At times I found it necessary to adopt strategies to avoid conversations with tourists. Entering the house (going backstage) until they had passed by was the easiest avoidance strategy.

I also took the 'complete observer' stance when doing research into the narrative of non-local guides. I noticed that non-local guides felt threatened when they knew I spoke the local language and knew about the culture and they avoided giving cultural explanations in my presence. In order to record their narratives I acted as a tourist.

Again I was trying to avoid problems of reactivity.

Some data collection in the villages was also as a 'complete observer', especially in my latter two residencies when I was living in the centre of the villages. I would sit on the terrace, observe and write. Sometimes my observations were directed, for example, at what the villagers did when a group of tourists arrived. At other times I observed and took notes on activities that were seemingly unrelated to my research but which became the rich data that could be pieced together to provide a deep understanding of Ngadha society.

Although observation was an important part of the data collection technique, for the majority of the research, I was a 'participant-as-observer', which, as Burgess (1984) points out, allowed me the freedom to go where the action was. 'Dialogue is the backbone of ethnography' (Monaghan and Just, 2000: 23). Interviews are central to the ethnographers' participant observation. Interviews, conversations with a purpose (Robson, 1993), are subdivided into three types, depending on the degree of structure: structured, semi-structured and unstructured (Punch 1998; Frey and Fontana, 1991). All types were used at different times during the research process.

I used structured interviews with personnel from various government departments and semi-structured interviews with key individuals that I needed to talk to but rarely had the opportunity for spontaneous chats with. The majority of 'interviews' were conversations or casual chats. While a general purpose, to collect data, always existed the casual undirected approach was best suited to the local ways of articulating and transmitting knowledge (cf. Forth, 1998). Asking direct questions led to problems for two reasons: first, Indonesia has 'a high power distance culture where emphasis is on obedience, conformity, authority, supervision, social hierarchy and inequality' (Reisinger and Turner, 1997: 141). Although non-hierarchical relationships between respondent and researcher would have been preferable, this was clearly difficult to achieve. As an educated white

researcher, my status was ascribed. By making interviews non-directive, allowing villagers to talk at length in their own terms and by using self-disclosure and reciprocity the hierarchical pitfall (Reinharz, 1992) was minimized. Second, Indonesians are well known for 'telling you what ever they think you want to hear' (Draine and Hall, 1996: 79). When an elder male had provided an opinion in front of other villagers this opinion was repeated as *the* opinion they assumed I wanted.

In order to overcome the problems of 'conformist responses', fear of giving the 'wrong answer' and of villagers being too shy because of my ascribed status I adopted a strategy of chatting. I avoided direct questions and was sensitive about taking notes. Villagers who were at home would be on their terraces chewing betel, mending mats, threading looms, shelling maize, etc. and could be easily spotted and approached. I would, where possible, join in their activity. As conversations developed I would attempt slowly and subtly to steer conversations on to useful topics. This took time and patience. I had to accept that the villagers wanted to ask me questions, to interview me and to learn from me. Recounting the four seasons in England for the fifth time, discussing the merits of the British monarchy or the normality of 'thirty-something' westerners not having children could all, with patience, lead to data-rich conversations.

Analysis

The analysis of ethnographic data involves a multiple array of tasks, which often lack a coherent order. Participant observation involves two activities concurrently: the dual roles of participation and data collection. At times, I relied on memory. On other occasions, I took condensed notes. Much of the time, on-the-spot interpretation took place. Frequently, I gathered and analysed data concurrently.

Although I tried to keep my notebook with me at all times and unashamedly took notes whenever it was appropriate, frequently I could not do so. Whilst cooking, threading a loom, picking coffee, de-seeding maize or playing cards, it is not possible simultaneously to take notes. I, therefore, had to rely on memory and write up when I could. Sometimes I would break off from a task, perhaps briefly, to jot down a key word or two to remind myself to make more detailed notes on a subject. When playing cards with one key informant, I would play my turn and then jot something down while he thought about his next move. However, if I asked a question, he would accuse me of attempting to distract him from the cards. Once or twice when making notes at meal times, another key informant would exclaim 'Eat first: you can catch up (with your note-taking) later'. At times, when important new information was being revealed, my head felt as if it would explode as I was trying to carry so much in my memory.

Usually at the end of the day, but also as an opportunity arose, I turned rough notes into more coherent notes under subtitles. This process was part coding as I was going along, part checking my recording of data, and part analysis. I asked informants to help me check and recheck data as I tried to make sense of my observations and analysis. I believe that my informants' patience in back-tracking over the same ground was made easier by the action orientation of my research.

Two points about the data analysis process are worthy of particular comment. First, the data was collected over a 10-year stretch, during which time I undertook research in a number of guises. During my formal academic research I was able to return to the field and talk over my analyses with the villagers, to double-check my interpretation of their voices, and to fill in gaps in my data. Second, with the advent of global communication I had regular e-mail contact with a key informant who moved to Jakarta. This has allowed for 'respondent validation' as I tested my accounts and analyses with him. At times, he took sections of my analysis and translated them to his father and uncles, elders respected for their intimate cultural knowledge, in order to get further feedback for me.

Conclusions: From Data to Action

As I have suggested, the aims of my research were twofold: to produce an ethnography of tourism and to make my research useful to the researchees. I was addressing both theoretical and practical concerns at the same time. The work was both applied and interpretative.

The action orientation of my work had significant benefits for the research process. Interviewees or participants readily gave up their time and informants would show extraordinary patience with my need to back-track over the same ground. At times I would be sought out and stories shared because it was believed I could influence policy. Indeed, the regency heads of both the Department of Education and Culture and the Department of Tourism sought interviews with me, to learn from my findings.

Undertaking research as a trusted practitioner also had a number of advantages. Being well known to the villagers meant rapport was easily re-established. The villagers' experiences from when I took tours to the village provided examples for us to draw upon in discussions. Importantly they trusted my knowledge in the area of research and wanted to gain from it.

Although I wanted the research process to be reciprocal, balancing the applied and interpretative aspects of my research proved more of a challenge than I had expected. As I became more accepted by the communities they increasingly asked my opinion, probed my knowledge and used me as a sounding board for their ideas. Balancing the giving and taking of knowledge proved increasingly difficult during my stay. The process whereby *my* interviews would be turned into *their* interviews, and I would be the giver rather than the taker of knowledge, while particularly apparent during focus groups (cf. Cole, 2004), extended to many interviews.

Knowledge of the tourism system and decision making processes is essential if the villagers are to participate in the planning and management of tourism. During my research the process of transferring knowledge into the community began. I was able to de-mystify the discourse of tourism and clarify issues and positions held by official-dom. I could also provide examples of how problems were dealt with in other destinations. I could feed back what I had learnt from tourists. My research became a two-way learning process.

The multi-method mix of participant observation is an appropriate methodology where learning is to be shared. Although data collection may take longer than with other methodologies the rapport and trust developed during participant observation allow that knowledge to be transferred into the community. This flexible opportunistic method with an adaptable and patient researcher can pay dividends for both the research process and the researchees.

On completion of the research I facilitated a 1-day seminar. While a detailed discussion is beyond this chapter it provided a forum for the researchees to discuss and debate tourism issues. Villagers, government officials and local guides enthusiastically turned up and actively participated. They were keen to hear my recommendations. Although well known and trusted by all the participants, I was an outsider and therefore I was in a good position to chair a debate on some of the thorny issues. The seminar allowed the participants to draw up an action plan for their future tourism development.

For tourism research to get beyond lecture halls and libraries and to reach those most affected by tourism, more researchers need to address the utility of their research and how it can benefit researchees. Further, examples are required on the practice of tourism research and how the knowledge so gained can be shared with those most affected.

References

Angrosino, M. (1986) Son and lover: the anthropologist as non-threatening male. In: Whitehead, T. and Ellen, M. (eds) *Self, Sex and Gender in Cross-Cultural Fieldwork*. University of Illinois Press, Chicago, Illinois, pp. 64–83.

Bernard, R. (1988) *Research Methods in Cultural Anthropology*. Sage, London.

Berno, T. (1996) Cross cultural research methods: content or context? A Cook Islands example. In: Butler, R. and Hinch, T. (eds) *Tourism and Indigenous Peoples*. International Thompson Business Press, London, pp. 376–395.

Burgess, R. (1984) *In the Field. An Introduction to Field Research*. Routledge, London.

Burgess, R. (1990) *In the Field. An Introduction to Field Research*, 2nd edn. Routledge, London.

Burns, P. (1999) *An Introduction to Tourism and Anthropology*. Routledge, London.

Cole, S. (1997a) Anthropologists, local communities and sustainable tourism development. In: Stabler, M. (ed.) *Tourism and Sustainability*. CAB International, Wallingford, UK.

Cole, S. (1997b) Cultural heritage tourism: the villagers' perspective. A case study from Ngada, Flores. In: Nuryanti, W. (ed.) *Tourism and Heritage Management*. Gadjah Mada University Press, Yogyakarta, Indonesia.

Cole, S. (2004) Shared benefits. Long-term research in Eastern Indonesia. In: Goodson, L. and Philimore, J. (eds) *Qualitative Research in Tourism: Ontologies, Epistemologies and Methodologies*. Routledge, London.

Din, K. (1988) Social and cultural impacts of tourism. *Annals of Tourism Research* 15(4), 563–566.

Draine, C. and Hall, B. (1996) *Culture Shock: Indonesia*. Kuperard, London.

Forth, G. (1998) *Beneath the Volcano: Religion, Cosmology and Spirit Classification among the Nage of Eastern Indonesia*. KITLV Press, Leiden, The Netherlands.

Frey, J. and Fontana, A. (1991) The group interview in social research. *The Social Science Journal* 28(2), 175–187.

Gardner, K. and Lewis, D. (1996) *Anthropology, Development and the Post-Modern Challenge*. Pluto Press, London.

Geertz, C. (1973) *The Interpretation of Cultures*. Fontana, London.

Golde, P. (1986) *Women in the Field: Anthropological Experiences*. California University Press, Berkeley, California.

Hammersley, M. and Atkinson, P. (1983) *Ethnography Principles in Practice*. Routledge, London.

Hammersley, M. and Atkinson, P. (1995) *Ethnography Principles in Practice*, 2nd edn. Routledge, London.

Hendry, J. (1999) *An Anthropologist in Japan. Glimpses of Life in the Field*. Routledge, London.

Hitchcock, M. (1991) *Indonesian Textiles*. British Museum Press, London.

Humberstone, B. (1997) Challenging dominant ideologies in the research process. In: Clarke, G. and Humberstone, B. (eds) *Researching Women and Sport*. Macmillan, Basingstoke, UK.

Jorgensen, D.L. (1999) *Participant Observation*. Sage. London.

Kottak, C.P. (1999) *Assault on Paradise: Social Change in a Brazilian Village*, 3rd edn. McGraw Hill Higher Education, Burr Ridge, Illinois.

Kuper, A. (1983) *Anthropology and Anthropologists. The Modern British School*. Routledge and Kegan Paul, London.

MacCannell, D. (1989) *Empty Meeting Grounds: the Tourist Papers*. Routledge, London.

MacClancy, J. (2002) Keeping watch on the seats of power. *Times Higher Educational Supplement,* 21 June, p. 20.

May, W. (1980) Doing ethics: the bearing of ethical theories on fieldwork. *Social Problems* 27(3), 358–370.

May, T. (1997) *Social Research Issues, Methods and Processes*. Oxford University Press, Buckingham, UK.

Monaghan, J. and Just, P. (2000) *Social and Cultural Anthropology: a Very Short Introduction*. Oxford University Press, New York.

Nash, D. (1996) *Anthropology of Tourism*. Pergamon, London.

Preister K. (1987) Issue-centered social impact assessment. In: Wuff, R. and Fiske, S. (eds) *Anthropological Praxis Translating Knowledge into Action*. Westview Press, London.

Punch, K. (1998) *Introduction to Social Research: Quantitative and Qualitative Approaches*. Sage. London.

Reisinger, Y. and Turner, L. (1997) Cross-cultural differences in tourism: Indonesian tourists in Australia. *Tourism Management* 18(3), 139–147.

Reinharz, S. (1992) *Feminist Methods in Social Research*. Oxford University Press, New York.

Robson, C. (1993) *Real World Research: a Resource for Social Scientists and Practitioner Researchers*. Blackwell Publishing, Oxford, UK.

Silverman, D. (1993) *Interpreting Qualitative Data: Methods in Analysing Talk, Text and Interaction*. Sage, London.

Umbu Peku Djawang (1991) The role of tourism in NTT development. In: Barlow, C., Bellis, A. and Andrews, K. (eds) *Nusa Tenggara Timor: the Challenge of Development Political and Social Change*. Monograph 12, ANU University, Canberra, Australia.

Van Willigen, J. (1986) *Applied Anthropology*. Bergin and Garvey, Westpoint, Connecticut.

Wolcott, H. (1990) *Writing up Qualitative Research*. Sage, Newbury Park, California.

7 Tourism Research Practices and Tourist Geographies

DAVID CROUCH

University of Derby, Kedleston Road, Derby DE22 1GB, UK

Introduction

The literature on tourism research methods has begun to be influenced by the significant conceptual developments in cultural geography and related disciplines of the 1990s. These developments offer research methods and practices through which to understand the increasingly complex character of being a tourist; the tourist–space encounter; the construction and constitution of space–destination–site–landscape. Therefore it becomes possible to more critically evaluate and empirically investigate the wider contexts through which tourism operates: brochures, marketing, destination branding, and so on. The significant component for geography here is the ways in which *space* is activated, constructed and constituted by the tourist. Above all, this discourse orientates around research methods that can enlighten our understanding of the *encounter* with spaces created by the tourist through 'doing tourism' (Crouch, 1999). It is this arena of work that is addressed by the present chapter, which seeks to explore the ways in which such new insights can be critically tested, developed and advanced in research approaches and research practice.

Space has long been at the core of geographical thinking. However, new methods have emerged to complement the more familiar, traditional, geographic research methods of spatial measuring and long-

distance mapping; of tourist movements to and between destinations. Space has often been mapped into fairly static models, emphasizing trends rather than processes: business models of production and consumption. Landscapes and destinations have been refigured in the early 1990s in the light of landscape geographies, but posited as constructed *for* the tourist (Ringer and Hughes, 1998a,b).

Here, I examine research methods that result from recent insights concerning the subjective, involved character of the tourist and her/his interface with space in relation to, rather than pre-figured by, particular contexts. The timely contributions of Urry (1990, 2002) follow the emphasis (if not the singularity) of context 'from the middle' (Doel, 2000), momentarily stripping away presumptions of how things work, or have been presumed to work, and 'enter' with research methods that connect with the individual, the tourist. Translated into very explicit tourist terms, the tourist makes (amongst other things) an encounter with space. This chapter presents an empirical analysis of the processes through which the character and significance of space is constructed for the tourist.

In trying to make sense of the 'meaning' of tourism, and the 'production' of destinations, tourist motivation becomes more complex due to the rapidly changing, increasingly nuanced world of contemporary tourism. Such a world influences the future preferences, choices and choice-processes of the tourist and in so doing affects how heritage is constructed and consumed; how cities and rural places are refigured, and how the industry responds to the processes through which tourism shifts. More broadly, the relationships between the tourist and tourism operators and producers becomes problematic, the working of tourism consumption more complex. Similarly, with issues of heritage and the critique of authenticity, the position of the tourist as the object of management and regulation is raised in new ways. The anticipation of tourism changes; for example niche markets turn on a more sophisticated interpretation of what the tourist is doing and how s/he makes sense of the world around him or her. Consequently, the role and mode of policy in tourism may need to be re-thought. There is a strong professional interest in understanding how people make sense of their experiences, places and events. In professional decisions and in research practice, imagination and creativity are essential in this unstable and changing market. The panoply of tourism research on tourist behaviour and motivations has tended to work from the producer's perspective, presumes rationality and linearity in the tourist and seeks to discover how to situate what the tourist does within the framework of formal production, management and policy. In this chapter I position the discussion of methods and research in a brief summary of the theoretical arenas currently contributing to the fuller understanding of contemporary tourism geographies.

Focus on the tourist mobilizes the discussion of *practice* and *performance*. 'Practice' refers to the encounters tourists make with their surrounding material space, a complex arena infused by metaphor and imagination. 'Performance' (as used in this chapter) concerns the tourist-in-action rather than the staged events and displays that resemble the more familiar tableaux of representations found in brochures, televisual and filmic contexts; representations through which places may be experienced *by* the tourist. Of course, all of these con-textual components are interplayed. It is in the articulation between what the tourist does, the industry and wider culture that the methods discussed here are operated.

These methods are situated within a philosophy of social constructionism, a humanistic postmodernism, and concern the everyday production of knowledge and the subject's subjective processes, which are fluid, contingent and complex. An empirical case study is explored that acknowledges the critical reflexivities required of this method. The following section examines the philosophical approach underpinning the research methods. The potential for insight that may derive from such a research approach, through the method, is examined, along with its utility for the wider set of concerns in tourism analysis.

Contextual Grounding for Research Practice

The investigative work on the tourist encounter in geography develops from a phenomenological perspective. It is concerned with interpretations, processes of making sense and of lay geographical knowledge that are fluid, contingent, subjective, multiple-informed and informing. It is post-structuralist, and connects aspects of postmodernism, but not those that claim the world as un-knowable and inaccessible to empirical research. It is also situated in a humanist tradition that acknowledges the dynamic human subject. Using the in-depth qualitative approaches discussed, this work is deductive and is positioned within a social constructionist position. Investigating subjectivities requires critical reflexivity by the researcher. This means acknowledging the researcher's own (subjective) position in relation to the research subjects, and her/his social and cultural position in relation to that of the subjects, and the practices and encounters being investigated. The researcher is involved with a self-awareness of expectations that s/he may project upon the situation, destination or tourist group that may prohibit or interfere with the data collection and handling process.

One particular social constructionist perspective, i.e. the world constructed and constituted through experience, understands ontology as practical, and sense and significance as being built through what is done and the ways in which it is done (Shotter, 1993). Individuals produce their own geographical knowledge through what they do and think (Crouch, 2001), in semi-attachment to contexts and representations. Being a tourist is part of the individual's popular culture, and rather than occurring in a tourist 'bubble', the tourist is a 'consumer-participant', again connected and semi-attached to other areas of human and cultural activity.

The particular focus of 'practice' developed in this chapter is 'embodied practice'. 'Practice' is a widely used term in the social sciences, for example in the work of Bourdieu (1984), socially constructed and situated ways of living produce and reproduce class distinctions. His empirical research in France evidenced practice as 'structured process' in even the most everyday activities and actions that individuals carry out, from the material objects used to decorate a room to the way they eat fish. Tourism choices are also examples of such mundane practices. However, an increasingly critical debate developed of this notion of practice through the post-structuralist focus on the subjectivities and flexibilities inherent in the ways in which individuals negotiate and adjust their lives, as illustrated by Miller's (1998) examination of the anthropologies of consumption and material culture, of which tourism is a part. Focus on embodied practice acknowledges that mind/body processes such as thinking and engaging with the world occur simultaneously. The individual not only thinks but also does, moves and engages the body practically and imaginatively, in relation to material objects, spaces and other people. Such aspects may inform the character of reflexivity, as noted below. The individual is surrounded by spaces which s/he engages with rather than experiences as an onlooker (Crouch, 2001, 2002; Coleman and Crang, 2002).

The French philosopher Merleau-Ponty (1962) built on extensive empirical research to argue that the individual is engulfed by space and encounters that space both multi-sensually and multi-dimensionally. Touch, a feeling of surrounding space, sight, smell, hearing and taste are worked interactively through the way the individual uses her/his body expressively – it turns, touches, feels, moves on, dwells, and in so doing the world is given significance. In an investigation of tourism branding and marketing in New Zealand, Cloke and Perkins (1998) have explored the possibilities of the individual acting bodily in a discussion of white water rafting. Things, artefacts, views and surrounding spaces become signified through how the individual feels and how s/he feels about them.

Whilst avoiding the familiar trap of romanticizing tourism, the individual can be poetic, and thereby lend distinctive significance to places, events and things. Veijola and Jokinen (1994) explored the enactment of the bodily sense through a discourse on the body and the beach. Their work is formulated not merely through the appearance of the body as inscribed with conventions, expectations and projected desire, but in terms of the bodily practice of the beach by sensuous, and sensual, and poetic beings. Individuals can overflow the boundaries of the rational and the objective and be playful, imaginative and go beyond what is evidently 'there' in an outward, rational sense. This capture of space may be described as a poetics of practice, as Birkeland explored in her discussion of the experience of the North Cape in Norway (de Certeau, 1984; Birkeland, 1999). The tourist acts alongside others, s/he is not the individual alone as so often imagined in tourism. Acting inter-subjectively, the character of events, experiences and sites is additionally attributed through what people do and how they feel (there) in relation to others (Crossley, 1995). Burkitt (1999) has discussed the 'embodied' character of this process of practical ontology and its emergent ontological knowledge, highlighting its potential role in refiguring the self and negotiating identity. Embodied practice is engaged in the flow of reflexive thinking that the individual employs (Lash and Urry, 1994) to make sense of their relatedness to the world around them.

Similarly, performance is a profoundly embodied act; expressive, potentially poetic, inter-subjective (Tulloch, 2000) and potentially elusory (Radley, 1995, Dewesbury, 2000). Performance concerns the enaction of life through protocols of engagement, surrounded by ritualized practice, working to pre-given codes, habitually repeated; conservative in nature and working to cultural givens. Yet it can also be potentially disruptive and unsettling, or at least have the potential of openness in refiguring space and the self in relation to those protocols (Carlsen, 1996; Crouch, 2003). The tourist experience may, then, be sought and used in ways that both reassure and pursue risk, in different proportions and tensions. The general discourse on performance, informed by performance studies, understands the individual's actions to be done in relation to the self or to others, 'performed for', including self-regulation and negotiation, inter-subjectively. Individuals may seek to move life forward, and individuals have the potential both to secure where they are in life and what things mean to them, and to change it: 'holding on' and 'going further', becoming something new. The expressive character in performativity is especially significant in 'becoming'. Dance has been considered in terms of its potential for opening up possibilities in the individual through what s/he does. Dance can combine choreography and freedom to express oneself creatively; dance is a significant constituent of the tourism experience, and Malbon's (1999) work on clubbing in London bears comparison with youth tourism in Ibiza and Rio.

The tourist is active in making the geographies of tourism, and taking these in different ways in relation to her/his own life. For example, Edensor (2001) has explored the performative nature of tourism. In his work on the Taj Mahal he has identified the diverse ways in which different groups of visitors make their way around the site, amble and queue and make sense of their experience and the spaces they occupy (Edensor, 1998). These diverse performances interact with, but may not be simply pre-determined by, social category, marketing frameworks and destination management. Indeed, particular social-cultural life contexts may interact in specific ways along the processes of the encounter, and, as a result, distinctive and hybrid knowledges, attitudes and values may emerge.

But tourism can also be used to regulate the self, to sustain or achieve security in life, to 'hold on' to life-references. Even in the apparently extreme tourism of white water rafting there is considerable effort to achieve security in the way things are done. Similarly, dance can be enacted 'safely' through repetition, rather than daringly by 'going further', by extending the boundaries of possibility (Radley, 1995; Thrift, 1997; Malbon, 1999). The care that tourists may give to identifying the minutiae of their travel, of knowing what to expect in advance, and the frequent repeated visits they may make, points to tourism as both 'holding on' and 'going further'. To investigate the ways in which these different elements may be negotiated by the tourist offers the potential to understand better the tourist consumer and how s/he may develop her/his own significance through events, places and things; and in so doing provide insights as to the limitations in the messages offered in tourism representations, brochures and staged events. Individuals negotiate things, and tourists are no exception. Practice and performance colour the character of consumption, the work of product and destination image and so on.

Such approaches are in no sense anti-contextual, nor do they privilege the individual and her/his subjectivities. Instead, they refute the privileging of contexts, of the gaze, and of traditional industry-determined perspectives of what tourism is and how it works (Nash, 2000). Being able to investigate empirically the potential insights requires a sensitive and responsive methodological approach and a carefully constructed research instrument that includes the identification of subjects, in-depth data capture of tourist–space encounters and a mode of analysis that can unpack and make connections. In the following section one particular investigation and investigative approach are identified with reference to an empirical investigation (Crouch, 1999, 2001, 2003).

Method and Research Practice

The research method explored in this section applies the conceptual orientation sketched in the preceding section through a consideration of an empirical investigation into touring caravanning in the UK, elements of which have been presented elsewhere (Crouch, 1999, 2001, 2003). In this chapter the ways in which the philosophy discussed has been applied to the setting up of a methodological approach, and how it has influenced the practice of the method, are discussed sequentially. In addition these components of method are considered through an examination of how the analytical method may be used critically to interpret the events through the philosophical debate presented, and the cautions and care needed in undertaking both the data collection and its analysis.

The case

Caravanning does not bear the romantic character of more familiar, more exotic cases in tourism analysis, consequently it has received little theoretical or empirical attention. This makes it a very attractive research avenue. Rather than the research being contextualized by the more familiar and powerful industry- and folklore-led contexts, the case was approached in a much more open, objective, and almost wary way. However, caravanning has its own contexts and folklore, and in popular culture it is often rendered obscure; but caravanning has for the last decade and more experienced an increasingly up-market and more stylish image such that touring sites have been re-designed, partly as a result of tourist experiences of other European locations and partly as a result of industry changes. The mediated contexts and folklore of caravanning have been the subject of semiotic investigation by Ravenscroft and myself (Crouch and Ravenscroft, 1996; Crouch,

1999, 2001). However, these contexts focused on the subjects themselves and where they directed us through what they said. Whilst we did not seek to pre-determine the character of the contexts, we came to acknowledge how they worked 'from the middle' (Doel, 2000: 421).

Research intentions

This investigation sought to understand the processes involved in visiting tourist locations. It sought to gather varied and diverse data, hermeneutically, to construct a kaleidoscope of the components that comprise the encounter a tourist makes in relation to material and metaphorical geography. Furthermore, it identified and tracked how these diverse components may be welded together through the ongoing knowledge the tourist constructs and constitutes. In other words it explored how these contingent knowledges may be reflected upon at a later date, and how these reflections may influence decisions over which destinations and events to choose in the future.

Informant identification: identifying the research frame

Initial informants were identified through clubs whose members were visiting particular locations. The locations were determined by the clubs, as the interviewing necessarily followed where individuals were visiting. The location choices were moderated by the practical time/accessibility for the researcher. From the initial contacts made, usually a committee member attending an event, snowballing was used as a means to meet further subjects. Of course, some subjects were unwilling to respond.

Thirty households were interviewed in three general locations (Essex, in south-east England; South Yorkshire; and Weardale, both in northern England). These general areas were chosen in an effort to relate to, but not be prescribed by, certain generalizations in terms of the socio-economic character of each club's membership and differences in general location. The overall aim was to provide a rich and diverse, yet reasonably accessible, set of spaces/landscapes. In all, 12 long weekends were spent in the field by the researchers.

Data capture

In-depth, intensive ethnographic-type interviews were conducted with those participants who had agreed to take part in the research. The qualification of 'ethnographic-type' is given because this approach clearly differs from the more familiar, classical anthropological method of immersion in a sub-culture over an extended period of time, such as 1 calendar year. However, as Pink (2000) has recently argued through empirical ethnography, this time-limitation is not necessarily the only form of ethnography, especially in investigations of cultural events in contemporary, Western societies.

Each interview took place over a period of between 2 and several hours. These interviews consisted of a small number of prepared questions, and 'conversation lines' through which a more exploratory and responsive engagement with the subjects was able to occur. It was thus semi-structured, with the emphasis on the 'semi'. Sometimes the interviews were continued intermittently and merged with other research activities such as participant observations, and sometimes they merged into larger interviews whereby groups of individuals participated in the process. This multiple character of the 'interview' is appropriate where the actual character of the events examined merges in a fluid way too. This approach offered opportunities for observing interactions and inter-subjective processes at work. Crucially the interviews were associated with participant observation. This included the self-awareness and reflexivity of the researcher and the more semi-detached observation of the identified subjects. In addition to observation of identified subjects the researcher/s noted other subjects and their practices across the times of the research period. This allowed the researcher to gather further examples of the

practice of caravanning, whilst being limited in terms of how these examples may be connected to particular individual narratives.

The research methods, then, focused upon a range of caravanning activities and spaces, including pubs, barbecues, going for walks (with the informants), playing games and sharing a beer. This enabled a flow of conversation between groups of varying size, different exchanges and some checking of narrative. Given the respective (in)competences of the researcher/s with the activities involved, neither had more than a cursory understanding of caravanning, then making these encounters was a very varied experience. Although these were not spaces we had encountered before, we felt able to translate and transfer encounters from other spaces and other forms of tourism to the investigation. We experienced what Katz (1994) has called the 'in between' character of the researcher, joining in socially, yet maintaining a semi-detached position. What we felt ourselves in the moments of our own encounters with these spaces, then, was not necessarily to be equated with our subjects. In any case, as researchers, we had a distinctive 'learnt' as well as experienced set of ideas of what these kinds of places, and their events, might signify. Moreover, our subjects had not asked us to do the work, yet we sought to encounter them. We both *Othered* ourselves and felt *Othered*. We felt difficulty in encountering because our subjects were 'on holiday'; presumably enjoying themselves. This kind of intervention as research practice can inevitably disrupt, detract and formalize. Our subjects had distinctive responses to us. Some subjects felt that we were there to understand site landscapes, destination images, which we were not, but talk like this often opened up further areas of exploration. Others sought to use the interviews to promote their sites, and to disrupt their stereotypes. Most subjects sought to make us feel comfortable and welcome, but not all. For example, an individual wearing many decorative chains who was pulled along by a dog 'trained for manwork' approached one researcher sitting calmly in a deckchair talking and drinking tea. The individual asked the researcher what he was doing. To his reply the man said, 'You must be fucking mad'. Even researchers are human beings; we too feel discomfort, have fun, enjoy human relations, behave practically and feel romantic.

A researcher caravanning alone tended to hinder conversation. Most caravanners were in families, or with partners, so we began to go with our partners. Caravanners seemed to be 'straight' and 'ordinary' individuals, and sought to present themselves as such in order to cope with their own 'Othering' by popular culture, pulling an awkward-looking and rather anti-*style* box along the road and parking for a few days at each location. In these several remarks it is evident that every tourist activity has its own character to which the researcher needs to attend, and to be open-minded, responsive, engaging, tolerant. Different tourist activities and locations may be, to us, respectively dramatic, mundane or otherwise. In no case should such research practice be seen as academic 'slumming', but rather an opportunity to understand lay practices and knowledges and potentially disrupt particular academic prescriptions of what is happening, what it all means (Katz, 1994: 72). At the same time, we do not pretend to be the same, but claim to be able to understand through the nature of the encounters we construct in the fieldwork. Our field of inquiry is a bundle of loosely bounded practices that happen in relation to space/time; a site of research encounter (Clifford, 1997).

The wealth and richness of data generated by these ethnographic-type encounters can be analysed by computer packages such as ATI and NUDIST. However, the character of this work, and the insights it can deliver, are likely to require close involvement with the data to avoid too prescriptive an interpretation that can ignore the processes it seeks to unpack and to explain.

The character of data collected and its analysis

What follows is an extract from one researcher's 1997 field diary from Weardale in Suffolk:

I am just out ambling, 'mooching about' as caravanners seem to call it. I walk across the site, from the green where the 'van is and onto the track that leads to the shop. I am momentarily aware of people moving and the smell of breakfasts cooking is significant all around me. I hear people talking behind me and notice a group of children cycling around. I am still tired from a night in the 'van and feel my body to be slow. Two women have just met, apparently not come across each other for over a year, but they are animated in conversation standing along the track. The soft grass under my feet gives way to a hard path and I turn and feel the wind as I step out from the relative enclosure of the 'vans. My next steps are more hurried as I express a sense of freedom by shuffling down the slope that leads to a calm hollow surrounded by trees; my walk feels looser. I wonder where to go next, so far having been moving at random. Rejoining the track I note several people walking back from the shop and some half nod to me, I gesture to them. My body feels gradually alerting to the morning, and as I half bend round I pick up the activity from several 'vans, a little away from my track, in different directions, as people spill out and across the wider field around which they are parked. I arrive back, having wandered through what feel like private spaces close to the 'vans and Jock offers me coffee.

In these field-notes I, as the researcher, sought to pick up a sense of activity and movement, of how I am performing in space and responding to it. I spent time amongst individuals who are on a weekend caravanning rally. I made an effort to report how I felt about my own performativities and awareness in relation to myself. I note the multi-sensual encounters I make with spaces, the inter-subjectivity apparent in the way others move and gesture and influence each other in the space I/they cross. I am not a regular to caravanning and my intervention is one of visitor and observer. I am using someone else's van and share few of the necessary tasks that I notice the others doing, although I join in with getting things ready. Such an intervention perhaps idealizes the everyday awareness individuals have of what they are doing as they may be more focused on tasks; at the same time I may interpret the world in a way that is too rationally performative. Some of the individuals are getting routine tasks done – collecting water and so on, others are out enjoying a 'mooch' too. These seem to be everyday, uneventful things. In this fieldnote, components of the performative are realized in a heightened awareness of hyper-reflexivity. How much do these notes record and communicate the ways in which individuals perform activities, space and time?

These performances happen across spaces in relation to the surrounding physical world of objects and other people amongst which the individual moves, acts and enacts responses; they are contained in setting up the van, grouping-up with friends to have tea, sorting the barbecue, resting and just 'hanging out'; in fact various activities. Each activity is marked by protocols that can include times for some activities, ways of doing things and so on. The material spaces are a flat field on which to park vehicles likely to be surrounded by evident physical boundaries. The individual handles equipment, just sits, greets or ignores others and copes with anxieties in relationships. Each of these doings is performed bodily, contains numerous gestures, mobilities, turns and touching. They may be envisaged tasks and may be done according to a pre-considered performance, club rules, routine practical tasks, habitual performances that fill the time between one and the next.

However, an individual's understanding of what they do and the space where they do it is more nuanced and complex than it may seem and thus not easily second-guessed; nor does the behaviour of individuals comply with obvious or pre-set categories, as the following exemplified statements and actions illustrate:

> **Tim talks:** Caravanning, it all makes me smile inside. I mean, everyone just comes down to the ford and just stands there and watches life go by. It's amazing how you can have pleasure from something like that. I just sit down and look and I get so much enjoyment out of sitting and looking and doing nothing. We wake up in the morning, open the bedroom door and you're like

> breathing air into your living ... We walk and talk ... I love to cycle and fish.

His moving to the edge of the ford by the water, and 'just stand[ing]' is a performative act. He discovers feeling by doing. His performance comprises haptic vision, caring, relating and finding it uplifting, touch and other performativities as he feels his body encounter the space between the van and the water's edge. He smells as he breathes what feels like different air. He is aware of this and constructs his representation of what he does through an interpretation of how he constitutes space as spacing. The space becomes his own through what he does and the way he does it. He gathers his sense of what he is doing through these components of performance, not just from other-figured information. In drawing on individuals' talk I acknowledge the significance of what they say. Their practice and performance occurs in a flow of gestures, plural and unrelated moments in a collection of nodes, gatherings, moments, collisions along flows where the particular character of what they do is felt to be significant. This may be important in terms of lay geographical knowledge, sense of the self and its identities, as components of an ongoing and fluid practical ontology.

Members of the caravanning club, for example, are familiar with its orientation towards activities and the club slogan of going 'where you like when you like'. Members refer to these in describing what they do. Other, possibly less self-conscious, contexts such as gender influence what they do and the way they do it, but these contexts may be drawn into their performativities rather than crudely pre-figure what that performance is. These individuals do not merely perform in an expressivity of anything as such, of anticipations or contexts. Through performance they engage, discover, open, habitually perform and enact, reassure, become, create in and through the performance. So expressivity is both engaging and momentary, now, not necessarily prefigured by either 'contexts' or representations or even wanting to respond to what is felt 'out there'. They do not bring expressivity 'with them' but constitute it in the now. As Burkitt (1999: 75) argues, our selves and the surrounding world are not engaged as data but our expressive relation with it.

Tim's narrative, time spent at the caravan site, is expressed very much in terms of his son's disability. At the site, the son is able to (re-)discover his confidence, interact with other people, feel at ease. The family cycles and walks, enjoys barbecues. Particular places on the way to the site are marked with the significance of doing the journey ('Once you pass C – you feel different'). Tim feels that in what he is doing not only his son, but he himself is opening into a feeling that moves further than what is discovered, of himself and the world about him that may be said to 'open up'. He feels a suspension of concern and constraints over how to feel. He is *feeling* doing. Thereby he constructs gaps in his life that he performs and fills. Thus he feels (as) he becomes. He recounts this as something he does from time to time, but re-discovers its feeling every time. He is aware of others feeling the same thing, or so he feels. He encounters this performance as his own, and inter-subjectively. He expresses his feeling and becoming in language, but constituted performatively through his poise and disposition.

When caravanners value being able to 'go where you like when you like' and compare it with 'the humdrum' of life they 'touch base', but their life moves on through what they are doing. To say 'go where you like when you like' captures the feeling of freedom they discover themselves, but also reiterates the slogan of one of their clubs even though the planned freedoms are within the choice confines of local club-arranged weekly venues in agreement with landowners. In both cases there are regulations and constraints yet these do not necessarily have a priori constraining influences on the ways in which individuals may performatively space them.

Things they do may not seem so different in isolation from other things. However, they encounter and 'know' they are doing something in immediate intimate contexts

they have created (by choosing to go, by moving to do something) that may use ordinary objects but be touched, shared, engaged in space differently. Sitting outdoors in a deckchair may seem hardly significant, but for the caravanner Doris it was, because of the way it was performatively achieved. Standing and staring at a view of water and grass is similarly felt significant for the caravanner Tim because of the whole series of movements in which it involved him, and the plurality of situations that it invoked, as is discussed below.

Space and landscape can be ambiguous, suggesting that the significance of destinations is inflected with other elements of the tourist encounter: 'No, it's not the countryside that matters so much ... (yet) we were in the middle of a horrible field ... Sometimes there's fishing and long walks ... the other... really nice, deer walking round and forest *all around us*' (my italics). Sometimes space is very 'straightforward': in the middle of a field, a barbecue and good booze. All you need is a few vans, a bit of a field. Memory is inflected too in making this intimate geography. Mick visited the same location as a child, '... childhood is another important thing, the memories you've stored up. If you were hot you put the orange juice in the river to cool'. Again these notes are drawn from an embodied practice through which space can be memorialized (Radley, 1990).

Some of those people interviewed may have talked for some time, yet in the content of their conversation/interview spoke of very little more than descriptions of journeys made, in terms of lists of B roads, rather than reflections upon those journeys. This content was felt less powerful in lending insight to the analysis, yet demonstrates a practical and objective, rather than playful and subjective, encounter, and this was noted.

Conclusions

In changing destinations the individual may seek to continue the possibility of change, however frustrated their desire may be. In any of these cases, people negotiate what they are doing, how they feel, and cope with, or reject, staged performances and visual or aural tableaux that precede and follow, and may seek to reconstruct memory in the present. Memory is temporalized and can reinvigorate what one is doing 'now', but also is reinvigorated and can be re-routed in the 'now', but not in an exact re-run of the past (Crang, 2001). Performing time/spacing appears to be more than a linear 'moving on' from ideas, and memory is operated as an active character of performativity. Representations of tourism events and sites do not act on a *tabula rasa*. Most individuals have experienced a tourist site or event, or find it resonant in other parts of their own lives. Individual places, and objects too, are remembered as significant because of the ways in which they were encountered (Radley, 1990). The significance of places and artefacts is not merely constituted through significance that is pre-given and projected, but also is gained in the practice and in combinations of the two, and through reflection.

The tourist 'gaze' is an important component of a deeper, wider practice (Urry, 2002). Looking is complex too. There is an engaging, connecting, caring content and character of looking, rather than merely a detached, observing, exploitative one. Of course, these different elements work together, or may figure more prominently at certain moments than others. Yet it is insufficient to argue that the presentation of a sight for sight-seeing necessarily enforces the detached gaze. The achievement of regulation is complicated through the diversities of consumption. The diversities, partly through social distinctions, of tourism enable individuals in contemporary culture to experience something different in their world outside from being a tourist (Urry, 2002). Yet rather than comprehend the tourist acting in a tourist bubble, there is increasing evidence that tourism overflows the boundaries of its apparent tight contexts and is rather a component of ongoing life (Crouch *et al.*, 2001). Moreover the individual may use tourism to discover, reaffirm or change his/her identity. Desforges (2002) argues that individuals back-packing in the

Andes may use this activity in an active negotiation of their identity. They may enact this through their bodily practice in particular places, in cultural contexts and in ways in which the individual makes sense. Along the way they may enact adjustments, negotiations and also tensions in their lives, relationships and identities. Tourism emerges from this discussion as a less stable component of contemporary culture, less easily controlled and managed in terms of contemporary society.

The intensive method explored in this chapter offers access and insight to the ways in which geography matters in tourism through addressing the tourist. The geographies of tourism emerge through this research practice as complex, fluid, subjective. The discourses of embodied practice and performativity concern the individual and thereby seek to comprehend more completely what, for example, the tourist does, and the sense he and she makes of what s/he does. These interpretations offer new components for research methods too. In-depth and ethnographic work, including visual methods and participant observation, are some of the key mechanics that provide insight into practice and performance and demand reflexivity of the researchers. Heritage, sustainable culture and environments and indeed the notion of authenticity are enabled to address new grounds through which tourism generates significance and value. The power of tourism in the contemporary world may also need to be refigured through the discourse on practice and performance. Whilst the power of investment and global capital movements, of major redevelopment and the erasure of local cultures and environments need not be rehearsed (Meethan, 2001), the cumulative, and diverse, consequences of tourism need to be comprehended from an awareness of the tourist's competencies in refiguring the world. There is considerable potential in engaging the insights of practice and performance in relation to the diverse contexts of tourism – brochures and other aspects of visual culture – with what individuals do at home. Thus whilst the idea of embodied practice may appear ephemeral, practice constantly informs knowledge, holds on, reshapes and refigures. The approaches considered in this chapter enhance the understanding of tourism consumption.

Recent work in material and visual culture studies points to the more active, subjective work that the consumer does in making things matter (Miller, 1998). The relative power of particular site-visits in the flow of tourist activity may be more complex than the guidebook privileging may imply.

Tourism analysis, whether in terms of the power of geography, and landscape in terms of individual sites/'sights', or the power of the individual in gazing upon them, has tended to extract particular moments of experience, taken as 'the big issues', and to work with one line of enquiry (MacCannell, 1999; Urry, 2002). Instead of such over-arching perspectives, the complexity of tourism needs to be unpacked since the tourist can refigure the significance attached to particular sites.

References

Birkeland, I. (1999) The mytho-poetic in northern travel. In: Crouch, D. (ed.) *Leisure/tourism Geographies*. Routledge, London, pp. 17–33.

Bourdieu, P. (1984) *Distinction: a Critique of the Social Judgement of Taste*. Routledge, London.

Burkitt, I. (1999) *Bodies of Thought: Embodiment, Identity and Modernity*. Sage, London.

Carlsen, M. (1996) *Performance, a Critical Introduction*. Routledge, London.

Clifford, J. (1997) *Routes: Travel and Translation in the Late Twentieth Century*. Harvard University Press, Cambridge, Massachusetts.

Cloke, P. and Perkins, H.S. (1998) Cracking the Canyon with the awesome foursome. *Environment and Planning D: Society and Space* 16, 185–218.

Coleman, S. and Crang, M. (eds) (2002) *Tourism: Between Place and Performance*. Berghan, London.

Crang, M. (2001) Rhythms of the city: temporalised space and motion. In: May, J. and Thrift, N. (eds) *Time/Space: Geographies of Temporality*. Routledge, London, pp. 187–207.

Crossley, N. (1995) Merleau-Ponty, the elusory body and carnal sociology. *Body and Society* 1, 43–61.

Crouch, D. (1999) The intimacy and expansion of space. In: Crouch, D. (ed.) *Leisure/tourism Geographies*. Routledge, London, pp. 257–276.

Crouch, D. (2001) Spatialities and the feeling of doing. *Social and Cultural Geography* 2(1), 61–75.

Crouch, D. (2002) Surrounded by place: embodied encounters. In: Coleman, S. and Crang, M. (eds) *Tourism: Between Place and Performance*. Berghan, London, pp. 207–219.

Crouch, D. (2003) Spacing, performativity and becoming. *Environment and Planning A* 35(11), 1945–1960.

Crouch, D. and Lubbren, N. (eds) (2003) *Visual Culture and Tourism*. Berg, Oxford, UK.

Crouch, D. and Ravenscroft, N. (1995) Culture, social difference and the leisure experience: consuming countryside. In: McFee, G. *et al.* (eds) *Leisure Cultures: Values, Lifestyles, Genders*. Leisure Studies Association, Eastbourne, UK.

Crouch, D., Aronsson, L. and Wahlstroem, L. (2001) Tourist encounters. *Tourist Studies* 1(3), 253–270.

De Certeau, M. (1984) *The Practice of Everyday Life*. University of California Press, Berkeley, California.

Desforges, L. (2002) Traveling the world: identity and travel biography. *Annals of Tourism Research* 27(4), 926–945.

Dewesbury, J.-D. (2000) Performativity and the event. *Environment and Planning D: Society and Space* 18, 473–496.

Doel, M. (2000) *Postmodern Geographies, the Diabolical Art of Spatial Science*. Edinburgh University Press, Edinburgh.

Edensor, T. (1998) *Tourists at the Taj*. Routledge, London.

Edensor, T. (2001) Performing tourism, staging tourism: (re)producing tourist space and practice. *Tourist Studies* 1, 59–82.

Fiske, J. (1989) *Understanding Popular Culture*. Routledge, London.

Harre, R. (1993) *The Discursive Mind*. Polity Press, Cambridge, UK.

Katz, C. (1994) Playing the field: questions of fieldwork in geography. *Professional Geographer* 46, 67–72.

Lash, S. and Urry, J. (1994) *The Economies of Signs and Space*. Sage, London.

MacCannell, D. (1999) *The Tourist: a New Theory of the Leisure Class*. Macmillan, London.

Malbon, B. (1999) *Clubbing: Dancing, Ecstasy, Vitality*. Routledge, London.

Meethan, K. (2001) *Tourism in Global Society*. Palgrave, Basingstoke, UK.

Merleau-Ponty, M. (1962) *The Phenomenology of Perception*. Routledge, London.

Miller, D. (ed.) (1998) *Material Culture: Why Some Things Matter*. Routledge, London.

Nash, C. (2000) Performativity in practice: some recent work in cultural geography. *Progress in Human Geography* 24(4), 653–664.

Pink, S. (2000) 'Informants' who come 'home'. In: Amit, V. (ed.) *Constructing the Field: Ethnographic Fieldwork in the Contemporary World*. Routledge, London, pp. 96–119.

Radley, A. (1990) Artefacts, memory and a sense of the past. In: Middleton, D. and Edwards, D. (eds) *Collective Remembering*. Sage, London, pp. 46–59.

Radley, A. (1995) The Elusory Body and Social Constructionist. *Theory Body and Society* 1(2), 3–23.

Ringer, G. and Hughes, G. (1998a) Tourism and the semiological realisation of space. In: Ringer, G. and Hughes, G. (eds) *Destinations: Cultural Landscapes of Tourism*. Routledge, London, pp. 17–32.

Ringer, G. and Hughes, G. (1998b) *Destinations: Cultural Landscapes of Tourism*. Routledge, London.

Shotter, J. (1993) *The Politics of Everyday Life*. Polity Press, Cambridge, UK.

Thrift, N. (1997) The still point: resistance, expressive embodiment and dance. In: Pile, S. and Keith, M. (eds) *Geographies of Resistance*. Routledge, London, pp. 124–154.

Tulloch, J. (2000) *Performing Culture*. Sage, London.

Urry, J. (2002) *The Tourist Gaze*, 2nd edn. Sage, London.

Veijola, S. and Jokinen, E. (1994) The body in tourism. *Theory and Society* 11, 125–151.

8 Revisiting Delphi: the Delphi Technique in Tourism Research

BRIAN GARROD[1] AND ALAN FYALL[2]

[1]Institute of Rural Sciences, University of Wales Aberystwyth, Llanbadarn Campus, Aberystwyth, Ceredigion, SY23 3AL, UK; [2]International Centre for Tourism and Hospitality Research, Bournemouth University, Poole, UK

Introduction

The Delphi technique belongs to a set of qualitative research methods that rely on the judgement of individuals presumed to be experts in the subject under consideration. Other 'judgemental' research techniques include juries of executive opinion, subjective probability assessments, and consumer intentions surveys (Frechtling, 1996). First developed in the 1950s by researchers at the RAND Corporation in the USA, the Delphi technique has found many and various applications across a number of topics, including tourism. Indeed, the Delphi technique is widely recognized to represent a very flexible research method, and one that can lend an added dimension of rigour to addressing the kinds of questions and issues that are difficult to research using more conventional methods. The technique is also much admired for its ability to dig beneath the surface of issues and to tap into expertise and insight that would otherwise be unavailable to the researcher.

The Delphi technique has nevertheless raised considerable controversy among academics and research professionals more generally, particularly with respect to its value as a research methodology. Hence while there have been some ardent supporters of the Delphi technique, there have also

been many fierce critics. The intense academic debate over the methodological worth of the Delphi technique, along with a long-standing lack of rigorous and widely agreed guidelines as to when and how best it should be applied (Rowe and Wright, 1999), and some 'sloppy execution' in the early years (Stewart, 1987), has arguably left the method with a tarnished reputation. Indeed, some commentators have concluded that the Delphi technique is of no value as a research tool. Bowers (1997: 141), for example, dismisses Delphi simply as 'discredited'.

The purpose of this chapter is to introduce the Delphi technique, to assess its major strengths and weaknesses, and to explore how the method might be applied in the context of tourism research using a case study of a Delphi study conducted into how the term 'marine ecotourism' might best be defined (Garrod, 2003a). The case study is instructive in that a number of innovative features were built in to the methodology, including the use of a straw model to guide experts through the Delphi process and the use of success criteria to determine whether or not the expert panel remained sufficiently well balanced. These innovations attempted to address some of the evident shortcomings of previous Delphi studies in the tourism field. The chapter then concludes by presenting some tentative operational guidelines for applying the Delphi technique in tourism research.

Philosophical Context of the Delphi Technique

The basic rationale of the Delphi technique is to elicit judgements on problems that are highly complex and necessarily subjective, requiring significant levels of knowledge and expertise on the part of respondents. Such problems are not easily dealt with using conventional questionnaire- or interview-based research techniques. For example, even generating a sampling frame may be impossible due to the limited number of individuals in a position to make valid responses to the survey. Potential respondents, being highly specialist, also tend to be broadly dispersed in geographic terms, so that the costs involved in bringing them together into a focus group or expert committee might well be prohibitive. The Delphi technique seeks to minimize these problems by making use of a small panel of experts and by enabling them to interact 'virtually', without actually having to meet one another. Similarly, it is widely recognized that asking respondents to make one-off judgements on issues that are highly complex and inherently controversial may result in false conclusions being drawn from conventional survey-based studies. The iterative nature of the Delphi technique, in which respondents are given the opportunity to make their judgements again on the basis of informed reflection, is said to reduce the potential for respondents to make snap judgements. This is likely to increase the accuracy of the study findings and make them more reliable (Ayton et al., 1999).

The Delphi method would therefore seem to have a number of inherent advantages in comparison with other survey methods. It is important to recognize, however, that the Delphi technique was never intended to serve as a substitute for more statistically rigorous or model-based procedures – to which it has been shown generally to be inferior (Rowe and Wright,

1999) – but as a practical solution to the problems of analysing issues to which these more conventional techniques are not readily applicable. It is at the distant edges of research, where the standard research methodologies are not so easily applied, that the Delphi technique comes into its own. Indeed, a review of comparative studies undertaken by Rowe and Wright (1999) indicates that Delphi consistently outperforms both statistical groups and standard interacting groups in such situations.

What is the Delphi Technique?

Helmer (1972: 15) describes the Delphi technique as: 'a systematic method of collecting opinions from a group of experts through a series of questionnaires, in which feedback on the group's opinion distribution is provided between question rounds while preserving the anonymity of the respondent's responses' (cited in Masser and Foley, 1987: 217–218).

The Delphi procedure is thus deceptively simple, involving the anonymous elicitation of group judgements using an iterative survey technique with a feedback loop. Rowe and Wright (1999) specify four key features that may be regarded as necessary for a procedure to be regarded as 'Delphi': anonymity, iteration, controlled feedback, and the statistical aggregation of group response. The anonymity of respondents is preserved by conducting the Delphi survey by post, e-mail or, occasionally, personal interviews with a member of the research team. The purpose of maintaining respondent anonymity is to reduce the potential for peer pressure, organizational allegiances or personalities to enter into the respondents' judgemental processes. This means that the issues involved are more likely to be judged on their intrinsic merit alone, minimizing the potential for outside influences to enter into respondents' complex and often controversial judgements. Full respondent anonymity is preserved during the various iterations, or 'rounds', of the Delphi study. This iteration gives respondents several 'bites at the cherry', enabling them to think more deeply about the issues at hand, to cogitate on the problem, and ultimately to apply their expertise. Individuals are at liberty to digress from their initial opinions, and are able to do so without fear of losing face in the eyes of other experts in their field (Rowe and Wright, 1999). Controlled feedback is given between survey rounds in order to inform panellists of the group's aggregate judgement. Often this feedback is in the form of a median value, although sometimes this information is supplemented by anonymous written justifications of selected panellists (for example, those whose judgements fell outside of the inter-quartile range). In the 'classical' Delphi method, researchers look for a movement towards consensus among the experts. When a sufficient degree of consensus is achieved the Delphi process is ended and the resulting group judgement may then be applied to the problem at hand. It should be noted, however, that some of the applications to which the Delphi technique has more recently been put do not seek convergence, divergence in group opinion being considered equally valid.

Based on descriptions of the technique by Archer (1976), Richey et al. (1985), Smith (1995) and Frechtling (1996), Table 8.1 summarizes the basic steps involved in a typical Delphi study. To begin with, a panel of experts is assembled. Members are selected on the basis of their knowledge and expertise in subject areas related to the problem to be addressed. Panel size is not considered to be a critical issue. Indeed, Smith (1995) argues that the panel size should be determined by the number of experts available, which is typically 40 to 50, but adds that successful Delphi studies have been conducted with as few as four and as many as 904 panellists. Yong et al. (1989), meanwhile, suggest that a panel of between 15 and 20 is generally sufficient. What is considered to be critical, however, is that the Delphi panel needs to be 'balanced' in terms of the background and capabilities of its members, and to remain so throughout the successive rounds of the study (Wheeller et al., 1990). If the panel becomes unbalanced, their group judgement is likely to be biased in favour of individuals who have characteristics that are over-represented in the panel.

The first round of a Delphi study is often referred to as the 'scoping round'. Here the experts are encouraged to establish the central focus of the study in terms of the major issues that need to be addressed. Panellists are usually sent a questionnaire, with reminders normally given to those not completing it by a pre-specified deadline. An information pack is often also presented to

Table 8.1. Basic steps in the Delphi technique.

1. Choose the members of the coordinating group.
2. Develop criteria for evaluating potential candidates for the expert panel.
3. Identify potential candidates, perhaps on basis of a review of literature/professional associations.
4. Request their participation (perhaps by a prestigious person).
5. Finalize panel composition.
6. Identify issues to be considered and develop the initial (scoping) questionnaire.
7. Send the first questionnaire.
8. Collate the responses.
9. Develop the second (convergence) questionnaire, incorporating all new input; perhaps using a numerical scale or ranking system to calibrate responses.
10. Send the second questionnaire.
11. Collate the responses.
12. Undertake further iterations as necessary (perhaps until an acceptable level of convergence is achieved).
13. Send summary results to all respondents.
14. Apply the judgement(s) to solve the problem(s) being addressed through the Delphi study.

the panellists at the beginning of the study, so as to ensure that they all begin from a common starting point. The resources of the research team are also often put at the disposal of panellists who feel they need further information – perhaps in the form of an influential report or paper – in order to improve their judgement.

Subsequent rounds are normally termed 'convergence rounds'. Panellists typically receive a summary of the aggregate group judgement on the questions included in the previous survey round, along with a new questionnaire that asks them to make their judgement again. Responses may be quantified, ranked, measured on some kind of scale, or even textual. Individuals who in spite of one or more reminders do not return a given questionnaire before the next is administered need to be excluded from further participation in the study. This is because their responses will not have been seen by other panel members, nor built into the development of the questionnaire for the following round, so that reintroducing them into the Delphi process may seriously bias its findings. The exclusion of panel members who do not comply with the return deadlines does, however, often lead to problems related to panel attrition, the panel often becoming unbalanced as it shrinks.

The final stage is to apply the judgements achieved through the Delphi process to the problem at hand. In many cases, a measure of central tendency and a measure of spread will be sufficient, in which case the median and the inter-quartile range are generally preferred. The latter denotes the degree of consensus achieved and is said thereby to indicate the quality of the group judgement. Often a final feedback report is prepared and sent to all panellists as a matter of courtesy.

Origins of the Delphi Technique and some Applications to Tourism Research

In what is often claimed to be the first Delphi study, Dalkey and Helmer (1963) attempted to elicit expert opinions in order to assess, from the viewpoint of a Soviet military planner, the number of on-target atomic bombs that would be required to reduce US munitions supplies to one quarter of their current level within a 2-year period, exclusive of new investment. Since that time, the Delphi technique has found ready application in the area of forecasting, especially 'technological forecasting'. This field of study attempts to predict when particular technological advances would be made: a task that is not especially well-suited to more conventional empirical and model-based forecasting techniques. A prominent example of the early use of Delphi in technological forecasting is the now famous study by the UK Office of Health Economics entitled *Medicines in the 1990s* (Teeling-Smith, 1971).

A rather similar use of the Delphi technique is 'event forecasting', where experts are asked to make judgements on the likelihood and/or timing of the occurrence of specified events. There have been many interesting applications of the Delphi technique to event forecasting in the field of tourism. Yong *et al.* (1989), for example, assembled a Delphi panel of 23 judges who were asked to make judgements on the probability of occurrence and likely importance of 26 event statements relevant to the future of tourism in Singapore. Kibedi (1981), meanwhile, reports on a Delphi survey organized during an international tourism symposium in 1979 that asked respondents to identify and rank the events they felt would most influence international tourism business in the 1980s. Kaynak and Macaulay (1984), meanwhile, used the Delphi technique to investigate the likelihood, probable year of occurrence, and importance to the Nova Scotian tourism industry of a number of relevant possible events (such as prospective legislative changes to the length of the working week). More recently, Moutinho and Witt (1995) report the outcomes of a 'symposium Delphi' in which 25 experts meeting at a tourism seminar were asked to make judgements on the importance and probability of occurrence of a number of possible future developments affecting the world tourism industry, as well as to forecast the likely year of their occurrence. Lloyd *et al.* (2000), meanwhile, use the Delphi technique to predict changes in the Hong Kong hotel industry as a result of the transfer of sovereignty from Britain to China in 1997.

There have also been a number of prominent studies which have employed the Delphi technique in forecasting tourism demand variables. Indeed, the Delphi technique is widely identified as a useful 'qualitative' technique for tourism forecasting (Archer, 1976, 1980; Uysal and Crompton, 1985; Calantone *et al.*, 1987; Frechtling, 1996), and it is here that the technique would probably most readily be categorized by tourism researchers. A widely cited example is a study by Liu (1988), which employed a panel of 29 local and outside experts to generate forecasts on a range of features of the demand for tourism to Hawaii, all based on developments up to the year 2000. Experts were asked to forecast visitor arrivals, the share of domestic arrivals and Oahu's share of visitors, the visitor-to-resident ratio and visitor accommodation supply.

However, it is relevant to note that Delphi is now being used in more 'qualitative' ways, rather than simply to develop forecasts of quantitative variables. Green *et al.* (1990), for example, attempted to use Delphi to identify the range and extent of the potential environmental impacts of the development of a new tourism attraction, Salt's Mill in Bradford. Their rationale for using Delphi was that it would be cheaper to carry out than a full environmental impact assessment, and would take less time to complete, providing more timely results to help speed up the planning decision process. Another example illustrating the various applications to which Delphi has more recently been put is the set of three contrasting studies published by Pan *et al.* (1995). The first looked at whether the island of Gozo should be marketed as a destination in its own right rather than as part of Malta, the second at the factors affecting investment in tourism facilities in the People's Republic of China, and the third at events likely to affect the strategic mar-

keting of the Belizean tourism product in the UK.

Further examples of more qualitative applications of the Delphi technique include the study by Garrod and Fyall (2000), which applies the Delphi technique to investigate the expert opinions of issues important to the heritage tourism sector in the UK, and that of Miller (2001), which attempts to generate a set of quantitative performance indicators for sustainable tourism across a range of contexts.

Strengths and Weaknesses of the Delphi Technique

The Delphi technique has met with certain controversy since it was first used almost half a century ago. While much of this controversy is evidently due to the lack of rigour with which some Delphi researchers have gone about applying the technique, there are also a number of well-known critiques of the Delphi technique: on the basis of its methodological robustness and validity as a research tool (see for example Hill and Fowles, 1975; Sackman, 1975). Other writers, meanwhile, have staunchly defended the technique; most notably Linstone and Turoff (1975). Table 8.2 presents a synthesis of the main strengths and weaknesses of the Delphi technique, based on those works and others (see especially Rotundi and Gustafson, 1996). Most of the strengths of the Delphi technique are reasonably straightforward and have already been discussed above. The following discussion will therefore concentrate on some of the alleged weaknesses of the Delphi technique.

First, critics of Delphi have pointed out that the technique can be extremely sensitive to a number of design characteristics, including the level of the panellists' expertise, the panel composition, the degree of clarity with which the questions are posed, how outliers are reported on, and how the survey is administered. For example, Wheeller *et al.* (1990) present a critique of the Delphi study undertaken by Green *et al.* (1990) on the environmental impacts of the development of a tourist attraction. One of

Table 8.2. Strengths and weaknesses of the Delphi technique.

Strengths
1. The technique is flexible enough to be applied in a variety of situations and to a wide range of complex problems, for which there is often no other suitable means of analysis.
2. The iterative approach allows experts to reconsider their judgements in the light of feedback from peers.
3. The process also gives participants more time to think through their ideas before committing themselves to them, leading to a better quality of response.
4. The anonymity of the approach enables experts to express their opinions freely, without institutional loyalties or peer group pressures getting in the way.
5. The potential influence of personality is also removed in this way.
6. Redundant 'noise' (issues that tend to side-track the debate) can be controlled by the project manager.
7. The process generates a record of the group's thoughts, which can be reviewed as required.
8. The method can be used to evaluate the spread of opinion as well as consensus points.

Weaknesses
1. Delphi can be extremely sensitive to:
    (a) the level of panellists' expertise
    (b) the composition of the panel
    (c) the clarity of the questions
    (d) the way in which the project manager reports reasons for outliers
    (e) the administration of the questionnaire.
2. It assumes that experts are willing to allow their judgements to be re-formed by the opinions of others.
3. The expert panel is vulnerable to high rates of attrition due to boredom with the subject matter, disillusionment with the process, or lack of time to complete the questionnaire before the following round commences.
4. Some Delphi practitioners use monetary payments or moral persuasion to encourage panellists to stay the course; however, this may bias the results of the study.
5. There is also a risk of 'specious consensus' being formed, whereby panellists conform to the median judgement in order to be left alone (or due to lack of time to think properly about the issues at hand).
6. Where consensus is being sought there is a problem in determining what actually constitutes consensus; and hence when the iteration process should stop and the final results be reported.
7. The technique often requires a substantial period of time to complete and can be costly in terms of the researcher's time.

the problems noted with the study was that the questions were not rigorously developed. For example, nowhere was it stated how many visitors were expected to visit the attraction in a given period of time. There appeared to be no pre-testing of the questions. Given the relatively small number of respondents in a Delphi study, misinterpretation of what is being asked of respondents may potentially impart a very severe bias to the findings, seriously calling their value into question.

A second criticism that is often levelled at the Delphi technique is that it implicitly assumes that experts are willing to allow their judgements to be re-formed by the opinions of others. In many cases, of course, this is not an unreasonable assumption to make. For example, many Delphi studies are undertaken among academics, who are generally used to working in learning environments where individuals are encouraged to allow their views to be shaped by others. In other cases, however, the assumption that the respondents are willing to modify their views towards a consensual group view is probably not so easy to make. When issues are being discussed that have a 'right' or 'wrong' answer, or a strong moral dimension, it is likely that some experts will become entrenched in their positions.

A third criticism of the Delphi technique is that studies often report high levels of panel attrition, which may result in the findings of the study being biased in favour of those remaining active panel members throughout. According to Wheeller *et al.* (1990), this was almost certainly the case with the study by Green *et al.* (1990), where the number of active panel members fell from 40 at the outset of the study to 21 at its completion. Thus, even supposing that the panel was well balanced in terms of the backgrounds, knowledge and expertise of its members in the beginning of the study (which was by no means clear), it was certainly not well balanced by the end. Some groups (such as academics) largely stayed the course and were hence over-represented in the final round of questions, while others (such as local residents) tended to drop out and were hence under-represented. Considerable doubt was shed on the findings of the study as a result. There are, of course, many reasons why expert panellists may drop out of the Delphi process: boredom with the subject matter, disillusionment with the process, or lack of time to complete the questionnaire. Some of these reasons are, however, more serious than others. Indeed, some may be symptomatic of serious flaws in the study's design or implementation. For example, if the type of question asked is such that the respondents need to invest a lot of time formulating their responses, panel members are likely to delay completing the questionnaire, and hence be more likely to get excluded from further participation in the study because they have missed the return deadline.

Some Delphi researchers have chosen to use monetary payments or moral persuasion to encourage experts to remain active in the panel, which forms a fourth criticism of the Delphi technique. Providing incentives for experts to remain active may help prevent bias due to panel attrition, but it may also open the door to different forms of bias in the study. For example, if monetary payments are used to encourage experts to complete and return their questionnaires there is a danger that mainly those experts who are motivated by financial gain will be left in the panel towards the end of the process. This subgroup is likely to express different views on the issues being considered in the Delphi study from those who are not motivated by monetary rewards, hence biasing the study findings. In a sense, therefore, the Delphi researcher enters into a 'no win' situation when monetary or moral persuasion is used to try to prevent panel attrition, and for this reason many Delphi researchers dislike the use of such incentives.

This leads on to a fifth criticism often levelled at Delphi, which is the risk of 'specious consensus' being achieved (Sackman, 1975). This is where the judgements made by the panel members appear to be converging, but this is simply because panel members are choosing to conform to the median judgement (which they are usually provided in the feedback on the previous round) so as to be left alone by the researchers. They may do this because they are too busy to think properly about the issues at hand or, indeed, because they in fact lack the knowledge or expertise necessary to make a genuine attempt at completing the questionnaire. While the potential for specious consensus to emerge through the Delphi process can never be fully removed, it can be minimized through careful study design. In particular, panellists need to be selected carefully on the basis of their demonstrated expertise in the subject area and the questions they are asked need to be tested carefully to ensure that panel members are capable of dealing with them. Suitable return deadlines also need to be set: ones that are neither so short that busy experts cannot find time to keep them, nor so long that experts lose their train of thought between rounds or get bored with the debate and disengage from the process.

A sixth criticism of the Delphi technique is that while most studies make it clear that full consensus is not what is being sought, not seeking consensus in the strictest sense of the term implies that a subjective decision must be made as to when the final round will be. Some Delphi researchers have suggested that agreement among 60% of the panel can be viewed as constituting sufficient group consensus (Hill and Fowles, 1975); others that the inter-quartile range should be no greater than 10% above or below the median (Frechtling, 1996); others again that time or budgetary limitations should determine how many rounds should be conducted. All of these methods of determining when to consider the Delphi process complete are, however, clearly arbitrary: there is no good reason why different rules of thumb would not be equally valid.

Finally, the Delphi technique has sometimes been advocated as a 'quick-and-dirty' research technique. This is not only to underestimate the potential methodological sophistication of the Delphi technique but also to misunderstand the rationale for its use. Delphi is intended as a method to explore and analyse issues that would be inaccessible to the researcher using conventional survey methodologies. It is not – and clearly never was – intended as a speedy or cheap substitute for longer-established research methods. Where conventional survey techniques are better placed to analyse the issues under consideration, these techniques should always be preferred to the Delphi technique. In fact, the claim that Delphi is 'quick-and-dirty' may simply be wrong: the technique often requires a substantial period of time to complete and can be costly in terms of the researcher's time. What is more, if corners are cut in the Delphi methodology in order to speed up the process (for example, setting unrealistically short deadlines for the return of questionnaires), the technique may yield results that are simply too 'dirty' (i.e. unreliable) to be of any real use.

Case Study: 'Defining Marine Ecotourism'

This section reports on the design and conduct of a Delphi study that was undertaken in 2000 as part of an EU Interreg IIc project entitled 'Marine Ecotourism for the Atlantic Area' (META-). The overarching aim of META- was to explore the potential for 'marine ecotourism' to contribute to the economic, social and ecological well-being of marginal communities located on the EU's Atlantic periphery (see Bruce et al., 2001; Garrod et al., 2001). It emerged at the early stages of the project that there was little consensus, even among members of the research team, as to what might reasonably constitute 'marine ecotourism' activities. While some team members preferred a fairly narrow definition, comprising observing marine fauna, scuba diving with a focus on interaction with nature, rock-pooling, and so forth, others sought to widen the definition to include additional activities such as walking on coastal footpaths, yachting, canoeing, and coastal and sea angling. Unfortunately, the existing ecotourism literature provided no clear-cut arbitration (see, for example, Fennell, 2000; Holland et al., 2000).

The Delphi technique was selected as a suitable method for enabling the team to firm up how marine ecotourism might best be defined for the purposes of the study. Delphi was chosen mainly on pragmatic grounds, there being few other suitable methodologies available for analysing definitions of complex notions such as marine ecotourism in depth. A postal survey was, for example, ruled out because of the difficulties of finding sufficient respondents with expertise in this highly specialized field to form a representative sample. The employment of consultants and the use of focus groups, meanwhile, were ruled out on the basis of cost, given the wide geographical spread of those experts who could be identified. It was also recognized that the use of the Delphi technique could bring further dimensions to the research that would not be possible using conventional focus groups. In particular, it was felt that in dealing with such complex and controversial subject matter, experts would need a substantial period of time to think and to formulate their responses, as well as to build the opinions of others into their deliberations.

A panel of 15 experts drawn from the three partner countries in the project, namely the UK, the Canary Islands and Ireland, was put together for the purposes of the Delphi study. Bearing in mind the evidence suggesting that the size of the Delphi panel tends to have little impact on study outcomes (Rowe and Wright, 1999), provided that the panel remains well-balanced, a panel of 15 was considered to be large enough for differing views to emerge among the panellists, yet small enough to facilitate timely implementation of the various study rounds. Candidates were identified by partner project research leaders, using their local knowledge and personal contacts. A fee of €300 was offered to respondents who agreed to complete all of the survey rounds.

Following the good practice of Richey et al. (1985), potential members were asked to complete a brief application form. This established each individual's professional and academic background, personal and professional interests in ecotourism-related fields, and place of residence. The purpose of this was to ensure that a good balance of expertise and knowledge would be represented on the panel. The following acceptance criteria were then used:

- Practical experience of developing marine ecotourism or a demonstrated interest in doing so.
- At least 5 years professional experience in a relevant field.
- Good knowledge either of a partner project location or a particular candidate type of marine ecotourism (e.g. whale-watching or scuba diving).

Panellists were also expected to have a high standard of written English, which was to be the working language of the project. It was decided that candidates who did not meet these basic criteria would be thanked for their interest but not invited to participate further in the study. In the event, however, it was not necessary to exclude any candidates from membership of the Delphi panel, the partner project researcher leaders being able to recruit individuals of sufficient calibre. It is possible that the offer of payment assisted in this, although it should be pointed out that in the end only one panel member actually claimed their fee.

As Wheeller et al. (1990) point out, establishing a balanced expert panel at the beginning of the Delphi process is not sufficient to ensure the reliability of Delphi judgements: the panel must also remain well balanced as the Delphi study progresses through its various rounds. In order to ensure this, three criteria for panel balance were established:

- The panel should comprise no more than 15 members (i.e. panel members who dropped out cannot be replaced).
- The panel should include no more than one-third of the members sharing the same profession, academic background or national location.
- The panel should have as little duplication of members' fields of marine ecotourism interest as possible.

It was decided that these criteria should be applied to the panel after every Delphi round and that if it were felt that they were no longer sufficiently met for the research team to have confidence in the study findings, the study should be terminated at that point. This is the first time, to the authors' knowledge, that such a 'quality-control' check has been used when conducting a Delphi study.

Having established the membership of the panel, the next task was to determine the format and subject matter of the project itself. Given that the Delphi study could run for up to 12 months, it was decided that six rounds could be comfortably undertaken. Panellists would be given 3 weeks to return their responses, leaving the research team 5 weeks to collate the responses, prepare a feedback booklet, and develop the questionnaire for the subsequent round.

In accordance with best practice recommended by Rotundi and Gustafson (1996), a 'straw model' was developed to help the panellists to understand what the exercise intended to achieve and what their role in achieving those objectives was expected to be. According to Rotundi and Gustafson (1996: 43) a straw model is:

> ... a conceptual model of a group's task [which] defines the parameters of the task and presents a perspective on how the task can be accomplished ... The model helps to make the group aware of the areas where they must concentrate their effort during the Delphi process [and] is intended

to be a target for the group to focus on and direct their efforts.

The straw model developed for the purposes of the Delphi project is shown in Fig. 8.1, which suggests that the expert panel might ultimately be able to construct a set of indicators for determining whether a given activity conforms to the characteristics required of genuine marine ecotourism. In the event, however, the Delphi study was terminated after only three rounds because, in spite of the best efforts of the research team, panel attrition had led to the panel becoming unbalanced. The objectives of the study were therefore moderated to comprise: (i) determination of a suitable working definition of marine ecotourism; and (ii) some information on the panellists' views as to the benefits and drawbacks of developing such a definition.

The first round of the study presented participants with a list of ten possible definitions of ecotourism drawn from books,

papers and reports. The definitions were selected to demonstrate a range of possible definition styles, lengths and contents. Some were adapted slightly so that they made more sense as 'stand alone' definitions. The experts were asked to perform three tasks. The first was to choose from the list the definition with which they felt most comfortable in the context of marine ecotourism in the EU Atlantic Area. The second task was to state how, if at all, they would improve the definition they had just chosen. Space was provided for respondents either to amend an existing definition or to write down their own. They were also asked to justify the changes they made and to state any sources of additional material they used. The third task was to give their view on why more formal definitions of marine ecotourism might be helpful or unhelpful to the sustainable development of tourism in their location.

The second-round questionnaire was sent out as soon as the last first-round questionnaire was returned. Only 14 panellists actually returned their completed questionnaires on time, even after an e-mailed reminder, but the panel characteristics when tested by the acceptability criteria established for panel balance were still considered to be acceptable. The second-round questionnaire was accompanied by a feedback document which detailed the anonymized responses of the panellists to the first-round questions. The second-round questionnaire comprised two tasks. The first asked the experts to reconsider their preferred definition of ecotourism and to choose again from the expanded list of 20 definitions (there being ten new definitions suggested in round one). Panellists were reminded that they were entitled to stick to their original choice, but they had to justify whatever judgement they came to. The second task presented respondents with a list of reasons why defining marine ecotourism may be helpful and another list of reasons why doing so may be unhelpful, these being drawn up from the information collected in round one. Respondents were asked to choose their first and second most important reasons from each list. They were also invited to add to the list if they felt so inclined.

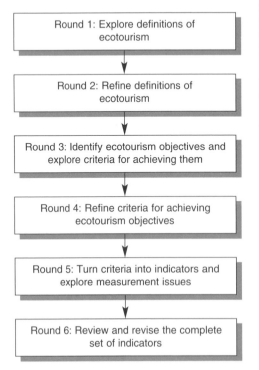

Fig. 8.1. The 'straw model' used in the Delphi study.

A third-round questionnaire was constructed on the basis of the second-round responses, but there were only ten responses to this questionnaire, despite the research team extending the return deadline and sending out reminders to those falling behind. The characteristics of the panellists fell outside of the acceptability criteria for panel balance, so it was decided to end the study at this point and not to use the results of the third-round questionnaire in determining the outcomes of the study.

The results of the Delphi study were then subjected to a manifest content analysis, using the computer package QSR N-VIVO to help keep track of the various definitions and justifications involved. Full results and analysis are to be found in Garrod (2003a). Regarding the determination of an appropriate definition of marine ecotourism, the study suggested the following important elements:

- Marine ecotourism should aim to educate tourists about the natural environment and its conservation.
- Management of ecotourism operations is required with a view to making them more sustainable.
- Marine ecotourism should attempt to provide benefits to local communities as well as to tourism operators and the environment.
- The focus of marine ecotourism should be primarily on promoting the conservation of species and habitats.

Interestingly, however, the panel's judgement was that marine ecotourism need not be based in natural areas and, perhaps worryingly, that the involvement of local people in the planning and management of an activity was not necessary for it to be described as ecotourism (see Garrod, 2003b). It is interesting also that the findings of this analysis – which is essentially a 'normative' study – generally confirm those of a 'positive' content analysis of 85 actual ecotourism definitions listed by Fennell (2001), although there are also some evident differences.

With regard to the panel's opinions on why defining marine ecotourism might be

helpful or unhelpful in developing sustainable tourism, among the most popular reasons why definition might be helpful were that it would act as:

- A means of putting the fundamental concept of ecotourism across to local people.
- A constant reminder to everyone involved of the reasons for creating ecotourism projects.
- A means of focusing and bringing together the disparate stakeholder groups involved in ecotourism.

Meanwhile the most popular reasons why defining marine ecotourism might be unhelpful were:

- Too narrow a definition of ecotourism can be unhelpful if it does not allow the concept to be applied in certain circumstances or if certain stakeholders feel excluded by it.
- The danger that, as the concept becomes more widely known and fashionable, large organizations will use it merely as a 'green label' for their existing activities, cynically exploiting people's goodwill towards the idea.

Conclusions

For a number of reasons, the reputation of the Delphi technique has suffered since it was first introduced. Unfortunately, the Delphi technique has too often been viewed as a 'quick-and-dirty' method of cutting corners with research and keeping down research costs. This had led to the Delphi technique being applied in contexts where it was never intended, and too often this has been accompanied by sloppy execution. For example, some Delphi studies have continued to operate even when they have experienced very high rates of panel attrition. There has also been a widespread failure to apply even basic statistical analyses, such as the construction of the medians and interquartile ranges. Similarly, Delphi researchers have often neglected to pilot test their questionnaires. In these respects,

Table 8.3. Some suggested guidelines for conducting Delphi.

1. The Delphi technique should not be seen as a main tool of investigation but a means of supporting/extending studies with better established and more reliable methods of investigation.
2. The topic must be appropriate, for example there must be no widely perceived 'correct answers' to the questions posed.
3. Every effort must be made to make the questions unambiguous; piloting the questionnaires can be particularly useful at the early stages.
4. Panellists should be recognized experts in their field (a self-assessment selection procedure may be useful in this respect); the use of students is therefore not recommended.
5. The panel should comprise a good balance of different disciplines and areas of expertise.
6. Adequate time must be given to experts to think deeply about the questions at hand.
7. Once a subsequent round has commenced, those completing the previous round late should nevertheless be excluded from continuing.
8. Attrition of the panel should be minimal; one way to improve retention is to select experts who already have a strong interest in the outcome of the project.
9. This is preferable both to using monetary payment and moral persuasion as a means of ensuring that experts remain committed to the project.
10. Criteria for panel balance should be established at the outset; should the panel composition at any stage fail to meet these criteria, further rounds should not be undertaken.
11. Experts must also believe that the Delphi technique is a valid way of going about the task at hand.
12. A 'straw model' may be helpful in enabling experts to see where the study is taking them and for them to feel confident that the study will produce useful results.
13. Full anonymity must be preserved at all times between the panellists (although not necessarily between the panellists and the coordinating researchers).
14. The coordination group should make themselves available as a resource for locating further information on specific subjects or clarifying the questions.
15. The coordination group should intervene in the process as little as possible.
16. The panellists must do the initial scoping themselves; the coordination group should not set the agenda for discussion.
17. Where consensus is being sought, the coordination group should determine the criteria for bringing the consensus rounds to a close before the project begins.

and others, it may be argued that critics of the Delphi technique have a very strong case.

It should be recognized, however, that to a greater or lesser degree all of these problems can be minimized through the adoption of more rigorous research procedures. Table 8.3 makes some tentative suggestions as to what steps might be taken in order to improve the methodological rigour of a given Delphi study. The need to establish and maintain a well-balanced expert panel is perhaps the most important principle underlying these guidelines. Unlike more conventional survey techniques, the Delphi technique does not have the rigour of representative sampling to ensure its reliability. Rigour must therefore be achieved by ensuring that the expert panel comprises a reasonably representative cross-section of experts according to their knowledge, areas

of interest, expertise, background and location. This balance must be maintained throughout the study. A panel that becomes less and less well balanced is likely to generate less and less reliable results.

Delphi researchers would do well, therefore, first to ensure that the panel is well balanced at the outset. This can be done by conducting a pre-survey of each expert's characteristics and mapping these at the panel level. Where there are shortfalls in certain characteristics, further panellists should be recruited to fill the gaps. Second, steps should be taken to minimize panel attrition. This might include, for example, ensuring that the experts have a stake in the outcomes of the study (the use of a straw model may be valuable in this respect). Ensuring that there is minimum delay in the turn-around time between rounds may also help to prevent experts getting bored or losing faith in the Delphi process. Third, the researchers can ensure that the panel remains balanced by introducing a quality-control check, through which acceptability criteria for panel balance are established and periodically monitored. Should the expert panel fall outside of these acceptability criteria, the Delphi study should be terminated and only the results from rounds previously undertaken be reported.

Possibly the most important improvement to the Delphi technique that can be made, however, is for researchers to recognize that it is not the 'quick-and-dirty' technique it has somehow come to be widely seen as. In this respect it is interesting to speculate how the Delphi technique got its name. Although staff at the RAND Corporation responsible for developing the Delphi technique have denied this to be true, presumably the technique is named after the Delphic Oracle of Greek mythology. The problem with this analogy is, of course, that the wisdom of the Oracle was untrustworthy, being capable of meaning more than one thing. Fools consulting of the wisdom of the Oracle interpreted the answers they received according to what they wanted to hear, with inevitably tragic results. Perhaps this should be taken as a warning to some Delphi researchers of today.

Acknowledgements

The 'Defining Marine Ecotourism' Delphi study was conducted as part of an EU Interreg IIc project (No. EA-C1UK-No.3.14) entitled 'Marine Ecotourism for the Atlantic Area'. Thanks are due to Julie C. Wilson and David M. Bruce for their collaboration in this project.

References

Archer, B.H. (1976) Demand forecasting in tourism. *Bangor Occasional Papers in Economics*, No.9. University of Wales Press, Cardiff, UK.

Archer, B.H. (1980) Forecasting demand: quantitative and intuitive approaches. *International Journal of Tourism Management* 1, 5–12.

Ayton, P., Ferrell, W.R. and Stewart, T.R. (1999) Commentaries on 'The Delphi technique as a forecasting tool: issues and analysis' by Rowe and Wright. *International Journal of Forecasting* 15, 377–381.

Bowers, J. (1997) *Sustainability and Environmental Economics: an Alternative Text*. Longman, Harlow, UK.

Bruce, D.M., Hoctor, Z., Garrod, B. and Wilson, J.C. (2001) Genuinely sustainable marine ecotourism in the EU Atlantic Area: a blueprint for responsible marketing. Project Report: University of the West of England, Bristol, UK.

Calantone, R.J., Di Benedetto, A. and Bojanic, D. (1987) A comprehensive review of the tourism forecasting literature. *Journal of Travel Research* 25, 28–39.

Dalkey, N. and Helmer, O. (1963) An experimental application of the Delphi method to the use of experts. *Management Science* 9, 458–467.

Fennell, D. (2000) Comment: ecotourism on trial – the case of billfish angling as ecotourism. *Journal of Sustainable Tourism* 8, 341–345.

Fennell, D. (2001) A content analysis of ecotourism definitions. *Current Issues in Tourism* 4, 403–421.

Frechtling, D. (1996) *Practical Tourism Forecasting*. Butterworth Heinemann, Oxford, UK.

Garrod, B. (2003a) Defining marine ecotourism: a Delphi study. In: Garrod, B. and Wilson, J.C. (eds) *Marine Ecotourism: Issues and Experiences*. Channel View, Clevedon, Australia, pp. 17–36.

Garrod, B. (2003b) Local participation in the planning and management of ecotourism: a revised model approach. *Journal of Ecotourism* 2, 1–21.

Garrod, B. and Fyall, A. (2000) Managing heritage tourism. *Annals of Tourism Research* 27, 682–708.

Garrod, B., Wilson, J.C. and Bruce, D.M. (2001) Planning for marine ecotourism in the EU Atlantic Area: good practice guidance. Project Report: University of the West of England, Bristol, UK.

Green, H., Hunter, C. and Moore, B. (1990) Assessing the environmental impact of tourism development: use of the Delphi technique. *Tourism Management* 11, 111–120.

Helmer, O. (1972) On the future state of the Union. Report 12–2, Institute for the Future, Menlo Park, California.

Hill, K.Q. and Fowles, J. (1975) The methodological worth of the Delphi technique. *Technological Forecasting and Social Change* 7, 179–192.

Holland, S.M., Ditton, R.B. and Graefe, A.R. (2000) A response to 'Ecotourism on trial: the case of billfish angling as ecotourism'. *Journal of Sustainable Tourism* 8, 346–351.

Kaynak, E. and Macaulay, J.A. (1984) The Delphi technique in the measurement of tourism market potential: the case of Nova Scotia. *Tourism Management* 5, 87–101.

Kibedi, G. (1981) Future trends in international tourism. *Revue de Tourism* 36, 3–6.

Linstone, H.L. and Turoff, M. (eds) (1975) *The Delphi Method: Techniques and Applications.* Addison-Wesley, Reading, Massachusetts.

Liu, J.C. (1988) Hawaii tourism to the year 2000: a Delphi forecast. *Tourism Management* 9, 279–290.

Lloyd, J., La Lopa, J.M. and Braunlich, C.G. (2000) Predicting changes in Hong Kong's hotel industry given the change in sovereignty from Britain to China in 1997. *Journal of Travel Research* 38, 405–410.

Masser, I. and Foley, P. (1987) Delphi revisited: expert opinion in urban analysis. *Urban Studies* 24, 217–225.

Miller, G. (2001) The development of indicators for sustainable tourism: results of a Delphi survey of tourism researchers. *Tourism Management* 22, 351–361.

Moutinho, L. and Witt, S.F. (1995) Forecasting the tourism environment using a consensus approach. *Journal of Travel Research* 33, 46–50.

Pan, S.Q., Vega, M., Vella, A.J., Archer, B.H. and Parlett, G. (1995) A mini-Delphi approach: an improvement on single round techniques. *Progress in Tourism and Hospitality Research* 2, 27–39.

Richey, J.S., Mar, B.W. and Horner, R.R. (1985) The Delphi technique in environmental assessment. I: implementation and effectiveness. *Journal of Environmental Management* 21, 135–146.

Rotundi, A. and Gustafson, D. (1996) Theoretical, methodological and practical issues arising out of the Delphi method. In: Adler, M. and Ziglio, E. (eds) *Gazing into the Oracle: the Delphi Method and its Application to Social Policy and Public Health.* Jessica Kingsley Publishers, London, pp. 34–55.

Rowe, G. and Wright, G. (1999) The Delphi technique as a forecasting tool: issues and analysis. *International Journal of Forecasting* 15, 353–375.

Sackman, H. (1975) *Delphi Critique, Expert Opinion, Forecasting and the Group Process.* Lexington Books, Lexington, Massachusetts, 160 pp.

Smith, S.L.J. (1995) *Tourism Analysis: a Handbook*, 2nd edn. Longman, Harlow, UK, 320 pp.

Stewart, T.R. (1987) The Delphi technique and judgemental forecasting. *Climatic Change* 11, 97–113.

Teeling-Smith, G. (1971) Medicines in the 1990s: experience with a Delphi forecast. *Long Range Planning* 3, 69–74.

Uysal, M. and Crompton, J.L. (1985) An overview of approaches used to forecast tourism demand. *Journal of Travel Research* 23, 7–15.

Wheeller, B., Hart, T. and Whysall, P. (1990) Application of the Delphi technique: a reply to Green, Hunter and Moore. *Tourism Management* 11, 121–122.

Yong, Y.W., Keng, K.A. and Leng, T.L. (1989) A Delphi forecast for the Singapore tourism industry: future scenario and marketing implications. *International Marketing Review* 6, 35–46.

9   Interviewing: a Focus on Qualitative Techniques

GAYLE R. JENNINGS

School of Marketing and Tourism, Faculty of Business and Law, Central Queensland University, Rockhampton, Queensland 4702, Australia

Introduction

In the latter half of the 20th century and in the early phases of the 21st century, interviews maintain their position as the research method of choice within the social sciences and, as a consequence, also within the field of tourism. So much has the interview method dominated that we have been described as living in an 'interview society' (Silverman, 1993, 1997; Fontana and Frey, 2000; Gubrium and Holstein, 2002). In an interview society, interviews are used to make sense of and understand on a daily basis the world in which we live, at either the informal or formal level. Whilst such a society is primarily associated with the Western world, due to globalization, internationalization and the spread of the knowledge economy as well as Western research practices, interviewing is becoming a global research method for understanding and making sense of the lives of the peoples of this world.

However, interviews are not all the same; each follows different 'rules', procedures or guidelines, and they are embedded in different philosophical backgrounds. As a consequence, the purpose of this chapter is to consider the overall continuum of interviewing, different types of interviews and then to hone in on qualitative interviewing. In particular, the chapter will overview some of the differing definitions of qualitative interviewing, the philosophical underpinnings of qualitative interviewing in contrast to quantitative interviewing, some practical guidelines for qualitative interviewing, debates associated with qualitative interviewing, representations from a case study informed by qualitative interviewing, and final reflections regarding the place of qualitative interviewing in tourism research.

Background

While the interview society is noted as a contemporary phenomenon, the use of question–answer interactions (informal and formal interviews) has been embedded in all our histories for centuries, for example, the collection of early census information (Babbie, 1998), interactions between parents and children (Gubrium and Holstein, 2002), teachers and learners, 'medical practitioners' and patients. However, after the First World War, the proliferation of interviews (including opinion polls, particularly credited to George Gallup in 1935) as a formal means by which to gather information on the social world has increased (see Benney and Hughes, 1956; Fontana and Frey, 2000; Gubrium and Holstein, 2002). Moreover, the time since the Second World War has seen a marked increase in the use of standardized interviews (Gubrium and Holstein, 2002). Throughout the 1950s to date, the use of the standardized/structured interview continues to maintain dominance as a research method, especially in comparison with other interview techniques. However, whilst not in a dominant role, other interview methods (semi-structured and unstructured/in-depth interviews) and other research techniques have also emerged and gained acceptance, as is evident from the various methods discussed in other chapters of this book. Subsequently, given the prolific documentation of the standardized/structured interview within and without the fields of travel, tourism and hospitality, this chapter will focus in detail upon in-depth/unstructured and semi-structured interviews. Such a focus provides a counterpoint to the hegemony and body of literature associated with standardized/structured interviews.

Types of Interviews

In the preceding section, three interview methods were mentioned: structured, semi-structured and unstructured. The words formal and informal were also used. The latter refer to the context in which an interview occurs and the former relate to the structure of the interview. However, it should be noted that within the research literature, formal and informal are also used to differentiate between structured (standardized or formal) and unstructured (non-standardized or informal); albeit that in this latter sense the use of formal and informal is sometimes applied pejoratively to distinguish respectively between a 'hard' science and 'soft' science approach. For the remainder of this chapter, the formal/informal differentiation in regard to structure rather than context or approach will be applied.

There are other ways to classify interviews than by context and structure. Interviews may be classified by the methodology that informs the overall research process, the number of people who are involved, the purpose of the interview and

the composition of the people involved in an interview. First, the methodology that informs the overall research process may be quantitative or qualitative, or in some instances a mixed methodology. To be specific, structured interviews are associated with the tenets of a quantitative methodology, and semi-structured and unstructured interviews with a qualitative methodology. The major differences between each, as a result of the informing methodology, are listed in Table 9.1.

Second, the number of people participating may also be used to classify the interview. Under this classificatory rubric are group interviews, paired interviews and individual interviews. Group interviews have a variety of forms: focus groups, focused interviews, Delphi, panel and nominal group techniques. Overall, group interviews tend to be classified as focus groups. The term 'focus group' was coined by Merton, et al. (1956). Paired interviews involve two related persons in an interview, such as a couple in a relationship or parent/carer and child/dependent person. Individual interviews are conducted between the interviewer and the participant. An alternative to the latter is the self-interview, where the participant interviews her or himself using diaries and autobiographies (Douglas, 1985). Group, paired and individual interviews may be associated with quantitative or qualitative methodologies depending on the nature of the 'protocol' for the interview.

Third, interviews may be classified by purpose. A number are associated with forecasting trends such as Delphic and panel techniques. Others are associated with achieving consensus such as nominal group technique and focus groups, whilst still others may be used to achieve an understanding of diversity of opinions, attitudes and values, such as focus groups, panel techniques and focused interviews. (Readers should refer to Garrod and Fyall, Chapter 8, Ritchie, Chapter 11, and Weeden, Chapter 14, this volume.) Interviews may also be associated with achieving life stories or oral histories. Additionally, a fourth dimension may be applied to classify interviews and

Table 9.1. Comparison of structured, semi-structured and unstructured interviews.

Descriptor	Structured	Semi-structured interview	In-depth interview, unstructured interview
Style	Specific protocol of question and answer	Conversation-like	Conversation
Design	Structured	Semi-emergent	Emergent
Researcher stance	Objective	Subjective	Subjective
Researcher perspective	Outsider (etic)	Insider (emic)	Insider (emic)
Consequence of researcher stance and perspective	Limited reflexivity	Reflexivity	Reflexivity
Exchange issues during the research process	Limited reciprocity	Reciprocity	Reciprocity
Language used	Subject/respondent	Informant, participant co-researcher	Informant, participant co-researcher
	Data	Empirical materials	Empirical materials
	Representation	Slice of life	Slice of life
Material/Data collection	Checklist	Field notes	Field notes
	Some open-ended questions	Transcription and recording	Transcription and recording
Basis of analysis	Mathematical and statistical analysis	Textual analysis	Textual analysis
'Findings' expressed as	Numeric representation	Depthful and thick descriptions	Depthful and thick descriptions
Writing style for reporting research	Scientific report	Narrative	Narrative

that is by nature of the composition of people involved in the interview interaction. Interviews may be classified as expert panels (Delphic, panel, nominal group techniques and focus groups). In expert panels, the group would be constituted of experts pertaining to the issue of focus. Alternatively, interviews may be classified by predominant sociodemographic features and as being gendered, indigenous, or cross-cultural interviews. Of these four dimensions, the structural and methodological classificatory motifs will be the ones consistently applied in this chapter.

Towards a 'Definition' of Interviews?

Before venturing further into this chapter, it is timely to consider what exactly the term 'interview' means. To this point in the chapter, I have assumed that we (you, the reader, and I, the writer) have a shared understanding. This may not be the case. When using the term 'interview', I am referring to face-

to-face interactions (sometimes voice-to-voice) rather than interactions mediated via written text transfers; these I refer to as questionnaires (see further comments on this in Fontana and Frey, 2000). In saying this, I am not disputing the fact that face-to-face (voice-to-voice) interactions produce written text units. Nor am I disputing that questionnaires may be administered by interviewers. What I am emphasizing is the nature of social interaction that needs to occur in a qualitative interview as a result of its philosophical underpinnings and subsequent methodological guidelines. So, to return to the question, what is an interview? Depending on the methodology applied, an interview may be defined as an interaction following a question–answer format (stimulus–response) or an interaction more akin to a conversation (refer back to the *Style* row in Table 9.1). The question–answer format (structured interview) is associated with a quantitative methodology and a conversation style (semi- or unstructured interview) with a qualitative methodology.

Table 9.2. The nature of qualitative interviews.

Writer and Year	The nature of qualitative interviews
Palmer (1928: 169)	'The conversations of human beings are an important part of the data of social research, as well as an important part of social research technique.'
Maccoby and Maccoby (1954: 499)	'... a face-to-face interchange in which one person, the interviewer, attempts to elicit information or expressions of opinions or belief from another person or persons.'
Dexter (1970)	Interviews are conversations with a specific purpose.
Oakley (1981)	Interviews are pseudo-conversations with historically determined protocols. Oakley (1981) argues that interviews should be founded on a 'relationship of mutual trust' and be 'non-hierarchical'.
Burgess (1982: 107)	'Conversation is a crucial element in field research.'
Hammersley and Atkinson, 1983: 126)	'Interviews must be viewed ... as social events in which the interviewer (and for that matter the interviewee) is a participant observer ...'
Mishler (1986)	'An interview is a joint product of what interviewees and interviewers talk about together and how they talk with each other. The record of an interview that we researchers make and then use in our work of analysis and interpretation is a representation of that talk.'
Denzin (1989: 103)	'An interview is like a conversation.'
Seidman (1991: 3)	'At the root of in-depth interviewing is an interest in understanding the experience of other people and the meaning they make of that experience.'
Bailey (1994: 176)	'The interview is a special case of social interaction between two persons ...' with related etiquette.
Kvale (1996: 14)	'The qualitative research interview is a construction site for knowledge. An interview is literally an *inter view*, an inter-change of views between two persons conversing about a theme of mutual interest.'
Rubin and Rubin (1995: 2)	'[Q]ualitative interviewing is more than a set of skills, it is also a philosophy, an approach to learning.'

Within a qualitative methodology, multiple definitions apply. Table 9.2 portrays representative quotations and texts drawn from social science literature to describe, define, explain or comment upon the nature of qualitative interviewing. The quotations are arranged chronologically.

A number of themes are evident in Table 9.2. Essentially, qualitative interviewing is a social interaction/interchange. It is a two-way exchange. Knowledge, understanding and learning are at the roots of qualitative interview engagements. There are also subtle differences due to refinement over time and different stances of the writers, and these demonstrate the multiple perspectives (explained later in this chapter) inherent in

defining the term 'interview' from a qualitative methodological and philosophical perspective.

However, while the definitions reflect synergy and appear to reflect a straightforward process, there are a number of cautions associated with interviewing. In the words of Gorden (1969):

[t]o the uninitiated, interviewing is 'just talking to people'.

p. 17

..., in comparing the interview with ordinary conversation we note that interviewing may include several possible functions of ordinary conversation, but that must be judiciously subordinated to the central purpose of gathering information. Habitual patterns of conversation must be modified in order to maximize the flow of relevant information in the interview.

p. 56

Moreover, whilst qualitative interviewing is similar to 'talking to people', it is much more sophisticated and complex. Hyman (1975: 1), although elaborating more specifically on survey research, that is, standardized interviewing, makes the following comment with regard to the complexity of interviewing:

> ... the very universality of interviewing as a method and the infinite variety of the procedures subsumed under the term create a difficulty. No single investigation – not even a score of investigations – could bear directly upon all the concrete forms and manifestations which interviewing takes...

How then to learn how to 'interview'? Rubin and Rubin (1995) suggest prudence, for while qualitative interviewing is like a conversation, qualitative interviewing also requires practice and skill. To assist the reader, later sections in this chapter deal with guidelines.

The preceding advice is historically situated, and this passage of time needs to be acknowledged further in regard to the movement of research between modern and postmodern discourses, Scheurich (1997: 73) advances:

> ... the interview interaction is fundamentally indeterminate – the complex play of conscious and unconscious thoughts, feelings, fears, power, desires, and needs on the part of both the interviewer and interviewee cannot be captured and categorized.

So having identified that qualitative interviews may on the surface appear easy to undertake, the very nature, diversity and complexity amongst qualitative interview forms and the resulting complex, dynamic and indeterminate nature of social interaction inherent in such interviews become problematic in attempting to capture that which is socially constructed and contextualized as well as historically situated in time. To commence addressing some of the issues to which Gorden, Hyman, Rubin and Rubin, and Scheurich amongst others alert us, the next section considers one of the 'broad' philosophical contexts informing qualitative interviews – the phenomenological, constructivist or interpretivist paradigm.

Philosophical Context of the Method Discussed

Qualitative interviews are shaped by a qualitative methodology, and subsequently by what may be generically described as a phenomenological or constructivist or interpretivist paradigm. A paradigm represents a set of beliefs about how the world operates. Within a theoretical research context, paradigms are constituted of ontological (world view), epistemological (knowledge construction), methodological (approach associated with information collection and analysis) and axiological (values and ethics) perspectives (Lincoln and Guba, 2000). In this chapter, I apply the dichotomous classification of research methodologies: quantitative and qualitative, albeit that mixed methods/ methodologies also exist (see for example, Brannen, 1992; Tashakkori and Teddlie, 1998; Creswell, 2003). I recognize that a number of disciplines draw on in-depth interviews as part of a mixed method design. In such designs, the in-depth interview, like the use of focus groups, is usually incorporated in the exploratory phase of a larger research project. The interview in this chapter assumes that in-depth and semi-structured interviews are the key components of a qualitative research project. Subsequently, as mixed methodologies are informed by quantitative and qualitative methodologies, and mixed methodologies are not the focus of this chapter, I will not go into a detailed discussion of mixed methodologies here. I will however, go into a brief discussion regarding the distinction between methodology and methods. A methodology being '[t]he set of guidelines of conducting research' and a method is constituted of '[t]he tools for data collection and analysis' (Jennings, 2001: 34).

Paradigms and methodologies

The use of in-depth and semi-structured interviews is associated with the phenomenological, constructivist or interpretivist paradigm, which holds an ontology (worldview) that recognizes multiple perspectives in regard to the research focus, an epistemological stance that is subjective in nature and a methodology which is predicated on qualitative principles. Axiologically, the research process is value laden, and the research purpose is intrinsic in nature. The outcome of the research should be educative and possibly transformative and/or emancipatory. As methods, in-depth and semi-structured interviewing are used by social constructivists, critical theorists, feminist perspectives, and postmodern researchers as well as chaos theorists when chaos is applied in a metaphoric sense. It is also used by positivists and postpositivists if using mixed methods. Positivists operate from an ontological perspective that supports universal truths, an objective epistemology, a quantitative methodology and an extrinsic, value-free axiology. Postpositivists acknowledge the fallibility of truths and their social and historical contexts as well as utilizing mixed methods. Further, postpositivists maintain an objective epistemology, albeit that they recognize that researchers can add bias to a research project; however, axio-

logically they essay to be value-free. The paradigmatic differences between positivism and phenomenology are presented in Table 9.3.

Informed by their ontological, epistemological, methodological and axiological principles, qualitative interviews are usually one of a suite of methods used to gather in-depth data about the phenomenon being studied, in this case tourism. For example, Jorgensen (1989) comments that interviews are supplements to information-gathering when using participant observation. Merton (1982) also reports on the complementary nature of using diaries and focused interviews together to get at more depthful information. In case study research informed by a qualitative methodology, interviews are a key material for gathering information (Yin, 1994). (See Beeton, Chapter 4, this volume, for further details.) However, qualitative interviewing can be used as the primary or only method of data collection.

Semi-structured and Unstructured Interviews

Semi-structured interviews differ from unstructured interviews in that the former have a flexible agenda or list of themes to focus the interview, although between interviews with different participants the order of discussion will vary. The unstructured interview is more open and more conversation-like with no set questions, just a theme, so

Table 9.3. Comparison of the paradigms of positivism and phenomenology.

Positivism	Paradigm	Phenomenology
Empiricism	Synonym	Social constructivism, interpretivism
Realism	Intent	Relativism
Explanation	Purpose	Understanding
Causal relationships	Ontology	Multiple realities
Objective	Epistemology	Subjective
Quantitative	Methodology	Qualitative
Extrinsic, value-free	Axiology	Intrinsic, value-laden
Scientific report	Genre	Narrative
Generalizable, representative	Representation	Localized, possibly generalizable to similar settings and contexts

that the interviewer and interviewee will become co-researchers in regard to 'topic' treatment. Subsequently there is great variability between interview formats in the unstructured or in-depth interview.

Table 9.4 outlines the different types of unstructured interviews available to qualitative and mixed methods researchers. Semi-structured interviews are variously noted within the table.

Some Guidelines for Qualitative Interviewing

As a starting point, one guideline is to remember that interviews are more than conversations, they are conversations with a purpose (Dexter, 1970). As Rubin and Rubin (1995: 2) state '[t]o conduct a qualitative interview and truly hear what people say requires skills beyond those of ordinary conversation and takes considerable practice'. Interviewers need to listen at least on three levels:

1. Active listening – listening with full attention to the participant, interacting and engaging with them, providing feedback regarding that engagement.

2. Interpretive listening – seeking clarification of terms that are socially acceptable in conversation such as 'the experience was interesting'. What exactly does 'interesting'

Table 9.4. Different types of unstructured interviews.

Types of unstructured interviews	Summary description
Open-ended, ethnographic (in-depth) interview (Spradley, 1979)	These interviews commence with a 'grand tour' question, then mini-tour questions, followed by questions which seek to elucidate information regarding examples, experiences and insider language, terminology.
'[I]ndepth, phenomenologically based interview ...' (Seidman, 1991: 9)	This interview is a mixing of the life history interview (Bertaux, 1981) and focused, in-depth interview grounded in the principles of phenomenology, particularly the work of Schutz (1967). There are three separate phases to this interview style: 1. Focused life history, which sets the context (approximately 90 minutes long). 2. Experience details phase, which focuses on gaining specificity in regard to the focused life history (90 minutes). 3. Reflection on meaning of experience phase based on the previous two phases (Seidman, 1991). Seidman (1991) recommends following the agenda of each interview phase rather than advancing into other interview phase foci. The argument is that the logic of the interview must be maintained so that sense-making will occur and detail will logically be determined. The benefits of these three interactions are the development of greater rapport, and that participants may reflect between interviews. Interviews need to be separated by 3–7 days.
Informal conversational interview (Patton, 2002)	Such an interview is open-ended, unstructured and the least formal of the interview approaches. Other synonyms are unstructured interview, ethnographic interview (Patton, 2002).
Life history (Thomas and Znaniecki 1918-19)	Also used by Bertaux (1981), the method involves the use of in-depth interviewing over successive occasions regarding the life experiences of an 'insider'. Questions and probes are used to gather as full a picture of the participant's life as possible.
Oral history	Contemporary method attributed to the work of Nevins in 1948 (Starr, 1984). Methodologically similar to other unstructured interviews. Focus is on telling a story about various aspects of a person's life (Fontana and Frey, 2000). *Continued*

Table 9.4. *Continued.*

Types of Unstructured Interviews	Summary Description
Creative interviewing (Douglas, 1985)	The mutual exchange of life stories on a one-to-one basis over extended periods of time at the one 'sitting' and consecutive 'sittings'. Both participants exchange information about self in order to achieve increased self-understanding. Douglas (1985) recommends the ousting of protocols and formulaic structures for the interview. The interview should progress creatively based on the interaction between both people equally sharing and reflecting upon their experiences.
Postmodern interviewing (see Scheurich, 1997; Fontana and Frey, 2000)	The interview is problematic. Language, interviewer–interviewee subjectivity, interviewer–interviewee interaction are all indeterminate and power relations should be considered as more than dominance by the interviewer and resistance or compliance by the interviewee (Scheurich, 1997).
Case study interviews (Yin, 1994)	These interviews draw on open-ended questions and move from positioning the participant as a respondent to an informant.
Focused interview (Merton *et al.*, 1956)	Conversational in style with the use of structured to semi-structured format. Used to confirm research information to date and to gain information regarding opinions, experiences, values and attitudes.
Focused interview	'Non-schedule standardized interview' is also known as the 'unstructured schedule interview' (Denzin, 1989). Specific information is required from all participants although the order of gaining that information may vary (similar to semi-structured interviews).
Informal interview (Jorgensen, 1989)	Similar to a conversation using questions and answers to gather information in a free-flowing conversational manner about a topic of interest. Another synonym is nonstandardized interview or unstructured interview (Denzin, 1989).
Formal interview (Jorgensen, 1989)	An interaction which has a fixed agenda and a structured question format that may use a specific set of questions of an open-ended nature with a fixed set of response choices.
Self interview (Douglas, 1985)	Diaries, journals, autobiographies.

mean? Probes are required to understand further the meaning of 'interesting' and other such everyday applied terms.

3. Process listening – monitoring the timing, where the interview has been, where it still needs to go, and any follow-ups. (Seidman, 1991: 56–57).

As well as the above listening skills, qualitative interviewers need to be conscious of empirical communication materials that need to be collected in interviews. These are oral, proxemic, chronemic, kinesic and paralinguistic communication materials (Gorden, 1969). See Table 9.5 for explanations of these.

Some other guiding principles for indepth interviews follow (based on Seidman, 1991):

- Listen more than talk.
- Ask for elaboration.
- Refrain from the use of leading questions.
- Use open-ended questions.
- Try not to interrupt, although judicious interruptions may save time budgets from being broken.
- Give of yourself, it is an interaction.
- Check your non-verbal interactions so that they do not bias interviewee reflections.
- Ask interviewees to explain laughter, hesitations and emotions.
- Trust your instincts – know when to ask hard questions or probe further.
- Use guides carefully.
- Feel comfortable about silences, they allow time for reflection.
- Be genuine.

Table 9.5. Empirical communication materials collected in interviews. (Based on Gorden, 1969.)

Communication type	Explanation
Oral	Interview notes or transcriptions.
Proxemic	Field notes regarding interpersonal spatial separations when discussing various topics.
Chronemics	Field notes regarding rate of oral communication and lengths of pauses.
Kinesic	Body stances, postures and movements.
Paralinguistic	Changes in voice quality, pitch and volume.

Finally, as the interviewer will be engaging in a community of space and time with the interviewee (Schutz, 1967), as noted before, the researcher needs to monitor the process and progress of the interview, the content of the interview (Cavana *et al.*, 2001) as well as the physiological well being of the interviewee. Take breaks when needed, reconvene, stop and reschedule if required and possible.

Qualitative Interviews: Other Considerations

In this section, six items will be briefly discussed: entering the field, establishing rapport, ethics, reciprocity, reflexivity, multivocality and polyvocality.

Entering the field – gatekeepers

To gain access to people whom we may wish to interview may mean gaining the support of a 'gatekeeper'. A gatekeeper, as the term suggests, is a person who may enable or prevent researchers gaining access to potential interviewees by way of sanction or veto. When approaching gatekeepers for access to the tourism field site, consider your attire, ensure it complements the situation, know your research project and present its purpose, impacts, processes and benefits clearly and articulately with language levels and style appropriate to the setting. Respect questions and answer them authentically.

Establishment of rapport

The success of an interview depends on establishing rapport with the participant. This means that the interview time will need to include time to establish a social relationship, as well as trust and respect. While 'genuineness, realness, or congruence' (Rogers, 1980: 116) are part of the humanistic psychology interviews, such attributes also have resonance with qualitative interviewing. However, Chirban (1996) comments that 'genuineness' may not be possible because of a participant's characteristics. The interviewer may not be able to summon 'positive regard', in which case Chirban advocates 'authentic interaction'. By this, should, for example, a tourist indicate that he or she engages in socially unacceptable activities, a researcher does not have to condone such activities but, rather, engage in authentic interaction regarding the activities to assist in information gathering.

Ethics

Interviews are conducted on the basis of informed or written consent. (Refer to Ryan, Chapter 2, this volume, for further discussion of research ethics.) However, sometimes after an interview has ceased and closure of the interview period has occurred, participants will continue to provide insightful details. This is an issue that must be addressed, since once the transcription book is closed and/or the tape is off, the participant may feel more relaxed to tell you more personal information. You have two choices:

(i) to not use the information as you do not have consent to do so; or (ii) to request that you make a note of that and include it in the interview text. The latter may generate some criticism as it could portray you as being a poor interviewer who cannot interview the person effectively. You could also be seen to be now extending the interview time period and seeking information that the interviewee has already chosen not to provide in the course of the interview.

Reciprocity

Reciprocity is about exchange. Exchanges may be of information, experience, time, reflection or monetary-based. In qualitative interviews, there should be a mutual exchange of information and/or experiences. As Anne Oakley comments (1981: 49):

> I have found, in previous interviewing experiences, that an attitude of refusing to answer questions or offer any kind of personal feedback was not helpful in terms of the traditional goal of promoting 'rapport'. A different role, that could be termed 'no intimacy without reciprocity', seemed especially important in longitudinal in-depth interviewing.

Interviews enable reciprocity from a time perspective in regard to the interview process providing time for interviewees to engage with another person, an opportunity that may not have otherwise occurred. Coupled with the provision of time is time for reflection via the interview process. Patton (1990) notes that the reflective process of an interview can assist the interviewee to learn about themselves. Monetary exchanges are sometimes used to increase participation rates and/or to pay people for their time. Debate exists in regard to the use of incentives (including payment). Fetterman (1989) proposes that incentives call into question the value of the information gathered – is it authentic or is it provided and shaped by the nature of the incentive? Regardless of the impact of an incentive, its use will cause the researcher to engage in reflexive processes.

Reflexivity

In qualitative interviews, the researcher assumes a subjective position. As a consequence of this epistemological stance, the researcher will engage in reflexivity throughout the entire research process. Reflexivity is the process by which researchers reflect and consider the impacts of their personal subjectivity and consequences of their participation in the research process and report on the same in their writings. This may be written up as 'The role of the researcher' (Cresswell, 2003), as a section outlining the 'social situatedness' of self (Harding, 1991) or as a discussion of the 'ethnographic presence' (Fetterman, 1989) of the researcher. Alternatively, the reflexive writings of the researcher may permeate the entire text (Cresswell, 2003).

Multivocality (multiple voicing) and polyvocality

The ontological perspective of phenomenologically aligned paradigms, and in this case materials generated by qualitative interviews, will generate and result in the analysis of multiple perspectives in regard to the tourism phenomenon being studied. The qualitative researcher does not attempt to reduce those multiple perspectives to a dominant view. All perspectives are valid and will be reported by the researcher. This is referred to as multiple voicing (Gergen and Gergen, 2000). Polyvocality on the other hand refers to identifying the multiple 'I's that as humans we are (Gergen and Gergen, 2000). At the time of writing this chapter, I am a researcher, a teacher, a writer, a learner, a partner, a daughter, a mother, a friend ... All of these voices are variously present in the construction of this chapter, just as multiple 'I's and their voices are part of the qualitative interview process for researchers and participants.

Table 9.6. Qualitative methods of analysis. (Source: Jennings, 2004, with permission from Elsevier, Inc.)

Types of Analysis	Discussion
Content analysis	Textual materials are read, annotated and coded. Categories are generated from reading, annotating and coding. Categories are evaluated in regard to relevance of emerging taxonomy in relation to the empirical setting from which they emerged. This involves reflection and questioning of assignment of codes and categories and the real-world context.
Constant comparative analysis	Constant comparative analysis involves two generic stages, coding and the comparison of codes to generate categories to build an ideographic representation of the study phenomenon. Theoretical sampling will also be applied to establish the repetitive presence of concepts. The method has similarities with grounded theory analysis.
Successive approximation	The researcher will iteratively and reflectively compare codes and categories to develop concepts, relationships and 'theory'. Questions in regard to 'goodness of fit' with the empirical world are posed constantly throughout the process. The method has similarities with constant comparison and grounded theory analysis.
Domain analysis	Categorizes study units using a 'cover term', 'included terms' and a 'semantic relationship'. Categorization is an on-going process during data collection. Domain analysis is founded in the work of Spradley (1980) and the study of culture.
Ideal types	Ideal types (models of social interactions and processes) establish a standard with which reality may be compared. Ideal types emanate from the work of Max Weber.
Event-structure analysis	The chronological ordering of events highlighting the causal relationships for their occurrence.
Matrices	Matrices demonstrate interactions between two or more elements of phenomena.
Grounded theory analysis	Grounded theory is attributed to the work of Glaser and Strauss. It is an inductive process, as are all the qualitative methods of data analysis. In its original form, theory is produced by identifying conditions that result in a phenomenon occurring that establishes a specific context, and concomitant actions and related consequences (Strauss and Corbin, 1990).
Other examples of analysis	Networks, models, typologies, taxonomies, conceptual trees, mind maps, semantic webs, sociograms.

Qualitative Interviews and Interview Material Analysis

To this point the chapter has focused on gathering materials; however, the analysis of interview materials is equally important. Researchers have a range of analytical tools available to them: content analysis, constant comparison, successive approximation, domain analysis, ideal type, event-structure analysis, matrices, grounded theory, and other analytical methods (refer to Silverman, 1993; Miles and Huberman, 1994). Table 9.6 outlines some of the ways interview materials may be analysed.

Depending on the nature of the tourism topic being studied, the researcher will draw upon one or more of the methods outlined in Table 9.6. Use of computer programs is also possible; however, computer programs are only as effective as the researcher who operates them (Dey, 1993). In the analysis phase, the voices of the participants are represented and/or reconstructed by the researcher. However, since interviewing is a social interaction, the researcher is involved and the subjectivity of the interview process means that the representations and reconstructions will also carry the 'brushstrokes' of the researcher.

Debates Associated with Qualitative Interviewing

The key debates relating to the use of qualitative instead of quantitative interview techniques are associated with differing paradigmatic views. As already noted, a qualitative interview will be associated with a phenomenological paradigm. On the other hand, a quantitative interview, a standardized structured interview, will be associated with a positivistic or postpositivisitic paradigm, which is predicated to an ontology that is expressed in causal relationships, an objective epistemology, a quantitative methodology and extrinsic and value-free axiology. See Table 9.3 again for a comparison between the two paradigms. The other differences, as expressed in Table 9.1, are the presentation of study findings in scientific report style as opposed to narrative style and the point that positivistic findings are generalizable and representative, whereas phenomenology is more localized. In the latter case, an in-depth understanding is achieved instead of explanation via causal relationships and findings may be generalizable to similar settings and contexts.

As noted earlier in the chapter, this debate may be described as one of the hard sciences (positivism) versus the soft sciences (phenomenology/constructivism) or quantitative versus qualitative research. In fact the debates that coursed throughout the 1970s–1990s are the ones that positioned researchers against each other, rather than drew researchers into dialogue with each other. In the 1990s, new positionings developed with the emergence of mixed methodologies and paradigm relativism (Tashakkori and Teddlie, 1998), paradigm relativism being the selection of whatever works for the research study, and the use of mixed methodologies. However, debate still circulates around the incommensurability of mixing between some paradigms (Lincoln and Guba, 2000), especially from a philosophical perspective. The dominance of quantitative survey research (standardized interviewing) and aspects of this debate are variously discussed in the writings of Dann et al. (1988), Cohen (1988), Hollinshead (1996), Walle (1997), Riley and Love (2000) and Jamal and Hollinshead (2001). Individuals will assume differing positions in regard to this debate. For me, such dichotomous positioning (hard or soft) masks the real issue, which is an alleged inability of researchers to engage in dialogue in regard to different paradigms that may inform research processes. Such dialogue would be more conducive to researching tourism in the ever-dynamic, changing, uncertain world of today, which is punctuated by unexpected and unprecedented events as well as conflicts. One of the aims of tourism has been postulated as increasing global understanding and world peace; researchers have a role to play in this aim and can do so by engaging in dialogue rather than pejorative positioning.

There are also a number of other debates when using a qualitative methodology, such as level of engagement of the researcher, interviewing in small numbers, power relationships, interviewer credibility, when to stop interviewing, using recording equipment or not, ways to report and publication constraints.

Level of engagement between researcher and interviewee or participant

Ticehurst and Veal (1999: 100) state, 'The interviewer is meant to listen and encourage the respondent to talk – not to engage in debate'. However, this is contrary to a phenomenological perspective of interaction and interchange (refer to Table 9.1 again) and particularly a feminist perspective, as noted by Oakley (1981: 49) in that there is 'no intimacy without reciprocity'.

Interviewing in small numbers – power relationships

Power relationships are evident in interview situations and may have impact on the quality of interactions. Under the phenomenological paradigm, postmodern, critical theorists and feminist researchers are particularly aware of power relationships, as are constructivists. In group interviews, researchers must be particularly attuned to 'power' so interactions and exchanges enable all to participate.

Gendered, indigenous and cross-cultural interviewing

Gendered interviews are also a site for power demonstrations. Men interviewing women and women interviewing men will gain differing insights from a man interviewing a man and a woman interviewing a woman. As Denzin (1989: 116) notes, 'It cannot be assumed that "gender-free" information is obtained in interviews. That is, one's gender shapes how one experiences and sees the world ... Gender is knowledge.' Similarly there are a number of issues associated with interviews of indigenous peoples and observance and understanding of social processes and practices that are inherent in indigenous cultures as well as topics which are culturally off-limits. Cross-cultural interviews are also sites for unequal power relationships, which may be compounded by limited command of interview language, literacy levels, different social mores and conduct protocols.

Credibility as an interviewer

The credibility of the interviewer links back to gaining access to the field. The gatekeeper(s) and participants need to see the interviewer as credible (and trustworthy) and the interviewer must be able to assume an insider role or be acceptable as an insider and subsequently use the language of the people being studied and be respectful of their values.

When to stop interviewing?

Qualitative material gathering is a different process from quantitative material gathering. Qualitative material gathering is guided by theoretical sampling. Theoretical sampling guides material collection and analysis and contributes to the determination of when to stop sampling. Qualitative interview texts and field notes are analysed as soon as materials are collected. The on-going process of material analysis drives the agenda to seek new areas in the research study or to follow-up on established areas of knowledge and understanding. Material collection will stop when there is sufficiency and saturation with regard to materials and their analysis (Seidman, 1991: 45) or when a qualitative informational isomorph is achieved (Ford, 1975; Lincoln and Guba, 1985). The term 'qualitative informational isomorph' refers to the collection of empirical materials until redundancy with regard to information is reached. Theoretical saturation occurs when materials fit identified categories and no new evidences or categories emerge (Charmz, 2000). Simply put, a qualitative researcher will stop when redundancy in regard to information is achieved.

Interview material recording

A number of authors who have written about interviews indicate that note-taking in interviews should be minimal in order not to interfere with the interview process (Young, 1939; see also Converse, 1987; Platt, 2002). Stake (1995) suggests that interviewers should take notes during interviews and not use a tape recorder. He argues this case because the intent of an interview is to gain understanding of the interviewee's accounts and the researcher should be able to expand notes after the interview has been completed.

On the other hand, interviews are participant observations (Denzin, 1989), within which the researcher will also be undertaking observations (refer to Table 9.5 again). Moreover, to facilitate participant observation, a good tape recorder enables the social interaction to be recorded authentically (Patton, 2002). Silverman (1993) also noted that transcripts of audio-recording provide superior accounts of the natural interaction within an interview. Of course, tape recorders can break down and also not record; interviewers need to monitor the equipment without fuss so as not to interrupt the flow of the interview interaction. When transferring recorded interviews into written text, a 90–120 minute tape takes approximately 4–6 hours to transcribe (35 words per minute typing speed). Researchers need to factor this into the overall design of the research process.

Reporting

The reproduction of material/information gathered in an interview will be transcribed either verbatim or minus pauses and repetitions depending on the analysis mode to be used. Full verbatim transcripts enable the researcher to monitor the communication styles mentioned in Table 9.5. Within the final research 'report(s)', excerpts from transcripts may be included to allow the voices of the participants to be heard and evident. The report will also be constructed using narrative genres and because of the subjective epistemological perspective associated with phenomenological paradigms first person, active voice will be used by the researcher.

Getting published

Qualitative research is not the hegemonic research methodology in tourism and as such the number of researchers able to review and comment effectively on qualitative research is limited. At times, quantitative researchers will review works and such critiques will often be misplaced as the wrong set of lenses has been applied in interpreting and critiquing the text. For example, requests are made for evidence to fulfil criteria from a positivistic paradigm and this reflects directly the incommensurability of the positivistic and phenomenological paradigms (as well as an understanding of

alternative paradigms). Sometimes reports of qualitative interviews have to be recast to fit the scientific report style which is evident in most structures outlined by journals. Researchers seeking to publish in journals reflective of a positivistic paradigm need to review writing guidelines and also engage in dialogue with editors or locate journals supportive of alternative paradigms.

Recommendations

Since qualitative interviews employ open-ended emergent designs, it is critical that researchers prepare, plan and consider the structure of their research projects (Seidman, 1991) and constantly monitor and review the processes and procedures and materials collected to guide the future steps and the closure of the study. While qualitative interviewing may appear to be deceptively simple, it is not. However, it is 'an adventure' (Rubin and Rubin, 1995) and one that generates great depth of knowledge, understanding and learning. The following case study of independent travellers demonstrates how some of the issues outlined above may be reconciled in the research process.

The Case Study: an Ethnography of Independent Travellers

There are a number of different types of independent travellers, for example, backpackers, caravanners, and long-term ocean cruisers. What makes these people move out of participating in mainstream society and adopt a lifestyle of long-term independent travel? How do they come to sustain the lifestyle? What is the lifestyle like? What are the impacts on family and relationships? Why do they terminate the lifestyle? What are their travel experiences? These were some of the questions that intrigued me about long-term ocean cruisers, that is, people who are self-supporting and live aboard their own boats for extended periods of time (3–5 years or more) while engaging in a circumnavigation of the world.

At their core, my intrigue focused on the lived experiences of these travellers, especially, the process of becoming, being and cessation of being such a traveller. Consequently, the phenomenological paradigm seemed the best fit with the research purpose and in particular the tradition of ethnography. Between 1992 and 1999, I engaged in an ethnographic study of long-term ocean cruisers. I became one of the independent travellers. My partner and I built a 40-foot steel boat and then joined the cruising subculture and embarked on a circumnavigation of the world. It was cut short by the 1990 Gulf War and safety issues associated with travel into that area. Our cruising adventure involved some 15,000 nautical miles and travel through Australia, Papua New Guinea and Indonesia.

The methods of data collection involved participant observation in all the various roles of participant observer, in-depth semi-structured interviews, visual ethnography and questionnaires regarding sociodemographics and boat details. To update the context of this earlier study, I have been engaging in further participant observation of long-term cruisers since 2000.

In the preceding section a number of debates and issues were raised in regard to qualitative interviewing. Entering the field was not an issue for me, I was living on a yacht at the time of interviewing my participants, I dressed and acted like a 'yachtie' (cruiser) – I had instant credibility. I was able to establish rapport with both men and women. Occasionally, the potential gendered nature of interviews became a test for me. Men in particular, would question me regarding my boat, its design, rigging, engine, power generation, refrigeration, and my navigation skills and cruising experiences. The grand tour question of the interview became part of the interview that the cruising men ran in order to see if they would spend time with me and how much information they would share. When I had answered all of their questions effectively, and using yachtie language, they relaxed and the interview would recommence with a strong rapport established. All interviews were conversational in manner and I also experienced 'no intimacy without reciprocity' (Oakley, 1981) when a woman cruiser said to me midway through an interview: '... you are being very professional ... now I want to know what you think!' (G.R. Jennings, unpublished).

As I had also sailed through the areas most cruisers were sailing into next, reciprocity was also associated with sharing knowledge of the cruising area they were about to enter, and examples of useful language for their Indonesian travels. Also at the time of the interview (either conducted on the participant's or my boat), I always took or gave something, a cake or a cooked meal. I emphasize here that this was not part of the agreement for an interview, that is, an incentive; it was my acknowledgement that the cruisers were giving of their precious time while in port. It was also a form of reciprocity and part of the culture not to arrive empty handed.

All possible participants who came into the study area were approached for an interview. To achieve maximum response rate, I would always wait until the second day in port to approach visiting yachts as I knew that the first day was frantic in getting tasks organized and underway. At the start of the second day, people had a better idea of their timeframe and space availability. At the first meeting, I dealt with the following aspects of ethics. I outlined the purpose of the study, for what and why it was being conducted, who would see the outcomes and what participation involved, including the time. I also gave my card with my name and yacht details on it. People usually agreed straight away or called by and let me know they were happy to be interviewed and a time was set up. For those who agreed straight away, and time allowed, I left several questionnaires dealing with socio-demographics and boat details to be completed prior to the interview. Others were given these when they called by to agree to participate.

At the commencement of the interviews, I revisited ethics and informed consent, and re-emphasized the point regarding stopping or not answering any questions. The majority of interviews were taped and this proved to be unproblematic; the tape recorder was small and positioned so that voices were effectively recorded but the recorder was not invasive. Several people did not want their voices recorded and for those interviews I took notes as the interview was conducted. I orally summarized parts and obtained feedback and then immediately following the interview wrote up my interview and field notes.

As interviews were conducted, I commenced transcription and analysis simultaneously. Some days, however, because of weather changes, numbers of boats would overwhelm me and there would be no time in the days or evenings for transcription and analysis. My field notes state:

> I have had two weeks of interviews,
> running three or four a day (from two to
> three hours each) they are starting to blur, I
> am not sure if we have talked about some
> aspects already and have had to do a
> check, this is not good, need to take a
> break from interviewing. But I don't have
> the luxury as I can't determine when boats
> will come in. Need to make memory
> checks to help as well as intense downtime
> in between interviews regardless how short.

The field notes enabled me to engage in reflexivity, and to consider aspects of theoretical sampling, which, along with grounded theory analysis, drove my material collection. I had no a priori theories although I did have some basic questions, as noted at the beginning of this section and as per Strauss and Corbin's (1990) style of grounded theory analysis. My literature review was conducted towards the end of my research process and determined by the analysis of cruiser materials. The literature review included: alienation and anomie; needs fulfilment, self actualization, flow theory; gender roles and relationships, equality and power, agency; authenticity, travel and tourism experiences and impacts; host–guest interactions; socio-economics; processes of moving from mainstream life into the margins, theories of subculture and positive deviance.

My sampling method was purposive and occasionally snowball sampling occurred as cruisers would tell me of other boats coming in and also tell others coming in that I was there. This assisted in my interview collection and also my credibility. Another note in regard to credibility is associated with issues of confidentiality. Within the culture of these independent travellers, part and parcel of living together is that you will interact. One cruiser in a non-research related session desired to know whether the social interaction was being studied or not. My credibility was so strong that others in the group said, 'You know Gayle, she is not like that, this is social time not research time', to which I also authentically acquiesced. But this demonstrates another challenge for qualitative interviewers: negotiating the multiple 'I's we assume as insider researchers and setting clear boundaries and expectations for self and others.

As is evident in this case study and in this chapter, the reporting of qualitative materials is different, the voice of the researcher is present and active rather than removed and passive. For some editors and publishers, this is problematic, for others not so, it is a matter of negotiation and of the editors putting on the appropriate lens with which to interact with the narrative style of text.

Conclusion

The use of qualitative interviews in tourism research is increasing incrementally; while the qualitative interview has been generally associated with tourism market research and mixed methods/methodologies, it also has a place as a primary tool of material collection within phenomenologically situated paradigms. Such paradigms give voice to the multiplicity of views and recognize the complex and ever changing nature of our lives. The multiple voices from which each of us as researchers speaks, coupled with the multivocality of participants when applied to the holistic study of the tourism phenomena, add depth and fulsome understanding which is socially, culturally, temporally, geographically and contextually situated. It is not a lesser or a better way of understanding but a different way of knowing to the dominant hegemony of positivism and its associated quantitative methodology and methods.

Acknowledgements

This chapter was written while on sabbatical leave. My thanks to my home institution, Central Queensland University, for granting and supporting the leave. The research reported in the case study was undertaken for my Doctor of Philosophy degree while a student at Murdoch University, Perth, Australia.

References

Babbie, E.R. (1998) *The Practice of Social Research*, 8th edn. Wadsworth Publishing Company, Belmont, California.

Bailey, K.D. (1994) *Methods of Social Research*, 4th edn. The Free Press, New York.

Benney, M. and Hughes, E.C. (1956) Of sociology and the interview. *American Journal of Sociology* 62, 137–142.

Bertaux, D. (ed.) (1981) *Biography and Society*, Sage, Beverley Hills, California.

Brannen, J. (ed.) (1992) *Mixing Methods: Qualitative and Quantitative Research*. Avebury, Aldershot, UK.

Burgess, R.G. (1982) The unstructured interview as a conversation. In: Burgess, R.G. (ed.) *Field Research: A Sourcebook and Field Manual*. Allen and Unwin, Boston, Massachusetts, pp. 107–110.

Cavana, R.Y., Delahaye, B.L. and Sekaran, U. (2001) *Applied Business Research, Qualitative and Quantitative Methods*. John Wiley and Sons, Milton, Australia.

Charmz, K. (2000) Grounded theory: objectivist and constructivist methods. In: Denzin, N.K. and Lincoln, Y.S. (eds) *Handbook of Qualitative Research*, 2nd edn. Sage, Thousand Oaks, California, pp. 509–535.

Chirban, J.T. (1996) *Interviewing In Depth, The Interactive-Relational Approach*, Sage, Thousand Oaks, California.

Cohen, E. (1988) Traditions in the qualitative sociology of tourism. *Annals of Tourism Research* 15, 29–46.

Converse, J.M. (1987) *Survey Research in the US: Roots and Emergence, 1890–1960*. University of California Press, Berkeley, California.

Creswell, J.W. (2003) *Research Design: Qualitative, Quantitative, and Mixed Methods Approaches*, 2nd edn. Sage, Thousand Oaks, California.

Dann, G., Nash, D. and Pearce, P. (1988) Methodology in tourism. *Annals of Tourism Research* 15, 1–28.

Denzin, N.K. (1989) *The Research Act, A Theoretical Introduction to Sociological Methods*. Prentice Hall, Englewood Cliffs, New Jersey.

Dexter, L.A. (1970) *Elite and Specialized Interviewing*. Northwestern University Press, Evanston, Illinois.

Dey, I. (1993) *Qualitative Data Analysis: a User Friendly Guide for the Social Scientists*. Routledge, London.

Douglas, J.D. (1985) *Creative Interviewing*. Sage Library of Social Research, Vol. 159. Sage, Beverley Hills, California.

Fetterman, D.M. (1989) *Ethnography, Step by Step*. Applied Research Methods Series, Vol. 17. Sage, Newbury Park, California.

Fontana, A. and Frey, J.H. (2000) The interview: from structured questions to negotiated text. In: Denzin, N.K. (ed.) *The Research Act, A Theoretical Introduction to Sociological Methods*, 3rd edn. Prentice Hall, Edglewood Cliffs, New Jersey, pp. 645–672.

Ford, J. (1975) *Paradigms and Fairy Tales: an Introduction to the Science of Meanings*, Vol. 1. Routledge and Kegan Paul, London.

Gallup, G. (1944) *A Guide to Public Opinion Polls*. Princeton University Press, Princeton, New Jersey.

Gergen, M.M. and Gergen, K.J. (2000) Qualitative inquiry: tensions and transformations. In: Denzin, N.K. and Lincoln, Y.S. (eds) *Handbook of Qualitative Research*, 2nd edn. Sage, Thousand Oaks, California, pp. 1025–1046.

Gorden, R.L. (1969) *Interviewing: Strategy, Techniques, and Tactics*. Dorsey, Homewood, Illinois.

Gubrium, J.F. and Holstein, J.A. (2002) From the individual interview to the interview society. In: Gubrium, J.F. and Holstein, J.A. (eds) *The Handbook of Interview Research: Context and Method*. Sage, Thousand Oaks, California, pp. 3–32.

Hammersley, M. and Atkinson, P. (1983) *Ethnography: Principles in Practice*. Tavistock, London.

Harding, S.G. (1991) *Whose Science? Whose Knowledge?: Thinking from Women's Lives*. Open University Press, Milton Keynes, UK.

Hollinshead, K. (1996) The tourism researcher as bricoleur: the new wealth and diversity in qualitative inquiry. *Tourism Analysis* 1, 67–74.

Hyman, H.H. (1975) *Interviewing in Social Research*. The University of Chicago Press, Chicago, Illinois.

Jamal, T. and Hollinshead, K. (2001) Tourism and the forbidden zone: the underserved power of qualitative inquiry. *Tourism Management* 22, 63–82.

Jennings, G.R. (2001) *Tourism Research*. John Wiley, Brisbane, Australia.

Jennings, G.R. (2004) Business and social science methods. *Encyclopedia of Social Measurement*. Academic Press, San Diego, California.

Jorgensen, D.L. (1989) *Participant Observation, A Methodology for Human Studies*. Applied Social Research Methods Series, Vol. 15, Sage, Newbury Park, California.

Kvale, S. (1996) *Interviews: an Introduction to Qualitative Research Interviewing*. Sage, Thousand Oaks, California.

Lincoln, Y.S. and Guba, E.G. (1985) *Naturalistic Inquiry*. Sage, Newbury Park, California.

Lincoln, Y.S. and Guba, E.G. (2000) Paradigmatic controversies, contradictions, and emerging confluences. In: Denzin, N.K. and Lincoln, Y.S. (eds) *Handbook of Qualitative Research*, 2nd edn. Sage, Thousand Oaks, California, pp. 163–188.

Maccoby, E.E. and Maccoby, N. (1954) The interview: a tool of social science. In: Lindzey, G. (ed.) *Handbook of Social Psychology: Vol 1. Theory and Method*. Addison-Wesley, Reading, Massachusetts, pp. 449–487.

Merton, R. (ed.) (1982) *Social Research and the Practicing Professions*. Abt Books, Cambridge, Massachusetts.

Merton, R.K., Fiske, M. and Kendall, P.L. (1956) *The Focused Interview*. Free Press, Glencoe, Illinois.

Miles, M.B. and Huberman, A.M. (1994) *Qualitative Data Analysis: An Expanded Sourcebook*, 2nd edn. Sage, Thousand Oaks, California.

Mishler, E.G. (1986) *Research Interviewing, Context and Narrative*. Harvard University Press, Cambridge, Massachusetts.

Oakley, A. (1981) Interviewing women: a contradiction in terms. In: Roberts, H. (ed.) *Doing Feminist Research*. Routledge and Kegan Paul, London, pp. 30–61.

Palmer, V.M. (1928) *Field Studies in Sociology: a Student's Manual*. University of Chicago Press, Chicago, Illinois.

Patton, M.Q. (1990) *Qualitative Evaluation and Research Methods*, 2nd edn. Sage, Newbury Park, California.

Patton, M.Q. (2002) *Qualitative Evaluation and Research Methods*, 3rd edn. Sage, Thousand Oaks, California.

Platt, J. (2002) The history of the interview. In: Gubrium, J.F. and Holstein, J.A. (eds) *The Handbook of Interview Research: Context and Method*. Sage, Thousand Oaks, California, pp. 33–54.

Riley, R.W. and Love, L.L. (2000) The state of qualitative tourism research. *Annals of Tourism Research* 27(1), 164–187.

Rogers, C.R. (1980) *A Way of Being*. Houghton Mifflin, Boston, Massachusetts.

Rubin, H.J. and Rubin, I.S. (1995) *Qualitative Interviewing: the Art of Hearing Data*. Sage, Thousand Oaks, California.

Scheurich, J.J. (1997) *Research Method in the Postmodern*. Qualitative Studies Series: 3. The Falmer Press, London.

Schutz, A. (1967) *The Phenomenology of the Social World*. (G. Walsh and F. Lehnert, trans.). Northwestern University Press, Chicago, Illinois.

Seidman, I.E. (1991) *Interviewing as Qualitative Research: a Guide for Researchers in Education and the Social Sciences*. Teachers College Press, New York.

Silverman, D. (1993) *Interpreting Qualitative Data: Methods for Analysing Talk, Text and Interaction*. Sage, London.

Silverman, D. (1997) Towards an aesthetics of research. In: Silverman, D. (ed.) *Qualitative Research: Theory, Method and Practice*. Sage, London, pp. 239–253.

Spradley, J.P. (1979) *The Ethnographic Interview*. Holt, Rinehart and Winston, New York.

Spradley, J. (1980) *Participant Observation*. Rinehart & Winston, New York.

Stake, R. (1995) *The Art of Case Study Research*. Sage, Thousand Oaks, California.

Starr, L. (1984) Oral history. In: Dunaway, D. and Baum, W.K. (eds) *Oral History: an Interdisciplinary Anthology*. American Association for State and Local History, Nashville, Tennessee, pp. 3–26.

Strauss, A. and Corbin, J. (1990) *Basics of Qualitative Research: Grounded Theory Procedures and Techniques*. Sage, Newbury Park, California.

Tashakkori, A. and Teddlie, C. (1998) *Mixed Methodology: Combining Qualitative and Quantitative Approaches*. Applied Social Science Research Methods Series, Vol. 46. Sage, Thousand Oaks, California.

Thomas, W.I. and Znaniecki, F. (1918–19) *The Polish Peasant in Europe and America*. University of Chicago Press, Chicago, Illinois.

Ticehurst, G.W. and Veal, A.J. (1999) *Business Research Methods: a Managerial Approach*. Longman, Australia.

Walle, A.H. (1997) Quantitative versus qualitative tourism research. *Annals of Tourism Research* 24(3), 524–536.

Yin, R.K. (1994) *Case Study Research, Design and Methods*, 2nd edn. Applied Social Research Methods Series, Vol. 5. Sage, Thousand Oaks, California.

Young, P.V. (1939) *Scientific Social Surveys and Research*. Prentice Hall, New York.

10 Applying the Mystery Shopping Technique: the Case of Lunn Poly

GRAHAM MILLER,[1] SIMON HUDSON[2] AND ROCHELLE TURNER[3]

[1]School of Management, University of Surrey, Guildford, Surrey GU2 7XH, UK;
[2]University of Calgary, 2500 University Drive NW, Alberta T2N 1N4, Canada;
[3]TUI-UK, Greater London House, Hampstead Road, London NW1 7SD, UK

Introduction

Mystery shopping is a rapidly increasing area of research. Wilson (2001) reports that the market for this form of participant observation has grown to be worth between $30 and $45 million per year in the UK. In addition, the range of industries applying mystery shopping programmes has increased to include most service industries, including the tourism industry (Hudson *et al.*, 2001). Despite this promotion in interest, Finn and Kayande (1999: 196) observe, '… surprisingly little discussion of the technique has appeared in academic literature'. This chapter considers the value of mystery shopping as a research instrument and its applicability to the tourism industry. The case study reports on a programme of mystery shopping developed by one of the four big travel agencies in the UK and focuses on the way mystery shopping research is used, and the validity, reliability, ethics and cost-effectiveness of such a programme of research.

Philosophy Underpinning Mystery Shopping

Patton (1990: 199) describes how 'To understand a world you must become part of that world while at the same time remaining separate, a part of and apart from'. Such a belief underpins observational research and has given rise to great cultural anthropological studies where researchers have immersed themselves in a setting to come to understand the traditions, language, values and attitudes of those being studied. Mystery shopping is a form of participant observation, which Lofland (1971: 93) describes as '… the circumstances of being in or around an on-going social setting for the purpose of making a qualitative analysis of that setting'. Qualitative analysis describes the goal of exploring a setting, discovering issues and applying inductive logic.

A principal benefit of observational research is that the researcher is able to observe the behaviour of interest directly as it occurs rather than asking respondents to describe events at a later point in time. This direct contact enables the researcher to achieve a deeper understanding than if the researcher only hears an interpretation of events. It may be of value to understand how a customer interprets events, but a customer satisfaction survey that asks a customer to describe a previous service interaction is unlikely to obtain an accurate description of events, only the customer's perception of events. A trained observational researcher can more accurately describe events, but can only serve as a proxy for understanding how a customer interprets these events. Hence, the mystery shopping method is one step removed from the actual actors involved in the event, but is one step closer to the event of interest.

An additional strength of observational research is that the researcher is able to witness events in their natural context, providing further value to the accuracy of the data (Frankfort-Nachmias and Nachmias, 1996). Patton (1990: 231) observes, 'If participants ... are not aware that an evaluation is taking place and are not aware that they are being observed, then reactivity is less of a threat to the validity of the evaluation'. This affords the researcher the opportunity to view behaviour in an open and inductive manner, unfettered by prior conceptualizations.

Change in Use of Mystery Shopping

From the philosophical traditions of participant observation, mystery shopping as it is increasingly applied is changing. As a form of qualitative research mystery shopping has previously been used to tell a story about customer service in a particular outlet, by a particular sales consultant at a particular time. From this, a hypothesis could be developed about the need to introduce changes to the training of staff, customer processing, etc. The lack of concern for demographics, regression analysis or statistical modelling is not due to the nascent form of the research method; instead, this is central to the nature of qualitative research. Mystery shopping has traditionally been a qualitative research method used to paint a picture, but more recently has been deracinated from this tradition. Instead mystery shopping is being re-planted as a quantitative, deductive research method, designed to test the strength of the relationship between previously identified elements of the customer service encounter and an increase in customer satisfaction and ultimately an increase in sales. Mystery shopping still retains some of its essence of qualitative inquiry, by relying on personal contact to

get close to the research and utilizing direct quotations to capture the experience. Yet, less and less of the researcher's own experience is of value as the range and freedom of consideration become more pre-determined and constrained.

Leeds (1995) argues that of all the forms of market research, mystery shopping is the first to be fully accepted by the banking industry because of its simplicity and the ease with which the concept is understood. The consequence of the increasingly widespread usage is the need to ensure reliability across all the different tests conducted. Responding to this challenge, Wilson (2001) identifies the increasing use of objective measures as a way to improve the reliability of mystery shopping. Yet, the use of objective measures constrains analysis and militates against the hypothesis development and exploratory nature of qualitative research.

Finn and Kayande (1999) argue that it is the measurement of objective elements of the customer service encounter that mystery shopping is best suited for. As such, assessing if the door is open or closed, whether the customer is greeted or offered a cup of coffee or if name tags are clearly visible prevents the subjectivity of the researcher from reducing the reliability of the research. However, Morrison *et al.* (1997) argue that this misunderstands the contribution mystery shopping can make as well as ignores the limitations of the mystery shoppers. Morrison *et al.* (1997) believe that human cognitive processes are such that mystery shoppers will perceive, encode and report all situations differently, whilst also all being subject to the processes of forgetting and the risk of reconstructing events. As such, the concept of 'objective measures' is exposed as weak and gives a falsely definitive air to such elements. 'Central' issues are more likely to be recorded accurately than 'peripheral' issues, but what is deemed to be central or peripheral is subject to the individual. Hence, if all the desks are tidy and free of clutter, this is likely to be recognized as such by a mystery shopper for whom this is important, but a person for whom cleanliness and tidiness is not of central importance will struggle to recall any evidence of this element and may reconstruct an answer to this objective element of consideration.

In addition to forgetting, the problem exists of our own prejudices, expectations and social attitudes influencing and distorting our memory. Morrison *et al.* (1997: 355) believe '... these ... biases occur most often in situations – such as those confronting mystery customer assessors – in which a large amount of information has to be remembered'; hence, it is important for mystery shoppers to be representative of the customer base to ensure that the same range of prejudices, expectations and attitudes are demonstrated. Yet, the difference lies in the fact that real customers are not forced to remember and score a service encounter on specific points, and, thus, the risk of re-constructing events is less likely. This leads Morrison *et al.* (1997) to recommend dividing the elements for assessment into the objective and the subjective, with the objective tested in an overt manner, aided by the use of a checklist. Such a visit would be announced only upon the arrival of the assessor, providing no opportunity for preparation by the shop staff, but with improved accuracy possible by not having to commit all the mandatory elements of the assessment to memory. The more subjective elements can then be tested secretly using mystery shopping, but there will be fewer elements to assess and so less risk of overloading and forgetting, reducing the potential need for reconstructing events.

While reliability has not widely been promoted through the separate assessment of subjective and objective elements, much more attention has been given in the literature to the more obvious need to match mystery shoppers appropriately to the product or service being investigated and to provide adequate training (Madden *et al.*, 1997; Wilson, 1998; Yeh and Kuo, 2003). Best practice requires that potential mystery shoppers are shown videos, or examples of what is understood to be varying levels of customer service. Madden *et al.* (1997) report that unless a shopper in training receives 85 per cent adherence with an expert panel, then the shopper is not allowed to take part in the main study. Hardin (1968) famously asked, 'Quis custodiet ipsos custodies?' (who shall watch the watchers?) and supervision of mystery shoppers in the field is difficult to conduct whilst retaining the pretence of the visit. Hence the mystery shopper is often alone from the first visit, with the associated risks to reliability, although Wilson and Gutman (1998) report on a study conducted by London Underground where 8 per cent of all mystery visits were either accompanied or spot-checked by a supervisor.

Sample Size, Validity and Reliability

Finn and Kayande (1999: 197) observe, '... published data on the reliability and validity of mystery shopping remains non-existent'. The authors are concerned that as the research method is being increasingly employed to test, rather than develop, hypotheses, increasing attention must be paid to the sample size if conclusions that can be generalized are to be drawn from the research. Such a position moves away from the qualitative tradition of the method, but reflects the reality of the way mystery shopping is being used. Further, the use of mystery shopping programmes as a method of calculating staff performance bonuses means that it must be possible for defensible conclusions to be drawn from any research conducted. Finn and Kayande (1999: 208) concluded from their research that '... it would be very unwise to rely on a single visit report when comparing outlets'; indeed, for subjective constructs the authors believe 40 visits are required, while 11 are needed for objective constructs to be statistically reliable. As an example, London Underground (LU) conduct at least seven mystery shopper visits of each platform at each of the 246 LU stations every quarter to assess 26 measures of their trains and 116 measures of their stations (Wilson and Gutman, 1998). Assuming two platforms for each underground station (this is the minimum number, many stations will have far more platforms), this means nearly 14,000 mystery shopper visits are made per year.

Yet, as mystery shopping programmes pursue greater reliability, it is apposite to consider what the effect is on the validity of the method. If the aim of the research programme is to replicate a customer's experience (but to enable this experience to be recorded after the encounter), then the mystery shopper should be as close to being a typical customer as is possible. However, typical customers do not pay attention to all the elements of service delivery that a company may be concerned with. A service encounter is a complex human interaction, and so the mystery shopper is trained to assess a vast range of elements that may or may not be germane for any particular encounter. Further, the participation of the ersatz customer is not complete in the way it is for an actual customer. The sense of risk, excitement and trepidation at making such a considerable purchase are all absent from the experience for a mystery shopper, for whom the process is their job and thus routine.

As the mystery shopper is trained, so they become hyper-aware of every aspect of service delivery, but therefore no longer typical of most customers that the outlet needs to face; instead, more like a researcher with a checklist of items to consider. A researcher with a checklist will be more reliable across a range of shops because they know they must look out for the same elements in every encounter. Further, reliability is enhanced across a number of shoppers who have all been trained to the same standards and to recognize examples of good and bad customer service. As such, the increase in reliability achieved through training and the development of objective measures to assess may come at the expense of risk to the validity of the pursuit of a realistic service encounter. The effect of this trade on the validity of the research method will depend on the effect of the training on the researcher in identifying issues of importance, whilst retaining the approach of an actual customer. However, to set this discussion in context, referring to advice given by medical doctors to mystery shoppers acting as patients, Madden *et al.* (1997: 1469) believe the method '... provides data which would be difficult or impossible to obtain through other methods'.

Cost Effectiveness of Mystery Shopping Programmes

As discussed above, if mystery shopping is to be used as a quantitative, rather than a qualitative, research method, then a substantial number of visits need to occur. Wilson and Gutman (1998) describe the programme undertaken by London Underground, which at a very conservative estimate must cost over £550,000 to run. With such an expense, the research needs to be utilized to produce outcomes of sufficient import to justify the cost, typically in a financial sense through cost savings or increased revenue.

LU operate their mystery shopper programme alongside an extensive programme of customer satisfaction surveys in order to assess the importance customers attach to various elements of the service delivery such as train punctuality through to the provision of public telephones on the platform. By assessing performance through mystery shopping and importance through customer surveys, in combination with information about the number of passengers using various services, the research is able to inform LU management of the investment priorities they should have. Hence, the provision of telephones on the platform edge may have scored poorly on the mystery shopping visits and require a substantial investment to raise the performance level, but as this is not important to customers, raising the mystery shopping score receives a low priority rating (Wilson and Gutman, 1998).

While the main benefit of the mystery shopping programme by LU is improved investment decisions, by linking several pieces of research LU are additionally able to bring research to the centre of management decisions and raise the profile of market research from its more usual peripheral role. Yet, having found itself occupying a more central role in management decisions than is typically the case for market research, the danger lies in the misuse of the mystery shopping research method, whereby the method is misapplied and suffers from validity and reliability issues. Such a situation risks devaluing market research as a discipline. The example of LU demonstrates the value that can be accrued from a well-conceived mystery shopping programme, while Finn and Kayande (1999) review many applications of the method that do not meet the standards that LU set.

Cost effectiveness from mystery shopping programmes can come not just in a change in operations or investment direction as a result of the research, but also through the signal sent out about the commitment of the organization to customer service. For the tourism industry, with limited product differentiation between the major tour operators, service differentiation is an important target. It may be an old maxim that 'what gets measured gets managed', but the lack of an assessment programme is likely to convey to staff, and ultimately to customers, that customer service is not taken seriously. Similarly, the mystery shopping of competitors can enable comparisons and the identification of areas of relative strength and weakness, signifying customer service to be an important area of competition. Thus, in the same way that research can be brought in from the margins of management, so mystery shopping can place customer service closer to the centre of decision making.

In order to further cement the importance of customer service in the minds of staff, Morrall (1994: 2) reports how increasingly organizations are '... tying mystery shopper programmes to merit and reward programmes'. Such a technique marks a further step in the quantification of the mystery shopping technique and necessarily so, as the determination of bonuses must be defensible against challenge. Wilson and Gutman (1998: 292) report that in the case of LU '... there is statistical proof that changes in mystery shopping scores will feed through to a change in customer satisfaction'. Conversely, Morrison et al. (1997: 355) observe, 'A mystery customer assessment is, by its nature, a report of an individual rather than of a representative sample of the cus-

tomer population' and where insufficient numbers of visits have been conducted to have confidence in the representative nature of the scores achieved, then front line staff and the management of the company share the risk of inaccurate levels of reward based on the research conducted. As staff are unlikely to be motivated to work harder by an undeservedly generous reward payment, but will be demotivated by an inaccurately reduced payment, so the cost effectiveness of the mystery shopper programme can be questioned.

Ethical Considerations

Jorgensen (1989) believes that mystery shopping research is ethical because it does not violate the right to privacy of the research participant. Mystery shopping takes place in a public arena where it is reasonable to assume that we do not engage in activities that we would not be happy for the general public to witness. Hence, mystery shopping does not violate our rights to privacy, but this is not sufficient to make mystery shopping ethical because the rights that may be violated are those of the research participant to avoid deception and exploitation.

In any social science research there may be the need to balance the rights of the researcher to conduct research against various rights of the research participants, including the right to privacy, to be free from exploitation and to avoid being deceived. Typically, this tension is relieved by the research participant giving informed consent to be involved with the research, and so waiving their rights not to be exploited or deceived. However, the four crucial elements of informed consent are that the research participant is competent to approbate, does so voluntarily and without duress, is fully informed of all aspects of the research and so fully comprehends what they are consenting to. While competence is unlikely often to be an issue for tourism researchers using mystery shopping, voluntarism is relevant. Where a company introduces a programme of mystery shopping research, it may be contractual that all staff agree to be mystery shopped. However, where such research programmes have been conceived after contracts have been issued, then consent is not explicitly given, but may be assumed under a general contractual clause such as 'acting in accordance with the wishes of your line manager'. With no prior consent the ethical pellucidity of the research is reduced.

A prescient programme of mystery shopper research will seek to avoid industrial relations problems by informing staff about the research programme and offering opportunities for concerns to be aired. However, it is crucial to the concept of informed consent that the staff are told the true reasons for the research. Clearly it is not always possible to achieve the real aims of the research if these intentions are made obvious at the beginning. Frankfort-Nachmias and Nachmias (1996: 93) state, 'Deceit of the participants should only be used if it is absolutely necessary, there being no other way to study the problem'. Yet research that claimed to be assessing customer service at an aggregated national or regional level, but actually used the data to assess individual members of the organization would be practising a deceit. Indeed, Berry (1995) holds that the attraction to management of mystery shopping is the ability to identify and evaluate the performance of individual employees. If such intentions are suspected by employees, then the programme is likely to meet with resistance. Similarly, the way the data is stored, who has access to this data and how it will be used in the future are important considerations to air before a research programme can claim to have received informed consent.

In order that the diminution of the rights of staff is balanced by the need for the research, some benefit should accrue from the research that will be of positive use to those staff suffering the loss of rights. Such a benefit may be as simple as feedback that leads to greater self-knowledge, or more extrinsic rewards such as financial bonuses. However, such benefits lead the discussion back to the dangers of conducting mystery

shopper research with poor sampling and to the risk of misjudging the contribution of an employee. In such an instance where the research has been of poor quality, the trade for the suppression of the rights of employees has not been equitable and the research can be deemed to be unethical. A further risk of poor research is that the research participants come to develop distrust of research itself and those in authority/management (Milgram, 1975). While it is to be hoped that tourism researchers will not design a research methodology using mystery shopping to compare to the horrors of Milgram's study, any research poorly conceived or conducted risks muddying the waters for future research, and so must also be considered unethical.

Case Study

Context

Lunn Poly is the main retail arm of Thomson tour operators, selling approximately 3 million holidays per year. Thomson is the largest tour operator brand in the UK, with a 20% market share, while Thomson in turn is part of the TUI travel group, which is the largest tour operator in the world.

Feeling that customer service was in need of review, in 2002 Lunn Poly decided to instigate a programme of mystery shopping amongst its retail outlets in order to assess the service provided by sales consultants. Lunn Poly had last used mystery shopping in 1993, and since then various regional managers have cooperated on a bilateral and informal basis to mystery shop each other. *Travel Trade Gazette* and *Travel Weekly* conduct mystery shopping visits on the leading travel agents and provide comparisons, but these are not specific to the needs of any single organization. This somewhat piecemeal approach has contributed to a lack of consistency of customer service standards across the country, types of travel agents and distribution channels.

Lunn Poly's new programme initially covered just 300 shops, split into two phases of 150 shops, plus 100 calls to call centres. This pilot programme recognized the need to ensure consistency of service in Lunn Poly shops across the UK and so it was decided to expand the programme to cover all Lunn Poly shops as well as other parts of the distribution channel, such as the direct sell element. In total, 766 Lunn Poly shops, 60 Travel House shops, 32 Callers Pegasus and 10 Sibbald Travel shops would receive four mystery shopping visits throughout the year from February 2003, giving a total of 3472 mystery shopping visits, plus 450 calls to the call centres.

Learning from the difficulties of previous research, the Lunn Poly mystery shopping programme sought to develop three different scenarios for the three types of retail outlets that Lunn Poly commonly divides itself into. However, the market research agency employed initially was not able to assure Thomson that sufficient efforts were being made to match the profile of the shopper with the scenario being enacted. This agency had its contract terminated and a second agency sought to match more closely the shopper profiles with the scenarios.

The formal aims of the 2003 programme of mystery shopping were to determine:

- The effectiveness and quality of staff.
- Sales and service performance (including transaction time).
- Whether the sales and service approach meets customers' expectations.
- Content of the sales delivery.
- The cleanliness and appearance of the shops.

However, informally there was a recognition that as this research was long overdue, then at least the first visit (referred to as the first phase of the research) was to be used as a 'dipstick' to see how the company was performing across a range of elements of customer service. Yet, once the intentions of the programme became known throughout the organization, so different departments came forward with research ideas that they wished to be included within the questionnaire. As an example, a number of shops had been entirely re-fitted and managers wanted to know what the mystery shoppers thought of these re-fitted shops and whether additions such as the coffee machine and coconut aroma machine were valued. While such requests will have been judged on their research merits, it is reasonable to assume that the items finally included on the questionnaire represented to some extent the political strength within the organization of different departments. As such, a variety of informal aims became manifest and despite the formal aim to assess 'effectiveness', it is fair to describe the research as exploratory in nature.

Use of mystery shopping as a research method

Lunn Poly conduct regular customer satisfaction surveys on genuine customers as they leave a shop, but these are conducted only in relatively small numbers and were felt to provide only a quantitative answer to the question of customer satisfaction as an end point rather than to examine the process of customer service. As more depth was required on understanding this process, so mystery shopping as a research method was decided upon. This desire to use qualitative research, coupled with the exploratory aims of the research, would make mystery shopping an appropriate method. 'We want to make sure that through the eyes of the customer we are doing what they are expecting because traditionally we have had a way that we have done things and who is to say that it is right' (Lunn Poly, 2003, personal communication). However, the insistence on asking questions about objective measures constrains the value of the mystery shoppers to use their own eyes to challenge the rubric and instead they are forced to see only what the questionnaire asks about.

However, as a result of the objective elements to the questionnaire some important changes have been made to operational practice. Transaction time in city shops was felt to be too long and so measures have been introduced to allow customers to leave their details and questions on a 'drop and go' leaflet and have a travel consultant contact the customer later. Such changes show the value of research, yet it is the perception of whether the time taken to be seen by a consultant is too long that is important and not the actual length of time taken. As such, the objective measure is of less value than the subjective measure and being alerted to the impatience of those using city shops could have been achieved with a much smaller and more qualitative focus than was the case.

Of 64 questions on the questionnaire, only 28 related to subjective questions such as 'Did you feel that the overall atmosphere in the shop was welcoming?', whereas the remaining 36 questions were objective and asked questions such as, 'How many customers were waiting to be served when you entered the shop?'. Separating the questionnaire into subjective and objective elements as recommended by Morrison *et al.* (1997) would enable the mystery shoppers to more completely view the shopping interaction with their own eyes and provide qualitative comments that might enable Lunn Poly to review the traditional elements of their distribution process.

Concern was expressed about the effect that the announced visit that was being made to assess objective issues would have on the staff, who would become aware that they were being mystery shopped. Although it is more standard practice in the USA to announce at the completion of the visit that a mystery shopping visit has been conducted, this has not been standard practice in the UK, where the approach has been considered too confrontational. Yet, making it obvious when certain elements of the service encounter were tested should increase the acceptance of the programme as the employees are able to acknowledge that they have been visited on a day when all was not well in the shop, if that was the case.

Additionally, if a non-representative number of visits is conducted, a shop with a normally high standard of performance could be reviewed on the four occasions throughout the year when service is not up

to its usual standards. Without knowing the dates on which the visits took place, the shop manager could justifiably feel aggrieved at the score received and question the veracity of the research programme. However, armed with the dates of the visits, a reasonable shop manager would not direct his/her dissatisfaction towards the research programme, but instead at the non-representative nature of the sample size.

Sample size, validity and reliability

The challenge to the non-representative nature of the sample is that one bad review is one bad review too many and even a new employee should be able to score sufficiently well on the visit with enthusiasm and a good, helpful attitude. Indeed, in a competitive market with little to distinguish between the major tour operators, it is essential for service to be a source of positive differentiation. The risk lies in whether it is possible in just four visits per year to distinguish accurately between the best and worst performers.

It is unclear how it was decided to make four mystery shopping visits to each retail outlet per year, but the decision was not made on the basis of providing a statistically reliable set of data. Instead, practical concerns such as cost and the length of time needed to visit all the retail outlets were cited as the main factors determining the number of visits undertaken. However, there was recognition of the problems of ensuring reliable outcomes. Those outlets that receive a maximum score from their four visits were to be identified in the in-house magazine, '… but what we didn't want to do was print it after the first phase because it could be that they score 100 this time, but then 40 next and so it isn't consistent' (Lunn Poly, 2003, personal communication).

Promoting the validity of the mystery shopper through being reflective of a typical Lunn Poly shopper has received some attention in this research programme, but the outcome is instructive as it reflects the tension between pure and practical research.

The market research agency contracted provided assurances that all their shoppers are trained and match the profiles of the scenarios set for the various outlets. However, it was then acknowledged that the age criteria to match shoppers to scenarios had to be relaxed because of the pressures of finding a sufficient number of shoppers to conduct the visits. Validity can be promoted by conducting two separate visits; each visit made to subjectively assess customer service would be shorter and more visits could be conducted using age-matched (and, ideally, matched in other demographics) shoppers. The objective assessment of the shop could be performed by researchers with any demographic background, while also having less need for training. Thus, the validity of the research is enhanced as the shopper faces less risk of reconstructing events that are not of central concern to him/her, while the reliability of the research is strengthened through the use of questions consistently applied.

Yet, what is of greater import is that those using the research understand that mystery shopping does not necessarily provide insight into what the customer is thinking. The mystery shopper is a researcher, working, who is pretending to be a customer at leisure, and as such can provide opinion on the service interaction, but cannot necessarily provide a view into the thinking of Lunn Poly's customers. Hence caution must be exercised in interpreting the findings.

Cost-effectiveness

The rationale for the expenditure on the mystery shopping programme is that if it generates an extra three sales per retail outlet per year the programme will have paid for itself. This target is felt to be achievable, but at present it is too early to determine whether this mark can be met. However, the principle of correlating sales figures with mystery shopping scores is sensible, whilst triangulating the findings does also provide a way to justify the research programme and argue for its continuance in the future.

A major theme to the research has been the need to use the mystery shopping visits to identify gaps in staff training and then to work to develop staff skills. An early finding of the research is that there is a variation in the ability of staff to meet customer needs across the three types of shops. This is to be expected as all sales consultants currently receive a standardized training package, but clearly the demands of serving a well-off and well-travelled customer will vary from the demands of serving a customer seeking a more traditional sun, sand and sea holiday. Hence, '... we are trying to make our staff individuals and people that the customers like and that they build a rapport with and hopefully they will remember us for that' (Lunn Poly, 2003, personal communication). Thus, Lunn Poly is now looking into the benefits of staff receiving training specific to the customer typical of the shop where they will be working, rather than training that is uniform across the organization.

In addition to the amount of sales generated, further measures of cost-effectiveness have developed from the research. Assuming a strong quantitative element to the mystery shopping programme, it may be possible in the future to compare scores for the mystery shopping visits against measures of customer satisfaction using more conventional survey instruments. Staff satisfaction surveys also represent a potential comparator to assess the effect of satisfied staff on service performance. For mystery shopping conducted via the telephone, the market research agency that conducted the research has a normative database of studies conducted on comparable organizations so it will be possible to relate service performance across industry borders. Such an action is useful given that on some metrics customers will not expect to receive a different level of service just because they are buying a tourism product as opposed to a financial, health or educational product.

Relating the mystery shopper programme to other aspects of research serves not only to justify this research programme, but also to strengthen the role of research within the organization. As an example, the mystery shopping programme has led to the hypothesis that the design of the shop window plays a significant role in whether customers enter the shop and thus are in a position to make a purchase. Analysis is currently underway to track the design of the window (clear of adverts and posters or complete with posters, etc.) against footfall (the number of customers entering the shop) and sales. Such a finding utilizes the contribution that research can make to the organization, but which so often has not been the case.

Ethical considerations

Typical of most commercial organizations, the consideration of the ethics of this research programme has been constrained to the practicalities of successfully achieving 'buy-in' from employees. In the case of Lunn Poly this has been made easier by the fact that mystery shopping was not new to many of the employees. 'They have known that it has always gone on, but it has never been formalized' (Lunn Poly, 2003, personal communication). Hence, while no consent was sought to expand the programme of research, its aims, administration and existence have been explained and made transparent. A briefing document was sent to all retail outlets explaining the proposed programme and time was set aside to explain to staff what was expected and what the outcomes of the research would achieve. By making explicit the programme of mystery shopping, the right to avoid deception and exploitation is not breached. In addition, the promised provision of training to employees can be seen as a 'quid pro quo' for the imposition upon existing working practices. Further, as few large organizations would explicitly seek consent from staff for mystery shopping research, Lunn Poly's approach can be seen as being consistent with its ethical context.

One remaining ethical concern is the ability of senior management to identify individuals from the data. Prior to the initial briefing document it had been the intention to provide feedback to retail managers that included the date and time of the visit and the name of the sales consultant shopped. However, '... what we have done now is just put the month they are visited and there are no names because we don't want it to be a witch hunt' (Lunn Poly, 2003, personal communication). One reason for this apparent corporate comity is the recognition of the fact that, given the way the programme has been set up, the data are best analysed at an organizational or regional level, rather than at the micro level of a particular outlet. A further reason is the preservation of the anonymity of the individual visited. The removal of the person's name and the specific time of the visit makes it impossible for the shop manager to identify which of his/her employees was responsible for the score achieved. As such, the manager must take responsibility for the whole shop over an extended period of time rather than focus attention on a certain individual's performance at a certain time. This second reason demonstrates the number of informal aims that lay behind this research programme and sets the use of the mystery shopping as a research method for the tourism industry in its proper commercial context. Yet, for verification purposes specific dates and names are still recorded by the market research agency conducting the visits and so at some levels of the organization it would still be possible to identify individuals. It is important that a statement be made about who can have access to this information and the purposes for which it can be used.

The only additional aspect of the research that was not made explicit to sales consultants was that the score achieved directly affected the bonus received by their shop manager. As has been discussed above, the provision of a financial bonus determined by mystery shopping programmes is contentious in many ways, not least in that it corrupts the research method and forces it to adopt an over-quantitative focus in an attempt to garner reliability. The attempt to promote the ownership of a shop through extrinsic rewards for managers is laudable, but this research programme is the wrong vehicle to use to arrive at this goal.

Conclusions

Lunn Poly should be strongly congratulated for the efforts they have made to introduce more research, and innovative research, into the tourism industry. This case study is based on outcomes from the research produced before the completion of the second wave of the visits, and there is much the company will be able to learn as the research evolves. The research programme was described as being exploratory and a 'dipstick' for understanding the position of the company. Valuable lessons can be drawn from this research to enable the programme to develop for the future and four suggestions are offered below for consideration.

First, the bonus payments received by shop managers create problems for the research instrument and the authors would suggest separating the payments from the scores received as a result of mystery shopping visits to their staff.

Second, the current length of the questionnaire is such that it risks events being reconstructed rather than recalled. The questionnaire might beneficially be separated into two questionnaires: one to cover the subjective elements of service delivery and conducted in a covert manner, the other to assess the objective elements of the customer's experience and conducted in an unannounced, but open, manner.

Third, further consideration should be given to how the sample size of the programme can better match the type of research conducted. If the programme is to be qualitative, then the sample size can be reduced and the customer experience can be seen more truly through eyes not blinkered by a strict questionnaire. By contrast, if the aim is to use the programme as a measure of customer service, then the sample size needs to increase such that the reliability of the results can be significant. Alternatively, the research can view the results at an aggregate level, in which case the number of visits conducted may be appropriate, but for a more micro level of analysis the number of visits would need to be increased.

Fourth, developing from this initial programme of mystery shopping research Lunn Poly will be able to tie in with other areas of research that they and Thomson are conducting. Linking with the sales figure, footfall in shops, staff satisfaction and customer satisfaction will serve to promote research to a more central role in decision making that frequently market research departments fail to occupy.

References

Berry, L.L. (1995) *On Great Service*. The Free Press, New York.

Finn, A. and Kayande, U. (1999) Unmasking a phantom: a psychometric assessment of mystery shopping. *Journal of Retailing* 75(2), 195–217.

Frankfort-Nachmias, C. and Nachmias, D. (1996) *Research Methods in the Social Sciences*. Arnold, London.

Hardin, G. (1968) The tragedy of the Commons. *Science* 162, 1243–1248.

Hudson, S., Snaith, T., Miller, G. and Hudson, P. (2001) Travel retailing: 'switch-selling' in the UK. *Journal of Travel Research* 40, 148–154.

Jorgensen, D.L. (1989) *Participant Observation: a Methodology for Human Studies*. Sage, Newbury Park, California.

Leeds, B. (1995) Mystery shopping: from novelty to necessity. *Bank Marketing* June, Issue 6.

Lofland, J. (1971) *Analyzing Social Settings*. Wadsworth, Belmont, California.

Madden, J.M., Quick, J.D., Ross-Degnan, D. and Kafle, K.K. (1997) Undercover careseekers: simulated clients in the study of health provider behaviour in developing countries. *Social Science Medicine* 45(10), 1465–1482.

Milgram, S. (1975) *Obedience to Authority*. Harper & Row, New York.

Morrall, K. (1994) Mystery shopping tests service and compliance. *Bank Marketing* 26(2), 13–23.

Morrison, L.J., Colman, A.M. and Preston, C.C. (1997) Mystery customer research: cognitive processes affecting accuracy. *Journal of the Market Research Society* 39(2), 349–361.
Patton, M. (1990) *Qualitative Evaluation and Research Methods*, 2nd edn. Sage, London.
Wilson, A.M. (1998) The use of mystery shopping in the measurement of service delivery. *The Service Industries Journal* 18, 148–163.
Wilson, A.M. (2001) Mystery shopping: using deception to measure service performance. *Psychology and Marketing* 18(7), 721–734.
Wilson, A.M. and Gutman, J. (1998) Public transport: the role of mystery shopping in investment decisions. *Journal of the Market Research Society* 40(4), 285–293.
Yeh, C. and Kuo, Y. (2003) Evaluating passenger services of Asia-Pacific international airports. *Transportation Research* Part E39, pp. 35–48.

11 Longitudinal Research Methods

J.R. BRENT RITCHIE

World Tourism Education & Research Centre, Scurfield Hall, Room 499a, University of Calgary, 2500 University Drive NW, Calgary, Alberta T2N 1N4, Canada

Introduction

This chapter deals with an area that has tended to receive relatively little attention in the published research of many, if not most, academics. Conversely, it is a methodology that is often of great interest to practising managers. Academics are under pressure to 'produce' – and since longitudinal research (LR) requires patience and a long-term commitment to a research topic (and adequate resources), many are reluctant to undertake studies requiring this approach.

In contrast, practising managers in both the public and private sector are very concerned about what is taking place both within their markets and in the economic and social environment as time passes. These concerns have both quantitative and qualitative dimensions. Quantitatively, managers need to keep aware of the extent to which their markets are growing or declining. Qualitatively, they need to maintain an ongoing understanding of why market levels and behaviours are changing. Both of the foregoing are often captured by the term 'trend analysis' – which seeks to monitor and understand how and why various aspects of the tourism market are changing over time, which is essentially the rationale of LR in tourism. However, before examining the applications of this particularly relevant approach to research for tourism, it is useful to have a clear understanding of the fundamentals of the method and the very special challenges it presents to researchers.

The Fundamentals of Longitudinal Research

Perhaps the most extensive single treatment of LR as a research methodology is the *Handbook of Longitudinal Research* (Mednick *et al.*, 1981). Other very useful collections of generic examinations of LR are provided by von Eye (1990), Nesselroade and Baltes (1979), Schulsinger *et al.* (1981) and Young *et al.* (1991).

One of the most insightful and more comprehensive reviews of LR and LR designs (see Table 11.1), and one to which more methodologically interested readers may wish to refer, is that provided by Menard (1991). He emphasizes that LR must be defined in terms of both the data and the methods of analysis that are used. As such, he formally defines it as 'research in which (a) the data are collected for each item or variable for two or more distinct time periods; (b) the subjects or cases analyzed are the same or at least comparable from one period to the next; and (c) the analysis involves some comparison of data from one period to another' (Menard, 1991: 4). In principle, the same variables are measured on the same units of analysis for at least two time periods. As such, LR distinguishes itself from simple cross-sectional research, where the data are gathered at one point in time.

Menard (1991: 4) further emphasizes

Table 11.1. Research designs for longitudinal data collection. (Source: Menard (1991).)

- Pure longitudinal research
  - Prospective panel design: a panel (sample) is established and tracked over time on identical measures
  - Retrospective panel design: a panel (sample) is established and asked to provide data on past behaviour with respect to identical measures
- Pure cross-sectional design
  Same measures gathered at given points in time with respect to individuals within samples having similar characteristics. Differences in results are assumed to be due to time rather than differences in sample members
- Not quite longitudinal designs
  LR on which assumptions of 'pure' LR are violated in relatively minor ways; details mainly of concern to 'statistical purists'!
- Repeated cross-sectional designs
  Researcher typically draws independent probability samples from the population of interest at each measurement period. The population from which the samples are drawn should be as comparable as possible from one period to another
  - Principal limitations are inappropriate for developmental patterns within a given cohort of people (i.e. those who have experienced the same significant life events during the period studied)
  - Is generally appropriate for measuring aggregate period trends
- Revolving panel designs
  Collect data on a sample of cases, either prospectively or retrospectively, for some sequence of measuring periods, then drop some subjects and replace them with new, comparable, subjects
- Longitudinal panel designs
  The same set of subjects (cases) is used in each period – although in practice there may be some variation from one period to another due to panel member attrition – resulting in 'missing cases'

that 'Longitudinal Research describes not a single method, but a family of methods – and that it might be defined in terms of both the data and the methods of analysis used in the research'. At a bare minimum, any true LR design permits the measurement of differences, or the changes in a variable from one period to another. In effect, then, it is the identification and understanding of these differences over time which are the essence of LR. These all-important differences in an area of interest reflect changes that are occurring within tourism or within a tourism market – changes that must be adapted to if a destination or firm is to achieve or maintain a strong competitive position.

Age, Period and Cohort Effects

In addition to the fundamental nature and purpose of LR, Menard identifies and discusses three theoretical constructs which are fundamental to an understanding of LR. He

defines these as age, period and cohort effects.

A *cohort* is defined by Glenn (1977) as 'those people within a geographically or otherwise delineated population who experienced the same significant life event within a given period of time'. When using LR, the goal is to examine the members of a given cohort (or population) so as to determine how their characteristics and behaviours may have changed over different periods as they age.

Given that it is not always possible to track a specific population over periods of time, an alternative model of LR is to execute a series of *cross-sectional studies* (CS) on different populations who have arguably had similar life experiences. For example, rather than tracking a market segment as it ages from 20 to 60 years old, one might study several samples of 20-year-olds and 60-year-olds at a given point in time. In the same vein, rather than following the same group of individuals to examine how their image of a given destination has changed as the result of a visit to the destination, one might undertake a CS study of several groups who have visited the destination and several who have not. While the repeated CS approach to LR clearly has its limitations, it may be the only possibility in certain circumstances. For example, should one wish to study the impact of hosting a mega-event such as the Olympic Games on possible changes in the image of the host destination, it may be very difficult to find and then interview repeatedly over time a significant number of people who have attended or followed the Games. Once the event is over, 'it's over', and no new attendees or 'fans' will be generated or influenced by the event. To overcome this difficulty, researchers may choose to study cross-sectional samples both before and after the event.

Some Particular Challenges of Longitudinal Research

Since LR is simply research that encompasses several time periods, it faces all the challenges of every piece of research. However, because of its efforts to examine issues over time, LR presents some particular challenges of its own. In addition to Menard's views on these challenges, there are two very insightful articles by Van De Ven and Huber (1990) and Pettigrew (1990) that provide some valuable theoretical and practical observations regarding the special challenges of LR, as well as useful discussion on how to overcome the challenges. In an effort to provide the reader with an initial understanding of the points made by these authors, Table 11.2 attempts

Table 11.2. Some particular challenges of Longitudinal Research – a summary. (Source: Summarized from Cutler (1979), Pettigrew (1990), Van De Ven and Huber (1990) and Menard (1991).)

- Longitudinal data collection exacerbates a variety of inherent weaknesses in data collection methods
- Demand for time commitment on the part of researchers
- The sheer labour intensity involved in LR
- Demand for dedication on the part of researchers
- Amount of data can accumulate astronomically over time
- Cost
- Attrition in panel/sample members
- Choice of time period to be studied is critical
- Choice of 'research sites' is critical
- Need to identify 'planned opportunities' for LR
- Need to build a 'network' of support researchers
- Need to identify situation where impact of time or event is 'transparently observable' (need for measures to be able to discriminate over time)
- Desirability of studying 'polar types' (highs and lows) in terms of performance
- Need for a high frequency of similar situations to allow for viable research
- Need for intensive access to situations that permit or facilitate LR
- Temporal order and causal effects are frequently not easy to establish
- May be a need for specialized skills on the part of good field workers
- Risk that repeated questioning over time may alter the 'underlying truth' in certain situations
- Need to manage the 'degree of involvement' of researchers who are gathering data within groups over time
- The fact that 'research is a reciprocal activity' can lead to special problems over time within the LR setting
- Much data used in LR has actually been gathered for other purposes and this is not always adequate for good comparisons
- Special need to clarify the nature of the research output
- Special difficulty in capturing the complexities of the 'real world' over time
- Replication to ensure reliability is often not possible, or at least successful
- It can often be very difficult to 'insulate' all panel members from 'life experiences' which may vary in ways which are uncontrollable – thus threatening the assumption of uniformity/equality
- High risk of collinearity in measures

Table 11.3. Some routes to structured understanding in longitudinal and comparative field research. (Source: Pettigrew, 1990.)

1. Being clear about research objectives (i.e. building on strengths and awareness of limitations)
2. Being clear about the unit of analysis and study questions
3. Coming to terms with time
4. Making explicit your theory of method
5. Making explicit your meta-level analytical framework
6. Making explicit the character of the generic propositions you are seeking
7. Identifying analytical themes which cut across the data
8. Using techniques of data reduction and display
9. Making prescriptive statements as an aid to analytical generalization
10. Making explicit the varieties and sequencing of research output

to identify and summarize the most important points raised by the above-noted papers. It should be emphasized, however, that the summary in Table 11.2 in no way does adequate justice to the original works. Readers who wish to truly understand the complex challenges facing LR researchers are urged to review the original papers. The Pettigrew paper is particularly valuable because the author, as well as identifying the challenges of LR, also puts forth suggestions for addressing these challenges. These suggestions are summarized in Table 11.3. In addition, Pettigrew, in discussing the need for clear research objectives, stresses that such goals must especially take into account some five crucial considerations. These are given in Table 11.4.

Longitudinal Research in Tourism

One of the few publications that explicitly examines LR and its importance in relation to tourism is by Jennings (2001). She defines longitudinal studies as the study of the same people, or a similar sample of people, over a period of time. She emphasizes, however, that data for LR may be collected using a variety of approaches, both quantitative and qualitative, including interviews, focus groups, participant observation and the documentation method. Jennings also provides a very useful summary of some of the general types of longitudinal study that are found in tourism settings (see Table 11.5). This provides a basic foundation for tourism researchers, and gives examples as

to how LR is typically used in a variety of managerial and research situations. In addition, Ryan (1995), in his examination of the research process as it relates to the study of tourism satisfaction, describes uses of the Longitudinal Research design in this important tourism application.

Another very helpful review of LR methods, in a field closely related to tourism, is one by Carpenter and Robertson (1999). They examine the use of longitudinal methods generally, but more specifically in research related to adult leisure. In this regard, they provide an excellent reference list for a number of long-term adult leisure behaviour studies. While many of the examples in the Carpenter and Robinson paper are indirectly relevant to tourism, there are a number of situational differences that need to be considered by researchers in travel and tourism.

In addition to the foregoing discussions of the use of LR in tourism and related areas, the present author has identified a number of selected examples of the application of the LR approach in tourism (see

Table 11.4. Some crucial aspects of research objectives for Longitudinal Research. (Source: Pettigrew, 1990.)

1. Precision of measurement
2. Generality over actors and situations
3. Realism of context
4. Theoretical and conceptual development
5. Contribution to particular and general questions of policy and practice

Table 11.5. Some general types of longitudinal studies in tourism settings. (Source: Jennings, 2001.)

Type of study	Characteristics	Tourism example
Panel study	Same group of people over time	Identifying a group of people who represent a specific sociodemographic market segment and studying their holiday patterns over an extended period of time
Time series	Different individuals over time, although one of the criteria remains constant, such as the study setting	An integrated resort determining the changing market segments that use the resort
Trend studies	Research over time with different subjects	Studying residents to determine their domestic and international travel patterns
Cohort analysis	Participants have an experience that is similar within a set time period	Identifying flight crew intakes trained during a specific year and then studying them throughout their employment to discuss working conditions
Case study	Intense observation or data collection over the short or long term	Studying a small seaside community located close to a major tourism precinct over a 20-year period using a variety of qualitative research methods such as focus groups, participant observation, interviews and the documentary method

Table 11.6). These examples provide readers with some idea of the range and scope of uses of LR in the efforts of tourism researchers to better understand different aspects of the complex phenomenon we call 'tourism' (Goeldner and Ritchie, 2003).

Finally, the chapter includes an in-depth look at two particular applications of LR that the author has personally undertaken. It is hoped that the detail of these studies, as they are presented first-hand, will serve not only to demonstrate the value of LR in tourism, but also to provide some indication of the complexities and challenges that can be encountered.

In-depth Example 1: Assessing the Impact of a Mega-event on the International Awareness and Image of the Host Destination: the 1988 Olympic Winter Games in Calgary

With all due humility, this example represents, in the author's view, one of the most exceptional studies using LR in the existing tourism literature. The announcement that the 1988 Winter Olympics had been awarded to Calgary was originally made in 1981. Since the author believed that the impacts related to the value of hosting such a major international event – particularly in view of the major investments and expenditures involved – were surprisingly ill-understood due to a failure to study previous editions of the Games, the present research was initiated immediately upon announcement that the 1988 Games would come to Calgary. In particular, efforts were undertaken to determine the extent to which this event might change the international awareness and image of the relatively small western Canadian city (population approximately 500,000 in 1981) that would, in 7 years' time, be the focus of television programming in many countries worldwide.

Towards this end, an LR programme was established to try to measure how the residents of Western Europe and the United States might have their views of Calgary altered from 1981 (the announcement) to 1989 (1 year after the Games) – and possibly even beyond.

A particular highlight of the study was the way in which a very serious resource limitation was overcome through the goodwill and cooperation provided at virtually no cost by academic colleagues throughout the

Table 11.6.   Selected examples of use of the Longitudinal Research methodology in tourism.

Research question/issue	Approach	Results
To monitor international travel patterns	Regular cross-sectional measures of visitor origin	WTO international travel statistics – reported annually
To track travel behaviours	Use of a panel of individuals selected to represent a given population	Commercial consumer panels (Ipsos-Reid, 2003)
To understand national travel trends and behaviours	Repeated samples from the national population	Canadian Travel Survey – conducted regularly
To determine the impact of a mega-event on image of the host destination	Repeated study of samples for the same cities over time	Longitudinal impact of 1988 Winter Olympic Games in Calgary (Ritchie and Smith, 1991). See Appendix 11.1
To determine the attitude of destination residents towards future tourism development	Study of samples of residents drawn at different points in time	Study of resident attitudes towards tourism in Spey Valley, Scotland (Getz, 1994)
To determine the perception of the impact of specific type of tourism development	Before-and-after measures of perception	Korean study on impact of a casino development (Lee *et al.*, 2003)
To determine public reaction to a land use policy change related to tourism facilities	Tracking of the attitude and behaviour of retailers in the facility areas	Land use change in Christchurch, NZ tourist tramway (Pearce, 2001)
To determine the stability of the public towards the policy recommendation of a federal government task force for future management and development of one of Canada's major national parks	Measure of reactions to policy recommendations from policy research	Banff-Bow Valley Study, Banff National Park, Canada (Ritchie *et al.*, 2002). See Appendix 11.2
To determine degree of compliance with defined actions and policies to achieve sustainability	Tracking of municipal actions over time to assess the extent to which policy proposals have been respected	European historic walled towns review (Bruce *et al.*, 2001)
To measure resident perceptions of the 1996 Olympic Summer Games	Telephone survey in 1992/1993 of resident perceptions regarding the 1996 Summer Olympic Games in Atlanta, Georgia, USA	Findings indicated decreasing support and willingness to attend (Mihalik and Simonetta, 1998)
The need to monitor visitor satisfaction at the local level	Regular visitor surveys	Case study of visitors to Cornwall, UK (Shaw *et al.*, 1990)
Examination of change and continuity in leisure patterns/perceptions	Respondents completed a questionnaire every year for 10 years	Study of leisure in adulthood (Carpenter and Robertson, 1999)
To determine the effectiveness of follow-up 'waves' of surveys	Analysis of data for subsequent waves of surveys to determine if follow-up survey had an effect on results	Variables analysed from 13 mail surveys that collected data from three waves of questionnaires to see if responses varied across waves (Crompton and Tian-Cole, 2001) (*Not strictly a longitudinal research, but an interesting time-sensitive methodological study*)

Need to determine how changing gasoline prices affect auto travel	Use of a consumer panel to track how consumers respond to price increases	Reports as a 5-year consumer panel study that demonstrated that vacation travel is affected by gasoline shortages and price increases (Trent and Pollard, 1983)
To better understand and improve the forecasting of travel patterns	To forecast travel patterns using Palmore's cohort analysis	Found that changes in travel behaviour are primarily due to period effects (Pennington-Gray et al., 2002)
To understand the long-term effects of festivals on communities	Case study of one particular festival	Factors influencing festival development for the Can-America Days Festival in Myrtle Beach, South Carolina, USA (Groves and Timothy, 2001)
Desire to understand how foreign nation perceptions of Barcelona are changed by the 1992 Summer Olympic Games	Use of a panel survey of 1154 foreign (Japanese) students	The level of positive feelings towards foreign nations generally increased over the 3-month period of the Olympics (Sakamoto et al., 1999)
To examine the changing market for heritage tours	Case study of historic houses in England	Records of historic houses over a 12-week season were examined (attendance, prices, net revenue) were studied to determine visitor sensitivity to price (Markwell et al., 1997)
To determine long-term impacts of tourists on host populations	Study of the 1961–1981 period in the Strathspey District of Scotland	Tourism brought about a reversal of population decline (Getz, 1986)
To improve the forecasting of business travel	Examination of seven different forecasting models and the number of time horizons over which forecasts are generated, from one to three	Found that relative forecasting performance is highly dependent on the length of the forecasting horizon (Kulendran and Witt, 2003)
To understand the impact of response problems in a vacation panel situation	Undertook a three-wave panel study to determine travel behaviour	Those who refused participation were most different from panel respondents in terms of travel behaviour
Review of the historical evolution of an 800-year-old festival in China	Using what they term to be a longitudinal methodology, researchers examined how the festival in question started, evolved and survived over an 800-year period	Exemplifies the key role which tourism is playing in the dynamics of change in China. Authors concluded that the historical methodology used was a useful tool for gaining insight into the dynamics which underpin tourism as sustainable development (Sofield and Li, 1998)
To understand how the nature of travel has evolved from the first work of Western travel literature to the modern era of mass tourism	A review of historical documentation on travel	Another demonstration of how industrialization has transformed travel and led to the use of mechanized mass travel (Leed, 1991)

study areas. While acknowledged most appreciatively in all publications resulting from the longitudinal study, the author wishes to again highlight the high degree of both professionalism and colleagueship demonstrated by all those who helped to gather the data for the study. It was this show of vision on their part that made this example of LR what I hope will come to be known as a 'true classic'. Again, I am most appreciative of the support received.

While a full reporting of various research projects related to the 1988 Winter Olympics is available in several publications over the years (see references), it is hoped that a focused summary of the key article on the longitudinal results of the awareness/image study may be useful here (see Appendix 11.1).

In-depth Example 2: Public Reactions to Policy Recommendations from the Banff-Bow Valley Study: a Longitudinal Assessment

Again, the author had the privilege of participating in what has also become a bit of a 'classic' in terms of the extent to which it has been cited in the tourism literature. In contrast to the study on the 1988 Olympic Winter Games, where resources were at a minimum, The Banff-Bow Valley Study (BBVS) was a 2-year, $2.4 million project designed to formulate guidelines for the future of a major National Park region in the Canadian Rockies. It provided a comprehensive set of over 500 policy recommendations for enhancing ecological integrity and managing sustainable tourism in this popular, environmentally sensitive destination (Page et al., 1996). In order for these recommendations to be implemented effectively, support from a broad range of stakeholders in the Canadian citizenry is essential. This study was undertaken in an attempt to assess the degree of public support for the major recommendations of the BBVS. The total assessment consisted of a two-phase longitudinal study (Ritchie et al., 2002). Phase 1 was conducted in 1996, following the release of the BBVS recommen-

dations. Phase 2, which sought to verify the stability of the initial results, was conducted several years later, in 2000. While some shifts in public support were identified, the most significant findings of Phase 1 were verified. Furthermore, the total study identified those recommendations most likely to be accepted or rejected by Canadians. Greater detail on the study, its methodology and its results are provided in Appendix 11.2.

Conclusion

While it is hoped that this chapter has succeeded in familiarizing the reader with LR and the particular challenges it presents, it is emphasized that the reader should not be discouraged from undertaking LR, because it can be particularly valuable and rewarding and can provide the kind of in-depth understanding that simple cross-sectional studies just cannot furnish. In brief, then, while LR can initially slow down 'academic productivity' it can also, if wisely designed and executed as an integrated programme of LR, be highly productive – and, more importantly, provide (in the author's view) a uniquely valuable legacy. It is hoped that the Olympic Games awareness impact study described in Appendix 11.1 makes this point especially clear. There was no other way to understand how the awareness of this 'once in a lifetime' experience for a relatively unknown host city was affected and evolved once the initial announcement of the awarding of the Games had been made. And if one also wishes to follow and understand how the 'peak levels' of awareness subsequently decay over time, then LR is a basic requirement.

However, to close, it should be again stressed that LR is not really a methodology in itself. Rather, it is simply the temporal manner in which virtually any set of research methods can be utilized. What the researcher needs to ask him/herself is what special insights the utilization of particular research methods over time can add to the understanding of the research question at issue. And it is only if it appears that the longitudinal utilization of research methods would improve understanding of the question/issue at hand, on a cost-effective basis, that the special challenges of LR can be considered worth the additional resources that must be committed.

Acknowledgement

The author extends his appreciation to Mr Stuart Levy for his valuable assistance in identifying and assembling the materials on which this chapter is based.

References

Bishop, R. and Heberlein, T. (1986) Does contingent valuation work? In: Cummings, R., Brookshire, D. and Schultze, W. (eds) *Valuing Environmental Goods: an Assessment of the Contingent Valuation Method.* Rowman & Allanheld, New Brunswick, New Jersey, pp. 123–147.

Bruce, D.M., Jackson, M.J. and Cantallops, A.S. (2001) PREPARE: a model to aid the development of policies for less unsustainable tourism in historic towns. *Tourism and Hospitality Research* 3(1), 21–36.

Carpenter, G. and Robertson, B. (1999) A call for the increased use of longitudinal methods in research on adult leisure. *Leisure/Loisir* 24(1–2), 59–87.

Crompton, J.L. and Tian-Cole, S. (2001) An analysis of 13 tourism surveys: are three waves of data collection necessary? *Journal of Travel Research* 39(4), 356–368.

Cutler, F. (1979) Overview of the 'Longitudinal Research Design and Analysis of Panel Data' Workshop. *Advances in Consumer Research* 6(1), 31–33.

Getz, D. (1986) Tourism and population change: long-term impacts of tourism in the Badenoch and Strathspey District of the Scottish Highlands. *Scottish Geographical Magazine* 102(2), 113–126.

Getz, D. (1994) Residents' attitudes towards tourism: a longitudinal study in Spey Valley, Scotland. *Tourism Management* 15(4), 247–258.

Glenn, N. (1977) *Cohort Analysis.* Sage, Beverly Hills, California.

Goeldner, C.R. and Ritchie, J.R.B. (2003) *Tourism: Principles, Practices, Philosophies.* John Wiley & Sons, New York, 606 pp.

Groves, D.L. and Timothy, D. (2001) Festivals, migration, and long-term residency. *Teoros, Revue de Recherche en Tourisme* 20(1), 56–62.

Ipsos-Reid (2003) *Global Marketing Research & Public Opinion – Publicly Released Polls & News Releases,* Ipsos-Reid, Toronto, Ontario. Available at: http://www.ipsos-reid.com/media

Jennings, G. (2001) *Tourism Research.* John Wiley & Sons Australia Ltd, Queensland, 452 pp.

Kulendran, N. and Witt, S.F. (2003) Forecasting the demand for international business tourism. *Journal of Travel Research* 41, 265–271.

Lee, C.-K., Kim, S.-S. and Kang, S. (2003) Perceptions of casino impacts: a Korean longitudinal study. *Tourism Management* 24(1), 45–55.

Leed, E.J. (1991) *The Mind of the Traveler: From Gilgamesh to Global Tourism.* Basic Books, New York, 384 pp.

Markwell, S., Bennett, M. and Ravenscroft, N. (1997) The changing market for heritage tourism: a case study of visits to historic houses in England. *International Journal of Heritage Studies* 3(2), 95–108.

Mednick, S.A., Harway, M. and Finello, K.M. (1981) *Handbook of Longitudinal Research – Vol. 1: Birth and Childhood Cohorts.* Praeger/Greenwood Publishing Group, New York, 740 pp.

Menard, S. (1991) *Longitudinal Research.* Sage Publications, Newbury Park, California, 81 pp.

Mihalik, B.J. and Simonetta, L. (1998) Resident perceptions of the 1996 Summer Olympic Games – Year II. *Festival Management & Event Tourism* 5, 9–19.

Nesselroade, J.R. and Baltes, P.B. (1979) *Longitudinal Research in the Study of Behavior and Development.* Academic Press, New York, 386 pp.

Page, R., Bayley, S., Cook, J.D., Green, J.E. and Ritchie, J.R.B. (1996) *Banff-Bow Valley: at the Crossroads (Technical Report).* Banff-Bow Valley Task Force. Prepared for the Honourable Sheila Copps, Minister of Canadian Heritage, Ottawa, Ontario, Canada, 432 pp.

Pearce, D.G. (2001) Tourism and urban land use change: assessing the impact of Christchurch's tourist tramway. *Tourism and Hospitality Research* 3(2), 132–148.

Pennington-Gray, L., Kerstetter, D. and Warnick, R. (2002) Forecasting travel patterns using Palmore's cohort analysis. *Journal of Travel & Tourism Marketing* 13(1/2), 127–145.

Pettigrew, A.M. (1990) Longitudinal field research on change: theory and practice. *Organizational Science* 1(3), 267–292.

Ritchie, J.R.B. and Smith, B. (1991) The impact of a mega-event on host region awareness: a longitudinal study. *Journal of Travel Research* 30(1), 3–10.

Ritchie, J.R.B., Hudson, S. and Timur, S. (2002) Public reactions to policy recommendations from the Banff-Bow Valley Study: a longitudinal assessment. *Journal of Sustainable Tourism* 10(4), 295–308.

Ryan, C. (1995) Research design: an overview. In: Ryan, C. (ed.) *Researching Tourist Satisfaction: Issues, Concepts, Problems.* Routledge, London, pp. 16–39.

Sakamoto, A., Murata, K. and Takaki, E. (1999) The Barcelona Olympics and the perception of foreign nations: a panel study of Japanese university students. *Journal of Sport Behavior* 22(2), 260–278.

Schulsinger, F., Mednick, S.A. and Knop, J. (1981) *Longitudinal Research: Methods and Uses in Behavioral Science.* Nijhoff, Boston, Massachusetts, 326 pp.

Shaw, G., Williams, A. and Greenwood, J. (1990) UK visitor survey. *Tourism Management* 11(3), 247–251.

Sofield, T.H.B. and Li, F.M.S. (1998) Historical methodology and sustainability: an 800-year-old festival from China. *Journal of Sustainable Tourism* 6(4), 267–292.

Trent, R.B. and Pollard, C. (1983) Gasoline prices and discretionary auto travel: evidence from a panel survey. *Journal of Travel Research* 21(4), 12–16.

Van De Ven, A.H. and Huber, G.P. (1990) Longitudinal field research methods for studying processes of organizational change. *Organizational Science* 1(3), 213–219.

von Eye, A. (1990) *Statistical Methods in Longitudinal Research.* Academic Press, Boston, Massachusetts, 256 pp.

Young, C.H., Savola, K.L. and Phelps, E. (1991) *Inventory of Longitudinal Studies in the Social Sciences.* Sage, Newbury Park, California, 568 pp.

Olympic Bibliography (for the Programme of Integrated Olympic Games Studies Conducted 1984–2000)

Ritchie, J.R.B. (1986) *Results of a Workshop on Enhancing the Long Term Impacts of the XV Olympic Winter Games.* World Tourism & Education Centre, University of Calgary, Alberta, Canada.

Ritchie, J.R.B. (1989) Promoting Calgary through the Olympics: the mega-event as a strategy for community development. In: Fine, S.H. (ed.) *Social Marketing.* Allyn and Bacon, Inc., Boston, Massachusetts.

Ritchie, J.R.B. (1994) Calgary's Open House Theory: resident-responsive tourism is key to success in the '90s and beyond. *Acumen,* pp. 5–7.

Ritchie, J.R.B. (1996) *Mega-Events as Vehicles for Tourism Destination Development: The Calgary (1988) XV Olympic Games as a Possible Benchmark for the Hosting of the (2006) XX Winter Olympic Games in Poland.* World Tourism Education & Research Centre, University of Calgary, Alberta, Canada, 14 pp.

Ritchie, J.R.B. (1999a) Lessons learned, lessons learning: insights from the Calgary and Salt Lake City Olympic Winter Games. *Visions in Leisure & Business* 18(1), 4–13.

Ritchie, J.R.B. (1999b) *A Research Framework for the 2002 Olympic Winter Games in Salt Lake City – Discussion Draft.* World Tourism Education & Research Centre, University of Calgary, Alberta, Canada, 11 pp.

Ritchie, J.R.B. (1999c) *Turning 16 Days into 16 Years: a Calgary Perspective on Strategies for Enhancing the Success, the Long term Impacts, and the Legacies of the 2002 Olympic Winter Games on the City of Salt Lake, Utah – Final Report.* World Tourism Education & Research Centre, University of Calgary, Alberta, Canada, 70 pp.

Ritchie, J.R.B. (2000) Turning 16 days into 16 years through Olympic legacies. *Event Management* 6(3), 155–165.

Ritchie, J.R.B. and Aitken, C.E. (1984) Assessing the impacts of the 1988 Olympic Winter Games: the research program and initial results. *Journal of Travel Research* 22(3), 17–25.

Ritchie, J.R.B. and Aitken, C.E. (1985) OLYMPULSE II – evolving resident attitudes towards the 1988 Olympic Winter Games. *Journal of Travel Research* 23(3), 28–33.

Ritchie, J.R.B. and Lyons, M. (1987) OLYMPULSE III/OLYMPULSE IV: a mid-term report on resident attitudes concerning the XV Olympic Winter Games. *Journal of Travel Research* 26(1), 18–25.

Ritchie, J.R.B. and Lyons, M. (1988) *A Survey of Calgary Residents Regarding the XV Olympic Winter Games.* XV Olympic Winter Games Organizing Committee, Calgary, Alberta, Canada, 59 pp. + appendices.

Ritchie, J.R.B. and Lyons, M. (1990) OLYMPULSE VI: a post event assessment of resident reaction to the XV Olympic Winter Games. *Journal of Travel Research* 23(3), 14–23.

Ritchie, J.R.B. and Smith, B. (1991) The impact of a mega-event on host region awareness: a longitudinal study. *Journal of Travel Research* 30(1), 3–10.

Appendix 11.1. The Impact of a Mega-event on Host Region Awareness: a Longitudinal Study
J.R. Brent Ritchie and Brian H. Smith
(extracted from an article in the *Journal of Travel Research,* Summer 1991).

The research reported here had four very basic objectives. These were:
1. To measure the impact of the 1988 Olympic Winter Games on the awareness levels and perceptions of the host city in international markets.
2. To examine how these awareness levels and perceptions changed over different points in time prior to and following the event.
3. To compare these changes in awareness levels and perceptions with those of a control group of cities that had not hosted such an event during the period of study.
4. To compare the nature and extent of possible awareness and image changes across major international market regions.

While the research objectives and associated measures were conceptually simple, the organization and administration of the required data collection were both complex and demanding, particularly in light of the limited resources available to support the project. A total of 22 centres located in the USA and Europe participated in the data collection over a 4-year period (1986–1989).

Each of the collaborating institutions was requested to complete annually 100 interviews by telephone with individuals over 16 years of age selected at random from the local telephone directory. The actual number of interviews completed by each centre did vary, as not all centres completed exactly 100 interviews each year. Data were collected for 1986, 1987, 1988 and 1989. It should be noted that a certain percentage of the data for the 1989 reports was not collected until 1990. As a result of this process, what is believed to be a rather exceptional data bank was assembled.

While the complete data bank contained data on the awareness of the image of Canada, the ten Canadian provinces, selected Canadian cities, and certain future

Games sites, this summary will focus on the longitudinal data related to a selected set of ten Canadian cities, including Calgary (the host city) and a 'control' city, Edmonton, also located in the province of Alberta.

Awareness of Canadian cities (1986–1989)

Respondents were first asked, 'What cities come to mind when you think of Canada?' (unaided recall). For those of the ten cities included in the study which could not be identified without prompting, respondents were subsequently asked, 'Have you ever heard of the following other Canadian cities?' Interviewers then read the names of cities which were not mentioned without prompting and accorded a positive response if the individual claimed to have recognized the name (aided recall).

While detailed results for both aided and unaided recall are provided in the original paper (Ritchie and Smith, 1991), due to space limitations this summary will focus primarily on unaided recall, or, as many refer to it, 'top of mind awareness'.

Unaided recall

Tables 11.A1.1 and 11.A1.2 provide the percentage of respondents who were able to name each of the ten Canadian cities in the study without prompting. Table 11.A1.1 provides these figures for European respondents for 1986, 1987, 1988 and 1989. Table 11.A1.2 provides the responses for US respondents for the same 4 years.

As can be seen from Table 11.A1.1, there was a reasonable degree of stability in Europe in the levels of awareness of most Canadian cities over the 4-year period. In absolute terms, it is seen that Montreal consistently obtains the highest level of unaided recognition, averaging 57.3% of all European respondents. Toronto is second with an awareness level of 46.7% over the 4-year period. Perhaps the best basis of comparison is between the two major Alberta cities, Calgary and Edmonton. In 1986 and

Table 11.A1.1. European awareness levels of selected Canadian cities (unaided recall).

Canadian city	Percentage of respondents			
	1986[a] (n = 857)	1987 (n = 741)	1988 (n = 927)	1989 (n = 562)
Halifax	2.8	3.1	3.1	4.3
Quebec	41.4	47.1	41.4	40.7
Montreal	58.0	62.5	55.1	53.6
Ottawa	28.9	35.2	27.4	31.5
Toronto	46.6	49.8	41.6	48.9
Winnipeg	8.1	7.0	7.1	4.4
Regina	1.0	0.8	1.3	0.1
Calgary	10.1	12.0	40.0	31.9
Edmonton	5.3	5.0	6.6	5.3
Vancouver	34.3	37.2	32.4	27.9

[a]Year of survey.

1987, Calgary obtained unaided recall percentages of 10.1% and 12.0%, respectively. In the same two time periods Edmonton obtained figures of 5.3% and 5.0%. The true impact of the Games is shown in the 1988 figures where Calgary's unaided recognition level jumped to 40.0% while Edmonton's remained at just over 6%. This increase of over 28 points far exceeded any other variations recorded by European surveyors. However, the impact of the Games on Calgary's recognition level could be short lived. In 1989, 31.9% of the European respondents named Calgary as being a Canadian city without being prompted. This represents a decline of 8.1% from the 1988 figure of 40.0%. The result for Edmonton in 1989 was 5.3%, which is quite similar to what it has been since 1986.

The same impacts were observed in the USA (Table 11.A1.2), although growth in awareness between 1986 and 1988 was not quite so dramatic (approximately 23 points). Calgary was nevertheless the only city for which such a large increase was observed. A decline similar to that which occurred in Europe in 1989 also occurred in the USA. In 1989 (without prompting) 9.5% fewer respondents identified Calgary as a city in Canada compared with 1988.

Table 11.A1.2. United States awareness levels of selected Canadian cities (unaided recall).

Canadian city	Percentage of respondents			
	1986[a] (n = 822)	1987 (n = 988)	1988 (n = 929)	1989 (n = 772)
Halifax	2.4	2.2	2.2	2.3
Quebec	46.8	40.9	25.8	22.0
Montreal	66.3	57.7	57.2	54.0
Ottawa	9.9	9.1	13.1	7.1
Toronto	47.8	40.9	43.6	46.5
Winnipeg	9.6	13.1	10.6	14.9
Regina	1.1	1.4	2.0	1.6
Calgary	19.5	22.4	43.3	33.8
Edmonton	12.3	13.5	18.6	18.1
Vancouver	38.0	38.1	32.8	26.3

[a]Year of survey.

Total recall (unaided plus prompted)

It is also quite interesting to examine how total awareness measure (unaided plus prompted) evolved over the period of the study. In this case, the information is given graphically in Figs 11.A1.1 and 11.A1.2.

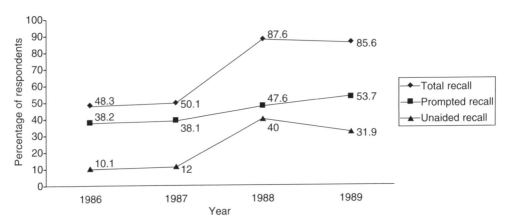

Fig. 11.A1.1. Awareness of Calgary by European respondents (1986–1989).

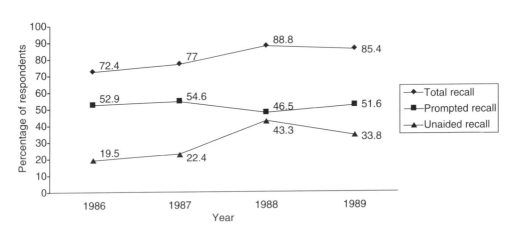

Fig. 11.A1.2. Awareness of Calgary by US respondents (1986–1989).

Appendix 11.2. Banff-Bow Valley Longitudinal Policy Study Summarized Extract from a Paper Describing Public Reaction to Policy Recommendations from the Banff-Bow Valley Study (BBVS) (Ritchie *et al.*, 2002)

The nature and significance of citizen support to Canadian public policy

Although the BBVS placed a strong emphasis on an assessment of the ecological integrity of the region under study, its policy recommendations reflected concerns for both the environment and human visitation to the region. Since these two concerns were addressed by the recommendations of the BBVS final report, it is essential from a public policy perspective to understand the degree to which Canadians support its broad range of recommendations, not only at a given point in time, but over an extended period of time. Also, if there are changes in the support for an individual recommendation, or the total set of recommendations, it is important to understand the nature and direction of these changes. Given that the current government is increasingly espousing 'National Parks' as an important 'Canadian Value', such an understanding is of growing significance to policy makers and politicians alike.

Research design and methodology

As noted earlier, the research consisted of a two-phase longitudinal study designed to measure the level of support of a select subset of Canadians (namely, residents of the city of Calgary) having a particular interest in the future of the Banff-Bow Valley region, since they are particularly heavy users of the park when compared with other Canadians. As such, they are particularly assertive regarding their interests. More specifically, the total study involved two samples of telephone subscribers drawn randomly from the metropolitan Calgary telephone directory. The first sample comprised 400 respondents who were interviewed in late 1996. The second sample consisted of 304 respondents, who were interviewed in early 2000. The gender structure of each of the samples is given in Table 11.A2.1.

The opening questions of the survey sought to establish baseline measures of awareness and attitudes regarding the study and development in general within BNP. In this regard, respondents were first queried in relation to their awareness of the study. As might be anticipated (see Table 11.A2.1), awareness of the study was lower (24.7%) in 2000 than in 1996 (35.8%). Regardless of their awareness of the study, all respondents were asked their views on BNP and the BBVS recommendations for its future protection/development.

A second benchmark measured respondent views on current levels of development

Table 11.A2.1. Size and gender structure of the samples and respondent awareness of the Banff-Bow Valley Study.

Respondent		1996		2000	
		Number	%	Number	%
Size and Gender Structure	Male	180	45	147	48
	Female	220	55	157	52
	Total (*n*)	400	100	304	100
		1996(%)		2000(%)	
Respondent awareness	Aware	35.8		24.7	
of the BBVS	Unaware	62.0		67.4	
	Unsure/neutral	2.3		7.9	

Table 11.A2.2. Views of respondents for Town of Banff and Rest of Banff Park.

		Town of Banff %		Rest of Banff Park %	
Benchmark		1996	2000	1996	2000
Views on current levels of	Under-developed	3.5	6.9	9.1	13.5
development	About right	37.8	38.2	66.2	60.9
	Over-developed	58.7	54.9	24.8	25.6
Support for limitation on	Yes	87.0	91.1	82.8	86.5
development	No	8.8	6.3	13.0	11.5
	Unsure/neutral	4.3	2.6	4.3	2.0
	Total	100.1	100.0	100.1	100.0

Note: figures do not always equal 100% due to rounding.

in both the Town of Banff and the Rest of Banff Park, a distinction that was found to be critical. As shown in Table 11.A2.2, roughly 40% of respondents felt that the current level of development of the Town of Banff was about right. Somewhat over 50% felt the town was over-developed, while less than 10% expressed the view that it was under-developed. As for the rest of Banff Park, in the order of 60% felt things were 'about right'.

A third benchmark measure assessed respondent views regarding support for limitation of future development. As for the Town of Banff (which, in 2000, 55% viewed as over-developed), it is not surprising that 91% supported limitation on development. Nevertheless, for the 'Rest of the Park' (which only 25% viewed as over-developed), support for limitation on development was also high at 87%.

A fourth benchmark measure revealed a perceived inconsistency on the part of respondents. Despite strong support for a limitation on development, a majority of respondents (over 53%) in both 1996 and 2000 did not support restrictions on access to the park (see Table 11.A2.3).

Views on Task Force policy recommendations

These results, shown in Table 11.A2.4, represent the core findings of the study.

As seen from Table 11.A2.4, there was strong support (strongly agree and agree)

Table 11.A2.3. Support for restriction of access.

	1996 (%)	2000 (%)
Yes	39.2	38.6
No	53.0	53.8
Unsure/neutral	7.8	7.6
Total	100.0	100.0

from both surveys for 'capping' the population of the Town of Banff (over 60%). The idea of fencing the town site was generally opposed by a majority of respondents (55%) in both studies. Opposition to imposing a quota on the number of visitors remained high at 49% over the 4-year period. As well, there was high support (over 50%) for imposing a quota on trail usage.

Table 11.A2.4 also demonstrates a strong (over 60%) opposition to new commercial leases within the park. In contrast, there was only weak support for public transportation (under 40%).

The concept of emphasizing education as a means of enhancing protection was viewed as generally unpopular, with more disagreeing than agreeing. In contrast, opposition to closing Lake Louise in the summer to protect wildlife remained high at nearly 60% in both 1996 and 2000. Similarly, the level of opposition to closing or removing hotels in the park also remained high at well over 75%.

Finally, a large majority (nearly 60%) of respondents were consistently opposed to the idea of charging higher fees for foreign-

Table 11.A2.4. Level of agreement with Task Force policy recommendations.

Recommendation	Strongly and generally agree (%)		Neutral		Generally and strongly disagree (%)	
	1996	2000	1996	2000	1996	2000
Cap population at 10,000	62.5	70.4	17.3	16.1	20.3	13.5
Quota on number of visitors	36.1	34.9	15.3	16.1	48.6	49.0
Fence Banff	21.6	31.1	18.1	13.7	60.3	55.2
Emphasize education	37.1	31.5	24.8	30.1	38.1	38.4
No new commercial leases	61.0	64.8	15.5	15.8	23.5	19.4
Quotas on trails	51.9	52.8	14.5	15.4	33.5	31.9
Public transportation	38.6	40.8	12.5	16.8	48.9	42.5
Higher fees for foreigners	32.4	33.2	7.8	9.9	59.9	56.9
Close Lake Louise in summer	15.5	22.4	22.6	18.7	61.9	59.0
Close/remove hotels	7.3	8.7	17.8	14.3	75.0	77.0

Note: figures do not always equal 100% due to rounding.

ers as one means of restricting visitation from non-Canadian taxpayers.

Managing visitation

A second major component of this study addressed the difficult issue of how best to manage visitation levels to the region. In this case, the figures for both 1996 and 2000, summarizing respondent views concerning the various proposals put forth by the Task Force, are given in Table 11.A2.5. As can be seen, proposals for auctions for access to the park, the use of tolls, and compulsory guiding tended to be strongly opposed. In contrast, proposals to restrict accommodation, to issue temporary permits, to impose booking limits and to impose fines were generally supported. The use of temporary closures received 'mixed reviews'.

Table A11.2.5. Respondents' views concerning the desirability of different approaches to manage visitation levels, 1996–2000.

Recommendation	Strongly and generally agree (%)		Neutral		Generally and strongly disagree (%)	
	1996	2000	1996	2000	1996	2000
Auctions of access*	3.8	2.6	4.3	2.3	93.7	95.1
Limit parking	31.9	32.5	37.6	28.9	40.4	38.5
Restrict accommodation	45.4	49.5	27.5	26.6	27.0	23.9
Impose tolls	17.3	19.7	20.3	14.3	62.5	66.0
Temporary permits	43.6	52.3	36.3	27.0	20.1	20.6
Temporary closures	31.6	38.1	27.8	19.4	39.7	42.5
Booking limits	50.0	57.2	26.4	19.1	23.6	23.8
Compulsory guiding*	29.6	26.4	20.0	15.2	50.5	58.4
Fines*	85.3	90.4	10.3	4.3	4.5	5.3

Note: figures do not always equal 100% due to rounding.
*Recommendations demonstrating a significant change over the period 1996–2000 (0.05 level).

Respondents' willingness to financially support environmental protection

As can be seen from the earlier sections of this paper, respondents generally indicated their support for a large number of the recommendations put forth by the Banff-Bow Valley Study Task Force. However, as most readers are well aware, there can be a considerable gap between what people say they support in ideal terms and what they will actually support when a commitment of time, energy or money is required to back up an expression of support. It was with this concern in mind that the final question in this study (using the contingent valuation approach) (Bishop and Heberlein, 1986) asked respondents how much per year they would be willing to contribute to maintain ecological well-being in the Banff-Bow Valley region. Given the apparent strength of expressed support for environmental protection indicated by earlier questions, one would hope that willingness to contribute or support this protection would also be strong. As shown in Table 11.A2.6, this did not prove to be the case. The percentage indicating that they wished to pay nothing ranged from 28% to 36.2%. While there was a slight decrease (from 38.2% to 38.0%) in those willing to contribute $1–$50, there was, however, a weak trend to an increased willingness to pay in all other categories, except for over $1000.

Did respondent views change significantly over the period 1996–2000?

An examination of the figures in Table 11.A2.4 and Table 11.A2.5 shows that in certain cases there appeared to be shifts

Table11.A2.6. Amount respondents are willing to contribute per year to protect the environment in the Banff-Bow Valley region.

Amount ($)	1996 (%)	2000 (%)
0	36.2	28.0
1–50	38.2	38.0
51–100	15.4	19.3
101–200	7.8	9.7
201–300	0.5	1.7
301–500	1.3	2.3
501–1000	0.3	1.0
> 1000	0.3	0.0

in the views of respondents over the 4 years between the two surveys. For example, the measured support to 'fence Banff' increased from 21.6% in 1996 to 31.1% in 2000. However, an analysis of variance between responses to the questions over the 4-year period found that only three significant changes (0.05 level) had occurred. All these related to approaches to the management of visitation levels. They were (as indicated by an asterisk in Table 11.A2.5):

- A fall in support for the use of auctions as a means for controlling access to the park.
- A fall in support for compulsory guiding.
- An increase in support for fines for improper behaviour.

All other shifts were found to be statistically insignificant.

To conclude, as expected in any longitudinal study, there was some small evolution in the figures obtained. However, there was also considerable overall stability in the picture provided by the 2000 results when compared with those of 1996.

12 Framing Analysis: Examining Mass Mediated Tourism Narratives

CARLA ALMEIDA SANTOS

Department of Recreation, Sport and Tourism, University of Illinois at Urbana-Champaign, 104 Huff Hall, 1206 South Fourth Street, Champaign, IL 61820, USA

———————

Any message which either explicitly or implicitly defines a frame...gives the receiver instructions or aids in his attempt to understand the message included in the frame.
(Bateson, 1972: 188)

Traditionally utilized in political communication research, the emphasis of framing theory has been on the analytical identification and examination of the ways by which language codes establish power relations and manifest themselves in the final stage of a decision. Additionally, framing theory has been identified as a viable resource in areas such as negotiation research (Fischer and Ury, 1981; Neale and Bazerman, 1985), and mass media research (Gamson, 1992; Entman, 1993; Berger, 1997). When adopted in mass media research, framing theory argues that frames are used to emphasize and magnify a specific portion of 'perceived reality', therefore contributing to the notion that journalists produce and reproduce similar narratives while claiming objectivity (Hackett, 1984; Berkowitz, 1997). In this chapter, I address how framing theory can assist tourism research by shaping textual analysis of mass mediated tourism narratives; as such, framing analysis in the context of this chapter refers to the drawing of textual procedures. These textual procedures, which consist of flexible strategies developed for the identification of terminology utilized, as well as general

narrative characteristics and thematic use, allow the researcher to progress from studying tangible realities, such as tourism narratives promoting specific tourist destinations and hosts, to providing a conceptual interpretation that furthers our understanding of those realities. As an approach, framing analysis allows tourism researchers to look at a variety of mass mediated tourism messages and identify the interplay of media and tourism practices, socio-cultural forces and framing approaches. Therefore, framing analysis facilitates not only the distinguishing of the variety of frames utilized by travel writers, but also the understanding of how individual stories add up to something bigger. Within the context of tourism research, framing approaches allow for the identification of the angles travel writers capture, which in turn reveals the organizing principles that make it natural for information to be included or excluded in a variety of tourism narratives (Reese *et al.*, 2001).

With this in mind, framing theory and analysis permits tourism researchers to advance conceptual and theoretical discussions regarding tourism narrative-production practices and reveal the embedded socio-cultural components of tourism marketing, the aim being to understand the narrative models of differentiation that mass mediated messages employ, and that we share of destinations and the 'Other' by examining and understanding the socio-cultural working parts of narrative-production. Ultimately, the concern is not with how realistic mass mediated tourism narratives are as much as how destinations and the 'Other' are organized and recognized in the minds of the mass media, since this organization and recognition will dictate, create, and reproduce social hierarchies and degrees of differentiation between us and them.

In my work, by identifying terminology, general narrative characteristics and thematic use, I was able to identify and examine the representational dynamics utilized by the *New York Times, Washington Post, Los Angeles Times* and *USA Today* travel sections' coverage of a particular tourism destination: Portugal. This analysis allowed me to identify the destabilizing framing practice of using contradictory frames – labelled as traditional versus contemporary – in the selected newspaper travel articles (Santos, 2004). Ultimately, findings allowed for the discussion of how global identities, and cultural–political relationships between nations, are framed by tourism narratives which are anchored in the socio-cultural and political ideologies of the writer and reader.

In the following pages, I summarize framing theory and analysis by discussing its paradigmatic positions and conceptualizations, assessing its strengths and predicaments and how it can be informed by textual procedures for the analysis of mass mediated tourism narratives, and discuss how tourism research can employ framing analysis in order to identify, examine and conceptualize representational dynamics in tourism narratives.

Framing Theory and Analysis

Goffman (1974), in his seminal work *Frame Analysis,* offered an account of how expectations are used to make sense of daily situations. He suggested that individuals organize their thoughts and experiences under a series of frames based on the individual's prior experiences and knowledge and, as such, these frames constitute the individual's reality. For that reason, he con-

ceptualized framing as 'rendering what would otherwise be a meaningless aspect of the scene into something that is meaningful' (Goffman, 1974: 21). Consequently, due to its interpretive nature, framing theory and its resulting analysis lend themselves as an analytical approach used by scholars to access and understand how a variety of issues are constructed, structured and developed by the mass media (Reese *et al.,* 2001).

Other scholars have also discussed framing theory and proposed complementary conceptualizations; Gitlin (1980: 7) described framing as 'persistent patterns of cognition, interpretation, and presentation, of selection, emphasis, and exclusion by which symbol-handlers routinely organize discourse'. Gamson (1989, 1992) conceptualized framing as the organizing theme in news media accounts and argued that the frames the mainstream media offer are used by audiences to construct their own themes for understanding social issues. And, finally, Entman's (1993) framing articulated selection and salience as its main conceptualizations. It emphasized not only what is there but also what is left out, or treated as not as important. When writers or journalists emphasize certain angles of an issue, they 'frame' the issue and, some would argue, influence how the audience understands it. Entman (1993: 52) states: 'to frame is to select some aspects of a perceived reality and make them more salient … in such a way as to promote a particular problem definition, causal interpretation, moral evaluation, and/or treatment recommendation for the item described'.

Moreover, there are two essential conceptualizations of framing: sociological and psychological. The sociological conceptualization concentrates on and embraces interpretative and rhetorical processes of media discourse, as well as the processes of news production and dissemination (Gitlin, 1980; Snow and Bendford, 1988, 1992; Gamson, 1992), whilst the psychological conceptualizations concentrate on the organizing structure of thought and the process by which audiences process and interpret information (Kahneman and Tversky, 1984; Iyengar,

1991; Pan and Kosicki, 1993). These conceptualizations, which serve to guide the theoretical and analytic nature of framing research, are rooted in paradigmatic positions that dominate the approach to framing theory. These main paradigmatic positions are: interactionism, structuralism and discourse analysis (Alasuutari, 1995). The first approach, interactionism, refers to how we can look at framing from a cognitive viewpoint in which different frames, when applied to the same specific situation, can turn out different interpretations and/or decisions. The second approach, structuralism, refers to how the interpretation of meaning takes place by combining and negotiating frames readily available and created by a variety of mass mediated messages and, finally, the third approach, discourse analysis, refers to how the 'framework constitutes the situation' (Alasuutari, 1995: 111).

In addition, framing research can explore frames as independent or dependent variables. Studies of frames as dependent variables usually involve the analysis of the different factors operating in the creation or modification of frames (Tuchman, 1978; Gans 1979; Schoemaker and Reese, 1996). Conversely, when media frames are studied as independent variables the research deals with issues of effects of framing and therefore involves issues of influence and impact by examining framing effects as media effects (Entman, 1993; Pan and Kosicki, 1993; Huang, 1996). Similarly, the study of individual frames as the dependent variable emphasizes that individuals' frames are the outcome of the different media frames they are exposed to (Iyengar, 1987, 1889, 1991; Gamson, 1992; Price et al., 1996). Of particular relevance to the study of individual frames is the work of Price et al. (1996: 496), who found that individuals' frames do not exclusively depend on media coverage of an event or issue, but rather that individuals 'demonstrated a capacity to introduce their own thoughts, going beyond the information provided and drawing out some basic implications on their own'. In addition, the study of individual frames as the independent variable has served to emphasize the connection between individual frames and information processing or political action prevalently studied within the context of social movements (Gamson, 1985; Klandermans and Oegema, 1987; Snow and Bendford, 1988, 1992; Gerhards and Rucht, 1992; Entman and Rojecki, 1993).

None the less, when analysed within the context of news media organization and production, framing suffers from two major predicaments. First, the definition suffers from being too broad, mainly because it has been used by different disciplines, in different ways, to mean different things. This conceptual indeterminacy can only serve to confuse. Second, scholars have often made assumptions based on the notion that differences in frames will automatically provide differences in outcome.

Often scholars put forth conclusions about the effects of news frames in the absence of evidence of consequences. In *The Pragmatics of Human Communication*, Watzlawick et al. (1967) made the differentiation between *what is said*, and how *what is said, is said*. The assumption here is that what a message is about and how it is presented have impact upon how the message will be understood, as well as the responses it will create. However, Iyengar (1987, 1989, 1991) found that the way the news media frame a story and how the audience frames exactly the same story are not always necessarily similar. As a matter of fact, while a writer or journalist may have an intended emotional identification with a character by framing the story in a specific way, it may none the less evoke a completely different reaction (Graber, 1988; Kintsch, 1988; Livingstone, 1990). Scheufele (1999) also argued that framing theory suffers from a lack of a clear conceptual definition and framework on which to base its research. Entman (1993: 51), among others, believed that framing suffers from being a 'scattered conceptualization', partly because it has been used to describe similar but definitely different approaches. An example of this is the work of Hamill and Lodge (1986) who analysed concepts of frame, schema and script and found only phrasing differences between them. In addition, framing has been operationalized along with concepts of agenda setting and priming (Iyengar and Kinder, 1987), and mass media scholars such as McCombs *et al.* (1997) proposed that framing is in fact an extension of agenda setting. As a result, Scheufele (1999) proposed, in the same way as Gitlin (1980) and Entman (1991), that we look at framing as mass media frames versus individual frames, providing a mass media focus to the analysis and orientation of framing research. This work follows Kinder and Sanders' (1990: 74) argument that frames serve as 'devices embedded in political discourse'.

Keeping in mind these predicaments, framing research must continue to explore and examine how media frames are formed, as well as which types of frames result from factors such as differing ideologies, professional values, content, form and organizational constraints and routines (Scheufele, 1999). In addition, framing research must continue to attempt to answer questions of difference between the perceived importance and salience of news frames, meaning the perceived importance given to frames by the audience and the ease of accessibility of previous frames by the audience. Framing studies have also neglected the processes linking the key variables, meaning that they have focused much on inputs and outputs and little on the connections between the two. Dunegan (1993) calls for the need to explore the possibility that framing may be a way to investigate different modes of cognitive processing. The pertinent questions here are whether audiences adopt media frames, and the degree to which the audiences use frames similar to the media frames to do their own information processing. Finally, there is a need to look at travel writers and journalists and whether they are susceptible to the very frames they use to describe events and issues.

The Use of Framing Analysis

According to Hanson *et al.* (1998), textual procedures seek to understand relationships and differences by looking at the use of terminology. Their main focus is on what occurs, when, how, and in which context. The label 'framing analysis' used throughout this chapter refers to the drawing of textual procedures to examine the content of various tourism narratives. As Babbie (1995: 312) argued, the content of messages contained within a text can be classified as either manifest or latent content. Manifest content refers to the 'visible, surface content of communication'. That is to say, there is an assessment of the frequency of word usage as an indicator of the content. This type of analysis is what is most commonly referred to as content analysis, where selected units of content (a word, phrase, or sentence) are organized and counted in order to determine frequency of use. However, latent content refers to the underlying meaning of the entire communication derived through personal interpretation of the material presented.

Textual procedures and analysis are performed when the researcher's goal is with understanding the meanings associated with the messages rather than the number of times message variables occur. Narrative approaches, for instance, will concentrate on themes and stories within certain texts; for instance, Berdayes and Berdayes (1998) analysed magazine articles on highway information and the world views they expressed, while Kreps (1994) analysed the narratives of health care experiences of nursing home residents in order to identify sources of satisfaction and dissatisfaction for elders in nursing homes, and Waitzkin *et al.* (1995) analysed major themes in narratives regarding ageing and social problems in medical encounters. Still other work, such as Altheide's (1996), blends quantitative and qualitative procedures and measurements by combining traditional objective analyses of messages with data interpretation made on the basis of observation. In his work, Altheide (1996) combined participant observation of electronic media with analysis of online messages in order to understand and provide useful interpretations of the uses and functions of new media technology.

This chapter and the framing analysis it

proposes represent the search for the latent content embedded in tourism narratives by drawing on textual procedures. For that reason, the focus is on the recurrence of certain types of content insofar as it reveals an implicit set of cultural beliefs and norms. Schudson (1987: 57) contended that cultural texts are 'ways a culture thinks out loud about itself'. In the case of tourism narratives, those narratives reflect what we think about the destination, hosts and their realities, as well as how our culture and its ideologies view function and the socio-cultural role in the world of the Other. Gergen (1985: 267) stated 'the terms by which the world is understood are social artifacts, products of historically situated interchanges among people'. If we accept the constructivist paradigm proposed by Lincoln and Guba (1985), then we must assume that reality is a construction in people's minds. Nevertheless, there are multiple and contradictory constructions provided by a variety of information sources. In the process of deciding which of these sources are 'most truthful', individuals tend to look at the truth proposed by those who are most knowledgeable on the topic and seem to command a bigger consensus (Schwandt, 1998). In this case, travel writers and journalists are viewed as most knowledgeable on the topic, and therefore should provide an image of the 'location's reality'. Finally, constructivism partakes of both science and humanism, therefore content methodologies owe much to it, in the sense that it allows for a merging of science and humanism (Smith, 1988). Analysis used to evaluate written or spoken records for the occurrence of specific categories of events, items or behaviours has been conducted with a variety of topics, such as mock juror deliberations (Horowitz, 1985) and television drama content (Greenberg, 1980).

In the context of tourism, an analysis of how travel writers and journalists describe, explain and situate tourism destinations and hosts provides insight into how discursive patterns serve to describe and define relationships of us versus them. Understanding these relationships, their creation and re-creation of the dominant ideology and para-digms, and their potential to reveal the ethical and socio-cultural components of tourism marketing and promotion is much needed considering that current tourism research involving social psychological theories is limited in its ability to analyse and understand mass mediated messages of tourism. As such, we need to search for a different 'frame upon which to examine our frameworks that condition and explain experience and action, question the ethics of our choices, and highlight the partiality of our knowledge and control' (Fox, 2000: 35). In its current state 'tourism research exposes a deep flaw in discipline thought. Specifically, a methodological commitment to, or at least a dependence upon, the assumption of cultural homogeneity within the various fields of study' (MacCannell, 1989: 2). Therefore, it is only logical and perhaps necessary to question tourism's research methodologies; this questioning illuminates interpretive approaches, allowing for further investigation and understanding of individuals' experiences in the context of their everyday actions and creation of meanings, particularly mass mediated cultivated meanings. Ultimately, organizing principles in mass mediated tourism narratives persistently promote destinations and events within a context that fits the organizing ideas of the writer and the audience. Correspondingly, the analysis of the factors that influence this frame persistence is possible through the use of framing analysis.

Framing Perspectives in the Context of Tourism Narratives

Organizations such as UNESCO propose that further theoretical frameworks be introduced in order to investigate and recognize the socio-cultural impact of a variety of mass mediated messages. One example of this variety is the promotional messages of tourism destinations and hosts. Through the power of contemporary mass mediated messages we are becoming increasingly aware of the various and distinct cultures of the world, and in the process we are constructing and forming opinions about these cultures. This mass mediated construction of cultures, along with the increasing accessibility of remote destinations facilitated by tourism, is transforming traditional cultural notions. People from remote areas and cultures are increasingly coming into contact with one another; all you have to do is look around you, and you will see that more and more we are coming into contact with individuals who are and look, at least on the surface, different from us. It is no longer uncommon for us to embark on journeys that take us half-way around the world. And the images we carry with us are increasingly determined by the mass media.

Within this environment, tourism has recognized the opportunity for its promotion and has enlisted the assistance of the mass media. Currently, there are many examples of this cooperation; in travel magazines, travel television channels and newspaper travel sections a discourse is taking place that stresses the need for travel, and promises in return, pleasure, relaxation and the development of a culturally responsive self. Van Doorn (1984) argued that while researchers must isolate tourism from other sources of social change (such as mass media), it is hardly possible to do so, especially from the standpoint of the tourist whose only knowledge of the locals comes from the media. Ultimately, the tourist enters the destination with a frame of reference of locals, who combine submissive-like attitudes with linguistic skills that allow them to do their job, 'and who in any case do not shatter the meticulously, prejudiced, preconstructed image of picturesque poverty' (van Doorn, 1984: 77). When it comes to tourism, the combination of people, ideas and images does not exist separately from the tourist; instead, Uzzell (1984) argued that they are given to the tourist in order to help to create his or her own fantasies and meanings. Considering this, Wearing and Wearing (1996) proposed that the personal and sometimes misleading meanings that tourists construct of the tourist space be included in the present day analyses of tourism. After all, tourists often look for the culture that the tourism industry has defined for them rather than seek a genuine, less

idealized version of a culture (Adams, 1984).

Morgan and Pritchard (1998) claimed that cultural meanings born from tourism processes possess a breadth of symbolism wider than the actual consumption of tourism products and places themselves. Identities are created according to the dominant value systems and meanings. 'Just as tourism sites are associated with "particular values, historical events and feelings", so values, feelings and events are used to promote such sites, reinforcing the dominant ideologies' (Morgan and Pritchard, 1998: 3). Therefore, when an individual's understanding of a destination and culture is limited, the media's framing can become the main reference. Considering that media coverage of a destination and hosts predates actual exposure, by the time exposure occurs one already has a dominant frame on which to rely. None the less, a variety of practices contribute to this framing of destinations and hosts. For instance, limited space and resources cause travel writers and journalists to frame another culture or group. When travel writers and journalists cover a destination they are given only a limited amount of space and resources to work with; with these types of limitations it is almost impossible to clearly define a culture or group; instead, facts and hard selling information are given priority.

Another common practice is the frequent use of simplification to describe reality. Bennett (1983) believes that mass media tend to look at the 'small picture' instead of the 'big picture' surrounding an event. There is also the story's angle, which requires, among other things, that travel writers and journalists choose an angle and introduce the destination and its hosts accordingly. By doing this, travel writers and journalists often give a subjective treatment to a destination and its hosts by ignoring other alternatives. 'Reporters can agree about the "facts" but still distort an event by pursuing one angle and thereby removing the event from the context in which it occurred, in which it would be more fully understood' (Altheide, 1996: 177).

By using the basic rules of fragmentation of news coverage, mass media with its enormous power to frame a given situation in any social framework can frame issues based on biases, prior knowledge and experiences. Domke (1997: 1) argued that 'in particular, scholarship suggests that the press may play a central role in shaping and reinforcing racial values and attitudes'. For instance, in the case of the coverage of tourist destinations and their people, labels used to describe tourist destinations and their residents imply evaluations and context. Such labels 'not only place and identify those events; they assign events to a context. Thereafter the use of the label is likely to mobilize this whole referential context, with all its associated meanings and connotations' (Hall *et al.*, 1978: 19).

Case Study: Framing Portugal

My approach to framing analysis proposes and embraces a sociological perspective which stresses that tourism narratives are performative, epistemological and not given to objective or value-neutral depiction, and, for those reasons, allow for the identification and revelation of representational dynamics developed within a dominant cultural system. In a study of the *New York Times, Washington Post, Los Angeles Times* and *USA Today* travel sections the goal was to reveal representational dynamics in the American coverage of tourism in Portugal so as to participate in the debate over news media and tourism (Santos, 2004). As such, I explored the various ways in which newspaper travel articles reproduce and articulate local and national socio-cultural realities. The *New York Times, Washington Post, Los Angeles Times* and *USA Today* travel sections were chosen because of their status as national newspapers being acknowledged as setting the national news media format. These newspapers provide an appropriate sample of the select few newspapers to make regular use of international travel writers; moreover, because it is common to find articles by the same writer in a variety of newspapers and magazines the same frames are likely to

reappear, and be duplicated, in other newspapers and magazines across the USA. Portugal was chosen mainly due to the insight it provides into Western European destinations exploring alternatives that will reposition their brand image from a low-cost 'sea and sun' holiday to an international cultural and heritage attraction.

All feature articles published between 1996 and 2002 were identified. Feature articles were selected since their reporting style offers greater detail and therefore reveals the tourism desks' approach to the significance of certain themes. Furthermore, since they concentrate on a particular destination they provide specific modes of socio-cultural representation. Letters to the editor, articles that made reference to Portugal in connection with other destinations, as well as articles with fewer than 500 words, were excluded from the analysis. The 7-year time frame was selected to trace any eventual changes in the newspapers' general focus. Articles in which the words 'Portugal' or 'Portuguese' appeared along with 'tourism', 'travel', 'leisure', 'discovery', 'journey' or 'vacation' were identified. This data collection process was done by first using the academic universe news database Lexis Nexis, then each newspaper's online database was searched to verify the Lexis Nexis findings. Finally, each original printed newspaper's travel section was found and all articles were photocopied.

Between 1996 and 2002 a total of 45 feature articles were published, and although this may be perceived as a small sample, it is representative of the limited variety of cultural observations. Next, articles were analysed in three stages by three individual coders. This was done to ensure that the frames identified were indeed perceived similarly by more than one coder. In terms of the analysis process, first, narratives were read individually by each coder in their totality for terminology use, ensuring a collection of the varied terminology. Second, a variety of descriptions based on terminology were assigned to each article by individual coders. Third, coders met to discuss terminology and description findings, allowing for similar descriptions to be combined and appropriately labelled. This allowed for frequently reappearing descriptions based on terminology to be sorted accordingly from more abstract to more specific descriptions. By developing descriptions and considering theme frequency, relationships and differences in framing are revealed and analytic focused frameworks are developed.

While framing analysis, with the aid of textual procedures, allows for the identification of frames, in itself it does little to explain the significance of the findings. The strength of framing theory and analysis is that it demands that findings be discussed within the theoretically sound context it provides; and, indeed, this can occur by simply taking one's distance to one's own field. With insufficient theoretical discussion of their findings researchers might end up with just descriptive accounts, thus there is need to incorporate a strong theoretical framework and discussion to better understand how, in this particular case study, tourism destinations are represented and why they are represented in the ways they are. Therefore, armed with analytic focused frameworks, and an analysis of the relationships and differences in framing, I was then able to explore the ways in which the identified narratives reproduced and articulated local and national socio-cultural realities, as well as where they located the writer and reader.

This process of contextualizing findings can only occur when the theoretical framework, as well as the research goal, is kept in mind. Since the goal of my study was centred on being able to provide a connecting point where news media, tourism and marketing meet and interconnect in order to reveal socio-cultural relationships, I was guided by a necessity to investigate mass media's capacity to address critical public issues; the exploratory nature of this study and its methodology allowed me to do just that. Ultimately, framing analysis relies not only on textual procedures but also on a need continuously to ask, why does it happen? And, so what? Why are these messages important? What do they say about our society and media practices? Where do

they locate hosts, writers and readers? Because mass mediated travel narratives are shaped by marketing efforts with the ultimate goal of generating audiences, they are sustained by a greater freedom to ignore questions pertinent to issues of inequalities and injustice, which I believe are important when it comes to safeguarding cultural identity. As Turner and Bruner (1986: 144) argued, 'narratives are not only structures of meaning but structures of power'.

Given the exploratory nature of this research, as well as the limited literature on the use of mediated messages of tourism destinations, much of the basis for my discussion and interpretation of the findings arose from my belief that American travel writers and journalists mediate the socio-cultural and political relationship between the USA and host countries by promoting American beliefs, priorities and perspectives. Ultimately, my findings allowed me to discuss how, by forcing destinations into the context of the reader, the reader is presented with his or her own views (Santos, 2004). For that reason, we must continue to reflect upon methods that bring tourism narratives into a frame of analysis that will ultimately show its representations as negotiated, constructed and partial (Clifford, 1986; Street, 1996).

Issues of Validity and Values

In view of the fact that I discuss how the basis for my research evolved from my beliefs regarding the creation process of tourism narratives, it is only necessary that I introduce a discussion regarding issues of validity and values in framing research. As a researcher, I believe that the question is not so much whether validity is important in the field of qualitative tourism research, but, rather, whether that validity is situated within qualitative research or is a remnant of quantitative tourism research. Kincheloe and McLaren (1998: 287) maintain that validity 'reflects a concern for acceptance within a positivist concept of research rigor'. A positivist rigour, therefore, should not be forced into qualitative work, whose researchers' preoccupation is with the traditional criteria utilized in order to evaluate and interpret qualitative research problems. After all, the traditional criteria utilized to assess validity and adequacy were formulated and essentially owned by positivism, which for centuries has justified the use of quantitative work (Altheide and Johnson, 1998).

As such, the call for the approach to validity should be replaced with a concern for trustworthiness in one's work. This trustworthiness can be accomplished through both the use of 'credibility of portrayals of constructed realities' and 'anticipatory accommodation', meaning the understanding that everyday situations cannot easily be studied through the application of generalizations, but rather require accommodation to the situation (Kincheloe and McLaren, 1998: 288). The problem exists, however, in deciding how to prove a document's authenticity. Throughout history numerous falsifications have been masterminded by individuals in order to appropriate money from the social sciences (Berg, 1998). Therefore, the notion of authenticity and reality, which are consequently interconnected, must be taken into consideration. An authentic document can 'produce' reality just as much as it can 'produce' supposition. The proof of reality lies not only within the document itself, but also with the intentions and readings of investigators, researchers and the audience. 'The qualitative researcher studies social action and cultural sensitivity situated in time and place; the move to generalize in the traditional sense is neither warranted nor particularly desirable' (Lindlof, 1995: 238). Ultimately, qualitative research is a process, in the sense that the tourism researcher approaches issues from within a set of ideas, a framework, and an interpretive community, and as such, its work must be constantly reviewed and contemplated.

Therefore, issues of validity may shift accordingly and, more importantly, appropriately. According to Janesick (1998: 50), 'validity in qualitative research has to do with description and explanation, and whether or not a given explanation fits a given description'. As Denzin and Lincoln (1998: 24) remind us, 'Any gaze is always filtered through the lenses of language, gender, social class, race, and ethnicity. There are no objective observations, only observations socially situated in the worlds of the observer and the observed.' Qualitative tourism researchers must continue to struggle to demonstrate how qualitative work accesses multiple tourism realities, human meanings and interactions from an insider's perspective. Kuhn (1970) and Toulmin (1972) believe that research is conducted from within a certain global perspective or world view which shapes the process of research itself; meaning, 'the mind of the observer has an inherent and active role in the process of knowing' (Pearce et al., 1982: 22). And, while a positivist notion insists on research as a 'value free' activity, others suggest that it cannot easily be separated from a set of values that dominate a culture or an individual (Longino, 1990). Furthermore, some have begun to address the importance of making the researcher's personal point of view known to the reader and how these same preconceptions actually work to shape the nature of the research (Creswell, 1998).

Conclusion

Mass mediated tourism narratives represent cultural products in which local, national and international ideologies, traditions, influences, trends and experiences are articulated, produced and negotiated by prospective tourists. These narratives are sites of knowledge production and identity formations. As cultural commodities these narratives reveal local, regional, national and international concerns, as well as systems of representation and construction, which intersect with transnational trends in tourism and mass media's tendencies to both shape, reflect and construct complex realities. These realities can sometimes be constructed without awareness of the local, regional and national and in the process place the travel sector and the tourist outside the social, political and cultural ramifications of tourism. It is here that framing analysis can contribute the most. Lea (1988: 2) argues that, 'there is no other international trading activity which involves such critical interplay among economic, political, environmental, and social elements as tourism'. Hence, due to its great influence, it is important that we look at how the mass media construct, describe and locate different populations, ethnic groups and nations, and how they choose to communicate those powerful cultural justifications and representations (i.e. framing). Ultimately, news media coverage of tourism, and its discourse, is not only universal, it is often unquestioned and presupposed.

The literature on framing asserts that media create frames about issues. These frames become the way the public 'knows' the information. Therefore, by using framing analysis to look at issues of tourism destinations and hosts, we are able to identify these frames. In addition, how the frames define the situations and the people involved in them, how production practices may contribute to them, and what are the ideologies transmitted by them are all important questions. Ultimately, I am interested in knowing how tourist destinations, events and issues are organized and made sense of by media professionals. Framing is particularly useful because it allows me to examine the available verbal and visual symbolic instruments used by media, as well as connect the private interests, culture, media production practices and more in order to understand the socio-cultural apparatus behind them. As Lutz and Collins (1993: 3), in their work *Reading National Geographic*, demonstrate: 'representations... are never irrelevant, never unconnected to the world of actual social relations'. While news media are often seen as straightforward evidence of the world, news media coverage reflects as much about whom it is writing about as it reflects about who is writing it and to whom it is being written. American travel narratives represent American desires, fears and special interests more than they reflect the desires, fears and special interests of those being covered (Santos, 2004).

References

Adams, K.M. (1984) Come to Tana Toraja: land of the heavenly kings. Travel agents as brokers in ethnicity. *Annals of Tourism Research* 11, 469–485.

Alasuutari, P. (1995) *Researching Culture: Qualitative Method and Cultural Studies.* Sage, London.

Altheide, D.L. (1996) *Qualitative Media Analysis.* Sage, Thousand Oaks, California.

Altheide, D.L. and Johnson, J.M. (1998) Criteria for assessing interpretive validity in qualitative research. In: Denzin, N.K. and Lincoln, Y.S. (eds) *Collecting and Interpreting Qualitative Materials.* Sage, Thousand Oaks, California, pp. 283–312.

Babbie, E. (1995) *The Practice of Social Research,* 7th edn. Wadsworth, Belmont, California.

Bateson, G. (1972) *Steps to an Ecology of Mind: Collected Essays in Anthropology, Psychiatry, Evolution and Epistemology.* Chandler Publishing, San Francisco, California.

Bennett, W.L. (1983) *News: the Politics of Illusion.* Longman, New York.

Berdayes, L.C. and Berdayes, V. (1998) The information highway in contemporary magazine narrative. *Journal of Communication* 48(2), 109–124.

Berg, B.L. (1998) *Qualitative Research Methods for the Social Sciences,* 3rd edn. Allyn & Bacon, Needham Heights, Massachusetts.

Berger, A.A. (1997) *Narratives in Popular Culture, Media and Everyday Life.* Sage, Thousand Oaks, California.

Berkowitz, D. (1997) *Social Meanings of News: a Text-reader.* Sage, Thousand Oaks, California.

Butler, R.W. (1999) Understanding tourism. In: Jackson, E.L. and Burton, T.L. (eds) *Leisure Studies: Prospects for the Twenty-First Century.* Venture Publishing, State College, Pennsylvania, pp. 97–118.

Clifford, J. (1986) Introduction: partial truths. In: Clifford, J. and Marcus, G.E. (eds) *Writing Culture. The Poetics and Politics of Ethnography.* University of California Press, Berkeley, California, pp. 1–26.

Creswell, J.W. (1998) *Qualitative Inquiry and Research Design: Choosing Among Five Traditions.* Sage, Thousand Oaks, California.

Denzin, N.K. and Lincoln, Y.S. (1998) Introduction: entering the field of qualitative research. In: Denzin, N.K. and Lincoln, Y.S. (eds) *Collecting and Interpreting Qualitative Materials*. Sage, Thousand Oaks, California, pp. 1–34.

Domke, D. (1997) Journalists, framing, and discourse about race relations. *Journalism and Communication Monographs* 164(4), 1–56.

Dunegan, K.H. (1993) Framing, cognitive modes, and image theory: toward an understanding of a glass half full. *Journal of Applied Psychology* 78(3), 491–503.

Entman, R. (1991) Framing US coverage of international news: Contrasts in narratives of the KAL and Iran air incidents. *Journal of Communication* 41(4), 6–27.

Entman, R. (1993) Framing: toward clarification of a fractured paradigm. *Journal of Communication* 43(4), 51–58.

Entman, R. and Rojecki, A. (1993) Freezing out the public: elite and media framing of the US antinuclear movement. *Political Communication* 10(2), 155–173.

Fischer, R. and Ury, W. (1981) *Getting to Yes*. Houghton Mifflin, Boston, Massachusetts.

Fox, K. (2000) Echoes of leisure: questions, challenges, and potentials. *Journal of Leisure Research* 32(1), 32–36.

Gamson, W.A. (1985) Goffman's legacy to political sociology. *Theory and Society* 14(5), 605–622.

Gamson, W.A. (1992) *Talking Politics*. Cambridge University Press, Cambridge, UK.

Gamson, W.A. and Modigliani, A. (1989) Media discourse and public opinion on nuclear power: a constructionist approach. *The American Journal of Sociology* 95(1), 1–37.

Gans, H. (1979) *Deciding What's News*. Pantheon, New York.

Gergen, K.J. (1985) The social constructionist movement in modern psychology. *American Psychologist* 40(3), 266–275.

Gerhards, J. and Rucht, D. (1992) Mesomobilization: organizing and framing in two protest campaigns in West Germany. *The American Journal of Sociology* 98(3), 555–596.

Gitlin, T. (1980) *The Whole World is Watching: Mass Media in the Making and Unmaking of the New Left*. University of California Press, Berkeley, California.

Goffman, E. (1974) *Frame Analysis: an Essay on the Organization of Experience*. Harper & Row, New York.

Graber, D. (1988) *Processing the News: How People Tame the Information Tide*, 2nd edn. Longman, New York.

Greenberg, B.S. (1980) *Life on Television: Current Analysis of US TV Drama*. Ablex, Norwood, New Jersey.

Hackett, R.A. (1984) Decline of a paradigm? Bias and objectivity in news media studies. *Critical Studies in Mass Communication* 1(3), 229–259.

Hall, S., Critcher, C., Jefferson, T., Clarke, J. and Roberts, B. (1978) *Policing the Crisis: Mugging, the State, and Law and Order*. Macmillan, London.

Hamill, R. and Lodge, M. (1986) Cognitive consequences of political sophistication. In: Lau, R.R. and Sears, D.O. (eds) *Political Cognition*. Earlbaum, Hillsdale, New Jersey, pp. 69–95.

Hanson, A., Cottle, S., Negrin, R. and Newbold, C. (1998) *Mass Communication Research Methods*. New York University Press, New York.

Horowitz, I.A. (1985) The effects of jury nullification instructions on verdicts and jury functioning in criminal trials. *Law and Human Behavior* 9(1), 25–36.

Huang, K.S. (1996) A comparison between media frames and audience frames: the case of the Hill-Thomas controversy. Paper presented at the Annual Conference of the International Communication Association, Chicago, Illinois.

Iyengar, S. (1987) Television news and citizens' explanations of national affairs. *The American Political Science Review* 81(3), 815–831.

Iyengar, S. (1989) How citizens think about national issues: a matter of responsibility. *American Journal of Political Science* 33(4), 878–900.

Iyengar, S. (1991) *Is Anyone Responsible? How Television Frames Political Issues*. University of Chicago Press, Chicago, Illinois.

Iyengar, S. and Kinder, D.R. (1987) *News that Matters: Television and American Opinion*. University of Chicago Press, Chicago, Illinois.

Janesick, V. (1998) The dance of qualitative research design: metaphor, methodolatry, and meaning. In: Denzin, N.K. and Lincoln, Y.S. (eds) *Strategies of Qualitative Inquiry*. Sage, Thousand Oaks, California, pp. 35–55.

Kahneman, D. and Tversky, A. (1984) Choices, values, and frames. *American Psychologist* 39(4), 341–350.

Kincheloe, J.L. and McLaren, P.L. (1998) Rethinking critical theory and qualitative research. In: Denzin, N.K.

and Lincoln, Y.S. (eds) *The Landscape of Qualitative Research: Theories and Issues*. Sage, Thousand Oaks, California, pp. 260–299.

Kinder, D.R. and Sanders, L.M. (1990) Mimicking political debate with survey questions: the case of white opinion on affirmative action for blacks. *Social Cognition* 8(1), 73–103.

Kintsch, W. (1988) The role of knowledge in discourse comprehension: a construction-integration model. *Psychological Review* 95(2), 163–182.

Klandermans, B. and Oegema, D. (1987) Potentials, networks, motivations, and barriers: steps towards participation in social movements. *American Sociological Review* 52(4), 519–531.

Kreps, G.L. (1994) Gender differences in the critical incidents reported by elderly health care residents: a narrative analysis. In: Sterk, H. and Turner, L. (eds) *Differences That Make a Difference: Examining the Assumptions of Research in Communication, Language, and Gender*. Bergin and Garvey, Westport, Connecticut, pp. 27–34.

Kuhn, T.S. (1970) *The Structure of Scientific Revolutions*. University of Chicago Press, Chicago, Illinois.

Lea, J. (1988) *Tourism and Development in the Third World*. Routledge, London.

Lincoln, Y.S. and Guba, E.G. (1985) *Naturalistic Inquiry*. Sage, Beverley Hills, California.

Lindlof, T.R. (1995) *Qualitative Communication Research Methods*. Sage, Thousand Oaks, California.

Livingstone, S. (1990) *Making Sense of Television*. Pergamon, New York.

Longino, H.E. (1990) *Science as Social Knowledge*. Princeton University Press, Princeton, New Jersey.

Lutz, C. and Collins, J.L. (1993) *Reading National Geographic*. University of Chicago Press, Chicago, Illinois.

MacCannell, D. (1989) Introduction to special issues on semiotics of tourism. *Annals of Tourism Research* 16(1), 1–6.

McCombs, M.E., Shaw, D.L. and Weaver, D.L. (1997) *Communication and Democracy: Exploring the Intellectual Frontiers in Agenda-setting Theory*. Lawrence Erlbaum & Associates, Mahwah, New Jersey.

Morgan, N. and Pritchard, A. (1998) *Tourism Promotion and Power: Creating Images, Creating Identities*. John Wiley & Sons, Chichester, UK.

Neale, M.A. and Bazerman, M.H. (1985) The effects of framing and negotiator overconfidence on bargainer behaviors and outcomes. *The Academy of Management Journal* 28(1), 34–49.

Pan, Z. and Kosicki, G.M. (1993) Framing analysis: an approach to news discourse. *Political Communication* 10(1), 55–75.

Pearce, B.W., Cronen, V.E. and Harris, L.M. (1982) Methodological considerations in building human communication theory. In: Dance, F. (ed.) *Human Communication Theory: Comparative Essays*. Harper & Row, New York, pp. 1–41.

Price, V., Tewksbury, D. and Powers, E. (1996) Switching trains of thought: the impact of news frames on readers' cognitive responses. Paper presented at the Annual Conference of the International Communication Association, Chicago, Illinois.

Reese, S.D., Gandy, O.H. Jr and Grant, A.E. (eds) (2001) *Framing Public Life: Perspectives on the Media and our Understandings of the Social World*. Lawrence Erlbaum & Associates, Mahwah, New Jersey.

Santos, C.A. (2004) Framing Portugal: representational dynamics. *Annals of Tourism Research* 31, 122–138.

Scheufele, D.A. (1999) Framing as a theory of media effects. *Journal of Communication* 49(1), 102–122.

Schoemaker, P.J. and Reese, S.D. (1996) *Mediating the Message*, 2nd edn. Longman, White Plains, New York.

Schudson, M. (1987) The new validation of popular culture: sense and sentimentality in academia. *Critical Studies in Mass Communication* 4(1), 51–68.

Schwandt, T.A. (1998) Constructivist, interpretivist approaches to human inquiry. In: Denzin, N.K. and Lincoln, Y.S. (eds) *The Landscape of Qualitative Research: Theories and Issues*. Sage, Thousand Oaks, California, pp. 221–259.

Smith, M.J. (1988) *Contemporary Communication Research Methods*. Wadsworth, Belmont, California.

Snow, D.A. and Bendford, R.D. (1988) Ideology, frame resonance, and participant mobilization. In: Klandermans, B., Kriesi, H. and Tarrow, S. (eds) *International Social Movement Research*. JAI Press, Greenwich, Connecticut, pp. 197–217.

Snow, D.A. and Bendford, R.D. (1992) Master frames and cycles of protest. In: Morris, A.D. and Mueller, C.M. (eds) *Frontiers in Social Movement Theory*. Yale University Press, New Haven, Connecticut, pp. 133–155.

Street, B. (1996) Culture is a verb: anthropological aspects of language and cultural processes. In: Graddol, D., Thompson, L. and Byram, M. (eds) *Language and Culture*. British Association for Applied Linguistics, and in association with Multilingual Matters, Clevedon, UK, pp. 23–43.

Toulmin, S. (1972) *Human Understanding*. Princeton University Press, Princeton, New Jersey.

Tuchman, G. (1978) *Making News: a Study in the Construction of Reality*. Free Press, New York.

Turner, V. and Bruner, E. (1986) *The Anthropology of Experience*. University of Illinois Press, Urbana, Illinois.

Uzzell, D. (1984) An alternative structuralist approach to the psychology of tourism marketing. *Annals of Tourism Research* 11, 79–99.

Van Doorn, J. (1984) A critical assessment of socio-cultural impact studies of tourism in the Third World. *Tourism Recreation Research* May, 178–183.

Waitzkin, H., Britt, T. and Williams, C. (1995) Narratives of ageing and social problems in medical encounters with older persons. *Journal of Health and Social Behavior* 35(4), 322–348.

Watzlawick, P., Beavin-Bavelas, J. and Jackson, D.D. (1967) *The Pragmatics of Human Communication*. W.W. Norton, New York.

Wearing, B. and Wearing, S. (1996) Refocusing the tourist experience: the 'flaneur' and the 'choraster'. *Leisure Studies* 15(4), 229–244.

13 GIS Techniques in Tourism and Recreation Planning: Application to Wildlife Tourism

PASCAL TREMBLAY

School of Tourism and Hospitality, Faculty of Law, Business and Arts, Charles Darwin University, Darwin, Northern Territory 0909, Australia

---

Introduction: General Definitions and Methods

Geographic information systems (GIS) refers to computer-based databases used to store, analyse, integrate in layers and display data of a geographical nature, in the sense that they are connected to discrete locations on the Earth's surface. General references on technical operations and applications include Johnston *et al.* (1993), Delany (1999), Grimshaw (2000), Longley *et al.* (2001), Walsh and Crews-Meyer (2002) and Chang (2004). Remote sensing methods refers to a set of techniques allowing for the capture of data from long distances and large scales, such as aerial photography and satellite imagery. These can be based on an increasingly wide array of 'sensors' (defining what spectral ranges or other phenomena are measured) and require sophisticated image processing techniques for data manipulation towards specific purposes (Campbell, 1996; Mather, 1997).

The extensive literature on applications is fairly recent (generally less than 15 years old) and has focused on applications attempting to utilize directly observable or measurable features of the landscape (obtained through remote sensing) for the sake of developing indicators of ecological characteristics and/or human-based features of spatial environments. In a sense, GIS methods have attempted to bridge some of the technical and policy gaps at the source of the business–social–environmental divide by providing a platform to combine information and knowledge measured from different sources and pertaining to social, economic and ecological domains. Most of the intended applications aim at providing planning and spatial decision making tools allowing for the identification of spatial interactions between landscape, ecological habitats and multiple forms of human activity. The main advance of GIS is the ability to consider such complex abstraction, integration and compression of information at reasonable time and resources costs. GIS outputs remain abstractions capable of simplifying the display of complex phenomena into spatial connections between data objects with images made out of points, lines, surfaces, zones, measurement, layers, etc. in formats that are increasingly cheap and accessible to decision makers and planners.

Main Applications of GIS

A brief overview of the literature shows that GIS (and related sensing methods) have found widespread use in the area of ecological monitoring and environmental planning. In wildlife management applications, a central role of GIS techniques has been to associate landscape features (such as land cover, soil, ground gradient, altitude, etc.) with ecological–spatial attributes for the sake of identifying habitat suitability and thereby to provide models predicting the occurrence of plants and animals in space, the extent of potential conflicts over land uses and possible threats to biodiversity in general (Berry, 1991; Pereria and Itami, 1991; Aspinall, 1992; Bridgewater, 1993; Griffiths *et al.*, 1993; Stoms and Estes, 1993; Akcakaya, 1994; Goodchild, 1994; Carver, 1995; Congalton and Green, 1995, Aspinall *et al.*, 1998; Griffiths *et al.*, 2000) as well as with land cover change assessment (Petit and Lambin, 2001; Aspinall, 2002; Brown *et al.*, 2002; Comber *et al.*, 2003).

Typically, the suitability of habitat refers to the extent to which a population of plants or animals, a species or a broad ecosystem is likely to be found in specific spaces or locations. This is assessed, modelled or simulated by combining knowledge of the land cover and landscape in the location studied with ecological niche knowledge associated with the living unit analysed, whether a species or biosystem (Congalton and Green, 1995: 17). Information about landscape provided by remote sensing methods includes such things as extent of plant coverage, ground slopes, water bodies and many other features. This is combined with knowledge of preferred habitat characteristics for a given species or group of species which have been derived from extensive empirical observations and include attributes such as food availability, preferred forest coverage, slope of the terrain, soil type for some types of species, indicators of human activity (usually modelled as constraints), exposure to predators, presence of bodies of water and distances between patches of ideal habitat and possibly many more (Bridgewater, 1993; Congalton and Green, 1995; Lopez, 1998; Griffiths *et al.*, 2000). Modelling is unavoidably arbitrary to the extent that the weights associated with vari-

ous features depend on judgement, are adjusted by trial and error and their predictive performance is ideally tested against field observations.

It is possible to use the spatial and temporal information produced by GIS to address deeper questions involving time, usually linked with the monitoring and modelling of ecological patterns and dynamic processes. Although still under-developed, the availability of discrete pictures of landscape and corresponding distribution of wildlife species allows one to query empirically the very complex relationships between changes in landscape, changes in land cover and changes in the distribution of wildlife species.

Most areas of GIS development attempting to bridge complex interactions between biotic, abiotic and human processes in space and time are likely to have great implications for recreation and tourism planning, especially those with the obvious purpose of being able better to assess the impacts of human activity on landscape and related ecological implications. It has long been proposed that GIS could hold the key to explicitly modelling complex phenomena occurring on related temporal and spatial spaces when they are grounded on fixed landscape elements (geological, ecological, man-made) and assumed to interact (Perez-Trejo, 1993). But the technical difficulties involved should not be under-estimated as the choice of appropriate and compatible spatial and temporal scales is a major challenge for GIS studies. This occurs because ecological and social data are usually collected using different methods, by different agencies and with different purposes. Data integrated through GIS usually come in different formats, social data being typically discrete, whilst data on land cover and landscape are usually continuous (Rindfuss, 2002: 7).

Applications to Recreation and Tourism

A number of surveys on 'GIS and tourism' can be found, usually in the park management, recreation and tourism literature. It is useful to first summarize some of the generic possibilities this literature identifies in the surveys published in the last decade, discuss in more detail those applications which are most often developed and bring together ecological or wildlife management with recreation or tourism planning, with a view to identifying converging issues and methods. The following section in the chapter develops such an application involving GIS used for tourism and recreation planning and wildlife management in Northern Australia.

Tourism

It is possible to find in the tourism literature a number of surveys on the potential and development of GIS applications for tourism marketing and information technology applications linked with mass tourism (Sussman and Rashad, 1994; Bertazzon *et al.*, 1997; Kilical and Kilical, 1997; Elliott-White and Finn, 1998; Bahaire and Elliot-White, 1999; McAdam, 1999; Van der Knaap, 1999). Recent developments of destination-based tourism information management systems incorporating user-friendly maps of routes and facilities abound and multiple applications or websites on the topic can be found (Allen *et al.*, 1999; Porter and Tarrant, 2001). Among the uses connected with the expansion of mass tourism, changes in land uses and patterns have been documented (Berry, 1991; Allen *et al.*, 1999). Dietvorst (1995) has examined through GIS the spatial connections between socio-economic origins of tourists and travel flows in and out of a given theme park and its region in The Netherlands. McAdam (1999) surveys a number of uses and applications of GIS in tourism originating from the private and public sectors. Results display a high degree of diversity and fragmentation in approaches and methodology. He observes that applications of GIS. have in general focused on 'remote localities or situations where tourism development is only at the consideration stage' and 'issues of sustainability are on the planning agenda because these environments

and cultures remain largely unspoiled and unprotected' (McAdam, 1999: 79).

Applications to recreation planning in natural environments

As a large proportion of GIS applications have developed by combining information about land and other spatial characteristics with ecological data to produce multi-layered maps capable of identifying habitats for various ecological units, such models were bound to play a role in early tourism and recreation applications in the area of protected areas and resources planning. For instance Bahaire and Elliott-White (1999: 162) view GIS as capable of enabling 'the integration of datasets representing socio-economic development and environmental capital within a given spatial setting'. Such models identified early conflicting uses of a resource and typically featured conservation and recreation (or tourism) as competing uses for a given area or set of resources (Carver, 1995). For instance, multi-layered GIS data allow the integration of data about habitat suitability for a wildlife species with data about recreational uses or spatial preferences to identify overlaps and potential conflict areas.

In a typical application, Harris *et al.* (1995: 562) assume that recreationists and mountain sheep in the Colorado National Forest compete for the same land resources and that park managers need to allocate such territory so as to minimize 'conflicts' or 'clashes', deemed undesirable for the animal but not necessarily for the recreationists. Data about recreationists' movements were associated with information about existing trails and survey-based data about movements away from trails for the sake of the exercise applying to a relatively small territory, but the authors recognized a number of difficulties in the integration. In the context of such an application, it is assumed that the regulation of human movements would constitute the appropriate policy to limit perceived conflicts over resource use (Bishop and Gimblett, 2000).

GIS models have also been used in the

realm of outdoor recreation for the sake of evaluating the appeal of a place or region or ultimately predicting the number of visitors to a recreational area. It is useful to describe a typical example in that tradition. Boyd and Butler's (1996) study of the ecotourism potential in northern Ontario attempted to model the suitability of various places by combining landscape data collected by remote sensing techniques on a scale and resolution that allowed for planning and management applications to tourism and recreation to be made. For the sake of describing ecotourists' preferences in the Ontario context, they do not use empirical knowledge; rather they combine common sense specifications based on an acceptable definition of ecotourists and expert knowledge about their behavioural attributes (Boyd and Butler, 1996: 385). Eventually they produce maps that combine a series of broadly acceptable attributes of place that are deemed to hold great appeal for ecotourists. For instance, they refer to such principles as ecotourists' respect for the integrity of host communities, the need for complementarity with existing resource-based uses present at the ecosystem level and other ideological and aesthetic considerations such as their dislike for visible habitat degradation. This allows them to blend generic characteristics of an abstract eco-

tourist market with characteristics of the place for the sake of computing ecotourism suitability scores. The rest of the procedure is conventional in following the GIS–ecological approach. A desirability index for ecotourism is built to take into account natural features (forest coverage, wildlife potential, relief, presence of water, etc.), access (distance from main road infrastructure), density of attractions and other features relevant for the region they investigate. Although the weights associated with the various features are arbitrary, the approach provides a typical attempt to combine ecological landscape knowledge with assumed behavioural preferences of a specific market segment.

A number of examples of applications related to recreation and tourism planning (reflecting a variety of locations, market segments, planning criteria and contexts) can be found in Table 13.1. These cases all entail prior ecological-landscape knowledge and combine it either with surveys of recreationists' preferences or with expert knowledge of resources managers. These applications constitute clear extensions of the ecological habitat paradigm as all the models entail determining the most suitable locations for tourists and developing mappings of suitable 'tourist or visitor habitats'. The similarities between tourists and wildlife becomes evident when authors use the ter-

Table 13.1. Examples of applications of GIS to recreation and tourism planning.

Reference	Location	Niche market	Criteria to determine habitat suitability
Lovett et al., 1997	UK – regional	Forest recreationists	Travel time, travel cost, woodland quality – empirical
Williams et al., 1996	Canada – BC	All recreation – general	Natural, cultural, built environment characteristics, aesthetics, land tenure – expert-based knowledge
Reed-Andersen et al., 2000	USA – Wisconsin lakes	Boaters and fishing recreationists	Access to fish, water quality, aesthetic values, public amenities, density and congestion – empirical survey
Gribb, 1991	USA – Wyoming	Reservoir recreation	Suitability for camping, boating, fishing, amenities – empirical survey
Manigawa et al., 1999	Indonesia – Lombok	Tourism – general	Tourism resources, facilities, infrastructure – planning experts
Bishop and Hulse, 1994	USA – Oregon	Locals and tourist users	Aesthetic aspects – scenic beauty or visual appeal – mix of experts and public survey

minology of tourists' 'niche' markets and recreational resources inventory.

As for models trying to predict wildlife occurrences in space, the validity of tourism and recreation applications usually depends on the reliability of the behavioural knowledge, the ability to verify it empirically and the degree of precision and relevance of the remote sensing process providing landscape attributes. Serious limitations in the availability, reliability and formatting of that data restrict the compatibility with prior landscape knowledge and this explains why most applications in tourism and recreation have been in large part restricted to inventory, monitoring or simulation studies usually only valid at a given point in time. Johnston *et al.* (1993) have noted that even within the limited realm of ecological applications, GIS studies have been mainly concerned with monitoring or predicting wildlife suitability and rarely extended to the possible dynamic impacts of changing animal or plant density on ecosystems and landscape. Applications in the area of human (recreation or tourism related) impact assessment hold even greater complexity and potential difficulties, as they require mixing various types of knowledge across time and space perspectives. By definition, impact assessment and observation hinge on time-dependent data and must provide reliable ways of establishing correlations between cause and effects.

In a similar way, tourism and recreation applications have mainly focused on the description of 'habitat suitability for tourists' at a point in time and have not yet been able to provide a basis for the evaluation of tourist or recreation impacts, whether based on simple presence in the landscape, visitor movements, action-externalities, industry development or infrastructure. The latter involves great theoretical and empirical challenges. Theoretical questions about the stability and meaningfulness of causal relationships (between human development, ecological and abiotic processes) emerge when contrasting spatial data at different points in time. Demands on data and empirical proxies for both human and ecological processes are also problematic. As noted by

Van Horne (2002: 697), the emergence of new tools in ecology or in other related fields often leads to increased efforts towards large-scale data collection but the main issue remains the compatibility of space and time frames when data sources differ considerably in their methods and their purpose. Illustrations of an attempt to connect tourism and ecological knowledge, and infer space and time relationships, are provided in the case study that follows.

Major Case Study: GIS Application to Wildlife Tourism

Research questions

The Top End of the Northern Territory in Australia is a relatively remote region featuring unique natural and cultural tourism attractions in a semi-tropical climate. It has been hypothesized – but never really established – that a number of its wildlife inhabitants hold an iconic status and play a central role in attracting both domestic and international tourists (Tremblay, 2003). Concerns are growing over the impacts of increasing, seasonally concentrated tourist visits on relatively unspoiled locations, including the habitats of its core wildlife assets. As property rights over land uses in the Top End are negotiated and access infrastructure is planned, a number of questions arise: What wildlife species really play a role in attracting tourists? Which areas hold the greatest potential for tourists seeking such wildlife experiences? How many sites and how much investment in potentially damaging infrastructure are appropriate? Is it possible that tourism and other forms of local development are having an impact on the habitats that hold the iconic species playing a role in such tourism development? While the project discussed below attempts to address some of these questions using a general GIS methodology, its impact on wildlife management and policy range have broad relevance in the region.

The project methodology falls in part in the tradition of those surveyed earlier as it attempts to combine knowledge of tourist behaviour with landscape features as well as ecological knowledge, allowing spatial connections between wildlife and that landscape. In fact, it makes explicit that the habitats sought by wildlife tourists are the regions inhabited by the preferred species. It is innovative in the way it attempts to establish a direct connection between tourist preferences and behaviour as well as in the way it proposes to examine the dynamics of the connection between tourism development indicators and the natural landscape features which affect the quality of tourism experience in the Top End. The whole project assumes that the opportunity to view wildlife constitutes a core attraction for the region and that it is useful to produce a wildlife-viewing tourism desirability index. An implicit hypothesis therefore is that it is possible to identify wildlife species which constitute the most valuable assets for the Top End. It is inferred that investigating whether such iconic wildlife-tourism resources are identifiable (as in the question of which species play a key role in attracting tourists in natural areas) and how well supported or managed they are (if viewing opportunities are sufficient or well managed) is useful for decision makers considering making decisions about land use and about infrastructure developments and contemplating alternative options such as the development of semi-natural wildlife attractions.

General methodology and data sources

The project as a whole uses GIS to integrate tourist demand information and knowledge, ecological–spatial knowledge and tourism supply-side knowledge in space (phase 1) and eventually in time (phase 2). Sources of these types of knowledge are, as usual, disparate and turned out to be quite difficult to reconcile. Differing measurement difficulties appear for each and conceptual or interpretation difficulties emerged too, especially when the time dimension was considered. Some of the difficulties are specific to the nature of this project whilst others are conventional issues found almost everywhere in the GIS literature. The approach for the

wildlife tourism application will be described in general terms first, and lessons derived from specific methodological challenges that need to be considered when using GIS in a tourism context will be highlighted after.

Tourist-demand knowledge acquisition

The first component of the project aims at uncovering the motivation of nature-based visitors to the Top End. Rather than identifying a particular market segment for that region, it was hypothesized that the opportunity to view wildlife constitutes a core attraction for the region and decided to produce a wildlife-viewing tourism desirability index by identifying the species which play the greatest role in local attractiveness to the majority of tourists. The secondary, implicit hypothesis incorporated in the proposed methodology is that the wildlife species identified above would constitute valuable assets for the Top End. This initial, static component of the analysis surveyed tourists in the Top End (through personal interviews) to identify wildlife species that they wanted to see and which they considered to constitute the most important attractors for this destination. The survey was very comprehensive in assessing tourist motivations (pre-trip), knowledge, perceptions of importance and recognition of wildlife. While most tourists do not visit the Top End region only to view wildlife, it is recognized that there is a high level of correlation between the landscapes they are interested in exploring, other cultural interests they may hold and the animal species they want to view (Tremblay, 2002, 2003).

Ecological–spatial knowledge

The market research-based knowledge of tourist preferences described above is then combined with ecological–spatial knowledge which can be integrated into the GIS framework. This component is more conventional in that it blends land coverage data and ecological knowledge (accumulated in the scientific community) about the identified wildlife species to build maps of wildlife-viewing suitability locations.

From that original arises a tourism-led perspective on the valuation of various environments and locations and a set of parameters built specifically for this regional space and its particular environment. It provides a way of utilizing demand-side knowledge of tourist preferences to provide socio-economic preferences over regional resources based on the most relevant species or habitats for the tourism industry. As a basis for planning, it obviously provides a greater legitimacy to recreational and tourism uses and is particularly relevant when the management focus is not on the conservation of a single endangered species, but on dispersed and threatened habitats associated with many species valued through the preferences of tourists.

Supply-side tourism knowledge acquisition

The next component examines medium-term linkages between landscape attributes and tourism (and other) development and plays a role in the dynamic phase of the project. A conceptual connection can be established between several indicators of residential, industrial and tourism developments and changes on the landscape. If such connections can be empirically represented in space and chronologically through time, it becomes possible to assess the extent to which tourism and related residential and industrial growth are impacting adversely on core resources. Despite the simple logic of this design, serious conceptual and empirical difficulties arise with that component and they are examined in more detail below. At this point in the discussion, it is useful to mention that the approach hinges on a leap of faith regarding the stability of motivations to visit the region studied. In particular, the approach assumes that the (static) data collected about tourist preferences (Tremblay, 2002) for wildlife viewing are sufficiently lasting so that the conceptualization of desirable tourism locations itself is stable throughout the period in which land cover has been investigated and useful to predict future needs. In retrospect,

the collection of wildlife species that have been identified and their habitats in the Top End are such that it seems justifiable to assume reasonable stability, but this might not hold true if the method were applied in other locations. The main indicators of tourism development used in the study include infrastructure (road and specific attractions) development, visitor movements (data related to road counts) and changes in land tenure (reflecting new uses) and these are contrasted to habitat–landscape attributes at specific points in time.

Secondary data sources

Such space- and time-based correlations, hopefully, point towards connections between tourism development and landscape evolution, but these remain correlations as the possibility of temporal causal feedbacks and the ensuing possibility of spatially identifying in greater depths tourism impacts on wildlife habitats cannot be deemed definitive without complementary theoretical or empirical work to support those observations. As a fair amount of technical detail must accompany such a study, it is possible to refer to related publications (Pearson et al., 2002; Robinson, 2002; Tremblay, 2002, 2003, 2004) and a more comprehensive overview is set to appear in the detailed CRC Sustainable Tourism report.

It is useful to mention that the digital data used in this study consist largely of digital AUSLIG 1: 250,000 topographic data, retrospective remotely sensed imagery from the last 20 years, combined with Transport and Works and Land Tenure data for various points in time. The AUSLIG topographic data provide digital maps for the local infrastructure, hydrography and relief. The satellite imagery used in this study is commonly referred to as Landsat data. Since the imagery has been collected over 20 years and technology has changed during this time, two types of scanner and different Landsat satellites have been used to capture the imagery. What are known as Landsat Thematic Mapper (TM) data have been captured for 1990, 1995 and 2000 and Landsat Multispectral Scanner (MSS) imagery is used for 1980 and 1985. A large number of manipulations and adjustments are required to allow for temporal comparability. The imagery is made up of several spectral bands that support the identification of key landscape characteristics and that are useful for mapping land cover and land use. Two images were needed for each year to cover the whole study site. One covers the Darwin–Outer Darwin region, the other extends to the western boundary of Kakadu National Park. Current digital land tenure data were also obtained from the Department of Infrastructure, Planning and Environment. Past tenure data were obtained in the form of paper maps, and these maps were used to add information on the status of change to the current digital data as an attribute in the database table (Robinson, 2002; Pearson et al., 2002).

Other ancillary information collected and entered in the GIS originated from secondary research into the main tourist attractions found along the Darwin-to-Kakadu corridor. This included collecting the grid reference for these tourist locations so that a spatial point data set of locations could be created within the GIS, and other information such as the dates of establishment of these attractions and visitor numbers were entered into the database. Other data sets such as vehicle counts were collected for specific points along the Arnhem highway to give a feel for how traffic flows along the highway as well as how visitor numbers to attractions have changed over time; these data sets were used as indicators of total residential, industrial and tourist traffics. However, there is a serious dearth of information about the relative importance of tourists, other recreationists and other users of the corridor. Rainfall data were obtained in tabular format from the Bureau of Meteorology.

Conceptual and measurement difficulties involved with the integration of spatial knowledge

This chapter does not aim at reporting the comprehensive set of results associated with the project (including many maps), nor even the main findings, but focuses on difficulties associated with knowledge integration. Complications of relevance in this project, and which are likely to appear in any efforts linking landscape changes and tourism impacts, include empirical (measurement-related) difficulties and conceptual difficulties usually linked with the connections between the types of knowledge, the proxies used to measure them and assumptions required. As these are often interrelated, the discussion will focus on methodological challenges and some findings presented for the sake of illustrating the difficulties. Descriptive results and preliminary tables can be found in Pearson et al. (2002) and Tremblay (2002, 2003, 2004).

Tourist preferences towards wildlife-viewing opportunities

In the first phase, the identification of tourists' expectations and motivations to see wildlife species led to interesting challenges in itself (Tremblay, 2002). Tourists do not conceptualize animals, their habitats and their activities along conventional or formal species categories compatible with ecological concepts. This caused difficulties because, whilst a few wildlife icons could easily be reduced to 'species' category, others had to be represented as groups of animals meaningful to casual observers, but not necessarily for the determination of ecological habitat. This had an impact on the degree of precision with which ecological knowledge could be superimposed to define with precision suitable habitats and locations. Taking into account knowledge limitations of tourists and trying to combine adequately their perceptions with ecological knowledge, the following icon species were identified and eventually used for modelling: saltwater crocodiles, buffalo, barramundi, waterbirds and kangaroos/ wallabies (Tremblay, 2002). While it is reasonable to infer a specific species for the first three categories, the latter two posed greater interpretation difficulties.

Another difficulty, which emerged only once suitability images were produced, is that the species (or groups) identified as iconic attractors showed great spatial overlap, largely with respect to their ideal habitats. This could be observed when indexes of wildlife attractiveness were derived combining the five-species group retained in the study. This difficulty might be specific to the Top End because similar images of the natural environment formulated by marketing agencies in the Top End repeatedly feature the wetlands landscapes and accompanying wildlife. This reduces the ability of the model to identify narrow hot spots and discriminate between locations of different recreational, conservation and tourism value, and generally points at the value of wetlands, where most of such species congregate.

Ecological–spatial knowledge about identified species

Ecological knowledge was assembled to reflect the habitat characteristics of each of those species or groups. These were then translated into meaningful structural characteristics of the landscape that have a high probability of: (i) hosting the animals listed; and (ii) being detected from remotely sensed data or other spatial data sources and therefore being reproducible within a GIS. For the two looser categories incorporating a number of species (waterbirds and kangaroos/wallabies), the criteria for habitat were slightly more subjective and required expert knowledge of wildlife movements as well as tourist preferences. In the case of waterbirds, it was assumed (from answers to open-ended questions and secondary sources) that tourists were expressing the desire to see locations where large numbers of birds gather near wetlands, referring both to bird density and species diversity. This led to an excessively broad range of habitats being included to reflect the inherent variety of wildlife experiences that can be found in the Top End's wetlands. With respect to viewing of kangaroo/wallabies, the demand is largely driven by international tourists and it seems reasonable that they indicate their desire to view any type of marsupial in a wild environment. Given the mobility and

widespread presence of the most common wallabies found in the Top End, this has proven problematic as these animals can be found almost everywhere, although they are not necessarily easily observed by tourists. In the case of the wallabies specifically, very local conditions (such as the presence of lawn close to a caravan park) determine critical viewability and these features do not occur on a scale allowing incorporation in a GIS. In the case of buffalo, conventional data were used (as if the animals could be seen in the wild as used to be the case), but it is clear that stable viewing opportunities are nowadays largely dependent on chance and human control over land use. Habitat suitability maps have been produced through the combination of habitat–ecological characteristics listed in Table 13.2.

Other difficulties emerge when attempting to analyse a number of species simultaneously as the ideal spatial and time scales to describe them and predict their occurrences are different. Related issues associated with ecological predictions based on GIS-type models apply generally and fundamental limitations have been observed and identified by Huston (2002: 7).

• Mismatches between the spatial and temporal dimensions at which hypothesized processes operate.
• Misunderstanding of ecological processes.
• Use of inappropriate statistics to quantify ecological patterns and processes.

Historical tourism supply and tourists' movements knowledge

In the latter phase of the data-gathering exercise, many indicators were derived to reflect the increasing importance of tourism in the region (Pearson et al., 2002; Robinson, 2002). The emphasis is placed mainly on analysing visitor numbers within the Darwin-to-Jabiru corridor over the 20-year period between 1980 and 2000, as well as examining infrastructure changes that have accompanied visitor movements within the corridor during that same time

Table 13.2. Icon species for the Top End and their habitat characteristics and map attributes.

Species	Habitat characteristics	Spatial data
Crocodiles	Coastal rivers, swamps and creeks; coastal wetlands and floodplains within 100 km of sea; downstream 10 km above tidal influence, 200 km upstream in major rivers and mangrove-lined tidal rivers	AUSLIG topo 250K
Buffalo	Less than 100 km inland; large coastal floodplains	AUSLIG topo 250K
Barramundi	Coastal swamps; upstream freshwater	AUSLIG topo 250K
Waterbirds	Sub-coastal floodplains; permanent wetlands; estuarine mangroves; retreat coastwards with dry season; swamps and marshes; saline flats, floodplains, tidal sections of rivers	AUSLIG topo 250K
Wallabies	Tropical lowlands; coastal and sub-coastal plains; between savanna woodlands and grassy plains of rivers, streams and billabongs; late dry around waterholes; open flat habitat/low relief; open grassy forest along rivers and streams; extend 100s km inland	Landsat classified image

period. Within that body of fragmented empirical evidence, the following sources proved the most useful and relatively dependable indicators of tourism growth and yet highly questionable in their measurement:

1. Data on the presence of attractions and visitor numbers at main tourist attractions situated in the Arnhem highway corridor (linking Darwin to Kakadu) at different points in time have been included; data sometimes indicate building, sometimes start of operation – activities included in each attraction changed over time and simple counts do not really reflect magnitude of potential impacts.
2. Records of vehicle counts on the Arnhem highway at a few strategic locations were also included; these include only point data, estimates rarely identify types of users and the traffic counts provide a poor indication of movements outside the highway corridor itself.
3. Changes in land tenure status in the central region (Mary River area) have also been examined for the sake of representing spatial and temporal changes connected with tourism development in the region – while these might reflect new purposes and uses, they are sometimes driven by political processes which have little to do with tourism development.

Robinson (2002) discusses in detail the complexities and data limitations associated with those and other indicators which were considered to reflect tourism development in this region. Lack of consistent records (for infrastructure development, attractions or tourists movements) and poor differentiation between users were particularly problematic. As land cover data have been acquired and processed for the equivalent 20-year period, the full analysis involves overlaying the tourism data with the discrete time-slices of landscape and examining the evolving connections between the two. To make better use of the limited available data, greater attention was eventually given to smaller tourism areas for which land tenure information is available at given points in time, providing a closer match to remotely sensed land cover data. Focus was also directed towards tourism buffer zones where detailed data for traffic flows and attractions were concentrated.

As was noted in the previous section, it is common to encounter mismatches between the spatial and temporal dimensions at which hypothesized ecological processes operate. This is even truer when ecological, landscape and human-made dynamics are combined. The spatial scales (and their visual representations) relevant for ecological research and for tourism activity differ because tourists in general operate along a few limited and narrow corridors (mainly highways and access roads linking tourists spots), which provides them with a linear relationship to the land and to the landscape (unless they undertake a scenic flight!). Ecological processes and diffusion, on the other hand are best understood in two or three dimensions, depending on the species or ecosystems studied. Differences between these knowledge platforms are compounded by the fact that data are collected by different agencies at different times, by different researchers, for different purposes and use different units of analysis and samples. Establishing spatial and dynamic connections through GIS methods requires a good understanding of how such measurement details can affect radically the ability to convince a wide and differentiated array of stakeholders about causal relationships.

This last obstacle becomes markedly conspicuous when one attempts to integrate as time series the dynamic relationship between complex phenomena, such as tourism development and wildlife icon habitat changes. In the project design, discrete slices of 5 years (1980–1985–1990–1995–2000) seemed meaningful to analyse changes in tourism infrastructure and flows in the region. Yet these cutting points turned out to hold limited significance for the sake of understanding ecological processes in the region examined. The sheer size of the area could be blamed, but it is the dynamic nature of the Top End wetlands which caused the major interpretation difficulties. Challenges arose when analysing results about land cover because of the latter's high sensitivity to natural seasonal fluctuations, e.g. yearly variations in rainfall, as well as the impact of fire regimes on that environment. Other more complex chemical and ecological processes less well documented can also influence the land cover over the longer term such as changes in coastal water salinity, invasion by introduced weeds and animal species, etc. It is fair to argue that for the excessively large region analysed, fundamental and powerful natural variations were likely to explain a greater proportion of changes in land cover measured by remote sensing (than human-related

movements, externalities and developments).

The ability to assess human impacts can be marginally improved by reducing the study area in which the sources of various transformations are analysed, and by trying to make tentative corrections based on weather data. It has therefore been found that when ascertaining the main causes for land cover changes in Top End wetlands, natural vagaries dwarf human effects. This is especially true when researchers can observe only discrete snapshots of the landscape and its environment. Land use changes associated with tourism have been examined in other studies (for instance, Allen et al., 1999) and they have led to more reliable predictions when clear trends could be established. In the Top End project, more detailed historical data were available when concentrating on the Mary River area, where a more reasonable analytical scale could be used. Even then, establishing an empirical relationship between tourism and other human developments, land tenure dynamics and changes in land cover is anything but straightforward.

Difficulties in connecting knowledge in time and space

As is apparent from the previous sections, a number of complex difficulties need to be addressed for the sake of progressing the integration of wildlife and tourism knowledge. To prepare for these challenges and provide an idea of their relative magnitude, it is suggested that researchers attempt to systematically anticipate them by categorizing the expected causal relationships which the GIS is supposed to be able to handle and the needed hypotheses supporting the analysis. This can be done by investigating the reliability and stability of the linkages specific to a project. For instance, in the case of the present study, the following needed investigation:

1. Connections between tourists' stated preferences and attractiveness of locations for wildlife viewing.

2. Connections between land cover (or landscape) attributes and presumed ecological habitat.

3. Connections between habitat identified and presence of wildlife species.

4. Connections between presence of wildlife species and observability of those animals by tourists.

5. Dynamic connections between presence of tourists or infrastructure in the region and impacts on habitat or land cover, as well as wildlife species of interest.

The first level of conceptual difficulties is discussed in Tremblay (2002, 2003). Like most empirical work dealing with motivations, it is rarely straightforward to obtain survey-based information about preferences. This usually encompasses conceptual difficulties linked with the great variance in tourists' actual knowledge and frames of reference. The choice of icons was supported by multiple tests, but it is clear that few reliable data of that nature can usually be found, even in major recreational and tourism areas, and this is why expert knowledge is often called on. It seems reasonable to presume that the identification of wildlife icons could be much more problematic in other locations than it was in the Top End. Furthermore, in other places, different market segments would be better served by viewing different wildlife species mixes. In that case, marketing ought to be considered an endogenous variable, which could be used to impact on those mixes.

With respect to the second and third types of connections listed above, they constitute primary concerns for all ecological modelling focused on predicting animal presence in various habitats (a summary of these widespread concerns can be found in Van Horne (2002: 70–72)). The degree of confidence in the reliability of the models depends on the scale of analysis (spatially and in terms of landscape variability) as well as the dependability of the ecological knowledge on which it rests.

The fourth question, of observability of the animals, is central to tourism and recre-ation management and holds implications associated with efforts to match the demand for wildlife-viewing opportunities with spatial and temporal factors that affect animal presence in various landscapes and their behaviour in those locations. Again, observability of different species takes place on different spatial scales, is largely affected by the approach of the 'observer' and can be difficult to plan. The management of vulnerable habitats potentially holding conservation and recreational values must consider the possibility of trading-off such values by investing in 'managed natural environments' which allow tourists to optimize the chances of viewing wildlife in acceptably wild-looking settings.

The last category holds the greatest opportunities as well as major challenges. Given recent interest in the impacts of tourists on wildlife, one would expect that the development of large-scale spatial management tools would constitute a priority. But conceptual difficulties with trying to establish the dynamic connections – even with the help of GIS – between tourism (and other human) development and habitat transformations remain overwhelming in terms of both depth and breadth. It must be repeated that the project only attempted to establish a correlation in time and space between ecological and tourist-behavioural attributes, not causation. Many intervening variables operate concurrently within the analysed space, as was observed in the previous section. It is difficult to assess whether changes in the landscape have played a role in removing natural constraints and have affected tourist preferences or whether, instead, the tourists themselves have been a source of impacts on the landscape. Spatial interconnections are numerous and their joint dynamic analysis is made especially difficult by the fact that other phenomena, some natural (e.g. natural disasters, climatic variability) some induced by humans (e.g. fire regimes, policy changes, politics), also operate on a scale and in manners which GIS techniques cannot necessarily differentiate.

Conclusion: Modelling Tourists and Wildlife

While the challenges posed by attempting to integrate geographical, ecological and tourism behavioural knowledge remain great, the establishment of information systems capable of pinning down spatial and dynamic connections between phenomena summarized by distinct sources and types of information constitutes a logical and promising analytical platform. The tradition of predicting wildlife occurrence by identifying suitable habitats can be, at least superficially, extended to the analysis of tourists' movements. While deliberately simplifying tourists' and recreationists' motivations to travel, it is suggested that modelling the latter as migrating bodies in search of suitable habitats has provided a natural path towards greater understanding of their likely behaviour and impacts for the sake of supporting planning.

Due to resemblances in the concerns with time–space connections, unavoidable similarities can already be found in the terminology of ecology and tourism planning fields. As for niches and habitats, ecological corridors can be contrasted to tourist corridors, whilst the identification of ecological hot spots and tourism hot spots point at interconnections through landscapes shared by tourists and wildlife species. The methodology proposed in the project described above effectively broadens the parallels by identifying tourist-based keystone species capable of playing a critical role in establishing future economic values of some species (to safeguard their habitats), in the same way that ecological keystone species play a critical role in ecosystem processes.

GIS techniques hold promises in testing the connections between types of knowledge that everyone recognizes as relevant for land planning and management and yet which up to now have remained excessively fragmented. Yet, the measurement and conceptual difficulties encountered in bringing together the various knowledge platforms remain overwhelming for widespread use. Increasingly, sophisticated objectives and applications are likely to require mixing with available secondary data (with variable formatting, reliability and continuity) with case-specific discrete information suffering from other types of biases and limitations. Prior knowledge of research methods appropriate for tourism research and understanding of data manipulation techniques associated specifically with fields such as ecological impact assessment, computer technology, remote sensing, landscape measurement, socio-economic, infrastructure and business development statistics will constitute necessary assets required to tackle such complexity.

Acknowledgements

The author acknowledges the funding from the Sustainable Tourism CRC, as well as the GIS expertise and main contribution of Dr Diane Pearson in the project, and the contributions of T. Robinson, M. Shires, J. Gorman and Y. Zhang to various components.

References

Akcakaya, H.R. (1994) GIS enhances endangered species conservation efforts. *GIS World*, November 1994.
Allen, J.S., Lu, K.S. and Potts, T.D. (1999) A GIS-based analysis and prediction of parcel land-use change in coastal tourism destination area. Paper presented at the World Congress on Coastal and Marine Tourism, Vancouver, Canada.
Aspinall, R. (2002) A land-cover change infrastructure for measurement, modeling and analysis of land-cover change dynamics. *Photogrammetric Engineering and Remote Sensing* 68(10), 1101–1105.
Aspinall, R.J. (1992) Spatial analysis of wildlife distribution and habitat in a GIS. In: *Proceedings of Spatial Data Handling Conference*, Charleston, South Carolina, pp. 444–453.
Aspinall, R.J., Burton, G. and Landenburger, L. (1998) Mapping and modeling wildlife species distribution for biodiversity management. In: *Proceedings of the ESRI Users Conference 1998*, San Diego, California, CD-ROM.

Bahaire, T. and Elliott-White, M. (1999) The application of Geographical Information Systems (GIS) in sustainable tourism planning: a review. *Journal of Sustainable Tourism* 7(2), 159–174.

Berry, J.K. (1991) GIS in island resource planning: a case study in map analysis. In: Maguire, D.E.A. (ed.) *Geographical Information Systems*: Volume 2 *Applications*. Longman, Harlow, UK, pp. 285–295.

Bertazzon, S., Crouch, G., Draper, D. and Waters, N. (1997) GIS applications in tourism marketing: current uses, an experimental application and future prospects. *Journal of Travel & Tourism Marketing* 6(3/4), 35–59.

Bishop, I.D. and Gimblett, H.R. (2000) Management of recreational areas: GIS, autonomous agents, and virtual reality. *Environment & Planning B: Planning & Design* 27(3), 423–435.

Boyd, S.W. and Butler, R.W. (1996) Seeing the forest through the trees – using geographical information systems to identify potential ecotourism sites in Northern Ontario. In: Harrison, L.C. and Husbands, W. (eds) *Practising Responsible Tourism: International Case Studies in Tourism, Planning, Policy and Development*. John Wiley & Sons, New York, pp. 380–403.

Bridgewater, P.B. (1993) Landscape ecology, geographic information systems and nature conservation. In: Haines-Young, R., Green, D.R. and Cousins, S.H. (eds) *Landscape Ecology and GIS*. Taylor & Francis, London, pp. 23–36.

Brown, D.G., Goovaerts, P., Burnicki, A. and Li, M.Y. (2002) Stochastic simulation of land-cover change using geostatistics and generalized additive models. *Photogrammetic Engineering and Remote Sensing* 68(10), 1051–1061.

Campbell, J.B. (1996) *Introduction to Remote Sensing*, 2nd edn. Taylor & Francis, London.

Carver, S.J. (1995) Mapping the wilderness continuum. Paper presented at the *GIS Research Conference UK*, University of Newcastle, UK.

Chang, K. (2004) *Introduction to Geographic Information Systems*, 2nd edn. McGraw Hill – Higher Education, Dubuque, Iowa.

Comber, A.J., Birnie, R.V. and Hodgson, M. (2003) A retrospective analysis of land cover change using a polygon shape index. *Global Ecology and Biogeography* 12(3), 207–215.

Congalton, R.G. and Green, K. (1995) The ABCs of GIS: an introduction to geographic information systems. In: Lyon, J.G. and McCarthy, J. (eds) *Wetland and Environmental Applications of GIS*. Lewis Publishers, Boca Raton, Florida, pp. 9–24.

Delany, J. (1999) *Geographic Information Systems: an Introduction*. Oxford University Press, Oxford, UK.

Dietvorst, A.G.J. (1995) Tourist behaviour and the importance of time–space analysis. In: Ashworth, G.J. and Dietvorst, A.G.J. (eds) *Tourism and Spatial Transformations*. CAB International, Wallingford, UK, pp. 163–181.

Elliott-White, M.P. and Finn, M. (1998) Growing in sophistication: the application of geographical information systems in post-modern tourism marketing. *Journal of Travel & Tourism Marketing* 7(1), 65–84.

Goodchild, M.F. (1994) Integrating GIS and remote sensing for vegetation analysis and modeling: methodological issues. *Journal of Vegetation Science* 5, 615–626.

Griffiths, G.H., Smith, T.M., Veitch, N. and Aspinall, R. (1993) The ecological interpretation of satellite imagery with special reference to bird habitats. In: Haines-Young, R., Green, D.R. and Cousins, S.H. (eds) *Landscape Ecology and GIS*. Taylor & Francis, London, pp. 223–236.

Griffiths, G.H., Lee, J. and Eversham, B.C. (2000) Landscape pattern and species richness; regional scale analysis from remote sensing. *International Journal of Remote Sensing* 21(13 and 14), 2685–2704.

Grimshaw, D.J. (2000) *Bringing Geographical Information Systems into Business*, 2nd edn. John Wiley & Sons, Chichester, UK.

Harris, L.K., Gimblett, R.H. and Shaw, W.W. (1995) Multiple use management: using a GIS model to understand conflicts between recreationists and sensitive wildlife. *Society and Natural Resources* 8(6), 559–572.

Huston, M.A. (2002) Introductory essay: critical issues for improving predictions. In: Scott, J.M., Heglund, P.J. and Morrison, M.L. (eds) *Predicting Species Occurences – Issues and Accuracy and Scale*. Island Press, Washington, DC.

Johnston, C.A., Pastor, J. and Naiman, R.J. (1993) Effects of beaver and moose on boreal forest landscapes. In: Haines-Young, R., Green, D.R. and Cousins, S.H. (eds) *Landscape Ecology and GIS*. Taylor & Francis, London, pp. 237–254.

Kilical, H.F. and Kilical, A.A. (1997) GIS as a tool for tourism information management systems. Available at: http:/www.esri.com/base/common/userconf/proc97/T0450/PAP426/P425.html

Longley, P.A., Goodchild, M.F., Maguire, D.J. and Rhind, D.W. (2001) *Geographic Information Systems and Science*. John Wiley & Sons, Chichester, UK.

Lopez, W.S. (1998) Application of the HEP methodology and use of GIS to identify priority sites for the management of white-tailed deer. In: Savitsky, B.G. and Lacher, T.E.J. (eds) *GIS Methodologies for Developing Conservation Strategies – Tropical Forest Recovery and Wildlife Management in Costa Rica.* Columbia University Press, New York, pp. 127–137.

Lovett, A.A., Brainard, J.S. and Bateman, I.J. (1997) Improving benefit transfer demand functions: a GIS approach. *Journal of Environmental Management* 51(4), 373–389.

Mather, P. (1997) *Computer Processing of Remotely Sensed Images*, 2nd edn. Macmillan, Chichester, UK.

McAdam, D. (1999) The value and scope of geographical information systems in tourism management. *Journal of Sustainable Tourism* 7(1), 77–92.

Pearson, D.M., Robinson, T. and Zhang, Y. (2002) Interim report on the production of maps – for the project: the sustainable management of wildlife tourism in the Top End: matching supply and demand for wildlife tourism icons by mapping the changing spatial distribution of tourists and habitats. The CRC for Sustainable Tourism, Darwin, Australia.

Pereira, J.M.C. and Itami, R.M. (1991) GIS-based habitat modeling using logistic multiple regression: a study of the Mt. Graham red squirrel. *Photogrammetric Engineering and Remote Sensing* 57(11), 1475–1486.

Perez-Trejo, F. (1993) Landscape response units: process based self organising systems. In: Haines-Young, R., Green, D.R. and Cousins, S.H. (eds) *Landscape Ecology and GIS.* Taylor & Francis, London, pp. 87–98.

Petit, C.C. and Lambin, E.F. (2001) Integration of multi-source remote sensing data for land cover change detection. *International Journal of Geographic Information Science* 15(8), 785–803.

Porter, R. and Tarrant, M.A. (2001) A case study of environmental justice and federal tourism sites in southern Appalachia: a GIS application. *Journal of Travel Research* 40(1), 27–41.

Reed-Andersen, T., Bennett, E.M., Jorgensen, B.S., Lauster, G., Lewis, D.B., Nowacek, D., Riera, J.L., Sanderson, B.L. and Stedman, R. (2000) Distribution of recreational boating across lakes; do landscape variables affect recreational use? *Freshwater Biology* 43(3), 439.

Rindfuss, R.R. (2002) Continuous and discrete: where they have met in Nang Rong, Thailand. In: Walsh, S.J. and Crews-Meyer, K.A. (eds) *Linking People, Place and Policy – a GIScience Approach.* Kluwer Academic Publishers, Boston, Massachusetts, pp. 7–37.

Robinson, T. (2002) An interim report on tourism infrastructure, volume and flow along the Darwin to Jabiru corridor 1980–2000. NT University, for The CRC for Sustainable Tourism, Darwin, Australia.

Stoms, D.M. and Estes, J.E. (1993) A remote sensing research agenda for mapping and monitoring biodiversity. *International Journal of Remote Sensing* 14(10), 1839–1860.

Sussman, S. and Rashad, T. (1994) Geographic information systems in tourism marketing. In: Cooper, C.P. and Lockwood, A. (eds) *Progress in Tourism, Recreation and Hospitality Management* (Vol. 6). John Wiley & Sons, Chichester, UK, pp. 250–258.

Tremblay, P. (2002) Tourism wildlife icons: attractions or marketing symbols? *Journal of Hospitality and Tourism Management* 9(2), 164–180.

Tremblay, P. (2003) Crocodiles and Top End visitors: a meta-review of tourist perceptions, motivations and attitudes towards a controversial local icon. In: Braitwaite, R. (ed.) *Riding the Wave of Tourism and Hospitality Research – Proceedings of the Council of Australian University, Tourism and Hospitality Education Conference*, CD-ROM, Southern Cross University, Coffs Harbour, Lismore, Australia.

Tremblay, P. (2004) Integrating tourism and environmental knowledge in space and time: challenges for GIS and sustainable management in the Top End of Australia. *Proceedings of CAUTHE 2004: Creating Tourism Knowledge*, University of Queensland, CD-ROM, Brisbane, Australia.

Van der Knaap, W.G.M. (1999) Research report: GIS-orientated analysis of tourist time–space patterns to support sustainable tourism development. *Tourism Geographies* 1(1), 59–69.

Van Horne, B. (2002) Approaches to habitat modelling: the tensions between pattern and process and between specificity and generality. In: Scott, J.M., Heglund, P.J. and Morrison, M.L. (eds) *Predicting Species Occurrences – Issues and Accuracy and Scale.* Island Press, Washington, DC, pp. 63–72.

Walsh, S.J. and Crews-Meyer, K.A. (eds) (2002) *Linking People, Place and Policy – a GIScience Approach.* Kluwer Academic Publishers, Boston, Massachusetts.

Williams, P.W., Paul, J. and Hainsworth, D. (1996) Keeping track of what really counts: tourism resource inventory systems in British Columbia, Canada. In: Harrison, L.C. and Husbands, W. (eds) *Practising Responsible Tourism: International Case Studies in Tourism, Planning, Policy and Development.* John Wiley & Sons, New York, pp. 404–421.

14 A Qualitative Approach to the Ethical Consumer: the Use of Focus Groups for Cognitive Consumer Research in Tourism

Clare Weeden

Centre for Tourism Policy Studies, University of Brighton, Darley Road, Eastbourne BN20 7UR, UK

Introduction

Focus groups are a qualitative research tool whose characteristic is 'the explicit use of the group interaction to produce data and insights that would be less accessible without the interaction found in a group' (Morgan, 1988: 12). This interactivity makes them different from many other methodological approaches (Smithson, 2000), and they are considered to be 'particularly useful for exploratory research where rather little is known about the phenomenon of interest' (Stewart and Shamdasani, 1990: 15). As a research method, they are highly flexible; not only can they be used to understand key issues at the outset of a research study, but they can also aid the development and design of quantitative survey instruments. Although they are often used as supplementary methods of gathering data they can be highly effective as a stand-alone method of gathering rich and insightful data.

There is some discussion in the literature that focus groups are not useful in all types of research and certainly they have their limitations. However, for the initial exploration of a previously unfamiliar topic they are hard to beat, and this is the central point of the present chapter. Focus groups can be guided or unguided, but their infor-

mal structure 'is intended to encourage subjects to speak freely' (Berg, 2001: 111) about their opinions and beliefs. Indeed, focus groups, through collective discussion, allow participants to explore underlying (possibly unconscious) influences on their actions and behaviours, what Bloor *et al.* (2001: 6) call 'retrospective introspection'. Although these data cannot be generalized across all populations of interest, the interaction can potentially reveal intensely personal views and values. These often powerful data can inform subsequent research and yield insights that may possibly be hidden from researchers using other, more quantitative, research methods.

The purpose of this chapter is to introduce the focus group as a tool for qualitative data collection. The chapter will briefly address their history and general contemporary use, as well as their application within tourism research. It will explain the key aspects of focus groups, exploring the various stages of planning, recruiting, conducting and analysing focus groups. The chapter will conclude with a case study that used focus groups to explore tourists' experiences of tourism, what the term 'ethical tourism' meant to them, and whether their opinions and concerns regarding the impact of tourism influenced their future purchasing behaviour. Emphasis in this section is placed on recounting the experiences associated with conducting focus groups, rather than on the findings and analysis of the research questions.

Philosophical Context and Origin of Focus Groups

Normally, a focus group consists of a small number of people brought together to concentrate on and then discuss a set of pre-determined research questions. The discussion is led or directed by a moderator, who may or may not be the researcher. Typically consisting of six to 12 participants, the focus group discussion may last up to 2 hours, with the interaction being recorded for later analysis. Very often an observer is present to take notes on non-verbal communication between the participants. Although Morgan (1988) describes them as a type of group interview, it is generally agreed that focus groups take the form of group discussions. Barbour and Kitzinger (1999: 4), for example, state that focus groups are 'group discussions exploring a specific set of issues', which Bloor et al. (2001) support by emphasizing that they can give a researcher access to in-group conversations that could not be sustained using the method of a group interview. This opportunity and potential for group interaction, and the resultant synergy, can be dynamic and exciting, allowing participants to almost brainstorm with each other (Berg, 2001). As such, focus groups are often promoted in social science research as they are considered to be ideal 'for exploring people's experiences, opinions, wishes and concerns' (Barbour and Kitzinger, 1999: 5).

Historically, focus groups have existed since the late 1930s when social scientists began exploring alternatives to the traditional individual interview (Krueger and Casey, 2000) that primarily used structured questionnaires with closed-response questions. It was thought that in order to discover people's experiences and to determine their understanding of certain issues an alternative approach, using non-directive interviewing would be better, taking control from the interviewer and placing it with the participant. This move away from the controlling direction of the interviewer, it was believed, would lead to a greater emphasis on participant's views (Morgan, 1988), thus gaining access to more insightful information.

As Berg (2001) highlights, focus groups then came into further predominance through the Second World War, when they were used to explore the nature of morale in the US Armed Forces (Krueger and Casey, 2000). Later, during the 1950s, focus groups became synonymous with marketing research, where they were quickly established as a cost-effective method of staying close to the consumer and gathering opinions about products and services being made available to them. Following their continuing success in marketing research, focus groups have been extensively adopted by the public sector, both in North America and Europe.

Academically, however, their adoption has been somewhat measured, not least because of some academics' preoccupation with numbers and quantitative studies (Krueger and Casey, 2000), and the suspicion that qualitative methods of gathering data may be somehow less valid. However, their use in academia is now becoming acceptable, and they are considered to be highly effective at adding in-depth meaning to all stages of the research process. Their use in the social sciences has become widespread in the last decade but in tourism research there is still a lack of studies using this method of data collection.

The Researcher's Concerns with Focus Groups

Although the use of focus groups has mushroomed during the last two decades, there are several limitations that need to be considered prior to a research study. First, focus groups are not a naturalistic setting for research, and are limited to verbal self-reporting of behaviour. The moderator controls them, and there is a trade-off between the quality of the data being collected and the unnaturalness of a contrived setting (Morgan, 1997). Focus groups, however, do allow for the gathering of concentrated data in a short time.

Second, as Catterall points out (1998: 71), focus groups have been criticized for being cheap and quick to execute, as well as being described as either supplementary to quantitative research or, at the very least, complementary to it. Indeed, focus groups, in their original arena of marketing research, were praised for their 'cheapness and speed', which has resulted in their overuse and often misuse (Catterall, 1998). Of course, this may in part be due to the general distrust of qualitative research by the more traditional academic, rather than the reality of their limitations. Certainly, Morgan and Krueger (1993) disagree with the premise of quickness, and suggest that focus groups require as much planning as other methodologies if they are to be an accurate and robust method of research.

Third, the number of people willing and able to take part in a series of focus groups necessarily limits the generalizability of the data generated, not least because they may be 'quite different from the population of interest' (Stewart and Shamdasani, 1990: 17). However, because of their agreeing to take part in the research, their interest in the topic could be inferred to be greater, which can only benefit the discussion and thus facilitate group interaction, to the ultimate advantage of the analysis.

Fourth, there is the question of expertise in conducting focus groups. The novice moderator may be intimidated by their personal lack of experience in moderating and running focus groups. This is a real dilemma but not the only one. There are also many other skills involved in planning and conducting focus groups, not least of which is analysis of the data. However, whilst it is true that skilled moderators could enhance a project, a novice moderator can be just as effective if they have had previous experience of working with groups and facilitating discussion (Morgan and Krueger, 1993).

Finally, the presence of a dominant individual among the group of respondents during a focus group can present certain challenges to the moderator. For example, intimidation of one or more of the others can occur and therefore a picture is presented that is not an accurate representation of what the individuals in the group really think. It is also important to remember that there might be a 'hidden agenda' – when recruiting people it is difficult to know why they want to participate – and it can be difficult to determine whether they have a particularly strong viewpoint they want to share or they want to participate for another, hidden, reason. Put another way 'for what purpose are participants using the focus groups?' (Smithson, 2000: 106).

However, given these concerns, focus groups have many strong points of recommendation and can act as a key method of gathering rich and insightful data.

Key Planning Points

The following section discusses the primary considerations common to the planning of focus groups. It will describe the preparation required, and include a discussion on the recruitment of participants. Ethical considerations, the recording of discussions and development of a question guide will all be addressed. This section will not discuss conducting the groups, nor the analysis, as this can be more effectively achieved through the case study in the latter half of the chapter.

As with all research, it is imperative that sufficient time be set aside for the planning of focus groups. As Morgan (1988) suggests, the two factors most important in the planning phase of any research are time and cost constraints. However, these are not the only constraints. The first decision to be made is whether focus groups are the most appropriate method of answering the research questions. As mentioned previously, focus groups are highly effective in the preliminary stages of a research study, particularly if the topic is new to the researcher. Indeed, one of the most important advantages to the use of focus groups in social science research is that they are useful in enabling the researcher to get close to the participants or respondents (Stewart and Shamdasani, 1990). This is particularly helpful when trying to understand their opinions and thoughts on a topic that is new to the researcher, not least because the meanings of a particular point can be checked at the time. This probing of responses can be instrumental in uncovering issues not previously known to the researcher.

Once the researcher has determined whether focus groups are relevant and appropriate to the study an important element of planning is to decide how many focus groups need to be undertaken. The advice varies, from two or three groups to a total of up to 40, depending upon the scope of the research questions and whether the groups are part of a stand-alone study or just one element in a research methodology. Generally speaking it is advisable to plan for three or four groups with any one type of participant (Krueger and Casey, 2000) or sub-group (Morgan, 1988), but this number will depend on the complexity of the research objectives. However, at the point where more groups are uncovering no new information, the researcher needs to determine whether carrying on with this type of sub-group will yield fresh insights. It is useful to remember, 'there are few economies of scale to doing many groups' (Morgan, 1988: 43). Clearly, practical considerations will also need to be addressed here and the number of focus groups conducted will be partially dependent upon the amount of funding made available to the researcher as well as the time frame of the study.

Focus groups, when successful, and effectively moderated, aim to provide a 'shared experience', by which it is hoped that the group will offer up more readily their feelings and thoughts regarding the research questions. Therefore, it is imperative that some consideration be given to where the focus group is to take place. If the purpose is to stimulate self-disclosure (Krueger and Casey, 2000) and encourage people to talk freely about their thoughts and experiences (Berg, 2001) then the venue (and atmosphere) will need to be non-threatening in order to create a safe space. The moderator's role in this process is to facilitate discussion by creating a safe atmosphere in which to do this.

Not only will the choice of venue be paramount to the success of the group, but it can also be instrumental in the actual attendance of participants. For example, an invitation to a focus group will not guarantee attendance and so a venue convenient to all participants will be important. Additionally, the venue must be free from interruptions, such as people wandering into the room or telephones ringing in the background, all of which can interrupt the flow of conversation. It is essential to remember that convenient times are vital to encourage participation.

With regard to moderating groups it is significant for the researcher to think about the level of moderator involvement. If one of the research objectives is to explore concepts that are new to the researcher then a low level of moderation is advised (Morgan, 1988) in order to encourage free-flowing conversation and discussion. Low moderation can also encourage the group to self-manage its time together – the less the moderator interrupts, the more the discussion will reflect what the participants think, rather than the moderator's opinion. However, the moderator will need to intervene if discussion goes off the point, or if a period of silence goes on for too long. Getting the balance right at this stage is a skill that will develop with experience.

When planning focus groups it is necessary to consider the use of incentives to encourage participation. Very often these are financial, such as book tokens, or shopping vouchers. Alternatively, offering something that is considered to be of value to the participants, as well as making it clear that expenses will be covered, are both necessary components of the planning process. Commercial organizations may give participants £25 each to attend, whereas a focus group organized by a postgraduate student, for example, may offer a book token to the value of £5 or £10. It is highly unusual for participants to give up 2 or 3 hours of their time for no remuneration!

The recruitment of participants is critical, as 'it is vital to have the right participants in a focus group' (Krueger, 1993: 71). However, there is some consideration in the literature as to who the participants should be and it is clear that 'the selection and recruitment of participants for a focus group is a critical task' (Stewart and Shamdasani, 1990: 51). Although it is suggested that care be taken over the composition of the group, given that the researcher has to rely on self-selecting volunteers, it is very difficult to pre-determine the group in terms of age, gender, life experience and so on. In reality, the moderator has to take 'pot luck' with whoever turns up at the location, and so planning group dynamics in order to ensure optimum interaction may prove to be a wasted exercise.

The groups are united by a common purpose and can be organized into segmented (or homogeneous) groups, for instance, all male or all female participants if it is judged that the issues raised may cause intimidation or embarrassment if groups are mixed. Groups should feel comfortable together in order for the conversation to be free flowing, although a shared sense of purpose may be insufficient to ensure that this happens. If it is important to gather views on a topic from a range of sub-groups it is better to conduct separate groups, in order to reduce the potential for either intimidation or inhibition. For example, if conducting research into tourism and its impact on small communities it would be advisable to keep non-experts separate from the experts. What can very easily happen if experts are put together with non-experts is that non-experts may feel inhibited and a range of viewpoints will not be collected.

However, no matter how much planning has gone into recruitment the moderator must always be prepared for the unexpected and make adjustments accordingly (Bloor et al., 2001). Indeed, conflict or disagreement may occur between participants during the course of the session for many reasons. What is most important to remember is that recruitment of participants must be governed by the objectives of the study (Stewart and Shamdasani, 1990), and it is therefore crucial to think about the composition of the groups in those terms.

It is relatively easy for researchers to develop questions on topics that they want addressed by a focus group. However, it is not easy to ask the questions in a manner that will encourage conversation and also in a language suitable for all participants. Therefore, it is crucial to take time to plan the questions, and a planned questioning route, or guide, is very useful. A questioning route is explained thus by Krueger and Casey (2000: 42): 'a list of sequenced questions in complete, conversational sentences'. This will be especially important for a novice moderator as it can form the structure for the session. However, the moderator will need to be flexible during the course of a discussion and probe behind certain statements. Sticking rigidly to a guide might be appealing but will not necessarily yield useful data. Ultimately, however, the topics to be covered will be determined by the study objectives and it is advisable to remember that over the course of an average focus group, participants could usefully discuss about four or five topic areas within a 90–120 minute period.

In order to ensure a relatively high level of comparability over the course of several focus groups it is advisable to have some structure in the form of a questioning guide. This is especially critical if the moderator is not the researcher or when different moderators convene separate groups. However, it may be that subsequent focus groups will be used to explore issues that were uncovered during earlier groups, in which case comparability is not essential. The researcher needs to spend time thinking through the objectives of the study and how they can be met, given the constraints of their particular project.

A particular issue in planning is to do with the recording of the group discussion. It is always advisable to audio-record a focus group, as the detailed transcript can facilitate a deeper analysis than that based purely on the moderator's notes of the group discussion. However, there is the question of how to record and whether the group should be videotaped or not. This latter can often be done very easily, but the researcher needs to reflect on whether the presence of the video with additional technical staff will prohibit a frank and open discussion. There is always a possibility of this occurring, in which case it may be more appropriate to audio record the group only.

Significant account must be taken of ethical considerations connected to disclosure. As Barbour and Kitzinger (1999: 17) state, 'ethical issues are relevant to all stages of focus group research design, implementation and presentation'. These considerations, such as the potential for invasion of privacy, and concerns to do with confidentiality, are especially important when a group of 'strangers' meets to discuss personal opinions and other sensitive topics. These issues are not restricted to focus groups but are common to qualitative methods in general (Morgan, 1993), not least because participants are revealing themselves, either to each other or to a researcher. The moderator needs to be made aware of these considerations at all times because by thinking about them it 'helps to keep them in perspective' (Morgan, 1998a: 85). Ultimately, ethical considerations can be brought to the group's attention by establishing ground rules at the start of the focus group, as well as possibly intervening or moving discussion forward if a participant upsets or conflicts with another. For an extensive examination of the ethical issues involved when conducting focus groups, see Chapter 10 in Morgan (1998a).

The Case Study: Exploring the Meaning of 'Ethical Tourism'

This section discusses a research project that was designed to provide insight into and explore the meaning of 'ethical tourism' and which comprised the initial stages of a much larger project into the decision making processes of ethical tourists in the UK. Clearly, it is difficult to define precisely the meaning of ethical tourism, and the

research project documented here aimed to move the debate forward on this issue, and sets out the findings of an exploratory focus group that took place in July 2002. As stated above, the objectives of this preliminary study were to provide insight into and explore the meaning of ethical tourism, and to understand the importance of ethical behaviour in tourism, for those tourists who incorporate ethical beliefs into their lifestyle and holiday purchasing choices. This exploratory group was planned to be part of an extended study and was to be the first in a series of focus groups exploring this topic. The following section will now describe the researcher's experience in planning, recruiting and conducting their first focus group, from the viewpoint of a novice moderator.

Context

The global tourism industry has long been seen as unsustainable and insatiable in its development and impact, and this is set to continue, notwithstanding the aftermath of 11 September 2001. The structure of the sector's operations has also attracted criticism; the global tourism industry is fiercely competitive and dominated by (mainly Western and First World) transnational corporations. These organizations lever huge economic power over the suppliers of the tourism product, creating unequal exchange and power relationships (Peet, 1991; Barratt-Brown, 1993) between tour operators, tourist destinations and host communities. As a result, one popular view generated is that all tourism is 'bad', most especially for those developing countries acting as host destinations.

In recognition of the potentially unequal power relations within tourism, some tourists have become concerned, and display unease over this, and consequently attempt to minimize their personal impact upon host communities. These people have been variously termed as responsible, alternative and/or ethical tourists and can be briefly described as people who share concerns over the impact their holidays have on the people and the environment of the country they are visiting. However, although there has been a rise over the past decade in the number of 'socially aware' consumers (Strong, 1996: 6), relatively little is known about the concept of ethical tourism, and whether this has any meaning to these 'concerned' tourists.

Given these constraints, and because of the sensitive and highly subjective nature of personal morality and ethical values, a qualitative research design was seen to be appropriate. The aim of the research was to understand the meaning of ethical tourism from the viewpoint of the tourist and, because only the consumer can determine meaning (Bogdan and Taylor, 1975), this suggested an in-depth approach to data collection. Qualitative research can never be statistically representative but in order to uncover how consumers interpret ethical issues involved in tourism, focus groups were thought to be appropriate. The use of focus groups is a method of gaining insight into consumers' thoughts, beliefs and attitudes (Bristol and Fern, 1996), and the researcher concluded that the valuable perceptual information could be used in the triangulation of subsequent data collection (Threlfall, 1999).

Planning

Focus groups can be used both as self-contained methods of data collection or as a supplement to quantitative data collection (Morgan, 1997). For this study they were used as the latter, and as a method of gaining insight from tourists about the concept of ethical tourism. Ethical tourism is not clearly understood, and with historical confusion over terms such as 'sustainable', 'responsible' and 'alternative' tourism being so well documented, one of the primary objectives of the focus group was to explore its meaning to the UK tourist.

The researcher spent time considering whether to undertake individual interviews with tourists or whether to conduct a short series of focus groups. The limitations and advantages of both methods were researched and it was decided that the inter-

action generated in a group discussion would result in a wider range of opinions being gathered. As the topics could be sensitive to the individual, there might be a problem with encouraging the respondents to discuss their private moral values with strangers in a focus group. In addition, 'an interest in individual behaviour might not be well served by data from group interviews' (Morgan, 1997: 12). However, to counter this limitation, the session was planned to be as inclusive as possible to all the respondents and the moderator was keenly aware of the need to avoid any perceived victimization of group members. The use of an observer also helped counter this possibility by recording non-verbal communication between participants throughout the session.

The issue of where the focus group was to be held was significant in the planning stage, as it would have an impact on the ease of the recruitment of potential participants (Stewart and Shamdasani, 1990). The public building chosen for the venue was set in a central location, close to transport links, in order to encourage attendance.

An important consideration to the researcher was the cost of conducting the research. As the focus groups were designed as part of a larger postgraduate study, financial support was limited to a £100 research grant per year from the sponsoring university. Therefore the reality of encouraging participation through the use of financial incentives was somewhat limited, as this amount would have to cover not only the cost of room hire, but also the cost of mailing participants and providing refreshments during the actual focus groups.

As the researcher was a novice moderator, there were initial misgivings about being able to facilitate the group effectively. However, as Morgan and Krueger (1993) point out, someone whose experience lies is working with groups can be a viable alternative to the professional moderator. As such, the researcher, who had spent several years working as a university lecturer, and had taken care in planning and organizing the focus group, took the role of moderator.

Recruitment of participants

It was important to consider at this stage not only whom to ask to take part in the group discussion, but also how to reach them. As the topic was a specialist area of concern it was important to speak to those people who already had an awareness of some of the key issues involved. It was also important to the researcher to be able to explore with the focus groups whether 'ethical tourism' was merely an academic construct or whether it actually had meaning in the wider world of tourism and holidaymaking. Importantly, the success of a focus group can depend largely on the extent of the conversation and communication thus generated. Therefore if the group consists of people who are interested in the topic this can aid discussion and hence the quality of the data generated (Morgan, 1998a). As such, participants were recruited who were members of Tourism Concern, an organization that campaigns for ethical and fairly traded tourism.

For recruitment, an advert was placed in *In Focus*, Tourism Concern's monthly bulletin, during May 2002, asking for volunteer participants who were concerned about the impact of tourism to take part in an informal focus group. The response to this was poor; with only two people offering to take part, one of whom worked for Tourism Concern. Tourism Concern, at the researcher's request, then wrote to all their subscribers in the Brighton area (n = 41) asking them to volunteer for a focus group, and clearly offered their support to the project. With an individual financial incentive of a £10 book token, and the promise of paid expenses, a total of ten responses were generated, with six positive replies. These six people were subsequently recruited to the first focus group in July 2002. One week prior to the focus group, the researcher reminded the participants of their promised commitment by mailing each one the details of the time and place to meet, plus a detailed street map of the venue's location, as well as a thank you for their help and participation.

Conducting the focus group

The focus groups were planned in accordance with the frameworks suggested by Krueger's Focus Group Kit (Krueger, 1998; Morgan, 1998a,b) and the purpose of the group was fully explained to the participants. The researcher explained that it was important to hear everyone's opinion, that there were no 'right' or 'wrong' answers to the questions raised and that the main objective was for the researcher to learn from the group in order to gain an understanding of the issues, through the views of tourists. The researcher explained what the research was to be used for and assured the group of confidentiality and anonymity.

The researcher also explained that it was important to hear as many perspectives as possible and that participants should be prepared to hear opinions different from their own during the process. The researcher also encouraged the participants to address their opinions to each other and not to the moderator to avoid moderator–participant conversation. Ground rules, such as one person talking at a time, and the right of everyone to be heard, were also established (Stewart and Shamdasani, 1990). Simple refreshments of tea, coffee, juice and biscuits were served prior to the focus group.

The focus group lasted for 90 minutes and was audio taped and fully transcribed. An observer, who sat behind the group, took notes. The observer's role was to check the recording equipment throughout the session, and to take notes about eye contact, the speed of the discussion, the enthusiasm noted on each topic raised and any non-verbal interaction that might be relevant to the analysis. These notes were later passed to the moderator, to add context to the resulting transcripts. There was medium involvement by the moderator, with the purpose of encouraging free-flowing conversation.

In accordance with Morgan's 'funnel strategy' (1993: 41) the session began with a free and unstructured conversation before the moderator brought it into a more focused and structured discussion of some specific questions. The funnel strategy was achieved using an icebreaker, or opening question (Krueger, 1998), where participants were asked to spend a few minutes getting to know their immediate neighbour, by introducing themselves and asking about their favourite holiday memory. They spent a few minutes doing this before introducing each other to the rest of the group, and explaining their neighbour's favourite holiday memory. The researcher believed this to be an important icebreaker function, as it would allow participants to relax and feel confident enough to contribute to the group. This part of the session was recorded but not transcribed.

As an introductory question (Krueger, 1998) the moderator asked the group to think back to the time when they first became aware of the impact of tourism and asked them to describe their thoughts and feelings. Introductory questions such as this typically allow participants to reflect upon their experiences and this question was designed to encourage conversation and interaction among the group, and to give a sense of shared meaning to the group. The researcher believed the experiences being shared here were intensely private and therefore no further probing was carried out. However, the insights gained at this point were used later in the discussion, when the term 'ethical tourism' was being explored.

After all of the group had described their experiences of tourism and its potentially negative impact, the researcher moved on to the transition questions, which helped to move the group towards the main focus of the discussion. In this instance, the participants were asked what was important to them when buying a holiday, and the researcher's intention was to make a link between the introductory question and the key questions (Krueger, 1998). After these points had been covered the moderator then took the group through the key topics, which included a request to explore the term 'ethical tourism' and whether it had any meaning to them.

During the discussion there were some periods of quiet when the researcher needed to stimulate the group conversation. These periods were minimal, however, but there was one moment when a conflict between two participants resulted in the whole group falling quiet. In fact, it was several minutes before one of the participants re-entered the conversation.

After 90 minutes the group conversation started to falter and the moderator sensed the group was becoming tired. Consequently, an ending question was posed in order to bring the session to a close. The suggestion at this stage of the process, made by Krueger (1998: 26), is to ask 'an all-things-considered' question, such as the one asked here: 'Of all the things we have discussed here tonight is there any one thing which you feel is the most important?' This allowed the individual respondents to make clear their personal emotions and feelings, in case they felt their opinion had been lost within the group discussion. After this, a summary of all the topics discussed was given and respondents were asked if that accurately represented the discussion. Subsequent to this, the group was asked if the discussion had missed anything – this was also followed up in an e-mail sent to the group the following day, thanking them for their input and also asking them for any further reflections upon the focus group discussion. This yielded further insights from the entire group.

Once the participants had left, the observer debriefed the moderator, with the main findings of the observation, including some discussion of the main non-verbal points. More detailed notes were sent to the moderator at a later date, and subsequently used to add context to the analysis. The audiotape of the discussion was fully transcribed by the moderator, a process that took a total of 8 hours and yielded 16 pages of data.

Analysis and Key Findings

Analysis of the transcript then followed, using a manual process, and consisted initially of coding the document according to several key themes that emerged. These are as follows:

- Critical incident, a recalling of the moment when the participants realized for the first time that the impact of tourism could be a negative experience for the host destination.
- The inequality associated with mass tourism.
- The participants' motivation for travelling.
- What the word 'ethical' meant, and the group's attempt to define 'ethical tourism'.

The analyst also being the moderator enabled the identification of the participants in the transcript. Not only did this help identify the context of speech but it also corresponded directly to the observer's notes, which supported the context further. Bloor et al. (2001) point out that identifying the participants is crucial as it enables the researcher to track any change of opinion that may take place during the course of the group discussion. When looking back over notes made as part of the analysis it appeared that no-one had changed their ideas as a result of the focus group – they all came with their 'prejudices' and left with them intact. Each person had their own ideas as to how they wanted to express their concern over tourism and its impact, and this preference was firmly in place at the end.

The following section will document the key preliminary findings from this focus group.

Critical incident

What is important to note here is that this insight came from the 'introductory question' and was not revealed as a result of a question that addressed the central focus of the discussion. This is an excellent example of how unexpected insights can be gleaned from a focus group and underlines the critical role of planning in focus group design. In fact, this insight may give the researcher

valuable information with which to guide future research.

The entire group could remember explicitly the moment that they realized for the first time that tourism could be a negative phenomenon. They spoke of their shock, and of the realization being a powerful experience. For example, 'I can remember the impact vividly … it really was a shock' and 'I felt so self-conscious, so different … I felt quite embarrassed about being there … it was quite a powerful experience'. One participant spoke of his self-consciousness regarding his clothes and also having a camera around his neck; he felt he stood out from the surrounding people as different and that this difference was a bad thing – a negative and anxious experience for him.

For many of the group this was a vivid recollection but an unexpected realization, when for the first time they felt a personal responsibility for the impact of tourism. Their coming face to face with the poverty and the different culture had a profound influence on them and transformed their holiday choices from that moment. The inequality of the world was brought to their attention and the group spoke of the shock of poverty, seeing it for the first time or having to confront it in person. The experience was profound and the entire group reported an emotional reaction to the impact of tourism, describing a bleak outlook for mass tourism, and a sense of loss of individual cultures, almost a sense of grief, for something lost. The group strongly identified that they did not want to be associated with mass tourism, as they saw it as being synonymous with destruction of what was good, in other words, local culture.

Inequality

The group strongly believed that the host community had cultural superiority, with different cultural values and superior family values. In addition, they felt that travelling was a 'Western' luxury, which highlighted what they perceived to be a huge economic gap between the tourist and the host. They professed a desire for there to be equality between host and tourist, of wanting to be seen as equals, of changing the balance of power away from the tourist back to the locals. Overwhelmingly, the group felt that local people's views regarding tourism development were very important and they wanted locals to benefit directly from their holidays. They believed strongly that their current holidays should allow the hosts to have choices regarding tourism, as they didn't want to impose themselves on the destinations.

The group consciously chose holidays that helped the local community, whether that was by staying in community housing with families or by using tour operators who worked closely with local communities to develop tourism. They spoke of autonomy being handed back to the local communities, of putting local people first and of restoring the balance of power. They also clearly wanted to reverse the perceived inevitability of mass tourism development seen by themselves in previous resorts.

Motivation for travelling

There was some confusion here in the group. Although the members agreed that a holiday for them meant a cultural learning experience there was disagreement about how different people and different communities/cultures viewed holidays and tourism. They came to no conclusion here except for their own personal reasons for travelling. There was some agreement, however, that tourism was different from holidaymaking and people's activities differed accordingly. Interestingly, independent discussion took place at this point, with group members addressing each other without referring back to the moderator. There was a strong motivation factor for going on holidays for this group – it was definitely an opportunity for learning and this (seemed to) override any negative impacts of tourism they felt their holidays produced.

Ethical tourism

Participants indicated that they were unhappy with the term 'ethical tourism', and this was indicated by a marked reluctance on their behalf to devise a definition. They expressed confusion but also a certain apathy about the term 'ethical tourism', as though it did not matter to them – they had their own interpretations of what was important to them as individual tourists and this was what they were interested in. The term 'ethical tourism' was irrelevant and meaningless. The following quotation from one of the group illustrates this point:

> Ethical tourism is so aspirational, because different destinations have different ways of behaving and if you are a thinking person, you've got to the stage where you have actually got to think about ethics you realize you are never ever going to achieve it. All you can do is just keep working at it, which is why possibly no one's saying 'I am an ethical tourist'. I'm trying to get there but I haven't got there yet because it's just so enormous.

Further focus groups need to be conducted to determine whether there is a trend or pattern to this opinion, and future research would need to address whether this view was widespread for all tourists. For this participant, compromise was the best way forward in achieving the balance between responsibility and having a good time on holiday:

> I would prefer to say I was a responsible tourist because it's less absolute than saying 'I am an ethical tourist' and for me, responsible tourism is easier to understand.

Conclusions

As a method of gathering rich and valuable data, focus groups can be excellent. The focus group reported in this chapter yielded the researcher insight from a small segment of tourists' emotions regarding mass tourism. The data indicated strongly their misgivings about tourism's impact on destinations, and it revealed some issues not previously considered by the researcher, such as the importance of the critical incident in shaping people's opinions and future actions. With regard to the larger research project, supplementary focus groups are planned to explore further the themes raised by this group. In terms of the contribution they have made to the project they have provided the researcher with a deeper understanding of tourists and strongly indicated areas for further research.

As a novice moderator (and researcher) the process of planning, conducting and analysing a series of focus groups was daunting. Many of the researcher's concerns, about both the usefulness of the method and the practical considerations in planning and conducting focus groups, have been fully documented in this chapter. However, the subsequent success in unearthing unexpected insight into tourists' concerns with tourism far outweighed these misgivings. To conclude, the learning experience provided by the use of this research method has been tremendous, and has enabled the researcher to plan further groups with more confidence and ability. For an exploratory investigation of unfamiliar concepts, focus groups are highly recommended.

References

Barbour, R.S. and Kitzinger, J. (1999) *Developing Focus Group Research: Politics, Theory and Practice*. Sage Publications, London.

Barratt-Brown, M. (1993) *Fair Trade*. Zed Books, London.

Berg, B.L. (2001) *Qualitative Research Methods for the Social Sciences*, 4th edn. Allyn and Bacon, Needham Heights, Massachusetts.

Bloor, M., Frankland, J., Thomas, M. and Robson, K. (2001) *Focus Groups in Social Research*. Sage Publications, London.

Bogdan, R. and Taylor, S.J. (1975) *Introduction to Qualitative Research Methods*. Wiley, New York.

Bristol, T. and Fern, E.F. (1996) Exploring the atmosphere created by focus group interviews: comparing consumers' feelings across qualitative techniques. *Journal of the Market Research Society* 38(2), 185–196.

Catterall, M. (1998) Academics, practitioners and qualitative market research. *Qualitative Market Research: an International Journal* 1(2), 69–76.

Krueger, R.A. (1993) Quality control in focus group research. In: Morgan, D.L. (ed.) *Successful Focus Groups: Advancing the State of the Art*. Sage Publications, Thousand Oaks, California.

Krueger, R.A. (1998) *Developing Questions for Focus Groups*, Focus Group Kit Vol. 3. Sage Publications, Thousand Oaks, California.

Krueger, R.A. and Casey, M.A. (2000) *Focus Groups: a Practical Guide for Applied Research*, 3rd edn. Sage Publications, Thousand Oaks, California.

Morgan, D.L. (1988) *Focus Groups as Qualitative Research*. Qualitative Research Methods, Series 16, Sage Publications, Thousand Oaks, California.

Morgan, D.L. (1993) *Successful Focus Groups: Advancing the State of the Art*. Sage Publications, Thousand Oaks, California.

Morgan, D.L. (1997) *Focus Groups as Qualitative Research*. 2nd edn. Sage Publications, Thousand Oaks, California.

Morgan, D.L. (1998a) *The Focus Group Guidebook*, Focus Group Kit Vol. 1. Sage Publications, Thousand Oaks, California.

Morgan, D.L. (1998b) *Planning Focus Groups*. Focus Group Kit Vol. 2, Sage Publications, Thousand Oaks, California.

Morgan, D.L. and Krueger, R.A. (1993) When to use focus groups and why. In: Morgan, D.L. (ed.) *Successful Focus Groups: Advancing the State of the Art*. Sage Publications, Thousand Oaks, California.

Peet, R. (1991) *Global Capitalism – Theories of Social Development*. Routledge, London.

Smithson, J. (2000) Using and analysing focus groups: limitations and possibilities. *International Journal of Social Research Methodology* 3(2), 103–119.

Stewart, D.W. and Shamdasani, P.N. (1990) *Focus Groups, Theory and Practice*. Applied Social Research Methods series, Vol. 20, Sage Publications, Thousand Oaks, California.

Strong, C. (1996) Features contributing to the growth of ethical consumerism – a preliminary investigation. *Marketing Intelligence and Planning* 14(5), 5–13.

Threlfall, K.D. (1999) Using focus groups as a consumer research tool. *Journal of Marketing Practice: Applied Marketing Science* 5(4), 102–105.

15 Content Analysis

C. Michael Hall and Andrea Valentin

Department of Tourism, University of Otago, PO Box 56, Dunedin, New Zealand

Introduction

Content analysis (CA) is arguably one of the fastest growing methods in social research (Neuendorf, 2002). Krippendorf (1980: 21) defined content analysis as 'a research technique for making replicable and valid inferences from data to their context'. Neuendorf (2002: 1) extended this definition further by describing content analysis as 'the systematic, objective, quantitative analysis of message characteristics'. Content analysis is therefore an observational research method that is used to systematically evaluate the actual and symbolic content of all forms of recorded communication (Kaplan, 1943; Berelson, 1952; Holsti, 1969; Krippendorf, 1980; Weber, 1985; Neuendorf, 2002). For example, when studying effects such as newspaper coverage on readers' perceptions or issue salience and public opinion (Downs, 1972; Nickerson, 1995; Hester and Gonzenbach, 1997; Schindlmayr, 2001). Content analysis is often used as a companion research instrument in multi-method studies employing diverse methods to enhance the validity of results by minimizing biases, although it can clearly be used as a research tool in its own right. Nevertheless, as Neuendorf (2002: 52) commented, it is not usually 'appropriate to make conclusions about source or receiver on the basis of an analysis of message content alone'. In recent years, the research technique has also been adapted to become an element in the evalu-

ation of new communication media, such as websites, and a component of data mining methods, as well as being an important element of hermeneutics and semiotic analysis both in consumer studies and in critical social science (Kaplan, 1943; Holbrook, 1977; Kassarjian, 1977; Matacin and Burger, 1987; Kepplinger, 1989; Kolbe and Burnett, 1991; Stern, 1993; Arnold and Fisher, 1994; Scott, 1994).

While the advantages of content analyses are numerous, the main drawback is the potential influence of the researcher. Researcher bias has the potential to constrain decisions on data collection, analysis and interpretation in favour of the research hypothesis (Neuendorf, 2002). Kassarjian (1977) therefore developed a content analysis methodology which allows more objectivity and suggested that in order to lessen reliability issues, at least two independent judges should be introduced to the subject and decode the information obtained. However, arguably, CA is no different from many other social science research methods in that the value of the application of the method depends on the skill and appropriate exercise of judgement on the part of the researcher and appropriate reflection on the research process. This chapter will provide an overview of the application of CA in tourism and will then turn to a case study of its application to issues relating to the impacts of the terrorist attacks in the USA on 11 September 2001.

Content Analysis in Tourism

The subjects of CA in tourism range from advertisement identification with respect to gender and place issues to an analysis of definitions published in academic journals. However, the utility of CA as an analytical tool in tourism studies has arguably been broadly neglected in comparison with other research methods (Athiyaman, 1995; Jamal and Hollinshead, 2001). The reasons for this are unclear, although it may be noted that areas such as public policy analysis, in which CA is a major tool (Waterman and Wood, 1994), are only relatively marginal areas of the field of tourism studies.

Nevertheless, attempts have been made to examine tourism policy issues by using CA. For example, Padgett and Hall (2001) sought to identify the significance of tourism as a political issue in the 1999 New Zealand General Election through an analysis of four major newspapers. Perhaps an indication of the relative significance of tourism in national elections can be noted in that only four tourism stories were identified during the entire election period! However, CA was also used to compare and contrast the tourism policies of the parties contesting the election. Another policy-related study was undertaken by Richter (1980), who completed a 4-month CA of newspaper articles from three daily newspapers in the Philippines. She suggested that tourism might have been used as a propaganda tool in the Philippines to promote the country's beauty and disregard the fact that martial law had been declared. A more recent study of the political use of images, including tourism images, is that of Zhang and Cameron (2003) who examined China's promotional campaigns in the United States. In the applied tourism policy field Bentley et al. (2001a,b) used CA of hospital discharge data to examine recreational injuries to visitors.

CA may also be conducted in order to identify different understandings of conceptual issues. For example, Sirakaya et al., 1999) conducted a CA of ecotourism definitions. Through their analysis they identified components that were generally agreed upon, such as non-consumptive or educational, and compared their findings with the results of a quantitative study in which ecotourism operators were questioned about various issues surrounding the topic. Interestingly, ecotourism components as identified in the content analysis corresponded to their quantitative findings (Sirakaya et al.,1999). A similar approach was taken by Garrod (2003), who attempted to define the term 'ecotourism' from a marine tourism standpoint. In this instance the CA was combined with a Delphi study by experts. Malloy and Fennell (1998) also utilized CA to examine codes of ethics in tourism. Another analysis with an academic information source was the CA of *Annals of Tourism Research* undertaken by Swain et al. (1999) in order to identify the main research areas over a 30-year period. This content analysis was purely descriptive since the aim was to provide a history of the journal's content. Main results included a list of frequent authors and a list of special issues, as well as the top headwords by number and citations ('impacts', 'organizations' and 'development' were the key words), to mention but a few. This type of approach has proven to be quite popular in tourism with respect to identifying such things as the topics of doctoral theses and graduate research (Hall, 1991) as well as dominance of certain nationalities in the editorships of tourism journals.

CA can also be undertaken to examine the context of text written by tourists themselves. Yagi (2001) undertook a CA of 120 samples of online travelogues written by Japanese and American tourists in order to investigate how tourist–tourist encounters are reported. A total of 838 episodes were extracted from the sample travelogues and coded according to the types of encounter (absence, direct presence or indirect presence of others), attitude of the writer (positive, negative or neutral) and also the types of tourist(s) encountered (same or different nationality). Another example of a CA of tourist writing or responses to a questionnaire is that of Chen et al. (2001), who conducted CA on the answers provided in a survey of over 1000 individuals visiting nine industrial heritage sites in southwestern Pennsylvania in order to ascertain what influenced them to visit the site. Based on the CA, eight major reasons, including interest in the site, families and friends, recreation, promotional information, been-here-before, having some knowledge of the sites, road signs and curiosity, were uncovered. The examination of text has also given rise to the development of computer-assisted data analysis programs, such as ATLAS/TI and NUDIST, that can be of assistance in examining not only print media but also the text written by tourists. Although the capacity and applicability of such methods are not discussed in this chapter, it should be noted that the relative value of such methods is still open to debate as the selection of criteria and the interpretive skills of the researcher remain more significant than the use of computers in the method *per se* (Hansen, 1992; Barry, 1998; MacMillan and McLachlan, 1999).

Much CA in tourism focuses on advertising and images (Albers and James, 1988; Peterson, 1998, 2000; Pritchard and Morgan, 2001; Andsager and Drzewiecka, 2002; Ateljevic and Doorne, 2002; Echtner and Prasad, 2003; Henderson, 2003). For example, tourism brochures of all US tourism offices were analysed in order to depict potential differences of gender representation (Sirakaya and Soenmez, 2000). The study found that women were portrayed in more traditional roles and were depicted as subordinate and dependent. Such research builds on a substantial body of literature on the analysis of representations of gender and the body, e.g. Miller (1975), Blackwood (1983) and Rintala and Birrell (1984). CA may also be utilized as a tool in critical social analysis (Jamal and Hollinshead, 2001). For instance, Cloke and Perkins (2002) used CA to examine the commodification of the adventure tourism product in New Zealand. Image analysis may also be used in the examination of the photographs travellers take while on holiday. Such research may indicate the relative relationships between landscape and people (Groves and Timothy, 2001) as well as the significance of various attractions. The sem-

inal work of Albers and James (1983, 1984, 1985, 1988) is particularly important because their use of CA to investigate the relationship between photography, ethnicity and travel laid much groundwork for empirically informed semiotic analysis in tourism. On the whole, the few studies that have used CA as their primary research tool did not review newspapers or other media such as television or radio, one notable exception being Nickerson (1995), who used CA to investigate representations of gambling in newspapers. Indeed, it should be noted that tourism scholars have all but ignored the fact that it is the general mass media, and not academic journals, that primarily influences public opinion. Yet research in this area is surprisingly scarce.

Content analysis and the Web

CA can also be usefully undertaken on the Worldwide Web. The Web is a tool for undertaking CA as well as being a subject for CA in its own right. However, when identifying a research sample for CA on the Web there are a number of different methods that could be used.

Internet addresses have been used for research (Ju-Pak, 1999; Musso et al., 2000) with the main focus on the domain name system (DNS) groupings. For example, in order to identify e-mail inquiries or website location the naming system can be broken down into two parts: generic top level domains (TLDs) such as .com, .org, .edu and .gov; country-specific top level domains can also be identified, such as .us for the USA, .uk for the UK and .nz for New Zealand. However, although this method may be of some use for identifying traffic, there are problems in this approach due to the lack of centralized regulation of the Internet and the DNS and the capacity to obtain an address in one country while living in another.

Search engines tend to be a popular source for statistical samples for CAs undertaken on the Web. According to McMillian's (2000) survey of 16 Web CA studies, 44% used one or more search engines to develop their sampling frame. The main advantages of this method are that it is relatively inexpensive and, unlike sample frames based on domain names, it is not limited to sites with first-level domain names. However, the greatest limitation is that the Worldwide Web is not catalogued very well. For example, Lawrence and Giles (1999) estimated that the 11 major search engines they examined collectively indexed only 42% of the total pages on the Web, and any single search engine indexed no more than 16% of the Web. Also, it has been found that the probability that a site is indexed increases with the number of other sites that link to it and that some search engines base their indexing decisions on the popularity of sites (Nicholson, 1997; Lawrence and Giles, 1999). Consequently, frames based on search engines will lead to samples that are skewed towards the more heavily trafficked parts of the Web. These biases may or may not be consequential depending on the specific research question, and that researchers interested in the population of sites that the average Web surfer will locate are likely to be well served by search engines.

Given the importance of the Web for e-commerce and tourism information and business systems there is surprisingly little analysis of tourism websites and their effectiveness (Tierney, 2000), particularly with reference to critical success factors. However, this area is developing rapidly with respect to tourism websites (Buhalis and Spada, 2000; Jung and Butler, 2000; Jeong and Lambert, 2001; Wan, 2002; Chung and Law, 2003).

The Content Analysis Process

In order to illustrate the potential utility of content analysis as a research tool in tourism, the chapter will now turn to an illustrative example of CA as applied to examining media coverage of the terrorist attacks of 11 September 2001 and the extent to which they may influence perceptions of tourism and travel safety. Previous research undertaken by Hall (2002) has suggested that tourism issues, such as that of terrorism and travel security, pass through an issue-attention cycle similar to that described by Downs (1972).

Originally applied to an understanding of social issues of the 1960s, and environmental issues in particular, the notion of an issue-attention cycle has also been found to be extremely important in explaining the relationship between domestic and foreign policy decisions, the media and the level of public interest in certain issues (Iyengar and Kinder, 1987). According to Downs (1972) the issue-attention cycle is divided into five stages, which may vary in duration depending upon the particular issue involved, but which almost always occur in the following sequence:

- The pre-problem stage.
- Alarmed discovery and euphoric enthusiasm.
- Realizing the cost of significant progress.
- Gradual decline of intense public interest.
- The post-problem stage.

Previous research that attempted to examine the issue-attention cycle has utilized content analysis (Iyengar and Kinder, 1987; Hester and Gonzenbach, 1997; McComas and Shanahan, 1999). However, such a situation had not been previously analysed in the context of tourism even though the media is recognized as being extremely significant in shaping perceptions of destinations as well as individual products (e.g. Jenkins, 1999). The wider study of which the content analysis was a part also conducted surveys of perceptions of tourism and travel safety as well as the selection of tourism as a career choice. However, for the purposes of the present chapter we will focus only on the conduct of the CA and associated results.

The process of CA research is outlined in Fig. 15.1, developed from Ahuvia (2001) and Neuendorf (2002). Significantly for this figure the process is shown to be enveloped in the socio-cultural linguistic-economic context of the researchers undertaking the study. Such a recognition also suggests that rather than CA being seen just as a method for quantifying the *content* of texts, CA should be viewed as a method for counting *interpretations* of content, therefore explicitly recognizing the subjectivity of the researcher (Ahuvia, 2001).

For the purposes of the present research the content relevant to the analysis was identified as being terrorism-related articles before and after 11 September 2001 coupled with tourism-related statements. The conceptualization stage indicates variables to be used in the study. In order to identify the variables, it is necessary to include a brief overview of the print medium which was to be analysed. In New Zealand there is no true national daily paper that covers all regions. The *Otago Daily Times* (ODT) is the local daily newspaper in the Dunedin district and covers both the Dunedin and the larger Otago regions. The ODT is New Zealand's only independently owned metropolitan daily newspaper. The ODT's regional importance is emphasized by its average circulation of 45,000 (in 2002), a market penetration of 76%, and a reach of almost 90% for some demographic groups (Allied Press, 2003). The ODT's main foci are based on interests and aspirations of the region; however, it also covers international and national news as well as strong business and sporting sections.

The content analysis of articles published in the ODT was mainly based on the ODT's online edition. The online edition consists of the full text of articles from all sections of the print edition and includes the local, national and international news pages as well as sport, business and features sections. The ODT's online search engine is a valuable tool to undertaking CA as it permits the researcher to search for key words appearing in the body or title of an article and a specification of date range in which the found titles should fall. After the identification of the relevant article through key words (e.g. terrorism), the 'back issue' option makes it possible to identify presentation, placement and origin of story. For this particular study it has to be mentioned that, even though the largest part of the material from the print edition is put online, not all material is transferred. Advertising features, tabloids and special inserts are not put online, which might cause minor bias to the outcome. However, the features excluded from the online edition were not regarded as over-significant to this research project.

Having examined the medium, namely the online edition of the ODT, the conceptualization stage further requires the identification of variables in order to define the given construct. As the issue-attention cycle has not been previously applied to media reports on terrorism and tourism, which might shape tourism perceptions, it was not possible to draw conclusions from earlier studies. Therefore, the process of variable identification required the adoption of a more practical approach: through conducting a qualitative scrutiny of a subset of the content of the message pool to be analysed. Based on this subset of messages, the following research question and variables were identified. The research question was: What issues did the *Otago Daily Times* address concerning terrorism and tourism before and after the 11 September attacks? Hence the variables for the stories identified were: presentation, placement, origin of story, its geographic focus and its main theme (see Table 15.1).

In order to achieve operationalization the appropriate measurement technique had to be determined. A census and in-depth content analysis was regarded as beyond the aim of the research, although it may have been very beneficial to the research outcome. Due to financial as well as time limitations, a computer coding method utilizing key word search methods was applied. Text coding with the online edition of the ODT was regarded as most appropriate due to its ease of use. The key words identifying the target articles were 'tourism OR travel AND terrorism'. This subset of the content was sampled by the time period identified in both the literature review and methodology. Hall (2002) undertook his research on low-publicized terrorism and tourism incidents up to the 11 September attacks in 2001 from January 2001 up to 11 September itself. This fact, coupled with the survey distribution date of October 2002, resulted in a review of articles published in the ODT in

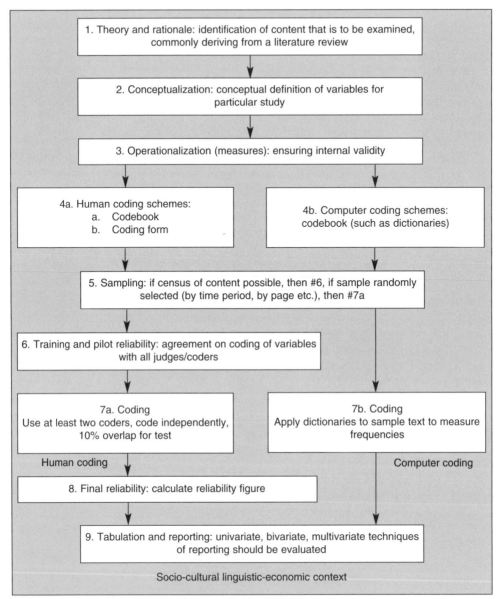

Fig. 15.1. The typical process of content analysis research. (Source: after Ahuvia (2001) and Neuendorf (2002).)

the period from January 2001 to October 2002 (Table 15.2).

Most content analyses usually involve at least two coders in order to minimize risks of researcher bias (Neuendorf, 2002). During training sessions the researcher and the coder developed the coding form and the codebook. This was felt necessary in order to avoid confusion and misunderstandings. In order to generate reliability about the decisions, it was decided to pilot-spot-check and select a few stories to make sure judgements were similar. It was necessary to develop the coding scheme including a coding form and a codebook to ensure validity and reliability of data, as this was the basis

Table 15.1. List of variables.

Variable	Reason
Presentation	To illustrate whether graphics, photos, sidebars, jumps have been used to tell the story
Placement	To analyse the section in which the article was presented: e.g. front, local, regional news, sports, business, food, lifestyle, etc.
Origin	To show whether international stories are covered by any other news service, such as Reuters and Associated Press, and if local stories are covered by ODT staff
Geographic focus	To determine if the stories have a geographical focus: local, regional, national, international, none
Theme	11 September, terrorism and tourism, travel safety, politics/government, war/international conflict, education, business/economics/finance, sports, parenting/relationships, science/technology, health/fitness/medicine, jobs/career

for measurement. For this, the coding form shown in Fig. 15.2 was developed.

Both the coding form and the codebook were based on the largest content analysis ever completed in the USA. In 2001 the Readership Institute examined 100 different newspaper titles, analysed 47,000 different stories in 700 issues in the USA and developed a 'how to' guide for content analysts. The guide is based on the well-tested methods of newspaper content analysis and proved to be useful for comparison and adaptation (Lynch and Peer, 2002).

Intercoder reliability issues were dealt with through the use of two coders and the reliability method of overlapping coding (Neuendorf, 2002). This meant that both coders coded the same units of articles and therefore maximized the reliability of the sample size. Coding for random sample stories was undertaken before the actual content analysis, which ensured intercoder reliability since the results were similar. In addition to the above CA, frequencies were run in order to capture the amount of general articles on terrorism, travel safety and 11 September. The final step in the content analysis process was the analysis and interpretation of the results obtained, which

Table 15.2. Content analysis sample

Sample:	All articles including the words 'tourism OR travel AND terrorism' – ODT search engine
Sample period:	January 2001–October 2002

required the ability to work with SPSS and Excel software.

The *Otago Daily Times* Content Analysis Results

Coverage of terrorism and tourism in *Otago Daily Times*, January 2001–December 2002

The *Otago Daily Times* covered the issue of terrorism to a far lesser extent before the 11 September attacks. In 2001 there were only 36 articles in total mentioning the word 'terrorism' before 11 September (Fig. 15.3). Media reports increased to a high rate in September and continued until November 2001. Interestingly, the number of articles started decreasing in December, a month which produced less than half of the articles than in the previous month (126 in November, only 60 in December 2001). Even though media reports were relatively constant throughout 2002, the diminishing interest in the issue of the 11 September attacks and its repercussions is shown with decreasing numbers of articles throughout the year 2002. The 1-year mark of the attacks in September 2002 resulted in increasing reports mentioning terrorism, which again increased in October 2002 due to the terrorist attacks in Bali, Indonesia (Fig. 15.3).

Downs' (1972) five stage model of the 'issue attention cycle', which begins with low attention during the pre-problem stage and continues with a dramatic rise in interest and

QUESTION	ANSWER
Story ID [six digit]	_____ [Day, Month, Year]
Section	❏ 1 Front ❏ 2 General ❏ 3 Local ❏ 4 Regional ❏ 5 World
Graphics	❏ 1 Yes, how many _____ ❏ 2 No
Photos	❏ 1 Yes, how many _____ ❏ 2 No
Origin or Source of story	❏ 1 ODT staff ❏ 1 Wire/News Service ❏ 2 Reader ❏ 4 Unknown
Geographical Focus	❏ 1 New Zealand ❏ 2 Dunedin, Otago ❏ 3 USA ❏ 4 Other
Main theme	❏ 1 September 11, Politics, Government ❏ 2 Tourism and Terrorism, Travel Safety ❏ 3 War, International Conflict ❏ 4 Education ❏ 5 Business, Economics/Finance ❏ 6 Jobs, Career ❏ 7 Other

Fig. 15.2. Coding form.

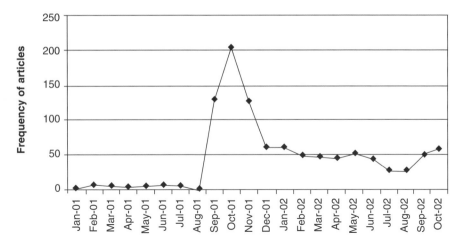

Fig. 15.3. Frequency of articles mentioning 'terrorism' in ODT by month, Jan. 2001– Oct. 2002 ($n = 1111$).

media coverage in the second stage, appears to fit well to the findings. As Fig. 15.3 illustrates, the *Otago Daily Times* did not publish much on terrorism before the 11 September tragedies, even though expert groups were alarmed before the tragedies (Hall, 2002). The second stage, 'alarmed discovery and euphoric enthusiasm', is well shown: a sudden high coverage of the issue 'as a result of some dramatic series of events' (Downs, 1972). The third stage is reflected through the decreasing frequency of media reports, which had already begun in November/December 2001. Downs (1972) also suggests that the cost and sacrifices of proposed solutions drive issues off the

agenda, whereas other theorists believe that it is simply boredom that enhances gradual decline of public interest (Hilgartner and Bosk, 1988; Kingdon, 1995).

The public suddenly became aware of the terrorism and tourism issue as outlined in Fig. 15.4, which is applicable to the 'alarmed discovery and euphoric enthusiasm' phase. The decline of articles happened relatively quickly, however, as already in November 2001 there were only five stories mentioning the key words. Overall, coverage of tourism and terrorism ($n = 49$) was far below coverage of terrorism in general ($n = 1111$). (Fig. 15.4).

Coverage of 'tourism safety' in the

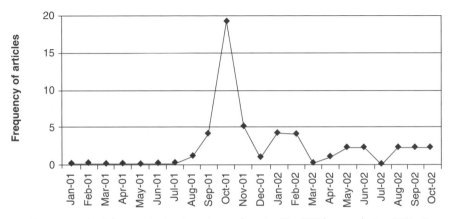

Fig. 15.4. Frequency of articles mentioning 'terrorism and tourism' in ODT by month, Jan. 2001–Oct. 2002 ($n = 49$).

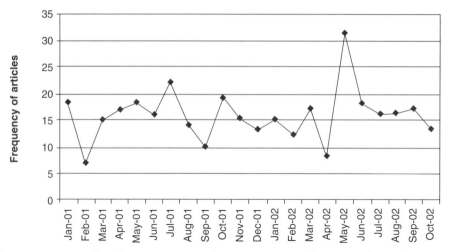

Fig. 15.5. Frequency of articles mentioning 'travel OR tourism AND safety' in ODT by month, Jan. 2001–Oct. 2002.

Otago Daily Times appeared to be fairly constant throughout 2001 and 2002. Figure 15.5 shows the frequency of articles mentioning the key words 'tourism safety'. The crucial months September and November 2001 do not show a significant increase of media coverage of these issues. In May 2002, however, media reports increased in regard to tourism safety because of a local issue in the region affecting safety in public transport. This finding particularly shows that the local focus of the ODT was relatively more important in newspaper coverage terms than the events of 11 September 2001.

To understand the findings, the body of main articles has been reviewed in detail. When screening through the 371 articles that mentioned the key words, it became clear that regionalism in New Zealand's print media is particularly evident with the *Otago Daily Times*. Many articles included a synopsis of why there is a 'safety problem on Saddle Hill motorway' (ODT, 12.03.2002) or 'tourist buses' speed risking lives' (ODT, 17.01.2002). Interestingly, the ODT did not show increasing media coverage after the 11 September attacks in regard to travel safety. Of the 57 articles mentioning the key words 'travel OR tourism AND safety' from September to December 2001 (which was identified in

Fig. 15.3 as the increased media coverage phase in issues relating to terrorism), only 10 focused on international travel safety issues. The remaining 47 articles discussed local issues as well as New Zealand's image as a safe destination.

As noted above, the contrast between news stories mentioning 'terrorism' ($n = 1111$) and articles mentioning 'terrorism and tourism' ($n = 49$) was enormous. It was assumed that similar results would be shown with the key words 'September 11 and terrorism' and 'September 11 and tourism'. Surprisingly, the differences were substantial. Even though the ODT covered the issue of 11 September and terrorism to a higher extent ($n = 518$) than the tourism issue ($n = 198$), coverage of both issues was similar (Fig. 15.6).

On the whole, the 'issue attention cycle' is, again, well applicable to the results. Interestingly, tourism did not peak as much as terrorism. One explanation could be that the ODT did not immediately associate tourism implications with the 11 September attacks. Overall, both topics received irregular attention throughout 2002 and, interestingly, in September 2002, coverage of terrorism-related articles increased again. As Hall (2002: 462) stated, 'Media coverage is therefore diminished and routinized with only sporadic review or anniversary stories

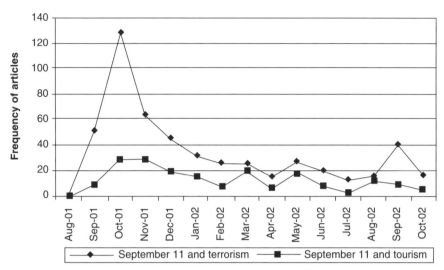

Fig. 15.6. Frequency of stories mentioning 'September 11' and terrorism ($n = 518$) and 'September 11' and tourism ($n = 198$) in ODT by month, Aug. 2001– Oct. 2002.

which mark the effects of the original event'.

Analysis of articles containing 'travel, tourism, terrorism'

In order to present findings along a time line, longitudinal data were collected in regard to newspaper stories concerning the issue of terrorism and tourism. The total number of articles in the *Otago Daily Times* mentioning the words 'tourism OR travel AND terrorism' in the time period from January 2001 to October 2002 was 89. These articles were analysed and interpreted with the statistical package SPSS, involving correlation and time series analysis (Neuendorf, 2002).

Figure 15.7 presents the time line of the portion of articles that appeared in the ODT from January 2001 to October 2002. Clearly, it is shown that before the attacks there were only occasional articles in April and July; however, issue coverage increased to a substantial degree during September and October 2002. Interestingly, issue coverage ceased fairly quickly. In December 2001 there were only four stories mentioning the key words. In 2002 the issue recaptured interest in March (realizing the effects

of 11 September on NZ tourism) and in June (local public transport safety issue). These findings show that media coverage of the 11 September attacks as reported by the ODT was intense, but relatively short.

Since the amount and type of media coverage influences public perceptions, a thorough content analysis followed surrounding the 89 articles identified above. Results were interpreted in regard to the codebook (see Fig. 15.2) and were statistically analysed. The findings were analysed relating to the day of newspaper publication, the articles' word count, the use of graphs and photos, the source of the newspaper story, its geographical focus and the major theme of the article reviewed.

The key words 'tourism OR travel AND terrorism' did not produce articles that focused on only these issues. For that reason, mutually exclusive categories were developed and applied to each story (see codebook). The outcome shows that the issue is very broad and encompasses various different subtopics (see Table 15.3). Of all stories reviewed, 25 centred on travel safety issues and the topic of travel and terrorism. A considerable 16 articles, however, dealt with international conflicts and wars (Israel, Palestine, Afghanistan, Iraq), which in turn affected travel worldwide. The attacks of 11

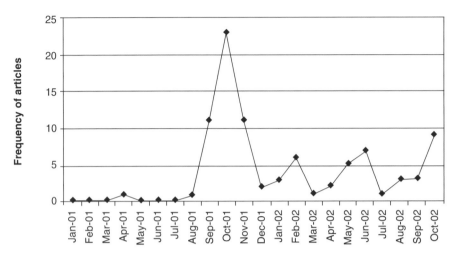

Fig. 15.7. Frequency of articles in ODT from, January 2001 to October 2002, key words 'tourism OR travel AND terrorism'.

September and their impacts upon politics and governments were discussed in 11 articles, whereas the tourism industry's business, economic and financial situation was reviewed in six of 89 stories. Interestingly, the major theme (30 articles) of the stories reviewed was 'other'. This was caused not only by the limitations through the relatively few categories, but also through the use of key words and the focus on regional, rather than international, issues in the ODT. Many articles appeared which unexpectedly included the key words but contained a completely different theme (e.g. golf).

Analysing these results on a basis of a time line, it is shown that the coverage of terrorism relating to tourism reached its peak in October 2001 with 23 stories focus-

ing on the categories. Most articles mentioning terrorism and travel safety, however, were published in September and November 2001 (Table 15.4).

Stories that were covered in September were entitled, for instance, 'Fear is the key to a vulnerable international tourism industry' (ODT, 20.09.01) or 'US has warned of further attacks' (ODT, 24.09.01). While this adds little to the previous articles, it suggests that the paper's editors believed there was a strong public interest in the stories, which gradually declined in the subsequent months (no article in December 2001). Indeed, the issue of media over-coverage arose only 2 weeks after the attack. Another story said: 'Many may complain of news overload, of being revolted by the continuing affront of

Table 15.3. Major theme of newspaper story.

	Frequency	Percentage
11 September, politics, government	11	12.4
Tourism and terrorism, travel safety	25	28.1
War, international conflict	16	18.0
Education	1	1.1
Business, economics, finance	6	6.7
Other	30	33.7
Total	89	100

Table 15.4. Issue coverage from September 2001 to December 2001.

	Sept.	Oct.	Nov.	Dec.
11 September, politics, government	4	4	1	–
Tourism and terrorism, travel safety	4	2	3	–
War, international conflict	–	3	4	1
Business, economics, finance	–	2	–	–
Other	3	12	3	1
Total	11	23	11	2

those appalling scenes of September 11. Yet we all know we are witnessing, potentially, the most important events since World War Two. We cannot help but be drawn to follow them with intense, almost morbid interest' (ODT, 22.09.01). Interestingly, some news stories also focused on the 'costs', which was described by Downs (1972) as the 'realizing the cost of significant progress'-phase. An article entitled 'Passengers may pay for higher airport security' (ODT, 31.10.01) showed concern at the prospect of increased costs as a result of 11 September: 'Dunedin International Airport chief executive John McCall said introducing permanent security could mean structural changes to airports and "Dunedin won't escape from that"'.

Of all stories reviewed, 21 were published on Tuesdays (24%). The ODT's sales are highest on Saturdays. A cross tabulation with the day of publication and major theme of the article revealed that most articles on terrorism and travel safety were published on Tuesdays.

It was also regarded as important to identify the sections in which the articles appeared because stories that appear, for

Table 15.5. Day of newspaper story publication.

	Number	Percentage
Monday	16	18.0
Tuesday	21	23.6
Wednesday	15	16.9
Thursday	14	15.7
Friday	11	12.4
Saturday	12	13.5
Total	89	100

Table 15.6. Newspaper section.

	Frequency	Percentage
Front	7	7.9
General	16	18.0
Local	4	4.5
Regional	3	3.4
World	25	28.1
Editorial	7	7.9
Features	8	9.0
Business	12	13.5
Sport	4	4.5
Other	3	3.4
Total	89	100

instance, on the front page possibly draw more attention. Table 15.6 provides a complete outline of the articles' section. Most stories appeared in the 'world' section of the ODT, while some were published under the 'general' section. Interestingly, of all articles reviewed, 12 appeared in the 'business' section, a part of the ODT that covers financial issues. The collapse of Ansett Australia, general airlines' problems post-11 September, as well as the impact of 11 September on the New Zealand tourism industry, were mainly discussed in this section. Surprisingly, only seven articles appeared in the front section, of which two were classified as 'September 11 and politics' and one as 'tourism and terrorism', whereas the remaining four articles were classified as 'other'.

Most articles reviewed for the CA were of 1001–1500 words. It is possible that such long articles may have drawn the attention of readers. Most other stories reviewed were in the 200–400 words range, which

Table 15.7. Word count of newspaper stories.

	Number	Percentage
101–200 words	7	7.9
201–300 words	16	18.0
301–400 words	17	19.1
401–500 words	0	0
501–600 words	12	13.5
601–1000 words	11	12.4
1001–1500 words	18	20.2
1501–2000 words	6	6.7
> 2001 words	2	2.2
Total	89	100

Table 15.8. Geographical focus of newspaper story.

	Frequency	Percentage
New Zealand	32	36.0
Dunedin, Otago	14	15.7
Australia	3	3.4
USA	13	14.6
Other	27	30.3
Total	89	100

included short opinion pieces or small pieces of information in regard to the issues (Table 15.7).

As the use of graphs and photos emphasizes the stories' importance and may draw the reader's attention, the use of photos was an important factor when analysing the news stories. Only one story that was reviewed made use of graphs to emphasize the stories' content. However, 29.2% of all articles made use of photos (mostly one photo per article). Of these almost one-third focused on international conflict such as war.

More than half of the stories (55.1%) were written by news or wire services such as Reuters or Associated Press. Staff of the ODT wrote around 38% of the stories. Of all articles, the authors of five stories were unknown or not stated (5.6%).

The geographical focus of the articles was also analysed, particularly to identify the extent to which the USA was discussed in the print media. Of the 89 stories, 32 focused on New Zealand and 14 on Otago (Table 15.8), followed by 'other geographical focus' including issues regarding Afghanistan, Pakistan, Israel or Palestine. Only 13 articles had the USA as their main geographical theme. This shows that despite the events that happened in the USA, the ODT had a substantial focus on local or domestic issues.

As outlined above, CA is usually undertaken in conjunction with other methods when dealing with social science issues. In the case of the present research the CA was complemented by a survey of students with respect to their attitudes and perceptions of travel, safety and terrorism issues in order to provide an empirical investigation of whether or not an issue-attention cycle existed with respect to travel safety policy (Hall, 2002). Although it is not the intention of the present case study to detail the results of the survey, we will briefly highlight the way in which the CA complemented the survey research.

The findings of the research suggested that the amount of media attention devoted to terrorism-related articles, amongst other factors identified above (e.g. area of study, work experience), influenced students' perceptions of travel and safety issues. This is consistent with previous results by researchers who discovered that the public often relies on the media for information (Freudenburg et al., 1996; Henry and Gordon, 2001). Moreover, the findings demonstrated that students' perception shifted between 2001 (Duval and Hall, 2002) and 2002 in regard to 11 September. Therefore, Fig. 15.8 seeks to illustrate the nature of the attention cycle through reference to the role of the media, which was analysed via content analysis, and respondent perceptions and attitudes, which were identified through surveys.

Conclusions

This chapter has indicated some of the potential applications of CA to tourism. The most significant aspect of CA is a clear

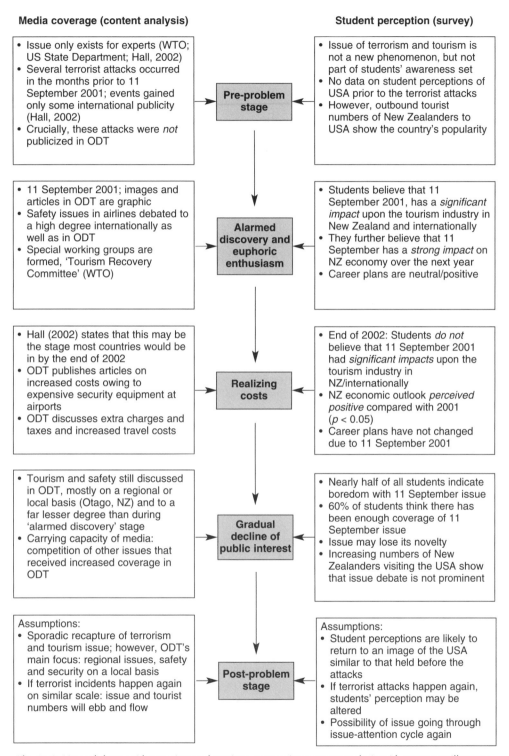

Fig. 15.8. Up and down with terrorism and tourism: connecting content analysis with surveys to illustrate the issue-attention cycle.

understanding of the process and the selection of appropriate categories. Historically, CA has not been substantially utilized in tourism with respect to its major role in analysing newspaper coverage with regard to an examination of public policy issues. However, its use in studying image and representation is much greater. Since the late 1990s CA has also been increasingly used as a tool in examining the effectiveness of tourism websites and in analysing Web traffic, although the nature of the Web itself means that there is only limited value in such traffic studies.

The case study illustrated both the process of undertaking CA and its application to a contemporary tourism issue. Significantly, in both the case study and several of the examples provided of CA in tourism it is important to note that CA is usually combined with other methods. Nevertheless, the case study did illustrate how CA may be used to investigate policy issues in tourism. However, of greatest significance, as with any research method, is consideration of the judgement and analytical skills of the researcher(s), as well as their capacity to write the results in a way that meets the questions posed and the audience to which the results of such analysis are addressed.

Acknowledgement

The authors would like to acknowledge the assistance of David Duval in the conduct and development of the case study.

References

Ahuvia, A. (2001) Traditional, interpretive, and reception based content analyses: improving the ability of content analysis to address issues of pragmatic and theoretical concern. *Social Indicators Research* 54(2), 139–172.

Albers, P.C. and James, W. (1983) Tourism and the changing image of the great lakes Indian. *Annals of Tourism Research* 10, 128–148.

Albers, P.C. and James, W. (1984) Utah's Indians and popular photography in the American West: a view from the picture post card. *Utah Historical Quarterly* 52(1), 72–91.

Albers, P.C. and James, W. (1985) Images and reality: post cards of Minnesota's Ojibway people, 1900–80. *Minnesota History* 49(6), 229–240.

Albers, P.C. and James, W. (1988) Travel photography: a methodological approach. *Annals of Tourism Research* 13, 134–158.

Allied Press (2003) Otago Daily Times *Profile*. Allied Press, Dunedin.

Andsager, J.L. and Drzewiecka, J.A. (2002) Desirability of differences in destinations. *Annals of Tourism Research* 29(2), 401–421.

Arnold, S.J. and Fischer, E. (1994) Hermeneutics and consumer research. *Journal of Consumer Research* 21, 55–70.

Ateljevic, I. and Doorne, S. (2002) Representing New Zealand: tourism imagery and ideology. *Annals of Tourism Research* 29(3), 648–667.

Athiyaman, A. (1995) The interface of tourism and strategy research: an analysis. *Tourism Management* 16(6), 447–453.

Barry, C. (1998) Choosing qualitative data analysis software: Atlas/ti and Nudist compared. *Sociological Research Online* 3(3). Available at: http://www. socresonline.org.uk/socresonline/3/3/4.html

Bentley, T., Meyer, D., Page, S. and Chalmers, D. (2001a) Recreational tourism injuries among visitors to New Zealand: an exploratory analysis using hospital discharge data. *Tourism Management* 22(4), 373–381.

Bentley, T., Page, S., Meyer, D., Chalmers, D. and Laird, I. (2001b) How safe is adventure tourism in New Zealand? An exploratory analysis. *Applied Ergonomics* 32(4), 327–338.

Berelson, B. (1952) *Content Analysis in Communication Research*. Free Press, New York.

Blackwood, R.E. (1983) The content of news photos: roles portrayed by men and women. *Journalism Quarterly* 60(4), 710–714.

Buhalis, D. and Spada, A. (2000) Destination management systems: criteria for success – an exploratory research. *Information Technology and Tourism* 3, 41–58.

Chen, J.S., Kerstetter, D.L. and Graefe, A.R. (2001) Tourists' reasons for visiting industrial heritage sites. *Journal of Hospitality and Leisure Marketing* 8(1/2), 19–32.

Chung, T. and Law, R. (2003) Developing a performance indicator for hotel websites. *International Journal of Hospitality Management* 22(1), 119–125.

Cloke, P. and Perkins, H.C. (2002) Commodification and adventure in New Zealand tourism. *Current Issues in Tourism* 5(6), 521–549.

Downs, A. (1972) Up and down with ecology – the issue attention cycle. *The Public Interest* 28, 38–50.

Duval, D. and Hall, C.M. (2002) 'People may finally realise just how important we are': New Zealand student perceptions of future career opportunities in the tourism industry following the events of September 11. *Journal of Hospitality, Leisure, Sport and Tourism Education* 1(2). Available at: http://www.hlst.ltsn.ac.uk/johlste

Echtner, C.M. and Prasad, P. (2003) The context of Third World tourism marketing. *Annals of Tourism Research* 30(3), 660–682.

Freudenburg, W.R., Coleman, C.L., Gonzales, J. and Helgeland, C. (1996) Media coverage of hazard events – analysing the assumptions. *Risk Analysis* 16(1), 31–42.

Garrod, B. (2003) Defining marine ecotourism: a Delphi study. In: Garrod, B. and Wilson, J.C. (eds) *Marine Ecotourism: Issues and Experiences*. Channel View Publications, Clevedon, UK, pp. 1–36.

Groves, D.L. and Timothy, D.J. (2001) Photographic techniques and the measurement of impact and importance attributes on trip design: a case study. *Loisir et Societe* 24(1), 311–317.

Hall, C.M. (1991) Tourism as the subject of post-graduate dissertations in Australia. *Annals of Tourism Research* 18(3), 520–523.

Hall, C.M. (2002) Travel safety, terrorism and the media: the significance of the issue-attention cycle. *Current Issues in Tourism* 5(5), 458–466.

Hansen, A. (1992) *Computer-assisted Analysis of Newspapers: an Introduction*. Discussion Papers in Mass Communications. Centre for Mass Communication Research, Leicester, UK.

Henderson, J.C. (2003) Managing tourism and Islam in Peninsular Malaysia. *Tourism Management* 24(4), 447–456.

Henry, G.T. and Gordon, C.S. (2001) Tracking issue attention. *Public Opinion Quarterly* 65(2), 157–177.

Hester, G. and Gonzenbach, W. (1997) The environment: TV news, real world cues, and public opinion over time. *Mass Communication Review* 22(1), 5–20.

Hilgartner, S. and Bosk, C. (1988) The rise and fall of social problems: a public arenas model. *American Journal of Sociology* 94, 53–78.

Holbrook, M.B. (1977) More on content analysis in consumer research. *Journal of Consumer Research* 4, 176–177.

Holsti, O.R. (1969) *Content Analysis for the Social Sciences and Humanities*. Addison-Wesley, Reading, Massachusetts.

Iyengar, S. and Kinder, D.K. (1987) *News That Matters: Television and American Opinion*. University of Chicago Press, Chicago, Illinois.

Jamal, T. and Hollinshead, K. (2001) Tourism and the forbidden zone: the underserved power of qualitative inquiry. *Tourism Management* 22(1), 63–82.

Jenkins, O.H. (1999) Understanding and measuring tourist destination images. *International Journal of Tourism Research* 1, 1–15.

Jeong, M. and Lambert, C.U. (2001) Adaptation of an information quality framework to measure customer's behavioral intentions to use lodging web sites. *Hospitality Management* 20(2), 129–146.

Jung, T.H. and Butler, R.W. (2000) Perception of marketing managers of the effectiveness of the Internet in tourism and hospitality. *Information Technology and Tourism* 3(3/4), 167–176.

Ju-Pak, K.-H. (1999) Content dimensions of web advertising: a cross-national comparison. *International Journal of Advertising* 18(2), 207–231.

Kaplan, A. (1943) Content analysis and the theory of signs. *Philosophy of Science* 10, 230–247.

Kassarjian, H.H. (1977) Content analysis in consumer research. *Journal of Consumer Research* 4, 8–18.

Kepplinger, H.M. (1989) Content analysis and reception analysis. *American Behavioral Scientist* 33, 175–182.

Kingdon, J.W. (1995) *Agendas, Alternatives, and Public Policies*, 2nd edn. HarperCollins, New York.

Kolbe, R.H. and Burnett, M.S. (1991) Content-analysis research: an examination of applications with directives for improving research reliability and objectivity. *Journal of Consumer Research* 18, 243–150.

Krippendorf, K. (1980) *Content Analysis: an Introduction to its Methodology*. Sage, Thousand Oaks, California.

Lawrence, S. and Giles, C.L. (1999) Accessibility of information on the web. *Nature* 400, 107–109.

Lynch, S. and Peer, L. (2002) *Analyzing Newspaper Content: a How-To Guide.* Media Management Center, Northwestern University, Evanston, Illinois.

MacMillan, K. and McLachlan, S. (1999) Theory-building with Nud.Ist: using computer assisted qualitative analysis in a media case study. *Sociological Research Online* 4(2). Available at: http://www.socresonline.org.uk/socresonline/4/2/macmillan_mcLachlan.html

Malloy, D.C. and Fennell, D.A. (1998) Codes of ethics and tourism: an exploratory content analysis. *Tourism Management* 19(5), 453–461.

Matacin, M.L. and Burger, J.M. (1987) A content analysis of sexual themes in *Playboy* cartoons. *Sex Roles* 17, 179–186.

McComas, K.A. and Shanahan, J. (1999) Telling stories about climate change: measuring the impact of narratives on issue cycles. *Communication Research* 26, 30–57.

McMillian, S.J. (2000) The microscope and the moving target: the challenge of applying content analysis to the world wide web. *Journalism & Mass Communications Quarterly* 77(1), 80–98.

Miller, S.H. (1975) The content of news photos: women's and men's roles. *Journalism Quarterly* 52(1), 70–75.

Musso, J.A., Weare, C. and Hale, M. (2000) Designing web technologies for local governance reform: good management or good democracy? *Political Communication* 17(1), 1–19.

Neuendorf, K.A. (2002) *The Content Analysis Guidebook.* Sage, Thousand Oaks, California.

Nicholson, S. (1997) Indexing and abstracting on the World Wide Web: an examination of six Web databases. *Information Technology and Libraries* 16(2), 73–81.

Nickerson, N.P. (1995) Tourism and gambling content analysis. *Annals of Tourism Research* 22(1), 53–66.

Padgett, M. and Hall, C.M. (2001) Case study 4.3: tourism at the polls. In: Hall, C.M. and Kearsley, G.W. (eds) *Tourism in New Zealand: an Introduction.* Oxford University Press, Sydney.

Peters, B.G. and Hogwood, B.W. (1985) In search of the issue-attention cycle. *Journal of Politics* 47, 239–253.

Peterson, R.T. (1998) The depiction of seniors in international tourism magazine advertisements: a content analysis. *International Journal of Hospitality and Tourism Administration* 1(4), 3–17.

Peterson, R.T. (2000) The utilization of ecological themes in state and local government tourism magazine commercials: an assessment. *Journal of Hospitality and Leisure Marketing* 6(4), 5–16.

Pritchard, A. and Morgan, N.J. (2001) Culture, identity and tourism representation: marketing Cymru or Wales? *Tourism Management* 22(2), 167–179.

Richter, L.K. (1980) The political uses of tourism: a Philippine case study. *Journal of Developing Areas* 14, 237–257.

Rintala, J. and Birrell, S. (1984) Fair treatment for the active female: a content analysis of *Young Athlete* magazine. *Sociology of Sport Journal* 3(3), 231–250.

Schindlmayr, T. (2001) The media, public opinion and population assistance: establishing the link. *Family Planning Perspectives* 33(3), 128–132.

Scott, L.M. (1994) Images in advertising: the need for a theory of visual rhetoric. *Journal of Consumer Research* 21, 252–273.

Sirakaya, E. and Soenmez, S. (2000) Gender images in state tourism brochures: an overlooked area in socially responsible tourism marketing. *Journal of Travel Research* 38(4), 353–362.

Sirakaya, E., Sasidharan, V. and Soenmez, S. (1999) Redefining ecotourism: the need for a supply-side view. *Journal of Travel Research* 38(2), 168–172.

Stern, B.B. (1993) Feminist literary criticism and the deconstruction of ads: a postmodern view of advertising and consumer responses. *Journal of Consumer Research* 19, 556–566.

Swain, M., Brent, M. and Long, V.H. (1999) Annals and tourism evolving: indexing 25 years of publication. *Annals of Tourism Research* 25, 991–1014.

Tierny, P. (2000) Internet-based evaluation of tourism web site effectiveness: methodological issues and survey results. *Journal of Travel Research* 39, 212–219.

Wan, C.-S. (2002) The web sites of international tourist hotels and tour wholesalers in Taiwan. *Tourism Management* 23(2), 155–160.

Waterman, R. and Wood, B.D. (1994) Policy monitoring and policy analysis. *Journal of Policy Analysis and Management* 12(4), 685–699.

Weare, C. and Wan-Ying, L. (2000) *Content Analysis of the World Wide Web.* Sage, Thousand Oaks, California.

Weber, R.P. (1985) *Basic Content Analysis.* Sage, Beverly Hills, California.

Yagi, C. (2001) How tourists see other tourists: analysis of online travelogues. *The Journal of Tourism Studies* 12(2), 22–31.

Zhang, J. and Cameron, G.T. (2003) China's agenda building and image polishing in the US: assessing an international public relations campaign. *Public Relations Review* 29(1), 13–28.

16 Using Cluster Analysis to Segment a Sample of Australian Ecotourists

David Weaver and Laura Lawton

School of Hotel, Restaurant and Tourism Mangement, University of South Carolina, Columbia, SC 29208, USA

Introduction

Binna Burra Mountain Lodge and O'Reilly's Rainforest Guesthouse, located adjacent to Lamington National Park in the Gold Coast hinterland, are established icons of the Australian ecotourism industry. As such, they provide an excellent opportunity to investigate the diversity of the ecotourist market, and specifically the proposition that ecotourists can be arrayed along a 'hard' to 'soft' continuum. This proposition has important implications for the planning, management and marketing of ecotourism products, since hard and soft ecotourists are purported to differ substantially with regard to their motivation, preferences and behaviour. A mismatch between market and product, therefore, is more likely to result in visitor dissatisfaction as well as negative environmental and socio-cultural impacts. To investigate this issue of ecotourist market diversity, the authors in late 1999 carried out a research project focused on overnight visitors to the above two ecolodges (Weaver and Lawton, 2002). This chapter critically focuses on the method, cluster analysis, that was used to identify distinct sub-groups within a sample of these ecolodge visitors. The first section considers the nature and philosophical underpinnings of cluster analysis as an analytical method, as well as associated issues. A discussion of the method's application to the actual research project, including questionnaire design, sampling procedure and data analysis, follows in the second section. The overall intent of this chapter, therefore, is to highlight the strengths and weaknesses of cluster analysis for those considering its application as a market segmentation technique.

Cluster Analysis

Essentially, *cluster analysis* designates a group of multivariate procedures that use a specified set of variables to classify a specified set of objects or subjects into relatively uniform clusters. In marketing research, this commonly entails the use of selected survey data to group survey respondents into distinct market segments. Target marketing and product development can be greatly facilitated if, for example, 1000 tourists can be reduced into four or five distinct groups whose members share important attitudinal and/or behavioural characteristics. *Hierarchical cluster analysis* using distance measures, the most commonly applied type of cluster analysis, employs a computer-based statistical package such as SPSS to assign a cumulative value to each respondent based on these responses. The two closest survey respondents in terms of this value are then grouped together to form the first cluster, which is assigned a new value that represents the mean between these two respondents. The second round of clustering could involve either: (i) a new respondent joining this first cluster, or (ii) a second cluster being created from two other respondents, depending on which scenario involves the smaller difference in value.

This process of cluster formation and amalgamation continues until all the respondents are grouped into just two clusters. For the researcher, a critical decision is then whether to accept this two-cluster solution or, instead, a larger number of clusters that better differentiate the respondents and are easier to interpret. The optimal or 'natural' solution is normally one in which the distance in value between members within each group is minimized while the distance between the groups is maximized (Hair *et al.*, 1995). Once an acceptable cluster solution has been identified and labels tentatively assigned to the clusters based on an analysis of responses to the discriminating variables, it is common practice for the clusters to be compared on the basis of gender, age and other relevant socio-demographic characteristics using statistical tests such as the *t*-test, ANOVA, and Chi-square, as warranted. The patterns that emerge from these comparisons may result in changes to the cluster labels that were initially assigned.

This brief outline indicates the need for the researcher to make a number of subjective decisions during the process of the hierarchical cluster analysis. These include:

- Sample selection.
- The choice of discriminating variables.
- The selection of an appropriate hierarchical clustering procedure to compute similarities among the objects or subjects.
- The identification of the 'best' cluster solution.
- Assigning suitable labels or names to each cluster as part of the interpretation process.

Each of these decision processes will now be considered below. For any non-specialist wanting a more detailed but accessible guide to cluster analysis and its application, we strongly recommend Hair *et al.* (1995).

Object or subject selection

The selection of objects or subjects is not problematic if the researcher is able to include the entire population of that which is being investigated. For example, a study might classify all the new cars released in North America during 2002 based on safety and performance, all countries based on 2003 indices for economic and social development, or the full British House of Lords based on voting and attendance patterns during the most recent session of Parliament. However, in situations involving very large populations, it is necessary to obtain a representative sample so that an undistorted picture of the population's actual structure will emerge. A detailed discussion of correct sampling techniques and protocol is not within the purview of this chapter and can be easily accessed elsewhere (e.g. Alreck and Settle, 1995; Burns and Bush, 2000).

Variable selection

The variables that are selected by the researcher for the purposes of performing a cluster analysis constitute the *cluster variate*. Since it is entirely on this basis that classifications are made, great care must be exercized when defining the cluster variate. This is not an issue in situations where the researcher's intent is to test relationships identified by prior research (i.e. *confirmatory cluster analysis*), since the same cluster variate is used. Far more common in the business and social sciences is *exploratory cluster analysis*, which typically uses hierarchical methods (see above) to estimate the relationships in the data. This often requires the researcher to compile the cluster variate 'from scratch'.

It is extremely important to note that each variable in the cluster variate is assigned equal weight in the classification of data. Thus, each variable in a five-member cluster variate contributes 20% to the resulting clusters, while the comparable contribution in a 25-member cluster variate is only 4%. Researchers must therefore carefully consider the rationale and objectives of their research as well as its practical and theoretical foundations, given that an irrelevant or marginal variable will carry the same weight as a critically important variable. Another danger is the inclusion of two or more variables that essentially capture the same idea, which has the effect of doubling or tripling the contribution of that idea to the cluster analysis. For example, this might occur in a survey containing the statements 'I am a frequent visitor to Florida' and 'I have been visiting Florida throughout my life'. Hair *et al.* (1995: 428) emphasize that 'cluster analysis can be dramatically affected by the inclusion of only one or two inappropriate or undifferentiated variables', thereby resulting in misleading outcomes. In this respect, it is recommended after running an exploratory cluster analysis that any variables which fail to significantly differentiate the sample (for example, a survey question to which everyone provides a 'strongly agree' response) be removed from the cluster variate, and that the cluster analysis be re-run using the abbreviated cluster variate. It is also common practice at this reassessment stage to eliminate *outlier* individuals who distort the classification structure because of characteristics that are very different from other individuals. An extreme example of an outlier in marketing research is a consumer survey respondent who reports (accurately or facetiously) that they consume only human flesh.

A final point concerns the widespread practice of using factor analysis to create a simplified cluster variate. This is attractive to the extent that factors represent the underlying structure of a set of variables, and a simplified cluster variate of (for example) five factors is easier to analyse and interpret than a cluster variate with the original 30 variables. However, bearing in mind that each item in the cluster variate is given equal weight, a problem is created wherein a factor that accounts for 40% of the variance in a data set makes the same contribution to the cluster analysis (i.e. 20% in a five-factor cluster variate) as a factor that accounts for only 5% of the variance. Such imbalances are more likely to result in a distorted structure, and hence it is probably better to use the original variables rather than factors when defining the cluster variate.

Technique selection

Before the above reassessment of the individuals and variables can occur, a suitable technique for identifying similarities between individuals must be selected. *Correlational measures* use a correlation coefficient to identify patterns in the values, while the more commonly employed *distance measures* define similarity in terms of differences in magnitude between values. *Association measures* are normally used when variables involve non-metric data such as a 'yes' or 'no' response to a survey. There are numerous procedures within each category, and a highly specialized knowledge of cluster analysis is necessary to understand fully the suitability of each technique under a given set of circumstances. For non-specialists, academic precedence is therefore an important if not necessarily optimal criterion used in making such a decision. Thus, the popularity of Ward's Method among social scientists is at least as much a self-reinforcing phenomenon based on the frequency with which it is encountered in the literature as a consequence of researchers' understanding of how it differs operationally from other procedures. Few non-specialists are aware that Ward's Method minimizes dispersion within groups and favours the formation of small clusters of roughly equal size.

Solution identification

As with the selection of the subject/object and the variable, there are occasions when the desired number of clusters is predetermined. For example, a World Bank project might require that all countries be divided into 'more developed' and 'less developed' categories to distinguish between those countries that qualify and do not qualify for special loans. The onus, however, is usually on the researcher to identify an appropriate solution from an array of options ranging from two clusters to ten or more, depending on sample size and other considerations. To achieve this, several factors may be taken into account. First, the distances between clusters can be observed visually on a *dendrogram*, or diagram that depicts all stages of cluster formation from the first linkage to the combination of all items into one cluster. This is convenient when the number of subjects or objects is small, but inconvenient when a large number of items are involved. Second, solutions that involve very small clusters should be reconsidered, as they may not be important or amenable to testing for statistical significance relative to other groups (that is, a large difference in responses between two small clusters is more likely to be the result of chance than an indication of statistically significant differentiation).

A third option is to analyse the cluster variate in terms of the values (e.g. means on questionnaire statements) that emerge for each variable against each cluster. Solutions that yield the highest level of statistically significant differentiation are the most desirable, since these indicate a strong level of 'distance' between the clusters (more detail is provided below in the case study).

A final consideration is interpretability. Even if all the other devices lead to positive assessments, do the clusters ultimately make sense from the perspective of intuition, theory, practicality, common sense, etc.?

Assignment of labels

Once an acceptable solution has emerged, the researcher must assign labels or names that best interpret or capture the essence of each group. There is scope for creativity in this process, particularly if subsequent comparative analysis in the case of a consumer survey yields significant differences in age, sex, ethnicity or other subject characteristics. Hair *et al.* (1995) cite the example of a fictitious soft drink consumption study in which the cluster containing individuals with a basically unfavourable attitude is labelled 'Health- and Calorie-Conscious', while the cluster of those with positive attitudes is labelled 'Get a Sugar Rush'. Investigating a

much broader array of value and lifestyle parameters, Ray and Anderson (2000) assigned labels of 'traditionals', 'moderns' and 'cultural creatives' to adult American clusters that respectively embodied conservative, mainstream and progressive tendencies.

More an art than a science?

Cluster analysis is an extremely useful, attractive and accessible method for classifying individuals or objects into relatively uniform groups. It is a method, moreover, that derives from a quantitative, positivist tradition of scientific inquiry that serves to convey a powerful sense of authority as well as confidence in outcomes. This authority and confidence, however, can be misleading due to the highly subjective decisions that underlie the veneer of objective output generated by the computer. The variables that a researcher chooses to include or exclude from the cluster variate, the individuals that are included or excluded from participation, the methods that are included or excluded from the analysis, and the clusters that are included or excluded in the final solution, all critically influence the final results. Moreover, this effect is cumulative and compound, as subjective decisions are made in response to results derived from earlier subjective decisions. No wonder then that Hair *et al.* (1995: 428) describe cluster analysis as 'much more of an art than a science' despite its positivist lineage.

Anyone who carries out or uses the results of cluster analysis must be aware of the interplay between subjectivity and objectivity that fundamentally characterizes this method. Quality research papers deal openly and honestly with the subjective decisions that were made in the course of a research project, revealing the options that were considered and the reasons for rejecting some options while accepting others. This implies that a continual process of experimentation, assessment of alternative outcomes, and revisitation of earlier stages is essential to this method. Ultimately, good experimental cluster analysis does not reveal a perfect picture of reality, but, rather, essential contours that form the basis for subsequent inquiry and 'fine tuning'.

The Lamington Ecotourist Case Study

The Lamington study was motivated by our desire to extend the research empirically into the contention that ecotourists could be divided into basic 'hard' and 'soft' ideal types. Laarman and Durst (1987) were the first to raise the notion of a hard-to-soft continuum, wherein hard ecotourists are committed environmentalists who travel in small groups within remote areas where services and facilities make minimal impacts. Soft ecotourists pursue a more superficial experience with nature focused around interpretation centres and other heavily serviced sites that experience high levels of visitation. Whether the 'hard/soft' or some alternative terminology (e.g. 'active'/'passive') is employed, this concept has become widely accepted and assumed by ecotourism researchers and practitioners (Lindberg, 1991; Queensland, 1997; Weaver, 1998; Orams, 2001). At least three previous empirical investigations using cluster analysis have corroborated the basic contours of the continuum despite differences in cluster variate, sampled population and procedures employed (Pearce and Moscardo, 1994; Chapman, 1995; Palacio and McCool, 1997). These differences may help to account for the variability in cluster descriptions and size that resulted from the studies.

Limitations in these studies include the use of factor analysis by Pearce and Moscardo (1994) and Palacio and McCool (1997) to simplify the cluster variate. In addition, the studies all involved samples and/or sites that were not confined to ecotourists or ecotourism, so that the results are diluted by the inclusion of a substantial non-ecotourist component. Other characteristics of these studies are described where appropriate for comparative purposes in the sections below, which follow the same sequence as the general discussion. Our own working assumption was that the Lamington project, in line with the assump-

tion of a bell curve distribution, would yield a 'hard' cluster, a 'soft' cluster', and an intermediate cluster comparable in size to the other two clusters combined.

Subject selection

One of our first priorities was to select a sample that actually consisted of ecotourists. Because Binna Burra and O'Reilly's are both widely regarded as iconic ecotourism products and are actually marketed as specialized 'ecolodges', we assumed that overnight visitors to these sites would self-identify as ecotourists. (Although soft ecotourists make up a much larger proportion of the overall ecotourist market than hard ecotourists, we further assumed that the two ecolodges would be skewed more towards the hard end of the spectrum because of the type of products they offer – hence our working assumption of a bell curve in which the two poles are evened out.) A second reason for selecting these two sites was that the scale of visitation at each (15,000–20,000 visitor nights per year) is large enough that we were confident about obtaining a large sample for the study. The largest study cited above in terms of sample size is Pearce and Moscardo (1994), who analysed 545 respondents. We hoped to obtain at least 1000 responses to ensure that the sample was representative of the target ecolodge population (see below). In addition, the two ecolodges are similar in terms of location, client profile, available activities, size and price, leading us to assume that there would be no significant differences between the samples collected, and that they could therefore be combined into one test group. Additional considerations included the proximity of the ecolodges to Griffith University (where the researchers were based at the time) and the willingness of the managers at each ecolodge to participate in the study by providing us with access to their overnight visitor databases.

To obtain the desired sample size of at least 1000, we randomly generated 1500 names from each lodge using their computerized client databases. Each name represented a 'visitor party' of one or more listed guests. Eligible guests were adults (over 16 years old) who had stayed overnight for at least 1 night during the 12-month period preceding the generation of the sample. They also had to be residents of Australia, since project funding did not allow for the translation of the questionnaire into languages other than English, or for expenses associated with pre-paid postal returns from overseas sources. Non-Australians in any case accounted for only a small proportion of the overnight clientele (estimated at 5–10% by the managers) at either site. Only one adult person was selected per visitor party, and the person chosen to receive the mail-out questionnaire alternated between male and female party members so that an equal sex distribution would be obtained. To increase the response rate, we provided pre-paid envelopes and a cover letter that explained the project and assured confidentiality of the respondent data. The cover letter also explained that respondents who completed the entire questionnaire would be eligible for an AUS$500 cash incentive draw.

Variable selection

As the basis for classifying our respondents, we composed a set of statements soliciting information about general ecotourism behaviour and attitudes (that is, not just in response to their Binna Burra or O'Reilly's experience). Five Likert-scaled response options were provided, ranging from 'strongly disagree' (= 1) to 'strongly agree' (= 5). Such a variable structure is commonly used in tourism-related cluster analysis (e.g. Fredline and Faulkner, 2000), including a study that we had done earlier on resident perceptions of tourism on Tamborine Mountain, a destination in the Gold Coast hinterland of Australia (Weaver and Lawton, 2001). We began by studying the empirical and theoretical literature to construct an 'ecotourism spectrum' that contrasted the purported 'ideal type' characteristics of hard and soft ecotourists (Fig. 16.1). Our intent was to minimize bias by wording half of the questions in favour of hard ecotourism (e.g. 'My idea of an ideal ecotourism destination is a wilderness setting') and half in favour of soft ecotourism (e.g. 'My ecotourism experiences are usually just one component of a multi-purpose trip experience').

In composing the actual statements, we sought to represent the three core criteria of ecotourism as defined by Blamey (2001), Weaver (2001) and others, namely, that ecotourism focuses on *nature-based attractions* (three statements), provides opportunities for *learning* (five statements) and strives to be *environmentally and socioculturally sustainable* (nine statements). Twenty 'miscellaneous' statements not directly related to the criteria were added (e.g. 'National parks should provide adequate infrastructure and services to accommodate those who want to go there' and 'I like my ecotourism experiences to be physi-

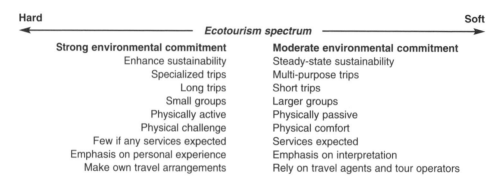

Fig. 16.1. Characteristics of hard and soft ecotourism as ideal types. (Source: adapted from Weaver and Lawton, 2002.)

cally challenging'). The final cluster variate of 37 statements was derived from an original set of about 50 statements that was reduced after exposing these to other ecotourism and tourism experts for redundancy, double meanings and other problems.

The 37 cluster variate statements were assembled in the first section of the 16-page mail-out questionnaire. Since cluster analysis cannot accept missing cases, it was crucial to inform respondents that they had to complete every statement to be eligible for the cash draw. Subsequent sections sought additional opinions about ecotourism and the natural environment more broadly, motivations for engaging in ecotourism, information sources, ecotourism destinations visited, ecotourism activities undertaken, usual trip duration and group composition, usual accommodation type and respondent characteristics (age, sex, place of residence, employment, political affiliation, education and income). We had some concerns about the length of the questionnaire, but assumed: (i) that ecotourists would be more willing than the public at large to complete a survey on this topic, and (ii) that the incentive would encourage a high level of response.

After a 6-week cutoff time, 1374 questionnaires were returned, of which 1180 (39.3%) were valid. Most of the invalid questionnaires were returned by the post office as 'undeliverable' due to incorrect addresses. Only 18 questionnaires were rejected because of incomplete responses to the statements. We would probably have attained a higher response rate had we sent out a reminder postcard after 3 weeks, but we decided against this due to funding constraints and an acceptable level of questionnaire return. Slightly more valid questionnaires were returned by the O'Reilly's sample, but statistical comparisons of the two sets of respondents revealed no significant differences on the statements or respondent characteristics. They were therefore combined into a single data set. We were also reassured that only five respondents noted that they did not really consider themselves to be ecotourists despite having stayed overnight at an ecolodge. This appeared to confirm our assumption that the respondents would self-identify as ecotourists.

Technique selection and solution identification

Moving to the stage of technique selection, we opted to rely on literature precedence (e.g. Fredline and Faulkner, 2000) and use Ward's Method (otherwise known as 'minimum variance'; see Ward, 1963), after becoming at least superficially aware of the strengths and weaknesses of this and other major hierarchical distance-based options. We requested solutions ranging from two to six clusters. Facilitating our analysis was the fact that (for example) a six-cluster solution is created by splitting just one cluster from the five-cluster solution, so that both solutions share four identical clusters. We sequentially rejected the six-, five- and four-cluster solutions, which produced at least one unacceptably small group and, more importantly, resulted in one or more clusters that were not substantially different from at least one other cluster in the solution, either in statistical or interpretive terms. The two- and three-cluster solutions both resulted in large clusters whose means were significantly different at the 99% confidence level in terms of all 37 statement ANOVAs (which meant that none of the statements needed to be discarded) and made sense from an interpretation perspective.

The decision finally to go with the three- rather than two-cluster solution was based on the fact that the former produced the 'hard', 'soft' and 'intermediate' categories that we were expecting, rather than just a 'hard/soft' dichotomy with substantial variability within each of the two groups. By accepting a three-cluster solution, it was then necessary to perform *post hoc* tests (we used Tukey's, but other tests are also commonly used) on the statements that would show which pairings of clusters were significantly different. Of the possible 111 combinations (that is, three combinations of pairs per statement – i.e. 1–2, 1–3 and 2–3

– times 37 statements) only 12 yielded no significant differences.

Assignment of labels

The first cluster contained 315 individuals (27% of the sample) who clearly leaned towards the criteria associated with soft ecotourism. For example, this cluster yielded a mean of 2.79 (indicating slight disagreement overall) on the statement 'I would be willing to go on a long hike in miserable weather if this was my only opportunity to see a unique plant or animal of interest to me'. Because these responses were not unequivocal (that is, none of the pro-hard ecotourism statements yielded a mean close to 1, or 'strong disagreement'), we elected to describe this first cluster with the relative term 'softer ecotourists'. The same applied to the second cluster with its 402 members

(34% of the sample). On the above statement, this cluster yielded a mean of 4.08 (out of a maximum 5), indicating here and in other statements a clear but not unequivocal affiliation with hard ecotourism. Hence, the label 'harder ecotourists' was applied. Upon reflection, the tendency of these two clusters to move away from the poles of the continuum (Fig. 16.2) was not surprising. Binna Burra and O'Reilly's both provide a comprehensive array of facilities and services, so that the extreme hard ecotourist is not likely to appear as an overnight guest – rather they would probably be found among the small number of Lamington visitors who participate in 'primitive camping' deep in the park's interior. For very different reasons, soft ecotourist ideal types are also less likely to stay overnight in an ecolodge, preferring to make a short day visit from a residence or resort on the Gold Coast.

Hard	Soft
←	Ecotourism Spectrum →

Cluster 2 = 'Harder'

Strong environ. commitment
Enhansive sustainability
Specialized trips
Longer trips
Smaller groups
Physically active
Few if any services expected
Emphasis on personal experience

Cluster 1 = 'Softer'

Moderate environ. commitment
Steady state sustainability
Multi-purpose trips
Shorter trips
Larger groups
Physically passive
Services expected
Emphasis on interpretation

Cluster 3 = 'Structured'

Strong environ. commitment
Enhansive sustainability
Physically active

Multi-purpose trips
Short trips
Larger groups
Services expected
Emphasis on interpretation

Fig. 16.2. Clusters obtained from the Lamington ecolodge sample. (Source: adapted from Weaver and Lawton, 2002.)

The third cluster, consisting of 463 respondents (or 39% of the sample), was in many ways the most surprising and interesting. As noted above, we expected this cluster to produce a consistent pattern of neutral responses (that is, around '3') to indicate an intermediate group between the hard and soft ideal types. This, however, is not what was encountered in the interpretation stage. Unexpectedly, the members of this cluster were similar to the harder ecotourists in terms of the desire to learn about the natural environment, preferring remote and wilderness-like settings and demonstrating strong environmentalist tendencies. However, they were also similar to the softer ecotourists with regard to factors such as preferring comfortable accommodation and services, and participating in ecotourism as one facet of a multi-purpose trip (Fig. 16.2). Even more surprisingly, the means yielded by this cluster were significantly higher than the other two groups in terms of seven statements that indicated a preference for product interpretation, National Parks that offered enough services to accommodate all those wishing to visit, making travel arrangements well in advance, and relying on travel agents and tour operators to mediate their travel experiences. In other words, these respondents were strongly associated with the three core criteria of ecotourism (i.e. nature-based, learning, sustainability), but preferred to facilitate their ecotourism experiences at all phases within the accommodation, travel agencies, tour operators and interpretive opportunities of the formal tourism and ecotourism industries. After much consideration, we decided on the label 'structured ecotourists' to describe such respondents; that is, they are ecotourists who prefer structure over spontaneity in the course of planning for and participating in their ecotourism experiences.

Analysis of the rest of the questionnaire confirmed our basic assessment of the cluster variate outcomes. The only major added insight was that the structured ecotourists were significantly more likely to be motivated by 'meeting new people with similar interests' (mean of 3.31 vs. 2.59 and 3.03 for the first and second clusters, respectively), having the 'opportunity to be with friends and/or relatives' (3.03 vs. 2.78 and 2.74), and 'being able to tell my friends about my experiences' (2.84 vs. 2.19 and 2.52). This suggests that a discernible social dimension accompanies the idea of 'structure'. That is, structured ecotourists, more than other ecotourists, enjoy interacting with other people, including travel agents, tour guides and other ecotourists. But because this is a moderate rather than overwhelming tendency (as indicated by the means), we chose not to label these respondents as 'structured ecotourist extroverts' or something similar. With regard to respondent characteristics, significant differences were found in age (structured ecotourists were slightly older), educational attainment (structured ecotourists were less likely to have a university degree) and political affiliation (harder ecotourists leaned towards the left of the political spectrum). Again, however, we felt that none of these differences warranted any changes in the labels despite their potential implications for marketing and product development.

Conclusion

We harbour no false illusions about the scientific objectivity of the cluster analysis that formed the basis of our Lamington study, and we recognize in particular that the selection of one particular ecotourist segment – overnight ecolodge patrons – does not capture the entire broadband of the ecotourist market. Yet, after a process that involved carefully considered decisions of both an objective and subjective nature, we are confident that our research has revealed the contours of some fundamental truths about the ecotourist market. The identification of the harder and softer clusters confirms what has already been conjectured and empirically identified in the literature. The structured ecotourists, however, are something new. While marketing and product development strategies that cater to hard and soft ecotourists are already well known, different and possibly hybridized strategies may be warranted in the case of the structured ecotourists. It seems to us that ecolodge and protected area managers would best appeal to structured ecotourists by treating them as hard ecotourists when they are 'out in the field' by providing physically and mentally challenging opportunities within a relatively undisturbed natural setting. However, at other stages of the tourist experience, including planning, transportation and rest and recuperation, they should be treated as soft ecotourists, and be provided with comfortable accommodation, gourmet food, sophisticated interpretation, specialized travel agency services, and, in recognition of the apparent social dimension, opportunities to engage in social intercourse with like-minded ecotourists. It is hard for us to imagine any other analytical technique that would have allowed us to identify this group so readily. The next logical phase of the research, if funding can be obtained, is to use the same questionnaire and cluster variate at other ecolodges and ecotourism products within Australia and elsewhere to confirm the reliability of our three-cluster solution.

References

Alreck, P. and Settle, R. (1995) *The Survey Research Handbook*, 2nd edn. Irwin, London, 470 pp.

Anon. (n.d.) Available at: http://www.mrs.umn.edu/~sungurea/introstat/history/w98/Tukey.html

Blamey, R. (2001) Principles of ecotourism. In: Weaver, D. (ed.) *The Encyclopedia of Ecotourism*. CAB International, Wallingford, UK, pp. 5–22.

Burns, A. and Bush, R. (2000) *Marketing Research*, 3rd edn. Prentice Hall, Upper Saddle River, New Jersey, 699 pp.

Chapman, D. (1995) *Ecotourism in State Forests of New South Wales: Who Visits and Why?* State Forests of New South Wales and the University of Sydney, Sydney.

Fredline, E. and Faulkner, B. (2000) Host community reactions: a cluster analysis. *Annals of Tourism Research* 27, 763–784.

Hair, J., Anderson, R., Tatham, R. and Black, W. (1995) *Multivariate Data Analysis*, 4th edn. Prentice Hall, Englewood Cliffs, New Jersey, 745 pp.

Laarman, J. and Durst, P. (1987) *Nature Travel and Tropical Forests*. FREI Working Paper Series. Southeastern Center for Forest Economics Research, Raleigh, North Carolina.

Lindberg, K. (1991) *Policies for Maximizing Nature Tourism's Ecological and Economic Benefits*. World Resources Institute, Washington, DC, 37 pp.

Orams, M. (2001) Types of ecotourism. In: Weaver, D. (ed.) *The Encyclopedia of Ecotourism*. CAB International, Wallingford, UK, pp. 23–35.

Palacio, V. and McCool, S. (1997) Identifying ecotourists in Belize through benefit segmentation: a preliminary analysis. *Journal of Sustainable Tourism* 5, 234–243.

Pearce, P. and Moscardo, G. (1994) *Final Report: Understanding Visitor Plans for, Visitor Expectations of and Visitor Reactions to the Wet Tropics World Heritage Area*. James Cook University, Townsville, Australia.

Queensland (1997) *Queensland Ecotourism Plan*. Tourism Queensland. Brisbane, Australia, 85 pp.

Ray, P. and Anderson, S. (2000) *The Cultural Creatives: How 50 Million People are Changing the World*. Three Rivers Press, New York, 370 pp.

Ward, J.H. (1963) Hierarchical grouping to optimize an objective function. *Journal of the American Statistical Association* 58, 236–244.

Weaver, D. (1998) *Ecotourism in the Less Developed World*. CAB International, Wallingford, UK, 258 pp.

Weaver, D. (2001) *Ecotourism*. John Wiley, Brisbane, Australia, 386 pp.

Weaver, D. and Lawton, L. (2001) Resident perceptions in the urban–rural fringe. *Annals of Tourism Research* 28, 439–458.

Weaver, D. and Lawton, L. (2002) Overnight ecotourist market segmentation in the Gold Coast hinterland of Australia. *Journal of Travel Research* 40, 270–280.

17   The Future of Tourism Research

C. MICHAEL HALL

Department of Tourism, University of Otago, PO Box 56, Dunedin, New Zealand

For tourism, a wide array of forecasting and predictive methods exist that try to increase the certainty of policy and decision making for governments and industry and the impact of those decisions. Tourism planning attempts to shape and understand the directions that tourism developments and the environment in which they operate will take. However, predicting the future is something that is fraught with difficulties and has proven many people and institutions to be wrong. For example, as Hall (2000) noted in an article on the future of tourism, one of the earliest books on the international tourism industry stated, 'There is, humanly speaking, undoubtedly no more potent force to allay the fears and hatreds which beset nations than the tourist movement' (Norval, 1936: 149). Written in early 1935, the author could likely not have forecast the chaos about to affect the international tourism industry. In the year the book was published, the Spanish Civil War had broken out, Japan was invading China, and Ethiopia, then one of the few independent countries in Africa, had recently been invaded by the Italians. Three years later, Europe, which already had substantial cross-border leisure and business travel, became embroiled in the Second World War. Indeed, the myth that tourism is a force for peace continues to be propagated by consultants, governments, business and even some academics despite ongoing conflicts around the world and the sometimes direct

attacks on tourists by militias and terrorists. All of which have enormous impacts on the patterns and distributions of tourists and tourism developments.

This chapter aims to look at both the means by which the future of tourism is researched as well as the future of tourism research itself. These two issues are related, particularly as some of the difficulties inherent in predicting the future highlight some of the problems in conceptualizing what the future of tourism research itself might be.

Predicting the Future

Attempts to influence, understand and have some measure of control over the future appear to be inherent to all but the most fatalistic of societies and cultures. Whether through prophecy or more systematic forms of 'scientific' forecasting, humans seek to determine their futures. The importance of understanding the future is such that there is now a well-established set of futurist associations and organizations providing advice to governments and businesses. The future, in the form of share and commodity prices, is even traded on the stock exchange. At the end of the 20th century concern over the future in much of the developed and developing world was such that 'our anxiety has naturally enhanced the position of our prophetic politicians, and of our futurologists and forecasters – they have the map of the future, they will tell us how to get there' (Dublin, 1991: 44). Such futurists can be extremely influential in not only affecting government and industry decision making, but also shaping popular perceptions of what the future will be (e.g. Beckwith, 1967; Kahn and Wiener, 1967; Fuller, 1969, 1981; Toffler, 1972, 1981; Bell, 1973; Masuda, 1981; Naisbitt, 1982; Hawken, 1984). Such is the influence of some futurists in policy making it could be suggested that they also help to shape the future. However, the map of the future is often not very accurate. For example, forecasts about the international economy and international tourism (e.g. Economist Intelligence Unit, 1995; World Tourism Organization, 1995, 1997; Qu and Zhang, 1997; World Travel and Tourism Council, 1998) were dramatically shaken in 1997 and 1998 by the Asian financial crisis. Moreover, as Law (2001) noted, not only were forecasting models unable to anticipate the impacts of the financial crisis but they also performed poorly in predicting the recovery from the crisis in terms of tourism arrival numbers in the Asian region. Indeed, the situation in the region, and for tourism internationally, has become even more confused since the terrorist attacks on 11 September 2001, the SARS outbreak of 2002/03, the American-led invasion of Iraq in 2003 and the Asian avian flu outbreak of 2004. All this serves to highlight the difficulties in predicting the future of tourism.

The choice of method to predict the future requires trade-offs between expected accuracy and precision and the various time, human resource and financial resources required for each method. Table 17.1 presents an overview of a number of different approaches towards forecasting tourism. The first three depend upon quantitative measures whereas the two qualitative modes rely upon the judgement of experts or consumers. Nevertheless, there is no clear conclusion as to which may prove to be more accurate (Witt and Witt, 1992).

Indeed, in some cases forecasts may be wildly wrong. For example, in 1973 and 1974 a Delphi study of a panel of 904 experts was undertaken in the USA to iden-

tify those developments likely to occur in the USA that would influence park and recreation management (Shafer et al., 1974 in Smith, 1995). The panel concluded, amongst other things, the following situation by the year 2000 (the actual situation is noted in brackets):

1. Five hundred miles (800 km) is considered a reasonable one-way distance for weekend pleasure travel (*this is only applicable to the small minority who undertake weekend pleasure travel by plane*).
2. Average retirement age is 50 (*average retirement age has remained at over 60*).
3. Middle-class American families vacation on other continents as commonly as they vacation in the USA in the 1970s (*middle-class Americans still vacation domestically much more than internationally*).
4. Electric power or other non-polluting engines replace internal combustion engines in recreational vehicles (*very few recreational vehicles use electric power or non-polluting engines*).
5. Travel in large parks limited to minimal-impact mass transit, e.g. tramways, air transport and underground rapid transit (*travel in large parks is still mainly conducted by cars on roads*).

Obviously the further out from the time of forecast the more likely it is that the prediction will be wrong. Nevertheless, evidence suggests, that forecasts based on expert judgement are seldom accurate. Indeed, there is a very large body of research that suggests that experts in various areas seldom generate better predictions than non-experts who have received some training, and that the predictions of experts are completely outperformed by those made by simple statistical models (e.g. see Camerer and Johnson, 1991). In his review of the work of future-predicting experts, Sherden (1998) concluded that meteorologists were not always correct, but had by far the best accuracy compared with economists, stock-market analysts, population researchers, management prophets and social-trend spotters. Similarly, research demonstrates that experts perform poorly in their prediction of stock markets and

Table 17.1. Summary of requirements and characteristics of tourism forecasting models. (Source: after Smith, 1995; Frechtling, 1996.)

	Trend extrapolation	Structural	Simulation	Qualitative (I) (Delphi; expert panels, environmental scanning)	Qualitative (II) (consumer/industry surveys)
Technical expertise required	Low to medium	Medium to high	High	Low to medium	Low to medium
Type of conceptual knowledge or data required	Time series data	Cross-sectional data and causal relationships	Time-series, cross-relationships, and change processes	Expert and experimental sectional data, causal	Expert and experimental
Required data precision	Medium to high	High	High	Low to medium	Low
Appropriate forecast horizon	Short	Short to medium	Long	Long	Short
Time required for forecast	Short	Short to medium	Long	Medium to long	Short to medium
Type of problem best suited for	Simple, stable or cyclic	Moderately complex with several variables and known, stable relationship	Complex with known and quantifiable relationships and some feedback effects	Complex with known relationships and elements of uncertainty	Simple to moderately complex, also useful for stable and cyclic problems

business trends (e.g. Mills and Pepper, 1999), while, in the area of predicting firm earnings, a model which simply assumes that there will be no changes might result in more accurate forecasts than expert judgement and advanced statistical models (Conroy and Harris, 1987). Furthermore, most experts overestimate their ability to perform accurately in comparison with non-experts, meaning that experts are over-confident (e.g. Ayton, 1992; Bolger and Wright, 1992; Allwood and Granhag, 1999), although some exceptions exist with respect to weather forecasters and expert bridge players (Bolger and Wright, 1992). The reason for such over-confidence is usually seen to be grounded in greater access to information for experts as compared with non-experts (Oskamp, 1982), with studies demonstrating that, for example, managers and online investors tend to exaggerate the accuracy of their forecasts (Aukutsionek and Belianin, 2001; Barber and Odean, 2002). Unfortunately, the accuracy of tourism forecasting has not been subject to the same degree of analysis as other fields of forecasting (although note Law, 2001). Indeed, Leiper (2000: 808) argues, 'If nobody foresaw the severe downturn in tourism across Asia that began in mid-1997, when all the official forecasting agencies were predicting strong growth, there seems little point in trying to predict, using existing research approaches, what will happen to tourism in the next century'. However, the present discussion does highlight some of the problems in predicting the future of tourism and tourism research.

Even with the uncertainties highlighted above, there are, perhaps, greater degrees of certainty over the future direction of some factors that influence tourism than others. For example, factors related to the physical environment have a greater degree of long-term certainty, for example with respect to climate change and ecological regeneration, while some demographic predictions, such as age structure changes, also have a high degree of predictability at the macro-level (United Nations Population Division, 1998). But, even in situations where there is seemingly reasonable predictability, the assumption is that 'wildcards'

– high impact, low probability events – will not occur, which will dramatically affect social and environmental processes (e.g. nuclear conflict). Yet in tourism, wildcards such as 11 September, SARS and the Asian financial crisis clearly have had dramatic impacts at various scales of analysis. This does not necessarily mean that tourism forecasting is without value. Qualitative methods such as environmental scanning and key force identification, as well as the results of quantitative techniques, are an important part of scenario building for government and industry which allows 'what if?' questions to be asked with appropriate preparations in response. What does not occur very often in tourism, however, is backcasting: the selection of desired futures and how they may be reached. Elements of the process are to be found in strategic planning with the formulation of visions, missions, goals and action plans, but they are generally not sophisticatedly applied to places. Indeed, such a change in direction may be significant as it also gives focus to the question of what sort of future we actually want; a question that applies as much to the field of tourism as an area of study as it does to forecasting tourism itself.

The Future of Tourism Research

Little has been written about the future of tourism research. Indeed, compared with other social science disciplines, there is relatively little self-examination of tourism as a field of study (although see the useful debate between Tribe (1997, 2000), Leiper (2000) and Ryan (1997)). Nevertheless, it is apparent that tourism as a field of study has developed hand-in-hand with the growth of international tourism. Does this then mean that tourism research will also continue to grow in the same vein? Possibly. Given that funding for research from government and industry is primarily driven by utilitarian motives, it may serve as a rough guide for determining the amount of funding available in the developed countries both for determining how to attract international tourists as well as solving issues and problems created by the consumption and production of tourism both at the destination and at the tourists' homes. Arguably, the former is a business studies function while the latter tends to be dealt with by the broader social and environmental sciences. However, increasingly tensions are developing within tourism studies because of the growing importance of government and industry funding of tourism research as compared with a substantially less-well funded but more critical approach. Indeed, in determining the future of tourism research I would argue that the most important factors are institutional and structural ones rather than mere selection of problem, although they are related. In a research environment that is increasingly driven by government and industry funding and directives as well as certain limited notions of quality, tourism does not escape. For me, while that is not a desirable future for the field as a whole, it is one from which I see little escape (Hall, 2004).

Instead, attention needs to be paid to the 'social game' (Weiner, 2001) and 'literacy practices' (Clark and Ivanic, 1997) of tourism, which include both the social and academic conventions, rules and regulatory frameworks that surround research and 'the physical, mental and interpersonal practices that constitute and surround the act of writing' (Clark and Ivanic, 1997: 12). 'Practices' are largely determined by dominant individuals or groups within the 'discourse community' of a subject at any historical moment. In order to enter and be part of a particular discourse community, individuals need to share certain characteristics including: a broadly conceived set of public goals; mechanisms for communication between members and circulation of information and feedback; utilization of specific language practices; and membership requiring a level of specific expertise and knowledge-base (Weiner, 2001). Similarly, Hall and Page's (2002) examination of the geography of tourism and recreation utilized the concepts of Johnston (1991) to highlight the fact that tourism and recreation geographers are 'a society within a society', academic life 'is not a closed system but rather is open to the influences and commands of the wider society which encompasses it' (Johnston, 1991: 1). The study of the development and history of a discipline is, 'not simply a chronology of its successes. It is an investigation of the sociology of a community, of its debates, deliberations and decisions as well as its findings' (Johnston, 1991: 11). The concept of 'discourse community' therefore reflects what binds specific groups of academics together, how others are excluded, the relative conservatism of such communities, and the potential difficulty of introducing changed practices (Swales, 1990). Because of the power of certain groups and individuals to shape and confirm the production of certain kinds of knowledge, it needs to be recognized that research has the power to control as well as generate knowledge. However, such communities are also sites of contestation which may lead to break-away communities that generate new discourses and disciplines (and new books and journals). As Apple (1982: 8) comments, 'reproduction and contestation go hand in hand'. As of the start of 2004 there were over 75 refereed academic tourism or tourism-related journals (Hall, 2004), yet while offering increased specialization in the tourism field many of these seemingly do not explicitly seek to provide ground for contestation (with the possible exception of Current Issues in Tourism and Tourist Studies). Nevertheless, arguably a new arena of contestation is developing.

Tourism and temporary mobility

Tourism is increasingly being interpreted as but one, albeit highly significant, dimension of temporary mobility and circulation (Bell and Ward, 2000; Urry, 2000; Williams and Hall, 2000; Hall and Williams, 2002; Coles et al., 2004; Hall and Müller, 2004). Figure 17.1 presents a model for describing different forms of temporary mobility in terms of three dimensions of space, time and number of trips. Figure 17.1 therefore illustrates the decline in the overall number of trips or movements, time and distance away from a central generating point which would often be termed as 'home'. The number of movements declines the further one travels in time and space away from the point of origin. The relationship represented in Fig. 17.1 holds true whether one is describing the totality of movements of an individual over their life-span from a central point (home) or for an extended period of time or whether one is describing the total characteristics of a population. Such distance decay effects with respect to travel frequency have been well documented. In addition, Fig. 17.1 also illustrates the relationship between tourism and other forms of temporary mobility, including various forms of what is often regarded as migration or temporary migration (Hall and Williams, 2002). Such activities, which have increasingly come to be discussed in the tourism literature, include travel for work and international experiences, education and

health, as well as travel to second homes and return migration.

From the perspective illustrated in Fig. 17.1, tourism may therefore be interpreted as an expression of leisure or recreation lifestyle identified either through travel or a temporary short-term change of residence. However, Fig. 17.1 also highlights that there are a number of different components of such travel behaviour which, as noted above, are increasingly studied under the rubric of tourism because of their leisure mobility orientation. Some of these categories could be described as 'partial tourists' (Cohen, 1974), nevertheless the leisure dimension remains important as a motivating factor in their travel behaviour. In addition, it should be noted that migration is often not permanent and individuals may return to their original homes many years

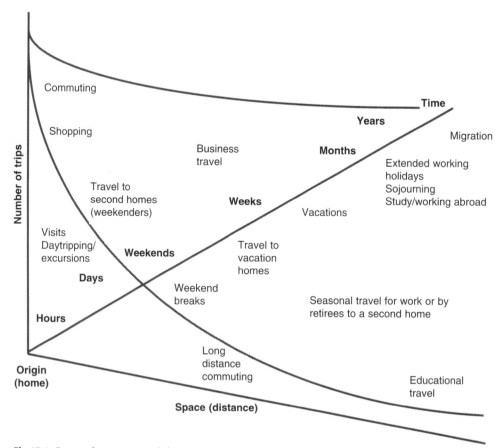

Fig.17.1. Extent of temporary mobility in space and time (after Hall, 2003).

after they left on either a permanent (e.g. for retirement) or a temporary basis (e.g. to a second home). Furthermore, for many migrants, relationships to the country of origin may be maintained through visits that are invariably described as tourism, while the development of transnational mobilities also assists us in understanding identities that often span multiple localities (e.g. Lee, 2003). Therefore, the study of tourism must have the capacity to formulate a coherent approach to understanding the meaning behind the range of mobilities undertaken by individuals, not just tourists (Coles *et al.*, 2004).

Such an approach means that tourism is roughly and conceptually analogous in scope and meaning to other forms of movement (e.g. travel to second homes, return migration, emigration). As Coles *et al.* (2004) have suggested, the conceptualization and development of theoretical approaches to tourism should therefore consider relationships to other forms of mobility, including migration, diaspora and transnationalism. Moreover, such a grounded approach necessitates reconfiguring tourism within those social, economic, political and technological forces that have enhanced mobility and the creation of extended networks of kinship and commu-

nity at regional, national and global scales. Indeed, Hall (2003) has argued that a focus on mobility provides a basis to integrate macro-level quantitative studies of tourism, e.g. through mathematical time series, space–time and spatial interaction modelling, with micro-level qualitative studies of embodiment – the individual body moving in space and time – thereby framing a relationship between the quantitative and qualitative traditions of tourism research.

Contemporary tourism is a synthesis, the resolution of a dialectic that has created new forms of migration, movement, place associations and life structures, yet contemporary tourism research must work towards constructing an epistemological and methodological toolkit that allows for fuller investigations of the range of mobilities undertaken by individuals, not just the category of overnight stays usually referred to as tourism. As Coles *et al.* (2004) have argued, recognition of the place of tourism within the context of mobilities goes some way towards a theoretical grounding, but the relationship of tourism to other forms of mobility should be embedded in the mainstream curriculum more fully, especially if tourism studies are to be centred on contemporary issues and current moments.

References

Allwood, C.M. and Granhag, P.A. (1999) Feelings of confidence and the realism of confidence in everyday life. In: Juslin, P. and Montgomery, H. (eds) *Judgment and Decision Making: Neo-Brunswickian and Process-tracing Approaches.* Lawrence Erlbaum Associates, Mahwah, New Jersey, pp. 123–146.

Apple, M. (ed.) (1982) *Cultural and Economic Reproduction in Education.* Routledge, London.

Aukutsionek, S.A. and Belianin, A.V. (2001) Quality of forecasts and business performance: a survey study of Russian managers. *Journal of Economic Psychology* 22, 661–692.

Ayton, P. (1992) On the competence and incompetence of experts. In: Bolger, F. and Wright, G. (eds) *Expertise and Decision Support.* Plenum Press, New York, pp. 77–105.

Barber, B.M. and Odean, T. (2002) Online investors: do the slow die first? *The Review of Financial Studies* 15, 455–487.

Beckwith, B. (1967) *The Next Five Hundred Years.* Exposition Press, New York.

Bell, D. (1973) *The Coming of Post-Industrial Society.* Basic Books, New York.

Bell, M. and Ward, G. (2000) Comparing temporary mobility with permanent migration. *Tourism Geographies: International Journal of Place, Space and the Environment* 2(3), 87–107.

Bolger, F. and Wright, G. (1992) Reliability and validity in expert judgment. In: Bolger, F. and Wright, G. (eds) *Expertise and Decision Support.* Plenum Press, New York, pp. 47–76.

Camerer, C.F. and Johnson, E.J. (1991) The process–performance paradox in expert judgment: how can experts know so much and predict so badly? In: Ericsson, K.A. and Smith, J. (eds) *Toward a General Theory of Expertise: Prospects and Limits*. Cambridge Press, New York, pp. 195–217.

Clark, R. and Ivanic, R. (1997) *The Politics of Writing*. Routledge, London.

Cohen, E. (1974) Who is a tourist: a conceptual clarification. *Sociological Review* 22, 527–555.

Coles, T., Duval, D. and Hall, C.M. (2004) Tourism, mobility and global communities: new approaches to theorising tourism and tourist spaces. In: Theobold, W. (ed.) *Global Tourism: the Next Decade*. Heinemann, Oxford, UK, pp. 463–481.

Conroy, R. and Harris, R. (1987) Consensus forecasts of corporate earnings: analysts' forecasts and time series methods. *Management Science* 33, 725–738.

Dublin, M. (1991) *Futurehype: the Tyranny of Prophecy*. Viking, New York.

Economist Intelligence Unit (1995) *Asia-Pacific Travel Forecasts to 2005*. Economist Intelligence Unit, London.

Frechtling, D.C. (1996) *Practical Tourism Forecasting*. Butterworth-Heinemann, Oxford, UK.

Fuller, R.B. (1969) *Utopia or Oblivion*. Bantam Books, New York.

Fuller, R.B. (1981) *Critical Path*. St Martin's Press, New York.

Hall, C.M. (2000) The future of tourism: a personal speculation. *Tourism Recreation Research* 25, 85–95.

Hall, C.M. (2003) Tourism and temporary mobility: circulation, diaspora, migration, nomadism, sojourning, travel, transport and home. *International Academy for the Study of Tourism (IAST) Conference*, 30 June–5 July 2003, Savonlinna, Finland.

Hall, C.M. (2004) Reflexivity and tourism research: situating myself and/with others. In: Phillimore, J. and Goodson, L. (eds) *Qualitative Research in Tourism*. Routledge, London, pp 137–155.

Hall, C.M. and Müller, D. (eds) (2004) *Tourism, Mobility and Second Homes: Between Elite Landscape and Common Ground*. Channelview Publications, Clevedon, UK.

Hall, C.M. and Page, S.J. (2002) *The Geography of Tourism and Recreation: Space, Place and Environment*, 2nd edn. Routledge, London.

Hall, C.M. and Williams, A. (eds) (2002) *Tourism and Migration: New Relationships between Production and Consumption*. Kluwer, Dordrecht, The Netherlands.

Hall, C.M., Williams, A.M. and Lew, A. (2004) Tourism: conceptualisations, institutions and issues. In: Lew, A., Hall, C.M. and Williams, A.M. (eds) *Companion to Tourism*. Blackwell, Oxford, UK, pp. 3–21.

Hawken, P. (1984) *The Next Economy*. Henry Holt and Co., New York.

Johnston, R.J. (1991) *Geography and Geographers: Anglo-American Human Geography Since 1945*, 4th edn. Edward Arnold, London.

Kahn, H. and Wiener, A.J. (1967) *The Year 2000*. Macmillan, New York.

Law, R. (2001) A study of the impact of the Asian financial crisis on the accuracy of tourist arrival forecasts. *Journal of Hospitality and Leisure Marketing* 8(1/2), 5–18.

Lee, H.M. (2003) *Tongans Overseas: Between Two Shores*. University of Hawaii Press, Honolulu.

Leiper, N. (2000) An emerging discipline. *Annals of Tourism Research* 27(3), 805–809.

Masuda, Y. (1981) *Computopia: Information Society as Post-Industrial Society*. World Future Society, Bethesda, Maryland.

Mills, T.C. and Pepper, G.T. (1999) Assessing the forecasts: an analysis of forecasting records of the Treasury, the London Business School and the National Institute. *International Journal of Forecasting* 15, 247–257.

Naisbitt, J. (1982) *Megatrends*. Warner Books, New York.

Oskamp, S. (1982) Overconfidence in case-study judgments. In: Kahneman, D., Slovic, P. and Tversky, A. (eds) *Judgment under Uncertainty: Heuristics and Biases*. Cambridge University Press, New York, pp. 287–293.

Qu, H. and Zhang, H. (1997) The projected inbound market trends of 12 tourist destinations in SE Asia and the Pacific 1997–2001. *Journal of Vacation Marketing* 3(3), 247–263.

Ryan, C. (1997) Tourism: a mature discipline subject? *Pacific Tourism Review* 1, 3–5.

Shafer, E.L., Moeller, G.H. and Getty, R.E. (1974) *Future Leisure Environments*. Forest Research Paper NE-301. USDA Forest Experiment Station, Upper Darby, Pennsylvania.

Sherden, W.A. (1998) *The Fortune Sellers: the Big Business of Buying and Selling Predictions*. Wiley, New York.

Smith, S.L.J. (1995) *Tourism Analysis: a Handbook*, 2nd edn. Addison Wesley Longman, Harlow, UK.

Swales, J. (1990) *Genre Analysis: English in Academic and Research Settings*. Cambridge University Press, Cambridge, UK.

Toffler, A. (ed.) (1972) *The Futurists*. Random House, New York.

Toffler, A. (1981) *The Third Wave*. Pan Books, London.

Tribe, J. (1997) The indiscipline of tourism. *Annals of Tourism Research* 24(3), 638–657.

Tribe, J. (2000) Indisciplined and unsubstantiated. *Annals of Tourism Research* 27(3), 809–813.

United Nations Population Division (1998) *World Population Projections to 2150*. United Nations, New York.

Urry, J. (2000) *Sociology Beyond Societies: Mobilities for the Twenty-First Century*. Routledge, London.

Weiner, G. (2001) *The Academic Journal: Has it a Future?* Education Policy Analysis Archives, 9(9).

Williams, A.M. and Hall, C.M. (2000) Tourism and migration: new relationships between production and consumption. *Tourism Geographies: International Journal of Place, Space and the Environment* 2(3), 5–27.

Witt, S.F. and Witt, C.A. (1992) *Modeling and Forecasting Demand in Tourism*. Academic Press, New York.

World Tourism Organization (1995) *East Asia and the Pacific*. World Tourism Organization, Madrid.

World Tourism Organization (1997) *Tourism 2020 Vision*. World Tourism Organization, Madrid.

World Travel and Tourism Council (WTTC) (1998) *APEC Travel & Tourism Millennium Vision*. World Travel and Tourism Council, London.

Index

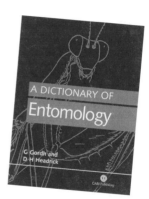
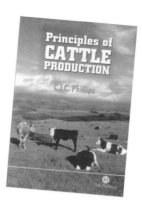